A Shattered Nation

CIVIL WAR AMERICA

Gary W. Gallagher, editor

A Shattered Nation

The Rise and Fall of the Confederacy,
1861–1868

ANNE SARAH RUBIN

The University of North Carolina Press

Chapel Hill & London

The paper in this book meets the guidelines
for permanence and durability of the Committee
on Production Guidelines for Book Longevity of
the Council on Library Resources.

Library of Congress Cataloging-in-Publication Data
Rubin, Anne S.
A shattered nation : the rise and fall of the Confederacy,
1861–1868 / Anne Sarah Rubin.
p. cm. — (Civil War America)
Includes bibliographical references and index.
ISBN 0-8078-2928-5 (cloth : alk. paper)
1. Confederate States of America—Politics and government.
2. Confederate States of America—Social conditions.
3. Nationalism—Confederate States of America—History.
4. United States—History—Civil War, 1861–1865.
5. Reconstruction (U.S. history, 1865–1877) 6. Southern
States—History—1775–1865. 7. Southern States—History
1865–1877. I. Title. II. Series.
E487.R925   2005
973.7′13—dc22   2004018013

cloth   09 08 07 06 05   5 4 3 2 1

Portions of Chapter 1 have been reprinted from Fitzhugh
Brundage, ed., *Where These Memories Grow*. Copyright © 2000
by the University of North Carolina Press. Used by permission
of the publisher.

FOR LODGE

CONTENTS

ILLUSTRATIONS

ACKNOWLEDGMENTS

I first began working on this project as a seminar paper in the spring of 1994. Along the way, I have amassed a collection of debts that I can never repay. So many people have helped me with this book, providing advice, suggestions, and support. This list is, I am quite sure, wholly inadequate, and I apologize for leaving anyone out. The staffs at the Historic New Orleans Collection; the Louisiana and Lower Mississippi Valley Collections, Louisiana State University Libraries; the Manuscript Department at the Howard-Tilton Memorial Library, Tulane University; the Gilder Lehrman Collection at the Pierpont Morgan Library; the Manuscript Department at the William R. Perkins Library, Duke University; the Southern Historical Collection at the University of North Carolina Library; the Manuscripts Department at the Alderman Library, University of Virginia; the Virginia Historical Society; and the Library of Congress were all unfailingly helpful. I received financial support from the University of Virginia, the Virginia Historical Society, the North Caroliniana Society, and the University of Maryland, Baltimore County, to help me complete my research and writing.

Over the years, many people have made helpful suggestions about all or part of this work, including Robert Bonner, Elsa Barkley Brown, Vernon Burton, W. Fitzhugh Brundage, Peter Carmichael, Jane Turner Censer, Karen Cox, Brian Dirck, Charles Eagles, Michael Fellman, Gaines Foster, Greg Kimball, Clarence Mohr, Emory Thomas, Trent Watts, and Charles Reagan Wilson. At the University of Virginia, Richard Handler, Michael Holt, Juliette Landphair, Gregg Michel, Amy Murrell, Peter Onuf, Will Thomas, and the Southern Seminar all provided excellent advice and support. I'm also grateful to my colleagues at UMBC, especially Marjeoleine Kars and Kriste Lindemeyer, for guiding me through the publishing process. James and Charlene Lewis, Mindy and David Patrón, and Beth and Tom Schweiger all gave me a place to stay while I did my research, and I thank them for it.

I appreciate that Catherine Clinton and Drew Gilpin Faust both took time out of their busy schedules to read early drafts. Gary Gallagher, David Perry, and the staff of UNC Press have been unfailingly patient and supportive throughout this process. I especially want to thank George Rable and the two anonymous readers for the press. They pushed me harder than I wanted to be pushed to rework sections, and this book is the better for it. The flaws that remain are solely mine.

Edward L. Ayers has been a teacher, a mentor, a colleague, and a friend. I could not have written this book without him. Whenever I despaired of having chosen a topic that was too big and at times indeterminate, he would remind me that I could use that to my advantage and just "skim the cream"—take the best of what I found. I hope that this book reflects his wisdom and generosity.

I could not have completed this project without the support of family and friends too numerous to list. My father died just as I was starting to write my dissertation, but his memory has been a constant companion. I could not ask for a better mother than Deborah Rubin. This book was supposed to be finished before Jack and Lucas Gillespie arrived, but they had other plans. Now they love "helping" by pulling the books off the shelves, scattering my papers, and begging to touch the "mouse with no squeak." In their own ways they have made contributions beyond measure.

Lodge Gillespie has lived with this project for as long as he has lived with me. It has been both a visible and an invisible presence in our lives. I dedicate this to him, for all that he does and all that he is.

A Shattered Nation

INTRODUCTION

It sometimes seems that the Confederacy is more alive today than it was in the 1860s. Conflicts over its imagery and symbols—its flags, its leaders, its memorial culture—have been almost constant over the past several years. These battles are all arguments about the meaning of the Confederacy, about the relevance that it has or does not have today. Each side tries to use history in its service, with the argument most often devolving into an "it was about slavery . . . it was about state rights," back and forth, neither side listening to the other, each side convinced it is right. But the question still remains: what did it mean to be Confederate in the 1860s? The men, women, and children who considered themselves Confederate during the 1860s created a nation, believed in it, saw that nation disappear, and re-allied themselves with the United States. The identity that they created as Confederates outlasted the Confederacy itself.

This book explores the myriad strands of ideology and identity that made up the Confederacy and shows the complexity and texture of people's attachment to their nation as an ideal, a state, and a memory. It is concerned with the experiences and ideas of those Southern whites who supported the Confederacy. Therefore, it excludes Unionists and African Americans from its analysis of nationalism and identity. While I have made an effort to be as specific as possible, the word "Southerner" should be taken to mean "white Southerner who supported the Confederacy." This population dominated the discourse over nationalism and identity during the 1860s.

Confederate identity and nationalism were constructed out of a combination of institutions and symbols. But, contrary to what we have thought, the construction or creation of Confederate nationalism was not a difficult problem. The speed with which white Southerners, many of them staunch Unionists through the election of 1860, shed their American identity and picked up a sense of themselves as Confederates was startling. Southern whites embraced the idea of a Confederacy with a minimum of backward glances. Where Confederates struggled, and where the growing pains of their new national identity are most visible, was in building an institutional framework for the nation. Thus each challenge to the national government —whether it came in the form of political squabbling, class resentment, or desertion—was perceived as a crisis of almost epic proportions. Problems that a mature nation like the Union could handle seemed that much more damaging and threatening to a Confederate nation fighting for its survival. And indeed, the Confederate *state* ultimately could not withstand a combination of internal and external pressures and collapsed in April–May 1865. But attachment to a symbolic or sentimental Confederacy, or at least to a separate Southern identity, existed independently of the political Confederacy, and thus was able to outlast the state.

This book also explores the ways in which white Southerners held on to vestiges of their Confederate identity. Recent works on nationalism, including Alon Confino's study of Germany and Partha Chatterjee's book on India, have examined the relationship between national and local identity, and I see similar processes at play in the Reconstruction South.[1] Former Confederates negotiated the boundaries of their American identity, struggling to hold on to local (and racial) control. In Reconstruction, the divided allegiances of white Southerners are easy to see. As they confronted their reabsorption into the Union they continued to cling to the idea of Southern independence. The remembered Confederacy was a place free of conflict; Jefferson Davis, now a martyred prisoner, had been a wise and pious leader; their slaves had not run away but had been loyal protectors of white families. Its imagined virtues stood in stark contrast to the ruins and radicalism that white Southerners believed hemmed them in on all sides. But at the same time, Southern men and women took the loyalty oath and applied for pardons in droves. They justified their decision on pragmatic grounds: they no longer had a Confederate government to pledge their loyalty to, and they wanted the rights and privileges that U.S. States citizens had, especially in terms of property and local political (and therefore racial) control.

Most scholarly work on nationalism has focused on nation-building, myths of origin, and the rise of the ethnic state, and scholarship on American nationalism largely conforms to this pattern.[2] From the perspective of the twenty-first century, when we have witnessed not only the fragmentation of the Soviet Union into a dozen ethnic states but also bloody ethnic fighting in both the Balkans and Central Africa, this narrow focus seems problematic. Nations, once created, do not always live forever. The story of the Confederacy's demise teaches us that identities are not so easily destroyed.

Nations, according to scholars like Wilbur Zelinsky and Richard Handler, are not the same things as states. A state is first and foremost a political construct and as such may encompass one or more nations. A nation, by contrast, is an emotional, ideological, and frequently sentimentalized construct, created by individuals who self-consciously share the belief that they are all united by a common culture, history, and social personality. Nations may or may not control their own political states; states have created nations more often than the reverse.[3] In the Confederate case, the idea of a Southern nation-state had gained currency among proslavery politicians throughout the 1850s, only to reach its culmination in the 1860–61 secession crisis.[4] Many white Southerners believed themselves to be a people apart from the rest of the United States: the Cavaliers to the Yankee Puritans. The idea of a Southern nation that preceded the war was qualitatively different from the one that followed: before the war, Southerners stressed their common origins and understanding of the Constitution, but during and after, they emphasized their Confederate experiences.

Confederates imagined their nation together and engaged in conversations about what it meant to be first a Confederate and then, later, a Southerner and an American.[5] They disseminated their culture and values through conversation, correspondence, and a variety of printed media, including newspapers, schoolbooks, music, and literature. By sharing reading material —both published and personal writings—they shared experiences over geographical spaces. Consequently, this book draws heavily on written sources, though many of these writings describe visual or public manifestations of national culture. Confederates also created new rituals to bind themselves together. They wrote new histories of the American and Confederate past in order to legitimate their national existence. They demonized their enemies and used metaphors of corruption and pollution, all in the service of inspiring a connection to their new nation and their new state.[6]

Confederates' and Southerners' silences and omissions were equally telling. Slavery was clearly a crucial component of the Confederacy—arguably its raison d'être—and preservation of the institution took pride of place in official documents like the Confederate Constitution. Yet private expressions of national identity, as well as public exhortations aimed at nation-building, all but ignored the question of racial slavery. Confederates feared enslavement at the hands of Northerners, but they seldom verbalized the connection between their fears and their own slaveholding country. Though it figured prominently in debates over the Confederate Constitution, and later in discussions over the draft exemption given to slaveholders in 1862, for the most part, Confederates took slavery as a given, albeit a sometimes problematic one, subject to neither challenge nor conversation.

Confederates had a second reason to keep silent on the subject of slavery, for they worried constantly about how their nation would be perceived by foreign countries. The ever-present search for diplomatic recognition, a sort of national status anxiety, underlay Confederate calls for indigenous schoolbooks and literature, and it influenced the language in which Confederates framed their national aspirations. They were sensitive to foreign, particularly British, opposition to slavery. By de-emphasizing bondage as a cause of secession, stressing instead state rights and political domination, Confederates were able to shift the terms of debate, thus making their cause more palatable to conditional Unionists, nonslaveholders, and outside nations.

Confederate identity did not evaporate with the end of the Confederate States of America in April 1865. Throughout Presidential Reconstruction, white Southerners continued to call for the preservation of their own values and to press for social separation from the North when they could no longer be politically divided. They worried about how best to remain true to their Confederate past, to make sure that the sacrifices their soldiers had made by fighting and dying were not in vain. They struggled to define new standards of appropriate behavior, whether that meant inviting investment from Northern capitalists or adopting a posture of public acquiescence to Republican rule. Women, who had enjoyed a measure of independence during the war years, found themselves caught between their new realities and a desire to return to the social status quo. They were praised for their wartime patriotism and chastised for not knowing when to let it go.

By 1867, Southern calls for separate nationhood had largely subsided, replaced by a desire for equal treatment within the American Union. Reconstruction under Andrew Johnson had been less punitive than white Southerners (and indeed Republicans) had initially expected, and whites took advantage of his leniency to reassert their vision of racial supremacy. The rise of the Radicals, however, brought a new harshness to relations between the federal government and former Confederates. Southern whites took the imposition of military government as a blow to their honor, a repudiation of the word they had given in their loyalty oaths. The Radicals' determination to accord African Americans all the rights and privileges of full American citizenship also struck many whites as an unforgivable affront. White Southern Democrats—the majority of ex-Confederates—reacted with anger and often violence directed against white and black Southern Republicans. These Southerners believed that they had emerged from the war with only their honor, their white supremacy, and their memories intact. Reconstruction challenged the first two, leaving them with little more than nostalgia for their Confederate past.

This book is broadly conceived in order to see what Confederate identity meant in a variety of places, times, and situations. Its focus is on nationalism as a felt experience, as a sentimental attachment first to the Confederacy and then to its memory. This project studies both men and women, because they experienced the war and Reconstruction together. It looks at soldiers and civilians, because the homefront influenced events and opinions on the battlefield and vice versa. Its chronological framework, covering both the war and the beginnings of Reconstruction, allows us to see patterns of thinking continuing or changing from the wartime Confederacy into the peacetime South. The end of the war did not mark a profound break in the ways in which Southerners imagined themselves but rather marked a shift in emphasis. Southerners might no longer have their independence, but they could maintain their sense of themselves as a culturally, indeed ethnically, distinct people.

This book cuts across several different areas of Civil War and Reconstruction historiography, touching on questions of nationalism, gender, the relationship between homefront and battlefield, political and social Reconstruction, and the myth of the Lost Cause. David Potter's 1960 essay "The Historian's Use of Nationalism and Vice Versa" has inspired military, social, and political historians to produce a voluminous literature on Confederate nationalism.[7] Beginning, too, with Potter's work, historians have tended to focus on the origins of Confederate nationalism, testing its "validity" against a range of theoretical precepts.[8] The primary question seems to be whether the Confederates were able to imagine themselves as different enough from the United States to endure as a nation. Thus, issues of Confederate nationalism seem, with few exceptions, always to be tangled up with questions of Confederate defeat.[9]

Other historians, in particular Drew Gilpin Faust and George Rable, have granted more credence to the strength of Confederate nationalism as a guiding ideology, and this book builds on their work in this area. In *The Confederate Republic*, George Rable argues that the Southern elite was engaged in a legitimate "revolution against politics," a cultural crusade to return to a purified form of the Founders' godly nation. He examines the myriad ways in which the government, especially President Davis, worked to define "a sacred center" around which to focus national identity. Where some historians saw the Confederacy foundering on the shoals of class conflict inadequately contained by weak nationalism, Rable contends that a system of political ideology founded on the principles of antipartyism could not control dissent and was thus doomed to failure. As far as nationalism is concerned, Rable seems implicitly to argue that the Confederacy passed Potter's institutional tests, that it was viable and self-sustaining.[10]

In *Creation of Confederate Nationalism*, Drew Faust takes Confederates' initial pronouncements about nationalism seriously. Faust uses a cultural approach to understand Confederate nationalism, paying close attention to Confederates' self-conscious creation of symbols and national myths, stressing the importance of evangelical religion and the proslavery argument to the Confederate sense of self. She shows Confederate nationalism as a work in progress, constantly being negotiated by all manner of Confederates.[11] In her most recent book, *Mothers of Invention*, and in her oft-cited 1990 article, "Altars of Sacrifice: Confederate Women and the Narratives of War," Faust expands her analysis of Confederate nationalism with a particular eye toward the role of women.[12] I am drawing on much of this work on the origins and creation of Confederate nationalism, using it as a foundation for my own work on the endurance of Confederates' attachment to their nation, even when their state ceased to exist.

In seeking to understand the nature of Confederates' feelings about their country, I have taken an expansive view, looking beyond the world of politics and opinion-makers to the broader population of soldiers and civilians. Confederates lived in a world where the battlefield and homefront were not two bounded entities but were instead intimately linked together. Soldiers and civilians were in constant communication, sharing news, opinions, and emotion. Those who argue that the Confederate homefront lost the Civil War neglect the fact that information flowed both ways. Soldiers sought to comfort civilians after losses, tried to minimize defeats, and assured their families that the men in the army were confident of eventual victory.[13] I also concur with Gary Gallagher's belief that the homefront and the battlefield need to be studied together, although where he stresses the importance of the Army of Northern Virginia as a unifying force, I emphasize the larger culture of nationalism and patriotism created by Confederates themselves. Confederates sustained their nationalism in the face of challenges, not through a centralized propaganda apparatus, but through countless personal exchanges. Thus, expressions of patriotism were not limited to published sources like newspapers and schoolbooks. I argue that the repetition of these themes in personal correspondence, and even more powerfully in diaries, shows that they were accepted by Confederates. Even if they may not have wholeheartedly believed nationalist and patriotic rhetoric, Confederates understood that it provided them with a common vocabulary.

All of these works on Confederate nationalism and identity share one important characteristic: they stop studying Confederate nationalism when the Confederacy ceases to exist as a political entity. For Confederates, however, the end of their state did not signal an immediate end to their sense of themselves as a separate people. Their belief in a Southern, if not Confederate, nation persisted into Reconstruction. Ex-Confederates struggled with conflicting loyalties toward their past and current nations. By shifting their focus from being "Confederate" to being "Southern," they were able to ease their transition to American citizenship. Just as books about the Confederacy rarely extend into Reconstruction, so, too, do books about Reconstruction and the Lost Cause rarely begin before Appomattox. One exception is *Masters without Slaves*, in which James Roark seeks to examine the moment of transition from the Old South to the New. However, he is most concerned with the impact of emancipation on the behavior of the Southern planter class. Although Roark does make reference to the social ideologies and philosophies inherent in planters' writings, he equates them almost exclusively with proslavery thought. Thus, the only ideological shift with which he is concerned involves slavery: his is the story of the transition from a plantation economy powered by slavery to one powered by free, or quasi-free, labor. He regards Confederate nationalism as a derivation of devotion to the slave-plantation system and argues that the planters swore their allegiance first to the latter and only incidentally to the former. For Roark, the Confederacy, even as an idea or ideal, ceased to exist when its government fell in April 1865.[14]

Books about Presidential Reconstruction have tended to focus on the politics of the period, especially at the state level.[15] They do not, however, address the plight of more ordinary people. All former Confederates, women as well as men, yeomen as well as elites, found themselves faced with questions of compromise and reunion. Southerners had to decide how much contact with the North was too much. Some could not stand any contact at all and emigrated to Central or South America. Women in particular found themselves torn, pressured to hate the Yankees but to do so in a quiet and ladylike manner. The more public positions that women had been able to take during the war were closed down, their energies channeled into more "female" outlets, like memorializing the Lost Cause.[16]

Confederate identity and nationalism, whether during the war or Reconstruction, were exquisitely sensitive to events, and I have structured this book to reflect that. Thus thematic chapters—about the ways Confederates maintained their nationalism, coped with challenges to it, or called for rebuilding during Reconstruction—are interspersed with shorter, more episodic "interludes." Part I describes the ways in which Confederates first inspired feelings of allegiance to their new nation and then faced a variety of challenges to it. It culminates in the collapse of the Confederacy in the spring of 1865. Part II explores the ways in which Confederates (now Southerners) redefined themselves as Americans while still holding onto vestiges of Confederate identity. It is this holding onto a Confederate ideal, even as they demanded political citizenship, that has endured, with profound consequences.

I

War

1 A Religious Patriotism

The Culture of Confederate Identity

The Confederate nation appeared to be born fully formed, going from vague idea to reality over a matter of weeks. South Carolina seceded on 20 December 1860, followed rapidly by the six other lower South states. The Montgomery Convention met in February, drafted its permanent Constitution quickly, and by the summer of 1861 the provisional government was ensconced in Richmond. The Confederacy, for all of its shortcomings, did possess all of the necessary apparatus of government—an executive, a legislature, a judiciary, a treasury, a postal service, a state department. Most important, for the Confederacy had no real existence apart from war, it raised and kept an army in the field. These institutions may not have always functioned well, or efficiently—indeed in many cases they barely functioned at all—but they did exist.[1] A state apparatus is important but does not a nation make: it alone does not ensure feelings of allegiance. But the new Confederacy did just that: almost from the moment of its creation, it inspired loyalty and commitment from its citizens. While there were Unionist minorities in every state, most Southern whites seemed willing, if not eager, to turn their back on the Union in favor of this new nation, and to do so with nary a backward glance. This was true not only of the fire-eaters who had been working for years to draw the South out of the Union but of conditional Unionists as well, of people who had done everything possible to avert secession.[2]

These new Confederates created a national culture in large part by drawing on the usable American past. But they also added a potent mix of fear and rage to it. The fear was of the end of slavery, couched often in the language of so-called black rule or race-mixing; the rage was against invading Yankees, demonized to the point of dehumanization. Confederates disseminated this culture largely through print—in particular through newspapers and journals—but also broadsides, songs, poems, and, of course, personal correspondence. Published words show the process of nation-building at work. Indeed, as Benedict Anderson argues in *Imagined Communities*, it was precisely the emergence of newspapers that provided the unifying means to allow nationalism to flourish. By transmitting a uniform version of events and ideology, newspapers give readers the sense of belonging to a larger imagined community, be it regional or national.[3] Nineteenth-century Americans were voracious consumers of news, and even people who did not themselves subscribe to a newspaper would borrow someone else's copy, or perhaps have the news read to them. Thus newspapers reached and influenced even the illiterate. Depending on their individual editors' proclivities, newspapers served as civics instructors, fostered party competition, provided household hints, and furnished readers with the latest poetry and serial fiction. A shared culture of print brought Americans together as a nation in the late eighteenth and early nineteenth centuries; it would do the same for Confederates during the Civil War.[4]

Antebellum and Civil War–era Southern newspapers were largely creatures of their editors. The tradition of "personal journalism" that was fading away with the rise of the Northern penny press held firm below the Mason-Dixon line. Southern and Confederate newspapers tended to have smaller staffs and older presses and technology and to be more sectional and partisan in orientation than their Northern counterparts. They also suffered greatly during the war, from a lack of supplies and labor, as well as from occupation and destruction at the hands of the Union army.[5]

Prior to the war, Southern editors gathered much of their news through a process of exchanges with Northern papers. After the war began, that was no longer a viable option, although Confederate papers continued to exchange news and anecdotes with one another. Confederate editors began casting about for other sources of military news and attempted to form news-gathering consortiums—one in Richmond and one in Atlanta. Neither was particularly successful, and eventually the editors of the Confederacy's forty-three daily papers met in Augusta, Georgia, in February 1863. This time they founded the Confederate Press Association and hired J. S. Thrasher to be the service's superintendent. Thrasher worked tirelessly on behalf of the PA, as it was known, negotiating telegraph contracts, challenging military censorship, and trying to instill objectivity and nonpartisanship in his reporters. The PA proved quite successful at news-gathering and dissemination, further adding to the Confederacy's shared print culture.[6]

Confederates were also united by a less public culture of words, through their writings for and to each other. One consequence of a war is that it separates people who might not have been apart under ordinary circumstances, and the Civil War provides historians with an almost limitless supply of personal correspondence. Husbands wrote to wives, fathers to children, distant friends to each other. Letters buzzed with rumors and gossip, war news and local happenings. Complaints about the Confederacy's erratic mails mingled with advice and gentle criticism, political opinion, and intimate endearments. No matter how personal and unmediated these letters appear, it is important to remember that nineteenth-century men and women wrote to one another in patterned ways, with formalized expressions and ideas of appropriateness. Too, especially in the case of letters written by soldiers to their families, one could expect a letter to be at least read aloud if not passed from hand to hand, which might have increased circumspection in observation and opinion. When Confederates told each other to keep their spirits up, to remain confident that victory was just around the corner, they might well have been lying to themselves as much as to their correspondents.[7]

Journals or diaries, which might seem to be the most personal and private sources of all, were no less bound by convention or secrecy than letters. Since the mid-eighteenth century, it had been typical for young women to keep journals, and many women continued the practice after marriage. Men, too, kept diaries, often recording both personal thoughts and business transactions. The sense that both men and women had that they were living through extraordinary times also increased the ranks of diarists during the war. Most wrote with the understanding that others, whether their contemporaries or posterity, would read their words. "My journal—a quire of Confederate paper—lies wide open on my desk in the corner of my drawing room," wrote one of the Confederacy's most famous diarists, Mary Chesnut. "Everybody reads it who chooses." Even less literary-minded folk then Chesnut kept their potential audiences near the forefront of their minds. "I write for the information of my Northern friends, should any of them have the curiosity to read this journal, & leave herewith the request that it may be forwarded to them at some future time if it should not be in my power to do it myself," explained a resident of Augusta County, Virginia, as she began a lengthy description of a Union raid. Though Confederates wrote with varying degrees of self-consciousness, their private writings tended to echo the themes and language of more public sources. Regardless of where they lived, Confederates received news through the same channels, read the same books, and sang the same songs. Words bound Confederates together, regardless of class or gender, allowing, for example, a man in Louisiana and a woman in North Carolina to imagine themselves part of a viable national whole.[8]

That process of national imagining began in earnest with the Montgomery Convention. Nations depend on myths of origin to inspire both domestic loyalty and foreign recognition. These new Confederates had one ready-made in the form of the American Revolution and they returned again and again to that deep well of national symbolism. Indeed, if Thomas R. R. Cobb, a member of the Georgia delegation to the Montgomery Convention, had gotten his way, the new Southern nation would have been known as the Republic of Washington.[9] His motion failed, and in a clear and conscious echo of the rejected United States, the country became the Confederate States of America. Thus did the national story created by Confederates have its roots in the story of the American nation. As Confederates went about the work of nation-building, they self-consciously drew on a ready-made myth of national origin, rejecting the recent American history of sectionalism and centralization and instead seizing on the American Revolution as the defining moment of their past.[10] Most interestingly, in looking to the distant Revolutionary past, Confederates rejected the antebellum bursts of Southern sectionalism as exemplified in the nullification crisis and the debates over the Compromise of 1850. Confederate nationalism would be propagated by antebellum moderates like Jefferson Davis; the fire-eaters like William Lowndes Yancey and Robert Barnwell Rhett would be largely shunted aside.[11]

Even before the shots were fired on Fort Sumter, Confederates were christening their struggle the "Second American Revolution" and praising Jefferson Davis as a second George Washington. Few, if any, Confederates actually remembered the Revolution, but its iconography—with its language of patriots and inalienable rights, heroes like George Washington and Light-Horse Harry Lee, stories of heroism and fortitude—gave Confederates a vocabulary and a conceptual framework with which to make claims for national legitimacy. Unionists were condemned as Tories, Yankee soldiers as Hessians. The Revolution of 1861 was the logical completion of the Revolution of 1776. In essays, speeches, newspapers, poems, and popular songs, Confederates told the story of a virtuous nation led astray by fanatical, greedy, and power-hungry Yankees. As Confederates sought first to inspire people to support the new nation and later to sustain them as their own struggle for independence seemed to founder, they drew on the patriotic example of colonists fighting for seven years, surviving material hardship, and eventually vanquishing a more numerous and better-equipped foe. Confederates were not destroying the Union; they were restoring it to its earlier glory. They were not rebels but patriots. Their ancestors had fought a glorious revolution to create a great nation; Confederates would do the same. Rather than representing a challenge to the ideals of the Founding Fathers, the Confederacy would be the perfection of their vision.

Confederates thus used the language of ancestry to emphasize their connection to the past. Whether an individual Southern soldier had descended from a Revolutionary fighter was largely irrelevant. What mattered was that Confederates, as a whole, cast themselves as a people apart. They were the Anglo-Saxon Cavaliers to the Northern Puritans and immigrants. Indeed, Northern Founders like Benjamin Franklin and Samuel and John Adams were rarely mentioned. In this construction, the courage and fortitude of the Revolutionary generation flowed through all Confederate veins: those of women as well as men, yeomen as well as aristocrats, Mississippians as well as South Carolinians.[12]

Too, when Confederates cast themselves as the guardians of Revolutionary ideals, they avoided discussing other causes of the war, specifically slavery. The word rarely appeared in evocations of the American Revolution, and when it did, it was usually in the rhetorical sense of Confederates fearing enslavement to Northern masters. This silence on the subject of racial slavery suggests that Confederates used the Revolutionary War to shift the terms of debate, and to make the war more palatable to conditional Unionists, nonslaveholders, and outside nations. A powerful example of this rhetoric can be seen in a *Richmond Enquirer* editorial clearly designed to urge Unionist Virginians to throw their support behind the Confederacy: it warned that "those who will hesitate to fly to arms at such a momentous crisis cannot be the legitimate descendants of the brave and chivalrous race of '76."[13] A war to recreate the glory of the Founders' nation was more honorable and less divisive than a war to protect the slaveholding prerogatives of a small percentage of the Confederate population. A war to recreate a virtuous America might appeal to conditional Unionists by convincing them that the Union as it existed needed to be destroyed in order to be replaced by a better one, a Confederate one.

The language of betrayal pervaded the rhetoric of Confederates who insisted on the essential conservatism of their actions. In his inaugural address as president of the provisional government in February 1861, Jefferson Davis explained, "We have changed the constituent parts, but not the system of government. The Constitution framed by our fathers is that of these Confederate States."[14] The author of "Too Much Nationality," in the *Southern Monthly*, stated simply, "The Government of the Confederate States is in conformity to that established by the fathers of the American Revolution, and a continuance of the Government they established." That government, this writer and others like him complained, had been perverted and betrayed by the Yankee tendency to (wrongly) place the interests and power of the nation above that of the individual states. That tendency, combined with the Yankees' generally corrupt and materialistic character, led to a "national decadence" that one writer dated to "the close of the administration of the last Revolutionary statesmen," James Monroe.[15]

This idea found reinforcement in the 1863 pamphlet *Our Home and Foreign Policy*, in which Henry St. Paul described a split between the Northern and Southern people that predated even the American Revolution. Northerners, St. Paul and others like him argued, were descended from the Puritans, whereas Southerners were the heirs of the more dashing Cavaliers. This divided heritage, and the different values implicit in it, necessarily fostered two separate societies.[16] During the years following the Revolution, the people diverged and "in the South, Northern stock got elevated and purified, and in the North, Southern blood became corrupt and degenerated. In less than a quarter of a Century, the North hated the South and the South despised the North." Constant association with immoral Northerners, who were tainted by their pursuit of money and power, according to St. Paul, "debased" Southern society, and the Missouri Compromise, with its limitations on the expansion of slavery, was "a standing insult and defiance." Only the moral fitness of Southerners allowed them to "steer clear of northern infamy" and escape "the contagious influence of northern immorality."[17]

A set of essays, collected under the title *The Confederate* and authored by "A South Carolinian," stressed the innate moral fitness of Southern men. "Trained to arms from boyhood, bold, hearty, active, and chivalrous," they were born to be soldiers. This was in marked contrast to their Northern opponents, who were "accustomed from infancy to the last, the needle, the axe, or the yardstick." In fact, over half of the dozen pieces in the collection were devoted to the social and ethical failings of the Yankee abolitionists and their "ruthless" and "unprincipled" Puritan ancestors. This characterization of Northerners as fanatical abolitionists was typical of Confederate rhetoric, as it provided Confederates with a justification for secession. They seceded not so much to protect slavery in the abstract as they did to protect themselves from an irrational and unreasonable North.[18]

The Civil War was thus, in the words of Rev. William Hall, a "Revolution" and "*a great historic protest, the only one of the sort in history, against philosophic infidelity and disorganizing wrong.*" It was a revolt against fanaticism, a separation that Hall's fellow clergyman, Benjamin Palmer, deemed essential, "for it separated us from a country that had become bloated in party corruption and was destined soon to fall into premature decay." God ordained the war, just as he had ordained slavery, and the Confederacy consequently represented the will of the Almighty.[19] Hall saw the situation in almost apocalyptic terms: "We are leading the great battle for the sum of modern history—for the regulated liberty and civilization of the age. It is conservative religion against atheism—constitutional law against fanatical higher law—social stability against destructive radicalism." In *Our Danger and Our Duty*, the Presbyterian theologian James Henley Thornwell framed the conflict as a battle between despotism on the Northern side and constitutional freedom on the Southern. Confederates were not, in his formulation, revolutionaries, but rather Conservatives, resisting the North's own revolt against the Constitution. Hall agreed with this explanation, reflecting that "the epithet, *rebels*, so fiercely hurled upon us by the Northmen is sadly amusing when it is remembered, that we are simply contending for the inherent right of self-government, which was so nobly vindicated by their fathers and ours."[20]

William Meade, the Episcopal bishop of Virginia, used the idea of Northern betrayal to argue that the new Confederate nation was in no way casting "contempt on the memory of our revolutionary fathers" and undoing "all which they so wisely did." The Founders had no way of foreseeing "all the unhappiness which has been felt for the last twenty or thirty years"; had they been able to, they surely would have provided for a means of separation. Moreover, Meade continued, if "those great statesmen" were alive to see the "failure of all their efforts and plans and warnings," they would side with the South. "Would they not rather say in tones of warning," asked Meade, "made more solemn as coming from the grave, 'Forbear this vain attempt. God himself has decreed the failure of our short-sighted devices. Yield then to his will. Still be brethren. Form a new alliance and be ready to combine against a common foe. Call not those who have departed from you rebels, traitors, conspirators, as our ancient foes did the noble fathers of our revolution; still be brethren of one great American family, honoring and being honored, and show to the world that a republic is not a failure; that it may divide, yet live and prosper.'"[21] Confederates' present revolution was legitimated by the past; they had no doubts the Founders would be with them.

Noted Southern polemicist George Fitzhugh also linked the Revolutions of 1776 and 1861, although with his own unique interpretation.[22] Rather than following the prevailing ideology that held the Confederate Revolution to be a continuation of the American Revolution, Fitzhugh claimed it was an improvement on the first. Fitzhugh deemed the first Revolution a reformation, and one that went too far in its Lockean doctrines of "natural liberty, human equality, and the social contract." The Confederates were "rolling back the excesses" of the American Revolution, excesses that meant that "liberty was degenerating into licentiousness." Fitzhugh, despite expressing his admiration for the English Cavaliers, stressed that he was not calling for a return to Toryism or monarchism. The general outlines of the American Constitution and the Union had worked well: "The only evil we have suffered under our institutions has arisen from our connexion with the North. That connexion dissolved, let us preserve our government in its present form until some great and pressing evil suggests and necessitates a change." The conservative nature of the Confederacy was highlighted by the decision to keep the basic format of the American Constitution. The Constitution was not generally flawed; it was simply that the American nation had run its course, had outlived its usefulness. The next stage in the perfection of America would come under Confederate rule.[23]

Constitutional legitimacy was crucial to the Confederates' sense of themselves. By fighting for their rights and the rule of law, and by emphasizing their Revolutionary antecedents, Confederate theorists gave their people a rich reservoir of national symbols upon which to draw, while at the same time downplaying the importance of slavery. Confederates, the prewar writings of their secession commissioners notwithstanding, knew that slavery alone would provide a shaky foundation for their new nation and they sought to buttress it by emphasizing the North's betrayal of the Founders' vision. Thus, the Confederate nation was not created out of whole cloth but rather represented a perfection of America; Confederates were not abandoning their old country so much as they were renewing it.[24]

All of these justifications for Confederate revolution shared an emphasis on the rightness of secession. In leaving the corrupted Union, Confederates were doing what God and their ancestors would have wanted. Who would dare challenge their actions? They believed they were the wronged party in this dispute, victimized by Northerners who changed the rules of politics midway through the game. The role that slavery and abolitionism had played in fostering sectional hostility, however, remained virtually unacknowledged. Confederates had no wish to engage in a debate about the rightness of slavery; that question had long been settled to their satisfaction and expounded upon by numerous proslavery theorists (George Fitzhugh and James Henley Thornwell among them). Furthermore, the Founders themselves—at least those who resided in Southern states—had held slaves, and so, too, should Confederates. A war for slavery would not necessarily have held the same appeal to nonslaveholders as one for white liberty and the honor of ancestors. For these reasons, Confederates were happy to highlight other reasons they had to be angry with the North.

Confederates not only rewrote the history of the United States with their own distinctive slant but also drew on the iconography of the American past in creating the symbolic foundations of their own nation. Detailed analysis of constitutional questions was generally limited to publication in pamphlets or literary and political journals, but evocations of the American Revolution were everywhere in Confederate popular culture. In poems and songs, conversation and letters, Northerners and Southern Unionists were repeatedly damned as "Tories" and Union soldiers as "Hessians" (the latter a wordplay on the many immigrants in the Northern ranks).[25] These more popular forms illustrate the tremendous resonance the American Revolution had among the general Confederate public. While comparatively few readers might have been expected to wade through detailed treatises on the true intentions of the Constitution's framers, even a child could appreciate the significance of a picture of George Washington on a stamp or adorning a broadside, or laugh at a new version of an old song. Revolutionary iconography had been a staple of political culture since the 1790s, and it provided a popular shorthand for expressing loyalty to party, state, or nation. Appropriating the instantly familiar to make the war comprehensible was a sure strategy for securing loyalty, for it meant that the new nation was not so different from the old. Holding on to the Revolution made it easier for new Confederates to reject the American present.[26]

Confederates sensitive to symbols sought every opportunity to express their continuing connection to the American past. Anonymous wags put new satirical words to familiar tunes, playing on past patriotism. "The Star Spangled Banner" became "The Stars and Bars," which began:

> Oh! say do you see now so vauntingly borne,
> In the hands of the Yankee, the Hessian and Tory,
> The flag that once floated at Liberty's dawn,
> O'er heroes who made it the emblem of glory?
>   Do the hireling and knave
>   Bid that banner now wave
> O'er the fortress where freemen they dare to enslave?

Oh! say has the star-spangled banner become
The flag of the Tory and vile Northern scum?

"The Southern Yankee Doodle," illustrated with Confederate flags, mocked Major Robert Anderson for failing to hold Fort Sumter against Confederate bombardment, while "The New Yankee Doodle" expressed Confederate contempt for Northerners:

Yankee Doodle had a mind
To whip the Southern traitors,
Because they didn't choose to live
On codfish and potatoes.
Yankee Doodle, doodle doo,
Yankee Doodle dandy,
And so to keep his courage up,
He took a drink of brandy.

The remaining verses described Confederates whipping Yankee Doodle at, strangely, both Manassas and Bull Run, all the while mocking his taste for brandy. No longer a symbol of home-grown resistance, Yankee Doodle had become a caricature of all that was weak and unmanly about Confederates' foes.[27]

Far and away the most often invoked icon of the Revolutionary War was George Washington. By 1861, he had come to symbolize all that was virtuous and heroic about the American Revolution, and he was beloved by both Northerners and Southerners throughout the antebellum period.[28] This love of Washington carried over into the Confederacy. Both Jefferson Davis and Robert E. Lee were dubbed "second Washingtons," and Davis consciously played up the allusions to Washington in his 1862 inauguration. Standing beside a statue of Washington on Washington's birthday, Davis invoked the Founder's values and sought his blessing, explaining that "on this the birthday of the man most identified with the establishment of American independence, beneath the monument erected to commemorate his heroic virtues and those of his compatriots, we have assembled to usher into existence the Permanent Government of the Confederate States. . . . The day, the memory, and the purpose seem fitly associated."[29]

Washington's image graced two physical representations of the Confederate government: postage stamps and the Great Seal of the Confederacy. In early 1863, as the Confederate Congress debated the seal's final design, an

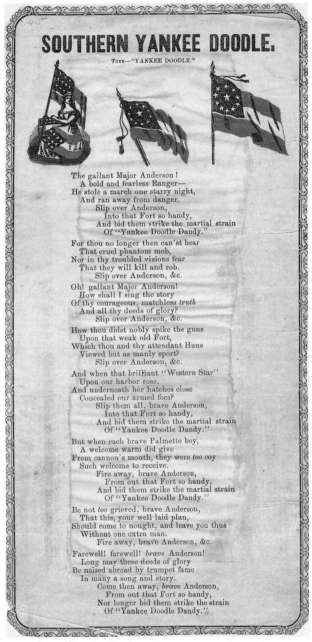

"Southern Yankee Doodle," Wake Forest Broadside Poetry Collection. Confederates drew on the familiar language and iconography of the American Revolution to create a usable past for their new nation. Confederate Broadsides Collection, Special Collections Department, Z. Smith Reynolds Library, Wake Forest University, Winston-Salem, N.C.

article in the *Southern Illustrated News* expressed agreement with the prevailing sentiment that it should bear the figure of a man on horseback— after all, Southerners were known for their equestrian abilities—but argued against it being a Cavalier. "We were not all Cavaliers, and we have no patrician order," the author claimed. "Far better were it to let the horseman be the well known and revered image of George Washington, as the loftiest development of the Southern Gentleman." This rejection of the Cavalier image may seem surprising in light of Confederates' frequent evocations of the Cavalier myth. In this instance, the author appears to have been making a conscious bid toward greater inclusion in the Confederate polity, by proposing a figure to whom Confederates of all classes would respond with positive associations.[30]

As Confederates sought to encourage enlistments, spur patriotism, and ultimately fight despair, they called upon Confederate men to live out the patriotism of their more direct ancestors, the common soldiers of the Revolution. Poems, songs, and stories invoked Revolutionary victories on Southern soil at Yorktown, Eutaw Springs, Cowpens, and King's Mountain and summoned the spirits of Washington, Richard "Light-Horse Harry" Lee, and Francis "The Swamp Fox" Marion.[31] Such invocations were not limited to generals but extended to the men under their commands as well. The image of the Revolutionary War soldier spurring on the younger generation pervaded Confederate calls to arms. In the poem "The Spirit of '76—The Old Rifleman," an old man put on his buckskin suit and ventured forth to inspire the new crop of soldiers:

> We'll teach these shot-gun boys the tricks,
>   By which a war is won;
> Especially how seventy-six
>   Took tories on the run!

The poem "Seventy-six and Sixty-one" sought to conjure up the "spirits of the glorious dead!" to lend their inspiration to their Southern sons, and "The Spirit of '60" referred to a resurgence of "the old spirit of '76." When Mrs. Frank Wilson of Raleigh presented a Confederate flag to the Oak City Guards in June of 1861, her husband read a poem of his own writing, encouraging "Patriots! Warriors! Freedom's Sons!" to "meet as your fathers met the foe!"[32] A poem directed at Marylanders called upon the "sons of Sires, of manly deeds, who died for love of right," to emulate their forebears and rise up in revolution against despotism. Apparently they were heeding the call, for the *Southern Monthly* reported that the Maryland regiments in the Confederate army "have adopted the title of 'the Maryland Line,' which was so heroically sustained by their patriotic sires of the first Revolution."[33]

Confederate women and men both turned to the Revolutionary experience to find comfort in times of trouble. And it was there for the finding, often in the form of public exhortations compelling Confederates to keep the faith. The war went on for much longer than Confederates had expected, and when the people feared that all might be lost, they were reminded of the bleak times in the Revolutionary War that eventually changed for the better. Confederates were repeatedly reassured that their ancestors had been in a much more difficult spot and had overcome far worse trials than those the Confederates were presently experiencing. Readers of the *Montgomery Mail* were told that "in the Revolution there was more suffering and more destitution than will happen to us if the war should last for fifty years. We are in a better position for carrying on a war than almost every other people, and should not complain of hardship." A piece in the *Charleston Mercury*, after the double defeat at Gettysburg and Vicksburg in July 1863, pointedly argued that "if Generals Lee and Bragg and Johnston were to-morrow beaten in the field, we would not be in as desperate a condition as our fathers were when General Washington, vanquished at Long Island, Germantown, and White Plains, and with a handful of men under his command, attacked Princeton in the dead of winter." The American Revolution proved that selfless dedication to the cause of liberty could triumph over a more numerous and better-supplied foe, and Confederates were encouraged to keep that lesson before them at all times. "Think of the men of the Revolution," Confederates were told in an article reprinted around the country in 1863, "when the entire South was overrun by the British and the Tories! . . . Are we any less than they?"[34]

These Revolutionary analogies emphasized the degree to which the North had become a foreign country to Confederates. As one might expect from a nation whose only experience was one of war and desolation, much of Confederate nationalist rhetoric had a negative tone—it was concerned with expelling the Yankees, fighting to the death if need be, consoling mourners.[35] The *Southern Field and Fireside* published an excerpt from the *Chicago Times* describing the murder of a young man in Memphis, shot by a Union soldier who had accused him of being a secessionist. "How," the accompanying commentary asked, "can we ever fraternize with a people whose brutality has crimsoned every section of our country they have occupied with the blood of innocent noncombatants?" diarist Emma LeConte scoffed at any talk of surrender—"a sea rolls between them and us—a sea of blood. Smoking houses, outraged women, murdered fathers, brothers, and husbands, forbid such a union. Reunion! Great Heavens! How we hate them with the whole strength and depth of our souls!" One Virginian preferred to die rather "than to have the Union with such a people restored," while another considered the Northern Christians who supported the war to be no better than the Catholics who had supported the Inquisition.[36]

Southern notions of honor and manhood influenced Confederate intransigence. Confederates saw themselves as patriots fighting an honorable and legitimate war, in contrast to the "dregs of the earth" believed to comprise the Union army. As such, they believed they could not be dominated by their social and moral inferiors. One typical article that appeared quite early in the war drew a stark comparison between "the very best portion of the population of the South," who would be facing "the very worst population of the North." Southern soldiers were "honorable, honest, moral and virtuous," their Northern counterparts, "desperadoes and dangerous men."[37] The rhetoric surrounding peace terms was laden with gendered language. In addition to expressing anxiety about Southern women, and their possible loss of position, it showed how closely intertwined the conflict was with notions of manhood. Southern men were accustomed to contests with clearly defined rules—be they horse races, card games, or dueling—and to the idea of never backing down or walking away from a fight. Confederates wanted peace on their own terms and peace with honor, both of which meant peace with independence. To accept anything less meant showing unacceptable weakness. This desire would, as we will see, hold with remarkable consistency throughout the years of the war.[38]

James D. B. De Bow warned, "We must succeed in this conflict or all is lost. *Reconstruction* is but a dream of fools, traitors, or weak-minded men at the South and deluded ones at the North." An author in the *Southern Cultivator* doubted that "peace can be obtained on any terms consistent with our manhood." Hearing the terms of Lincoln's "ten percent" plan for reconstruction prompted Gustave Breaux, the Confederate colonel in charge of Lafayette, Louisiana, to exclaim, "Comment upon the spirit of this document is almost unnecessary for any Southerner who has a spark of manhood. It is a burning insult to every person in the Confederacy, if an insult could be offered by so crass & vulgar a personage as Lincoln." Rather than appeal to Confederates through its moderate terms, Breaux continued, the plan "warns us that in successful rebellion is to [be] found our social & political safety."[39]

Confederate men and women, particularly as the war stretched from months into years, were concerned that the mounting death toll would be *for* something, that thousands of young men's lives "have not been offered up in vain" upon the "altars" of their country. In this way, and certainly until the final months of the war, Confederates who lost loved ones seemed more tightly bound to their new nation. Just as there was honor inherent in serving the Confederacy, so too was there honor in dying for it, as James Henley Thornwell reminded his readers: "The spirits of our fathers call to us from their graves. The heroes of other ages and countries are beckoning us on to glory. Let us seize the opportunity, and make to ourselves an immortal name, while we redeem a land from bondage and a continent from ruin." An Alabama mother, reflecting on the deaths of her two soldier sons, consoled herself, remembering that "their prayers have already gone up perfumed by the blood of attonement that their lives might exert a blessed influence on this country's revolution." She remained troubled, though, not only by her loss but by those of her fellow countrymen. Presaging the statues that would eventually dot the Southern landscape, she lamented, "Would that I could raise a monument in our own neighborhood to the memory of those noble young men who left neither wife nor child to tell that they had ever lived. But your countrymen will write an epitaph to your honor that has been sealed by your blood."[40]

SOUTHERN PENS TO RECORD THEIR FAME

Confederates, striving to establish their independence from the United States governmentally and geographically, sought to do so intellectually as well. In late 1862, Gertrude Thomas expressed frustration that the North remained more advanced than the South in terms of "literary attainments." She regretted that Southern newspapers still relied heavily on extracts from Northern papers and that Southern readers still favored Northern writers. Thomas attributed this dependence to lack of effort on the part of Confederates and feared for the future: "If this is so now, how will it be when peace is established between us? Will we resume the same old relations?" Her fears seemed to be about more than just literature. For Confederates, literary independence seemed to function as a symbolic, and frankly, a more attainable, stand-in for political independence.[41]

Confederate newspapers and magazines, especially in the early years of the war (before shortages of men and supplies forced them to cease publication), were optimistic in their assessment of Southern literary fortunes. The *Magnolia Weekly*, published in Richmond, was typical in its assertion that separating from the North freed "Southern Genius" to flower.[42] By far the most active booster of Confederate writings was the *Southern Field and Fireside*, published first in Augusta, Georgia, and then later in Raleigh, North Carolina. Described in an advertisement as "a rich casket of polite Southern literature," the eight-page weekly boasted over 10,000 subscribers and appeared more or less continuously until March 1865. It resumed publication in December 1865 as the *Field and Fireside*. Both the original wartime editor, James Gardner, and his successor, William B. Smith (who merged the paper with the *Raleigh Illustrated Mercury*), promoted Southern writers and encouraged patronage as a mark of patriotism. While most of the paper was devoted to serial fiction and poetry, as well as short articles culled from a variety of other sources (including British publications), the *Fireside* also had an editorial page to provide a roundup of recent war news. The last page, devoted to agriculture and home manufactures, furnished readers with a variety of hints for making the most of what they had in a time of shortages.[43]

Several articles in 1863 and 1864 devoted themselves to the connection between literature and "national greatness." "A people cannot take high rank in the scale of nations who neglect literature and the arts," an essay proclaimed in January 1863. Confederates were always concerned with proving their legitimacy as a nation. If their political independence would not be recognized, perhaps their artistic one would be. Another author reminded readers that "literature is the only power that can give immortality to the people." Comparing the lasting glory of Greece and Rome to the ephemeral leavings of Babylon and Ninevah, he warned that without a literary tradition to tell and retell stories of greatness, military might and power would eventually crumble. Like the frequent exhortations for Confederates to resist imported Yankee goods, these articles berated readers for not abandoning Northern writing in favor of local productions. The author praised his fellow citizens for their efforts to cut off commercial contact with the North but cautioned that "so long as we continue to patronize and read Northern literature in the shape of books, magazines, and newspapers, only the lesser half of Southern independence will be achieved." Confederates risked finding themselves in a "state of literary bondage," exactly the sort of commercial and political servitude that secession had been meant to prevent. The only impediment, the author argued, that stood in the way of creating worthy works was "the Southern people themselves; let them only patronize such efforts and there will be no difficulty in getting up works that the nation may be proud of."[44]

The article "Literature for the South" in June 1863 returned to the theme of self-sufficiency: "No such grand opportunity for building up Southern literature will occur again, if the present one is neglected, and the country will deteriorate instead of advancing in intelligence and learning. Shall the decision of the people be for home literature, or shall we return to dependence on foreign nations?" Here again literature served as metaphor. Confederate authors expressed concern about keeping up appearances before the rest of the world, important in the Confederacy's ever-present search for European recognition. Thus the editors of the *Fireside* appealed for support (and subscriptions) in late 1864, reminding readers that "the War should not so far absorb all our energies as to cause us to neglect our interests at home; we should show to the world that even in times of the greatest perils, we are able to do all that befits a great Nation, determined to be free." Southern stories had to be written by Southern authors, for only they could accurately "reflect our ideas and feelings," and thus "the deeds of our heroes lying dead on the field of glory, need Southern pens to record their fame, Southern flowers to deck their honored corpses."[45]

Indigenous literature would not only express appropriately patriotic sentiments but also protect Southerners from supposed Yankee moral degeneracy. Northern publications were characterized as "trashy, worthless, and poisonous," their degradation shared by the people who produced them. Nations, claimed the author of "Yankee War Literature," revealed their national character through their literature, and the people of the United States were consequently "eminently excitable, unstable, sensational, fickle, and extreme." While at one time the presence of Southerners had moderated these tendencies, the war had allowed the worst Yankee tendencies to flower. Particular scorn was heaped upon fashionably sentimental romances:

> The South is a favourite scene for the location of the Yankee writer's tale or poem, and in that South is sure to be represented some Union loving maid who remains true to the "gelorious" old flag in spite of the "treason" around her, discards her rebel lover who fights under the Southern cross, and only restores him to her good graces when, at the close of the tale, he comes back all repentant, ragged, wretched, and forlorn to claim the boon of serving seven years for his Rebecca under the "Stars and Stripes," keeping time to the air of Hail Columbia or what not.

These tales were not without variety, the article pointed out—sometimes the lover was a black soldier, sometime the action took place in East Tennessee or in West Virginia. Such "wild," "monstrous," "morbid," and "diseased" writing stood in marked contrast to the subjects of Southern letters, among them "patriotism and honour, household affection and a stainless love, the history of pure hearts and the life of the little ones, goodness, virtue, honest[y] and truth."[46]

The *Southern Field and Fireside* championed all aspects of Confederate belles lettres. In late 1864, upset at allegations that journalists exploited exemptions and unfairly attacked the government in Richmond, it endorsed calls for a convention of the Southern press. The editors defended Southern journalists as loyal to the cause and argued that a convention would show the unity of the press on questions of Confederate rights and independence. Similarly, it would show "Yankee scoffers . . . that in the assertion of its country's rights, and the maintenance of its own liberties that the Press is firmly knit as bonds of steel." The paper also praised the Confederacy's emergent book publishers, operating in Richmond, Mobile, Macon, and Atlanta, and their lists of histories, schoolbooks, and sheet music. While granting that the aesthetic qualities of Northern books, "that handsome display of gilt-edged paper, embossed covers, and gilt blazonry," outshone those of the South, Confederate books were "printed on tolerable substantial paper and with clear, readable type." This was not an insignificant achievement, given the severe shortages that the Confederacy faced. With the people's help, and with their purchases, "the establishment of Southern Political Independence" would be accompanied by "the establishment of Southern Literary Independence" as well.[47]

Confederates, as this explicit linkage between politics and prose demonstrates, tried to write themselves into existence. Southern calls for indigenous literature served two purposes. The first was as a marker or symbol of independence; the second had to do with content. Language transmitted identity and citizenship, and Confederates needed writings to explain to people why they were part of this new nation. This was especially true for children.

"WHAT ARE WE TO DO FOR SCHOOLBOOKS?"

For those concerned with forging a nationalist identity and traditions, children posed a pressing concern. If the Confederate nation was to survive, it would have to transmit its values and meaning to the next generation. Over three-quarters of the books published for children in the Con-

Pictorial envelope, "The Sunny South Our Country." Confederates wanted to make sure that their children learned the lessons of nationalism. Collection of The New-York Historical Society.

federacy were schoolbooks, and one historian has called the primers and spellers "the Confederacy's most important literary tradition." Because so many of these books were explicitly designed to teach children the rights and duties of Confederate citizenship, they provide a valuable window into ideas of Confederate nationalism.[48] "What Are We to Do for Schoolbooks?" asked an article in the *Field and Fireside*, lamenting prewar dependence on Northern-published texts. There was no excuse for the failure of the Confederacy to produce its own schoolbooks, for "a citizen of any country can make a better school-book for the youth of that country, than a citizen of the same qualifications of any other country." Part of the Confederacy's quest for international recognition rested on such foundations. The Confederacy needed to act like any other great nation; the English, for example, did not use American schoolbooks, so why should Confederate children be forced to do so? The article endorsed plans for an upcoming convention of Confederate teachers and called for Southern men to "go to the work of writing." Several men, and one woman in particular—Mrs. Marinda Branson Moore—heeded that call.[49]

Confederate schoolbooks fell into three main categories: arithmetic books, primers, and geographies, whose lessons frequently encompassed history as well as literature. Created as tools of socialization, schoolbooks reflected Confederate society. Arithmetic books, despite the oft-repeated math problems asking how many Yankees x number of Confederates could whip, tended to concentrate mainly on the subject at hand without devoting space to patriotic exhortation and the creation of nationalist identity. Some books were simply repackaged editions of older books, with the only change being a new title or preface; others, like John Neely's *Confederate Speller and Reader* or *First Dixie Primer* and *First Dixie Reader*, both written by the prolific Marinda Moore, claimed to represent improvements over Northern methods.[50] Neely sought to convince purchasers of his book's lasting merits: "The 'Speller and Reader' is not now published merely to fill up a gap for a time, and to be thrown aside when other books of its class can be procured from our former literary emporium. It claims at least equality with the very best of these productions; and is intended to hold its position *permanently* in the face of all such competitors." Moore's advertisement assured satisfaction, as her books were "composed by a Southern Writer and in Southern Style."[51]

A few of the primers and spellers showed the influence of war mainly through their illustrations—of cannons, Confederate flags, and soldiers in uniform.[52] Many readers contained short aphorisms or moral lessons designed to complement Christian teachings. The *Dixie Speller*'s lesson on cruelty urged children not to torment animals or slaves, reminding them that "the Bible tells us we must look after and correct both servants and stock." Emphasizing a main tenet of the antebellum proslavery argument, the lesson encouraged pupils to put themselves in their servants' place: "If we were servants and did wrong, we should expect to be punished according to the crime, but not to be abused. Then when we worked hard and made plenty to live on, we should expect to help eat it. It is not a sin to own slaves, but it is a very great sin to treat them cruelly." In this way children were taught that the Confederacy and slavery went together.[53]

Vocabulary lessons taught words that children probably heard and wondered about, like "cavalry" or "infantry." They also presented the Confederate view of the war: "An *enemy* is one who hates us. The Yankees are enemies to the Southern people."[54] Lessons similarly emphasized the responsibility everyone, even children, had to help the cause:

It is very common now to see ladies dressed in HOMESPUN. This is a very useful and becoming dress.

The man who proves TRAITOR to his country in time of war, must not expect to live.

You must not *taunt* the poor soldier because he is in rags; he fights for liberty and peace, which are priceless blessings to mankind.[55]

In "The Drummer Boy," a story in the *Child's First Book*, the young protagonist explains that his mother wanted him to join the army, but for the most unselfish of reasons: "It was not the pay sir; it was more than that; it was not the pay at all; for she said to me 'You can do your part, my boy, for the land. For if you will beat the drum, you will take the place of a man.' I am here for our land, sir—to help save my home." The *Confederate Speller and Reader* took a similar approach, explaining that "Troops who en-ter a State with hos-tile purpose, are in-va-ders. Let all who are able, take up arms to drive them back."[56]

Schoolbook authors sought to use children to combat desertion and shirking. "En-tice-ments to de-part from du-ty must be met with firm re-sist-ance," the *Confederate Speller and Reader* cautioned sternly. A lesson in the *Dixie Speller* appealed to children's sense of honor and duty:

If I were a man, and the laws said I must go to war, I would not run
    away like some do. . . .
I would soon-er die at my post than de-sert.
And O if my pa-pa had run a-way, and been shot for it, how sad I must
    have felt all my life!

Good citizenship demanded that all Confederates—rich or poor, male or female, young or old—put their nation before themselves.[57]

Most poignantly, several primers made reference to the horrors of war as experienced by children: the deaths in their families, the presence of maimed men around their towns, and the economic troubles that forced many of them into poverty. "This sad war is a bad thing," began a lesson in the *Dixie Speller*. "My pa-pa went, and died in the army. My big brother went too, and got shot. A bomb-shell took off his head." As if that were not enough for the poor fictitious family to cope with, "My aunt had three sons, and all have died in the army. Now she and the girls have to work for bread. I will work for my ma and my sisters." Another book taught that "of all that left the en-camp-ment to take part in the en-gage-ment, not more that one hundred sur-vived." A passage in the *First Reader* seemed guaranteed to provoke nightmares in small children:

Look at that boy's two hands
What would I do if I had no hand?
How glad I am that I can bend my arm!

That man's arm has been cut off.

It was shot off by a gun.

Oh! What a sad thing war is!

While acknowledging the war-weariness of its readers, the *First Reader* took care not to encourage subversion or griping, reminding them that "I must not speak evil of the rulers of my land."[58]

Primers and readers made occasional mention of the Confederate government. The *Confederate Speller and Reader* taught students that the Confederate president served for six years while the U.S. president held office for only four, and a lesson on war in the *Dixie Speller* cautioned children against electing "bad men" to office, for "if the rulers in the United States had been good Christian men, the present war would not have come upon us."[59] In general, however, detailed discussion of Confederate history and government were left to the geographies, and many of their lessons echoed the arguments presented to adults in publications like *The Confederate*. Kensey Johns Stewart's *Geography for Beginners* devoted a chapter to the history of the Confederate States, describing secession as a right and concluding happily that "the people of the Southern States have fought their own way to political independence and the respect and amity of the great nations of the world." The chapter closes with several review questions that do much to illuminate the issues Confederates thought important for their children to grasp: "Has one State a right to subjugate another? Who aided the South? Who is the King of Nations? Can a nation fail without His word? What will happen if we forget Him?"[60] Marinda Branson Moore's *Geographical Reader for the Dixie Children* reiterated some of the lessons contained in her speller, when the review section asked:

> Q. If the people of the United States had always elected good men for rulers what would have been the result?
>
> A. We should have had no war.
>
> Q. Why?
>
> A. Because every man would have been willing to treat others justly, and there would have been no cause for war.

Like Stewart, Moore expressed great confidence in the Confederacy's ability to survive the war and flourish. She praises the people for their ingenuity and resourcefulness, for helping themselves, and, consequently, securing God's assistance. "We were considered indolent, weak people," she explained, "but our enemies have found us strong because we have justice on our side."[61]

Moore's geography, while written for children, expressed the beliefs of many Confederate adults, especially regarding their new nation's origins and its supposedly intrinsic superiority. Moore began by detailing the various climatic zones of the world and describing the influences that climate has on race and personality. People of the "Temperate Zone"—where the Confederacy was located—are "generally industrious and intelligent." Of all the races, according to Moore, the Caucasians were the most civilized, followed by Asians and Indians. Africans left in their native continent were "slothful and vicious," as well as "cruel," but "the slaves who are found in America are in much better condition." The proslavery argument permeated all aspects of Confederate culture.[62] The lesson on North America devoted considerable space to the differences between the United and Confederate States, their leaders, and their people. Abraham Lincoln was condemned as a "weak man," whereas Jefferson Davis was "good and wise"; the Confederate military leadership was "pious," as were the Confederate people. Moore argued implicitly that separation was inevitable, for the Northern and Southern people were simply too different. Northerners were "ingenious and enterprising, and were noted for their tact in 'driving a bargain.' They are refined and intelligent on all subjects but that of negro slavery, on this they are mad." In contrast, "the Southern people are noted for being high minded and courteous. A stranger seldom lacks friends in this country."[63]

Moore had high praise for Virginians, both for their ability to withstand more than their fair share of war-related suffering and for the benevolent treatment they offered their slaves. North Carolinians were "noted for their honesty and for being 'slow but sure.'" Referring to the Unionist population, Moore took the opportunity to inculcate civic virtue in her readers. The few men who refused to fight for their country were "cowards," and "nearly all of them were of the ignorant class, and many of them did not know what patriotism was." She absolved South Carolinians from responsibility for starting the war, arguing that "the war would have come sooner or later." They were chivalrous, but hot-headed, and did not treat their slaves as well as masters from Virginia and North Carolina. Moore expressed confidence that the suffering of Missourians and Arkansans would soon end and the wrongs perpetrated against their Confederate people would be avenged. Regarding Kentucky, "when the matter is left to the people to decide, they will declare themselves Southerners. Many of her gallant sons are fighting for 'Southern Rights.'" She had high praise for Tennessee, oppressed and suffering but "nobly doing her part, and when the war is ended she will be one of our best states."[64] Moore, and one might assume her young readers, longed for peace, but it was a peace accompanied by independence, not re-union. She believed that only by repenting of their sins could Confederates win God's favor, and so she encouraged children to be good Christians, as well as good Confederates.[65]

"THE CAUSE IS NOT OURS, BUT GOD'S"

The connection between "Confederate" and "Christian" stressed in writings for children was integral to Confederate ideology. Religion was as important a foundation to Confederate nationalism as any other. Confederates believed themselves to be a chosen people, doing God's will by creating their new, more perfect nation. They believed themselves to be more virtuous, more pious than their opponents. Part of their mission to recreate the American nation in the Founder's vision was related to this. It gave the war a higher purpose than simply politics. Religion, or faith in God, was important in another way: Confederates needed to believe that God was on their side, for that meant that no matter the setbacks they faced they would eventually emerge victorious. As they looked around themselves, Confederates constantly turned to their faith in God to keep their spirits from faltering. Such religious faith, however, could be the proverbial double-edged sword as well. What God gave, some Confederates feared, he could also take away.[66]

"Who [is] so blind," asked a Virginian in 1864, "as not to be able to see the hand of a merciful and protective God in all this! in his wonderful deliverance of our army and people from the most powerful conflagrations ever planned for our destruction!" Confederates drew comfort from their faith, looking to God to lift their faltering spirits. A man in Mobile told a devout friend: "I intend to try and become religious and think as you do. If I could look at things as you do and have such faith as you have, I could have been much happier and better satisfied." Concerned about the news coming out of Vicksburg in June 1863, a Culpeper woman reminded herself, "Surely there never was a nation struggling for independence, whom an all wise providence has so repeatedly blessed. As a people we cannot be thankful enough."[67]

Such language, while ritualized to some extent, was also reflective of true emotions. Confederates needed to believe that the drastic decisions that they had made were the right ones. Believing that they were following God's will and that God would never forsake them was one way to make sure. This use of religious language as a foundation for national identity was not unlike the use of Revolutionary iconography—in both cases Confederates drew on the familiar not only to justify their choices but also to draw distinctions between themselves and Northerners. If Confederates were right, than Yankees had to be wrong.

Fannie Page Hume, a woman in her early twenties living with family in Orange County, Virginia, serves as a typical example of this relationship between religion and nationalism. Her February 1862 diary entries were full of bad news. She first lamented the loss of Roanoke Island: "Oh! Am too sorry—trust it may teach us a lesson, we have been too boastful, too confident of our strength." She greeted the news of the fall of Fort Donelson and that Nashville had been taken in much the same vein, noting first that "our dark day has certainly dawned," and later that "I trust this fearful reverse may rouse us to still greater exertions. We have relaxed vigilance too soon."[68] In this idea that Confederates almost deserved these losses, or were somehow being chastened or chastised for their failures of will or failures of humility, Hume expressed a powerful sense of the Confederacy's religious mission. This is not, however, the same thing as a sense of fatalism. Most Confederate civilians believed that their fate was in God's hands but that they could influence it: that is, they would be rewarded for their virtues, punished for their sins, but in a sort of parental, or correcting, way.

This relationship between faith and nationalism also comes through in Hume's remarks about Jefferson Davis. She first noted his inauguration on 22 February, hoping that the "rainy & gloomy" weather would not prove "ominous of the future of the Government." (Three days before, she had noted that the permanent Congress had opened it's first session "under gloomy auspices.") Davis quickly set aside 28 February as a day for fasting, humiliation, and prayer, as he would do almost a dozen times during the war.[69] Fannie attended her local church and declared the sermon "most excellent," even though the preacher "drew a gloomy picture of our present conditions attributing our reverses to our many sins; depravity in Camp & Capitol, &c." But it seemed to have immediate effect, for in the same entry, she noted rumors of advances emanating out from Centreville. A few months later, Fannie Hume mentions Davis again, this time noting approvingly his baptism and confirmation, "which event I trust augurs well for us."[70]

By the height of summer, the war had drawn closer to Fannie Hume in

Orange. Refugees from the West had passed through in the spring, and their singing "Dixie" did nothing to erase Hume's characterization of this development as a "sad, sad sight." Just before the anniversary of First Manassas, Union soldiers surrounded her home, arrested her grandfather and uncle, and raided their storehouses. In early August, she reported that there was so much fighting in the neighborhood that people were evacuating. Her cousin's slaves ran away, and rumors swirled that the Union forces had threatened to shell the village. At this her religious imagery returned, laced with anger: "Oh! that the day of retribution would speedily come! How long O Lord! How long!"[71]

Such religious language was not confined to the civilian population. Although many soldiers, liberated for the first time from the social strictures of parents, wives, and communities, took the opportunity to engage in the vices of gambling and drink, others looked to God as a form of comfort and security. Several revivals swept through the Confederate armies. Soldiers and civilians alike saw in the revivals the creation of a divine army and thus the hand of God. "How could a broader seal have been set upon the righteousness of our cause," asked a Virginia woman, who believed that the revivals signaled God's forgiveness, "to a certain extent at least," of Confederate sins.[72]

Men also found time to practice religion on a smaller scale. A rise in professions of faith was not surprising, given that men were asked to confront death—from both battles and camp sickness—every single day. Gustave Cook noted approvingly in early 1863 that in his camp near Shelbyville, Tennessee, "many who heretofore have either doubted outright or been criminally neglectful in religious matters are driven to the incontrovertible truth and acknowledge the fate of our Country and themselves to be in the hands of that true and trusty friend in whom we may safely confide." He urged his wife to share his faith, asking her to pray to God "for strength to sustain you in your part of the sacrifice. Make it for your own sake, for mine, and for the sake of our little ones and our dear Country." In another letter, he asked her to become his evangelist at home, sharing his thoughts with his friends, all in the service of praising God and ending the war.[73]

Cook was not asking his wife to do any more than he was willing to do. He saw a close relationship between religion and Confederate loyalty—one reinforced the other, together providing strength to continue the fight: "Oh! a religious patriotism is the most beautiful and glorious display of the better part of man." This notion of "religious patriotism," the way in which Cook linked personal and national salvation, was characteristic of Confederates. A nation of Christians, so they believed, would surely be saved by God. Margaret Wight, too, was struck by the faith of the Confederate soldiers encamped near her home outside Richmond in May 1864, praising them for singing hymns rather than swearing. "With such an army may we not look for his blessing? Every here and there one can be seen with his Bible in his hand." This was in marked contrast to their opponents, whom Wight reported had to be nerved with whiskey before they would fight. Piety was therefore linked to Confederate superiority, part and parcel with Confederate soldiers' supposedly greater courage and honor. Confederates also stressed the devout nature of their generals, especially Stonewall Jackson.[74]

"The parsons tell us every Sunday that the Lord is on our side. I wish, however, he would show his preference for us a little more plainly than he has been doing lately," complained one of Mary Chesnut's dinner companions at the end of 1863. Devout Confederates had an answer for his frustration. God was doing one of two things: he was either testing his people's faith by making them suffer, or punishing them for their lack of faith and their un-Christian behavior. The solution to either problem was simple—Confederates needed to have more faith, to pray more often, to be more grateful when God delivered them from the Yankees. James Henley Thornwell warned against committing the sin of pride by exhibiting a "presumptuous confidence." Confederates needed to remember that "the cause is not ours, but God's." Thornwell cautioned against misinterpreting battlefield losses: they were clear signs of God's displeasure, for "we had grown licentious, intemperate and profane; is it strange that, in the midst of our security, God should teach us that sin is a reproach to any people?" The Confederacy needed to rise to the challenges placed in their way by God, and in so doing they would show the world their national mettle and right to independence.[75]

Early in the war, Confederates felt more secure in their position as God's chosen, more confident that he would punish their invaders. As the conflict dragged on with no end in sight, however, people began to worry. Perhaps God was angry with the Confederate people, and that was why he kept them from winning the victories they needed. Zillah Haynie Brandon, who lost two sons in the Confederate army, exemplified this shift in attitudes. In January 1863, she reflected that the "savage barbarity" of the Union had been "turned to naught by the brave men under Jackson, the two Hills, Lee, Longstreet, Bragg, Forest, Wheeler, and a score of others whose men in God's name stand invincible." Christian generals in the service of the Lord would surely carry the day, she believed. But some eighteen months later, her confidence had given way to despair. She lamented, "The cruelties, the unrighteous deluge of blood, is fast destroying our time-honored name and nationality. Oh that a termination of this unnatural war would come. Oh sin what hast though wrought?"[76]

A sense of despair was hard to avoid, but some Confederate men and women tried to find a lesson in their struggle to win God's favor. Mittie Bond agreed with a friend who believed "that God had brought this war upon the south for her utter wickedness for her utter disregard to the sabbath and to the souls placed in her charge." Southerners needed to learn from their mistakes, for, "if peace should ever be ours, God grant it may and [if] we forget this chastisement, God will send worse plagues upon us [than] this war." Kate Cumming "firmly" believed that "there is not a state in the Confederacy that will not be scourged by the invader, for the sins we have committed in our prosperity, forgetting the Most High, who is the giver of all good." She hoped that the Confederate people would cease looking for outside salvation, in the form of European intervention, and instead look within. As bad as things looked for the Confederacy, Cumming believed that God would punish their enemies even more severely, that they, too, would have to answer for their sins. In another entry she reflected that "God is indeed trying us with the refiner's fire; may we come out of it purified."[77]

This belief that God's will would determine the course of the Confederate war for independence extended to the highest levels of government. Ten times during his term as president, Jefferson Davis issued proclamations to his people setting aside a specific day either for prayer and thanksgiving or (more frequently) for fasting, humiliation, and prayer. In doing this, Davis tapped into a powerful American tradition dating back to the Puritans. The use of fast days was another way, perhaps subconsciously, of drawing on the familiar past to legitimate the present. The connection between politics and religion in the Confederacy turned the Confederacy into the culmination of the Puritan "city on a hill."[78]

In each of these messages, Davis acknowledged the debt Confederates owed the Almighty for his support of their efforts and called upon his people to humble themselves before God. When times were good, as after Confederate victories at Second Manassas and Richmond, Kentucky, in 1862, Davis called his people together to "bow down in adoring thankfulness" and "to unite in rendering thanks and praise to God for these great mercies, and to implore him to conduct our country safely through the perils which surround us, to the final attainment of the blessings of peace and security." When the Confederacy struggled, Davis asked for "humble supplications" from the people toward God, asking him to forgive their transgressions and smile upon them once again.[79]

The response of Confederates to these fast days and to the sermons preached and often published remind us not only of how important religion was to the Confederate people but of how closely their national selves were tied into the notion of God's favor. The Presbyterian Synod of Virginia made that connection explicit in its 1862 annual report, which directly linked public fast days (such as had occurred in February and, more important, in May) to the second victory at Manassas. As the report explained, "At first God did not seem to smile on our defensive operations," but then "God put it into the heart of Davis to call for a day of fasting, humiliation, and prayer." The results were clear: following the "united supplication of the whole people . . . we were wonderfully delivered out of the hands of our enemies."[80]

A Presbyterian minister in Raleigh took as his fast-day text the psalm "Weeping may endure for a night, but joy cometh in the morning" and from that spun a sermon that not only dealt with the way that God was helping Confederates at the time but drew comparisons to the "first" American Revolution. Reverend Joseph Atkinson argued that this Confederate revolution was even more deserving of God's favor because its leaders—particularly Stonewall Jackson—were so pious. He reminded his listeners that there was more than one lesson to be drawn from the difficult times over the past winter and spring. Confederates tended to see times of trials as tests by God, or chastening. Atkinson put a more positive spin on them: they were not only "bitter medicine" but also a way for Southerners to come to understand their own "marvelous recuperative energy," their ability to bounce back from defeats and work their way to victory. Atkinson closed with a warning, a bit of a counter to the public urgings of invasion, telling his flock that in order to hold onto God's favor they needed to remain humble in victory.[81]

The Reverend Stephen Elliott, one of the Confederacy's best-known clerics, spoke on the subject of the Second Manassas in Savannah and took the opportunity to pat himself on the back a bit (though he denied it). Elliott returned to a sermon he had preached in May, when Jefferson Davis had called for a day of supplication and prayer. Elliott had believed that the "real troubles" were about to begin for the Union, that they would struggle in the summer heat, and that the Europeans were wavering in their adherence to noninterference. Elliott devoted much of his sermon to justifications of secession and slavery and then turned to praising Confederates—men and women—for their devotion to the cause. Like Atkinson, who ran counter to public calls for more action, Elliott, too, seemed inclined to go easy on the

Davis administration's war policy. Rather than complain that invasion of the North had been too long delayed, Elliott thanked God for restraining Confederates from "any premature invasion of the border states." Maryland and Kentucky were not ready a year ago for the Confederate mission, but now they were: "God wisely kept us back, by his inscrutable guidance, from invading those States a year ago, and we can now understand why the first battle of Manassas went to strangely and mysteriously unimproved, and why defeat so thickly pursued us in the West. It was that the presence of the Northern armies might discipline the people for a thorough union with the South and might bring them more heartily into the support of the institution he was protecting." Once that had been achieved, Elliott explained, God allowed for the second victory at Manassas. Elliott also put the whole question of European intervention into God's hands as well, echoing the themes of self-reliance that appeared in other venues. Confederates, Elliott argued, needed to earn their victories on their own, showing the world that slavery was an asset, "not a source of weakness or an object of fear." Elliott, almost alone among the post-Manassas celebrants, did not predict a speedy end of the war, though not because of any Confederate failings. Rather, their mission would not be complete until their independence was won and England and the North were "convinced that slavery, as we hold it here, is essential to the welfare of the world . . . a sacred trust from God."[82]

Davis wanted the Confederate people to accept their chastising from God and make amends, and they seemed happy to do so. Certainly the calls for fast days were rarely if ever met with criticism, and they were endorsed in public and private. A letter to the editor of the *Southern Recorder* detailing local prayer arrangements for the 21 August 1863 fast day was typical in its support for Davis's efforts and the author's belief that "we need the favor of God. Without it, we perish. God is angry with us for our sins. Hence the war itself, and hence the reverses of this summer." Even the *Richmond Examiner*, one of the newspapers most critical of Davis and his administration, grudgingly admitted that fast days, despite the fact that they "smack of Latter Day sanctity; savor of the nasal twang, and recall disagreeable reminiscences of Praise-God-Barebones, the Pilgrim Fathers, and their Yankee descendants," served a useful purpose, citing historical evidence for the presence of the hand of God on the battlefield.[83] Margaret Wight noted several fast days in her diary, as did many other Confederates. She was pleased that the 27 March 1863 day had been "generally kept" and thought "the admirable sermon on Extortion may have the desired effect for as long as it prevails we can expect the blessing of the Almighty upon our unhappy country." Cloe Whittle noted in August 1863 that "recently the Lord has not gone out with us to battle & I think our beloved [leader] has done very right to call our people to a public humiliation of ourselves before the Sovereign of the Universe."[84]

Jefferson Davis was not the only person to issue calls for public, communal prayer—governors, clergymen, and generals did so as well. Georgia governor Joseph Brown declared 10 December 1863 a day of fasting, humiliation, and prayer. The newly inaugurated governor of Alabama, Thomas H. Watts, concurred in the proclamation and asked the people of his state to humble themselves before God, "in view of our sin, and earnestly beseech Him that His face may shine upon us." In June 1864, the *Montgomery Advertiser* published a daily schedule of "prayer to Almighty God in behalf of our country, and for the success of our armies in the impending battles." Each night, the prayer meetings were held at a different church around town, an arrangement replicated throughout the Confederate South.[85]

In addition to requesting people's presence at various public prayer meetings and Sunday services, denominational leaders and organizations provided a variety of prayers and tracts designed to direct the faithful. Some were directed explicitly toward the soldiers in the armies; others appear to have been written and distributed for general use. One of the latter, "A Specimin of Southern Devotion; or, The Prayer of a Rebel Saint," published in November 1862, thanked God for the past and present successes he had given the Confederacy and asked that "the Federal Union be permanently destroyed." The one-page "Confederate Form of Prayer" began like most of these tracts by praising and thanking God for his efforts on the part of the Confederacy. Unlike the "Prayer of a Rebel Saint," it asked only that "it may please Thee to set at naught the efforts of all our enemies, and put them to confusion and shame." This pocket-sized publication, a model for Confederate Christians to utter privately, asked also that God see fit to "preserve our homes and altars from pollution and secure to us the restoration of peace and prosperity." The "Patriotic Prayer for the Southern Cause," complete with a red, white, and blue flag on its cover, addressed still more specific concerns, asking God to take his faithful Confederate subjects

under Thy nurturing care; give them wisdom in council and valor in the field; defeat the malicious designs of our cruel adversaries; convince the North of the "unrighteousness of their cause;" and, if they still persist in their sanguinary purposes, oh! let the voice of Thine own unerring justice sounding in their hearts, constrain them to drop their weapons of war from their unnerved hands in the day of battle.

Be Thou present, O god of wisdom and direct the councils of that honorable assembly; enable them to settle things on the best and surest foundation,—that the scene of blood may be speedily closed,—that order, harmony, and peace may be effectually restored,—and truth and justice, religion and piety prevail and flourish among Thy people.

Confederates thus believed that collective and direct appeals to God would turn the tide for the Confederacy and allow it to fulfill its national mission.[86]

All of these tracts, prayers, and sermons shared a common ideological message: Confederates were a godly people, best exemplified in the figures of Stonewall Jackson and Robert E. Lee, and God should therefore look with favor upon them. Their identity as a nation was tied up with an image of themselves as God's chosen people—chastised when they did wrong but protected and shielded when they did right. God was an integral part of Confederate society and ideology, but the reverse was also true. That is, by injecting the Confederacy into matters of religion like the liturgy, Confederates added legitimacy to their national aspirations. The Confederate nation was everywhere, a part of all facets of life. The secular was the sacred in the Confederate States.

Interlude

A Hope Fully Authorized by the Facts

By the summer of 1862, the war that was supposed to last for only weeks was over a year old, and those Confederates who looked beyond the platitudes and boasting that filled the pages of their newspapers had to know that there was no end in sight. The depth of Confederate anxieties about their future, anxieties that would temporarily be quelled by the battle of Second Manassas, is revealed by their assessments of their situation during the spring and summer of 1862. On 31 August 1862, Lucy Rebecca Buck, a young woman in Front Royal, Virginia, recorded the news of the "glorious" second Confederate victory at Manassas, one that made her feel "very hopeful and cheerful for our cause." More interestingly, however, she went on to describe six preceding months of "disaster and destruction":

> We had lost our stronghold and permitted the enemy to penetrate to the vitals of the country with his desolating armies, laying waste to the land with fire and sword. Then his ironclad gunboats were swarming on our coast and port after port, city after city were occupied by his ruffian horde and the whole South was being drained of its substance. So that there was nothing but starvation and ruin for the inhabitants. Our capital was menaced by a vast army of exultant and victory flushed foes. Our army seemed to have melted away, or were within the coils of a mighty serpent that must soon crush them—oh it was all disheartening enough![1]

Buck's palpable sense of relief at the Confederates winning the battle, a relief that would become delight when she heard about the invasion of Maryland, is typical of reaction to this news. Second Manassas played out against the backdrop of deep anxieties for Confederates, fears about their future independence and about their worthiness in the eyes not only of the world but of God.

The counter to this theme of Southern self-reliance, or, rather, reliance only on themselves and God's good auspices, came in the form of a yearning for foreign recognition that continued virtually unabated throughout the war years. A key component of Confederates' use of Revolutionary War analogies involved foreign intervention—every Confederate, indeed every American, knew how important the French had been to the Revolution. Confederates also wanted Britain and France to recognize them in order to break the power of the Union blockade, and they believed that their so-called King Cotton Diplomacy could achieve that end.[2] Beyond these very practical and diplomatic concerns, however, lay a more psychological desire for recognition. Confederates believed that they had created a legitimate nation, but they also knew how fragile it was. They also were a people to whom personal honor, in the form of public validation, was desperately important. They needed to have their choices, their independence, ratified by others. This yearning manifested itself in two kinds of expressions. The first was in newspaper articles and, to a degree, private writings, laying out the case for recognition, explaining why *this* time, after this or that battle, recognition would be forthcoming. This necessitated some intellectual gymnastics on the part of Confederates who seemed to argue that Britain and France were waiting either for the Confederate situation to become desperate before jumping in to save the day, or for Confederate victory to seem inevitable, at which point they would jump on the bandwagon. These articles tapered off considerably after the first year or so of the war, once it became rather obvious that no matter what happened, Britain and France were not going to recognize the Confederacy. Mary Chesnut summed this resignation up succinctly: "England's eye is scornful and scoffing as she turns it towards us—and on our miseries."[3]

This realization, however, had no appreciable impact on the other way these desires were expressed: through rumors of foreign involvement, usually centering on the French. These continued unchecked from the start of the war through to the days after Lee's surrender at Appomattox. Typical were these musings in Lucy Rebecca Buck's diary during the summer of 1862. Buck noted first that "the paper announced the recognition of the S C [Southern Confederacy] by France. I have lost all confidence and dependence in such rumors, but I would be glad if it were so." Less than two weeks later, she reported that France had recognized the Confederacy "and her determination officially announced at Washington of putting a speedy conclusion to this war." While Buck provided no comments on the believability of this rumor, she did note that rumors of Jackson's and Longstreet's deaths, and Early's and Stuart's captures were not credible. Chesnut herself got so caught up in rumors of French recognition at this same time that she joyfully noted, "Louis Napoleon does not stop at trifles. He never botches his work; he is thorough." That could not, however, be said of her source, none other than General Wade Hampton. These rumors, which Confederates dutifully recorded and reported to one another, even as they seemed to know they were untrue, were symptomatic of their anxiety about their national future. It almost seemed that they were trying to wish recognition into being.[4]

Such rumors continued to crop up at times of stress for Confederates. Thus, a resident of Dublin Depot, Virginia, confessed in July 1863 that he saw "but little prospect of Peace at present," unless European nations intervened. And he did not anticipate that happening until "our side is about to overthrow the other." Only then would "England & France step forward & demand a cessation of hostilities," for it was in their best interest to see "us cut up into separate nationalities, thereby better preserving the balance of power & enabling them to be the ruling powers of the Earth." Confederates could not count on European interest in them; they would have to fight for themselves.[5]

Confederates also used the question of foreign recognition as a way to motivate backsliders or make other points about the conduct of the war. For example, on 19 June, the *Charleston Mercury* somewhat testily attacked a piece in the *Richmond Examiner* that had attributed to nonrecognition two factors: a supposed "indisposition to encourage revolution" on the part of foreign nations and a more general ignorance on their part of the true causes and progress of the war. Nonsense, charged the *Mercury*. Foreign nations had recognized other countries' independence after revolutions (this, in fact, was a staple of the Confederate argument for recognition—essentially, that because Britain and France had recognized Mexico and other Latin American nations, they would have to recognize the Confederacy). And, if ignorance was the problem, the Confederates had only themselves to blame for not making a convincing enough case. No, argued the *Mercury*; the problem lay in the Confederates' own "inactive" war policy, in their failure to follow up after Manassas or Corinth, and in their failure to win a commanding victory in either Mississippi or Virginia. Confederate military policy in this first year of war had been "that of a beaten people . . . a policy of temporising weakness and timid surrender," not the policy of "an earnest people, really independent, or of a people manifesting the power to make themselves so." Europeans, this article charged, didn't believe in Confederate independence because the Confederates didn't seem to either. In this, of course, the *Mer-*

cury, a constant critic of Jefferson Davis, was actually pushing a policy of more offense, the very policy that made the editors of the *Southern Confederacy* so uncomfortable.[6]

More often, however, by the summer of 1862, Confederates were displaying an understanding that foreign recognition would not be forthcoming, and thus they concentrated on turning that into a virtue. In August, the *Memphis Daily Appeal* conceded that it had become obvious that England would not intervene in the war, "until, at least, the aspect of things is materially changed." Rather than be miserable about this, the paper suggested that Southerners should be happy with their independence. Indeed, perhaps the realization that Confederates would have to win or lose on their own would spur people to action. Victory was up to the Confederate people themselves. In one of the great juxtapositions that make newspapers such valuable and revealing cultural sources, this argument was reinforced by a letter just two columns over on the theme of "self-reliance," urging Confederates to trust themselves and fight for the recognition that they believed was their due. Such a hope was not entirely misplaced, for the *Richmond Daily Examiner*, which had made a similar argument in its pages, reported approvingly in an editorial (on the very day of the battle of Second Manassas) that since Southerners had become convinced of the futility of hoping for European action, their war spirit had taken a marked turn for the better. "Henceforth, the South fights the enemy, not merely to gain time, not merely to protect their homes and firesides; but they fight to conquer by arms an honourable and permanent peace."[7]

What prompted all of these calls about backsliding, and shirking? Why were Confederates, only a year into the war, so worried about the people's commitment? What could prompt the authors of "Be Courageous" to ask in July, "Whither are we drifting?"[8] I would argue that, in addition to the sort of pervasive anxiety that was only natural in wartime, particularly by the summer when battlefield victories had proved elusive in both the east and the west, and concerns about foreign recognition, Confederates had two other concerns: conscription at home, and their slaves, a problem exacerbated by the possibility of federally mandated emancipation.

Conscription, which the Confederate Congress first turned to in April 1862 (and then further refined over the next three years), was a necessary measure, for the armies were dreadfully short of manpower, a function not only of disease and battle casualties but of the fact that half of the original regiments had enlisted for only one year. Nevertheless, it was wildly unpopular, both with the prospective conscripts themselves and with politicians and editors, many of whom charged that such an expansion of centralized authority ran contrary to the Confederacy's founding principles. Editorials throughout the spring and summer complained about conscription—if not the law per se than about its uneven enforcement, or its overly violent enforcers. It seemed somehow insulting to force men into service, an affront to their honor. David Harris, a South Carolina farmer (who enlisted only under threat of the draft), noted that conscription for the men enrolling in his neighborhood was "a bitter pill for most of them, for they are the crew that does not want to fight for their country. I would hate to wate to be forced out in defence of my needy country." How else these men might have been induced to volunteer, when they had presumably turned deaf ears to literally thousands of exhortations and patriotic appeals, was left undescribed.[9]

Emancipation fears also began to rise during the summer of 1862. Slaveholders were always concerned about their slaves, a concern that paradoxically often revealed itself in near-constant professions of slave loyalty. Already in the summer months Confederates were complaining of their slaves' increased running away, and more frighteningly, their increased insubordination and plotting. The *Hinds County Gazette* proposed a renewal of nightly patrols in the town of Raymond, Mississippi, while a letter from Lawrenceville, Georgia, to the editors of the *Southern Confederacy* reported the discovery of an "alarming" quantity of gunpowder in slaves' possession. Rev. C. C. Jones, also in Georgia, reported the escape of over fifty slaves toward the coast in July.[10] What brought those fears to a head were two related events in the North: first, congressional debates over enlisting African Americans, and particularly former slaves, and second, the possibility of Lincoln issuing an emancipation proclamation of some sort. Both were discussed and debated in the pages of Confederate papers. The *Richmond Daily Examiner* actually went so far as to reprint Lincoln's letter to Horace Greeley, in which the president explained, "If I could save the union without freeing any slave I would do it, and if I could save it by freeing all the slaves I would do it; and if I could save it by freeing some and leaving others alone, I would also do that." What effect such a development might have on their already emboldened slaves was a sure source of consternation for Confederates.[11]

And then the tide seemingly began to turn for the Confederacy. As news of the second battle at Manassas trickled out and made its way through the Confederacy, people responded much as Lucy Rebecca Buck had—with mingled relief and elation. Even before the news of Second Manassas itself reached Memphis, the *Daily Appeal* cheered Pope's retreat from Cedar Mountain as the dawn after the Confederacy's many "dark hours," adding that "where was witnessed a few months ago so much despondency all is now hopeful," and, more importantly, "it is a hope fully authorized by the facts." The later news was deemed "electrif[ying]," and the *Appeal* promised that this one victory would have wide effects, inspiring "confidence in the bosoms of the wavering, doubting, and skeptical," inspiring troops in the other theaters of war, and, perhaps most significantly, might "prove the harbinger of recognition by foreign powers and the establishment of peace at home."[12] This reaction was largely to be expected—how else would people respond to a victory? What is interesting, however, is how quickly, in a matter of days, really, that elation gave way to more critical assessments of Confederate fortunes and actions. Too, the more ambiguous news that came out of Maryland and the battle of Antietam about three weeks later quickly overshadowed Second Manassas.

Newspaper editors in particular seized on Second Manassas (much as Lincoln would do a few weeks later with Antietam and emancipation) to make political points, often echoing or reinforcing their earlier concerns. In a brief notice, the *Charleston Mercury* described the community as "jubilant and sanguine" but in longer articles suggested that as "satisfactory" as the result was, "vain indeed, and costly would be our triumph if we should fail to grasp the advantages which it offers." Chief among those advantages would be an invasion of the North, and many Confederates expressed fervent hopes that the next news would be of Jackson and Lee leading columns into Maryland and Washington, D.C., and of Kirby Smith heading into Ohio. The *Richmond Examiner*, which praised the victory as nothing less than "gigantic," also seized on this idea, attributing the victories in Virginia to strategic shifts over the summer, specifically "a change from ditching and retreat, to attack and victory." The *Memphis Daily Appeal* praised as a "move in the right direction" a House resolution favoring invasion of the North.[13]

Confederates also drew on the victory as an excuse to support conscription, urging the Confederate Congress to act decisively, as the *Mercury* warned ominously that "procrastination is not paradoxically worse than murder—it is murder of the direct proportion—national murder." The *Richmond Examiner*, reported the *Mercury*, had made a similar endorsement. A few days later, the *Mercury* returned to this theme, pointing out the degree to which the tide had apparently turned in the Confederates' favor. But, the article cautioned, it could all change again. All of the good news could not obscure the fact that "we are now in the crisis of this war." The way out of this crisis was simple: "The stronger we prove ourselves in view of the next six months, the shorter the war, the easier the peace." And the way to shorten the war was to throw all available men into the fight, to call out all conscripts, with the upper age limit at forty-five, not thirty-five. Confederates understood the fragility of their independence and warned one another not to be too comfortable. In this we can see that victories and defeats were to some extent treated the same way as prods to greater patriotism and greater efforts.[14]

Because the Confederacy had no existence apart from war, it was exquisitely sensitive to shifts in its wartime fortunes. The war was the Confederacy, and one can hardly fault its citizens for seizing on victories as proof of the righteousness of their cause. Defeats were more complicated—privately, secretly maybe, Confederates feared that they were proof of wrongness. More often, they were seen as indicative of Confederate's need for change, and Confederates were willing to do that, at least to a point. What they were not willing to do, at least in 1862, was entertain thoughts that their experiment might fail—with or without European intervention.

Love of Country, Love of Self

Challenges to Confederate Unity

While Confederates from all stations and locations imagined themselves living in an independent, united, and virtuous nation, the reality of their daily lives did not always match that ideal. It was easy to pledge loyalty to the death in the abstract, more difficult to hold onto principles when faced with hostile soldiers, starvation, and death. Sacrifice, while glorious in theory, often proved less so in practice. So much of Confederate identity seemed bound up with demonstrating Confederate virtue and superiority. The problem, however, was that such ideals were unattainable. No population could ever put self-interest entirely behind them. The tension between ideals and reality is where loyalty and national commitment collide, forcing people to make difficult choices. As individuals struggled to reconcile their allegiances to the Confederate nation with the demands of their personal situations, they revealed the depth of their attachment to the Confederacy. This was not to say that people always put the Confederacy above all but, rather, that placing themselves first did not necessarily indicate a rejection of the Confederate nation. If Confederate nationalism was too weak to exert a hold over its people, they would not have worried so much about remaining true to their new nation and their new identities.

"THERE IS A SUBLIME MEANING IN SUFFERING"

Prior to the war, Southerners had frequently been accused by outsiders of being indolent, dissipated, and generally lacking in industrious virtues. Confederate commentators were eager to show that the war proved the lie to that stereotype. Thus the author of "Inquire Within" in the *Southern Field and Fireside* noted approvingly that "this revolution has developed the gratifying fact, that our Southern people though apparently lethargic and inert, are equal to any emergency when forced to call on their latent powers."[1] The idealized Confederate would suffer gladly and remain loyal and dutiful at all times. Newspapers were full of articles like the one touting "[t]he Moral Advantages of Public Calamities," or another reminding readers that "[s]uffering [was] the Price of Independence." James D. B. De Bow raised suffering from a virtue to a requirement, suggesting that "it be part of our religious creed in the future, that the only citizens of the Confederate States are to be those who are born upon its soil or who shared its fortunes in the dark hours of its history."[2]

Confederate men and women appeared to take this rhetoric of duty and suffering to heart, especially early in the war, and derived comfort from it. They were buoyed, at least through the 1864 campaigns, by a sense of patriotism and commitment that paradoxically was only deepened by their losses of both property and loved ones. For Confederates embroiled in a long, frightening, and difficult war, finding some higher meaning in their hardships might ease their burdens. Sarah Morgan, forced to leave her native Baton Rouge, melodramatically proclaimed her commitment to the cause, writing, "I have lost my home and all its dear contents for Southern Rights, have stood on its destroyed hearth stone and looked at the ruin of all I loved without a murmur, almost glad of the sacrifice, if it would contribute its might towards the salvation of the Confederacy." One former New Yorker reported that his friends in Charleston "are sustaining their misfortunes with a fortitude fully equal to that of the old Romans under similar circumstances, & are confident of ultimate success." Cloe Whittle was inspired by a church sermon on suffering, confiding to her diary, "Never will I forget one sentence, 'There is a *sublime* meaning in suffering.'" These homages to suffering were clearly an elite phenomenon—people who were truly suffering economically were presumably less likely to spend time writing about how wonderful it was and more time trying to put food on the table.[3]

An important component of patriotism involved service: for men of fighting age it meant joining the army, for women, contributing their sons, brothers, and fathers. Service to the cause ideally outweighed individual needs and fears, as Eliza Middleton Huger Smith explained in a letter to her daughter regarding her sons in the army: "If our boys only do their duty manfully & well we shall not be comfortless."[4] Just as women at home took comfort in their menfolk's patriotism, so, too, did men explain their absence using the language of duty, responsibility, and shared suffering. "I am sincerely anxious to do my whole duty to my country and my family," Clem Watson told his wife. Duty was not an ideal limited to soldiers; rather, all Confederates had a duty to their nation. Cleland Huger, Eliza Smith's nephew, consoled his younger cousin Daniel, a student at the University of Virginia, by reminding him, "We are all in our proper places. You, who are too young to come into camp, are preparing your mind to benefit your country hereafter, and are preserving and increasing those manly energies which will make you a good and efficient soldier, if the war is prolonged." As for himself and Daniel's older brother, Robert, "We are contributing our mite to protect our families and all that is sacred to us."[5]

Almost every one of Gustave Cook's letters to his wife, Lizzie, back in Texas mentioned how much he missed her, but he also took pains to explain to her why he could not be with her. Cook had been with the Army of Tennessee from the beginning of the war, had been promoted several times, and felt a deep attachment to his regiment, the Texas Rangers. He explained his commitment to his wife: "I could not think for a moment of quitting the service for a thousand times over would I die ere I would abandon the service of my beloved and needing country. The fatal bullet would be in a thousand times preferable." Nor should she want him "to do a thing so utterly repugnant to my own feelings and so recreant to my standard of honor" as to take a position in the local militia or Home Guard. Cook had no fear of dying in the service and tried to convince his wife that "my memory would be a thousand times more precious to you and my family should I be killed on the glorious field than would the person of so miserable a coward and a traitor as I should be to forsake my noble cause." He closed this letter by reminding his wife of the burdens and suffering that they shared and of the ways in which they could lighten them: "Let not your heart grow faint but pray to God for strength to sustain you in your part of the sacrifice. Make it for your own sake, for mine, and for the sake of our little ones and our dear Country. Though the labor is great and the sorrows heavy believe me the reward will be ampler and happiness will ten fold bless you for it." Again and again Cook returned to the themes of duty and obligation, trying to convince his wife, and perhaps even himself, that his individual needs and desires had to come behind those of his country. "I would give the world for the opportunity," Cook wrote to Lizzie regarding the possibility of getting a furlough for the first time in three years, "yes, everything save duty and honor. These must never be sacrificed." This language of duty and honor tapped into powerful cultural ideals about masculinity. This is not to say that all Confederates lived up to these lofty prescriptions (though all of the evidence indicates that Cook himself did), but they reveal the contours of Confederate identity.[6]

"GOD SAVE THE NOBLE WOMEN OF THE SOUTH!"

From the beginning of the war, Confederate men praised women for their willingness to sacrifice their men to the cause and their work on behalf of soldiers—sewing clothes, rolling bandages, and nursing the wounded. They were hailed as "Earth Angels" and as "The Mainstay of the South," and in the tradition of "republican motherhood," they were seen as the nurturers of the new, godly, and moral Confederate nation. Confederate newspapers, broadsides, songs, and poetry all paid homage to Southern women's patriotism, and articles drawing attention to one or another of their virtues were a staple of Confederate publications. "God bless our brave and noble Southern women!" read a typical piece, this one from the *Southern Cultivator*, praising a reader who cheerfully imbibed "wheat coffee without sugar" while making other culinary sacrifices. "Were all our men as true-hearted and self-denying, there would be no thought ever of failure," it concluded. Many of these homages drew comparisons to the women of Sparta or of the American Revolution. Despite the traditional social view of Southern women as the softer sex, prone to emotionalism and needful of protection, Confederate women were portrayed as the embodiments of strength and fortitude. One author compared them to Atlas, bearing the weight of the world upon their slim shoulders, "but we have learned too well how, in our day, when men might have fainted beneath the mighty burdens our women have stood up unbending beneath the crushing weight of all our wrongs, and fears, and cruel disadvantages."[7]

Such praise was a double-edged sword, however. Women were given so much credit for keeping the war spirit alive that they could not possibly live up to their public image. Early in the war, that didn't seem to matter, but as the war went on, and as women became less idealistic and more concerned with their personal or familial struggles (as opposed to those of the nation as a whole), their commitment to the Confederacy seemed to waver. Or did it? Perhaps their contemporaries (and historians) have judged Confederate women too harshly. Very few Confederate women wanted the war to end with a return to the Union. Many expressed war-weariness, in both word and deed, but that was not the same thing as rejecting the Confederacy itself. Women's experiences of the war, and their commitment to the war effort, varied considerably with class, with region, and with personality.[8]

Women were constantly being told how to be loyal to the Confederacy. One fascinating example of this campaign to praise (and by so doing influence and encourage) Confederate womanhood is the 1863 book *The*

Southern Women of the Second American Revolution. Our Naval Victories and Exploits of Confederate War Steamers, Capture of Yankee Gunboats, &c., published by Henry W. R. Jackson in Atlanta. Jackson's book is a compilation of anecdotes, many originally published in newspapers from around the Confederacy. The book included stories of female spies like Belle Boyd or Nancy McCartey, tales of Yankee violence toward women and guerrilla war in Missouri, and uplifting anecdotes about slave loyalty and female sacrifice.[9]

Paeans to Confederate womanhood generally centered around one of several themes or categories: women were praised for their defiance in the face of invaders, their patriotic sacrifices of food and clothing, and their benevolent organizations. Under the heading "A Brave Girl," Jackson reprinted an extract of a letter that first appeared in the *Columbus (Georgia) Times.* The writer was a young Savannah girl, "not all unknown to fame," who described her reaction to the news of the engagement at Port Royal and rumors that an invasion of Savannah was imminent. "I seated myself in the midst of all, and made a Confederate flag for the express purpose of waving it saucily in their faces when they landed. If they come upon us by land, they will have to pass this very door, and in spite of everything but *chains* I intend to wave my banner," she proclaimed, and continued angrily: "I intend to be the first Savannah girl to dare them, and to show them the South has not only brave *men*, but brave *women* also. How it makes my blood boil when I hear of a cowardly act done by any one bearing the name of *man*!" She went on to relate an incident in which Savannah men supposedly disguised themselves in bonnets and slippers to avoid being called to the front, and she vehemently expressed both her disgust and her desire to set a more positive example for women, by volunteering to "exchange my hat and slippers for the boots and breeches of the next man who had rather run than fight." She warned that "if the men prove cowards at a time like this, it is high time for the women to show what they can do; and if they cannot depend on them for protection, show them that they have bravery enough to meet them at their own doors, if they cannot follow them to the battle-field." Women then filled a dual role: they themselves were supposed to be brave and dedicated, and they could use the language of masculinity to spur men to greater heroism.[10]

Jackson reprinted and commented on a story from the *New York World,* which reported that several Winchester, Virginia, women opened fire on retreating Union troops from their bedroom windows. Although the comments began by dismissing the report as most likely false, if only because the women were "too glad to see the Yankees going to delay the departure of even one of them by a wound from a pistol shot," they went on to commend the impulse behind the act, wondering how the Yankees thought they could possibly defeat "a people whose women even take up arms against them." Too, the defiant women of Winchester were used as an object lesson for those Confederate men tempted to shirk their duty, noting that "if the rougher sex were as universally faithful as the women, this great struggle would have nothing to fear from enemies at home. God save the noble ladies of the South!—None of their sex, in any age or country, ever merited in a higher degree the admiration of chivalrous men or their most glorious deeds in arms in their defence." Thus, implicit in this praise for women is a call for Confederate men to reassert their masculinity by outdoing their women in the business of Yankee-fighting.[11]

Confederate women were encouraged to channel their considerable energies and devotion into more constructive outlets like nursing, sewing, and forming aid societies for soldiers and their families. The same rhetoric of duty and patriotism that encouraged men to join the army infused these calls for support, as women were asked to help ease the burdens of their defenders. In the *Southern Field and Fireside*, "Parker" issued "A Word to Southern Girls," in which he exhorted Southern women to do their part for the cause by going to school and then filling positions as governesses and teachers. It was their duty to educate—both intellectually and morally—the next generation of young Confederates. Teaching would provide an appropriate outlet for young women's fighting spirit. "I have heard many a dainty young lady affirm, 'O, how I wish I could be a soldier! I'd glory in fighting the hateful Yankees!' Here, my young friends, is a broad-battlefield. Ignorance is a hard enemy to overcome." Parker further reminded young women that they would be studying, not for themselves, but for the sake of the soldiers, asking women to "let them feel they have something to fight for save the broad, depopulated, desolate land. Let them feel that though they fall in the fierce conflict, they will gain liberty for a cultivated, an educated offspring,—a people whose intellectual refinement will ever adorn with fresh laurels, their martyrs['] graves." Confederate existence, it seemed, was ever linked to Confederate perfectibility.[12]

Nursing required a strong stomach, and a strong commitment to the cause. Kate Cumming, who left home to work as a professional nurse, frequently expressed frustration with the women who were unwilling to help out. She recorded a conversation she had with a lieutenant regarding the problems of civilian demoralization. Cumming rejected his romantic view and told him that "a man did not deserve the name of man, if he did not fight for his country; nor a woman, the name of woman, if she did not do all in her power to aid the men." Mary Chesnut was pleased with herself for deciding to volunteer at the Wayside Hospital in Camden, South Carolina, although she echoed some of Cumming's sentiments when she recorded that "I had excuses enough, but at heart I felt a coward and a skulker. I think I know how men feel who hire a substitute and shirk the fight. There must be no dodging duty." Emma Mordecai felt much the same and was happy to be able to do her small part to help the "pure highminded noble men" who lay wounded in Richmond. "Well may ladies devote themselves to attending their couches, & administering to their poor comfort." Although she found the work difficult, and almost fainted while helping a surgeon, she was re-warded by the men's gratitude—they "say they cannot fight hard enough for such ladies."[13]

An April 1863 appeal, looking to the future when the war would be over, asked women to pledge to continue their efforts on behalf of soldiers and their families. It noted ominously that "the ingratitude of Republics is prov-erbial, but let it not be said that Southern women forgot their brave de-fenders." Confederate women needed to be ever aware of the profound effect that their gentle and moral natures had on soldiers. "Reader," one author asked, "can you imagine what would be the moral condition of the Confed-erate army in six months if the influence of woman's love and charms were now withdrawn? What makes the Confederate soldier a gentleman of honor, courage, virtue and truth instead of a cut-throat and vagabond but home, sweet home, where his affections center in mother, sister, wife?" The answer, of course, was Confederate womanhood, in all its devoted glory. Women were expected to forgo luxuries, nurse the sick, uplift the living, and memo-rialize the dead.[14] Indeed, their responsibility toward soldiers extended lit-erally beyond the grave. A letter from a "Volunteer" in camp in Tennessee described the Cavehill Cemetery in Louisville as "a sight that should put to shame many who inhabit cities further South." In Cavehill, each Confeder-ate grave was raised and sodded, many were surrounded by flowers, and each had a headstone, neatly labeled with the deceased's name, state, and regiment, "around which hung a wreath of myrtle, the Christmas offering of the Southern ladies of Louisville, to the noble dead." As befitted them, the Federal graves were sunken, uncared for, and unidentified.[15]

Confederate women were not supposed to forget or neglect each other, either. In *Southern Women*, Henry Jackson reprinted several letters from Atlanta papers regarding the establishment of a new Home for Invalid Ladies. In a letter asking for donations, Abby Foot Farrar defended the women from charges of selfishness, explaining, "I have, in connection with other ladies, done all that was in my power to do for the soldier; but while doing this, I neither can nor will turn a deaf ear to the ways and means of affording relief to the afflicted of our own sex." Protecting women and orphans, Confederate women argued, served a valuable purpose in alleviating soldiers' worries about the families left behind. A request for contributions on the behalf of the Baptist Orphan Asylum in Montgomery assured readers that "it is really not a *charity*; it is a debt we owe the brave defenders of our land who have fallen to care for their children." Furthermore, establishing such institutions while the war was still ongoing would provide a valuable boost to morale, as "they will take the burden off many a father's heart, who goes into battle haunted with the thought—'if I fall, what will become of my children?'"[16]

Confederate women did respond to these appeals, and some even spoke —or wrote—for themselves in public forums. In the *Southern Field and Fireside*, "Lora" asked, "How are we as women of the South to evolve comfort out of this chaos; how derive strength to do and suffer to the end in the cause of truth, justice and freedom?" She reminded her fellow Confederate women of their duty to strengthen "the hands of those who toil through blood, suffering and weariness, in the erection of the great and glorious temple of liberty." Lora reminded her readers to never "despond, repine, or become cheerless and complaining," counseling them that faith in their armies, themselves, and, most important, in God, would see them through.[17]

The Ladies of Mobile, "realizing the imminence of the peril that now girdles our Land, and thoroughly convinced that all the sacrifices, trials and privations attending Revolution, are infinitely preferable to the horrors of subjugation and social and political slavery," printed up a broadside of resolutions pledging their support to the "Society of Loyal Confederates." These women resolved to discourage "all extravagant and giddy festivities," as such activities were not in keeping with a time of war and bereavement. In the same spirit, they condemned extravagance in clothing, preferring instead to see any extra money used for the relief of wounded soldiers and their families. These first three resolutions are all centered in the traditionally female sphere of home and dress, but the women of Mobile chose to exert their influence in the public sphere as well. In their fourth resolution, they pledged to discourage "absenteeism" by both deserters and shirkers, using some uniquely female tactics: they pledged to socially cut off any men who shirked their duty, describing them as "marked—as of leprous soul— and as unworthy [of] the respect of woman, whom they have not the manhood to defend"; and to make public their social opprobrium, to insure that all women knew which men were worthy and which were not. Essentially, these women declared that men who refused to do their duty and serve in the Confederate army were men without honor, and should be treated as inferior to Confederate womanhood.[18]

They went on to address politics and public discussion in the next two resolutions, though, again, from a carefully feminine position:

> *Resolved 5th.* Without pretending to enter upon political questions, we shall hold those public men, and those conductors of the press, and those candidates for public offices, *as the best friends to their country*, who endeavor to *unite* their countrymen, to uphold the government, to encourage the soldiers, and to preach the gospel of *faith* — of patriotic, heroic, sublime faith in the final and glorious success of a people struggling for country and home.
>
> *Resolved 6th.* That we will hold him who foments division and political strife, and him who disheartens by teaching distrust, and him who croaks only of evil, and him who withholds his means and his influence from our cause, whatever may be his name, whatever may be his position, or his intentions, as exerting a power against his country, and thus giving "aid and comfort" to the foe.

These women were serving notice to the men around them that they had subscribed to the vision of an independent Confederacy. And they did not want their influence limited to Mobile, for they closed by resolving to "let the world know that Southern women can dare the responsibilities of the hour, as inheriting the blood and spirit of those who suffered in Old Virginia and the Carolinas in the war of 1776." Thus, they, like Confederate men, were heirs of the Revolutionary generation, and these women, like their forebears, had a job to do. Only by working together, each within his or her role, could the Confederacy be saved; these Confederate women would do all in their power to make sure that duty was done.[19]

Women who before the war might have shunned men who were dirty and clad in rags were now supposed to vie for their attention and devote themselves to their care. Young girls were especially subject to these pressures, as described in the "Southern Girls Song":

> The soldier is the lad for me—
>   A brave heart I adore;
> And when the sunny South is free,
>   And when fighting is no more

I'll choose me then a lover brave
From out that gallant band.
The soldier lad I love the best
Shall have my heart and hand.

Mary Isabella Blackford was planning her wedding to J. Churchill (Church) Cooke in February 1865 when she received a letter full of instructions from her older brother Lancelot. Amid details regarding where to have the ceremony and whom to invite came this direction: "Be sure to let Church's *regiment* appear on the card. I would not have it appear you married anybody but a soldier; particularly now. Men that ain't soldiers may be very well in their way, but I prefer not to have any such in the family." Subject to these pressures, women were often loathe to criticize soldiers. When they did they felt ashamed at their own shallowness.[20]

Cloe Whittle struggled mightily with the burden of patriotic expectations. On her way to South Carolina in October 1863, she and her traveling companion, Mrs. Evans, encountered a group of North Carolina troops. They were the first Confederate soldiers Cloe had seen in eighteen months (as she had been living in occupied Norfolk), and she was surprised by her reaction. "I felt secretly ashamed to find how little patriotic emotion was called forth by this meeting with the Confederates & that I [could] coolly scan their faces as I [would] any strangers to see whether they were handsome or not."[21] While a few met her standard of attractive, she described the majority as "ordinary looking" and clothed in "coarse & plain dress." Despite her initial distaste for the troops, Cloe had internalized the messages about being a good Confederate and thus reported, "I forced myself to be very polite to the soldiers for I knew they deserved it at the hands of every Southern woman & whether I felt in the humor for giving it was not the question."[22]

Whittle's experience with the North Carolina troops and her self-critical analysis, however, did not bring about a real change in her attitudes. A few days later, while waiting for a train, she again encountered another group of Confederate troops, this time from her home state of Virginia. Again she was repelled by their appearance, recalling, "[I could] scarcely make myself believe that the queer looking, brown & grey & drab jackets around me were the actual garments of gentlemen." But again she was ashamed at her superficiality, and she berated herself: "I felt at the same time contempt and mortification at my fastidiousness—that I could be so unpatriotic not to feel a glow of joy in my heart at seeing Virginia's sons—her indulged & petted sons throwing away as objects of no value the wealth & luxury that they were accustomed . . . & all for the holy privilege of fighting Va's battles — & then to think that a daughter of Va [should] fail to recognize the stamp of Nature's nobleman because clad in a garb of homespun!" In her tirade, Whittle illuminates a theme running through Confederate rhetoric: war and soldiering had improved the "indulged and petted" Virginia (and Southern) aristocracy, forging them into true men worthy of an independent nation, which made her rejection of them all the more shameful. The war was supposed to heighten Confederate virtue, making the men more honorable and manly and the women more dutiful and feminine. As the people improved, so, too, would their chances, because God would never let so virtuous a population be defeated. Confederates believed in this rhetoric of self-improvement because it was tied up with notions of self and nation — all about perfectibility.[23]

Confederate women were subject to ever-changing public and private demands as the war went on. As women learned to live in a disordered society, and frequently without the men of their families and neighborhoods, some began to chafe against the restrictions that society had placed upon them. Many found fulfillment working outside the home for the first time as nurses or clerks in government offices. The praise heaped upon them gave women a public voice and the legitimacy to discuss politics among themselves and with men. But this newfound freedom came with costs and responsibilities. Confederates held women to almost impossible standards of patriotic self-sacrifice, and when women could not measure up to those ideals they were subject to public chastising and complaints about their lack of spirit.

One of the most interesting of these critical pieces, titled "Pictures — The Women and the War" and signed "Micare," appeared in the *Montgomery Advertiser* in June 1864, provoking an extended exchange of letters and responses. "Picture Number 1" was a typical flowery description of Southern women's patriotism and heroism as the war began. They were praised for encouraging men to join the army and for giving up their dances and parties: "while friends and lovers were exposed to the arrows of death abroad, they would know no joy at home." Women formed Ladies Aid Societies to help soldiers and their widows and orphans; "the love of fashion and dress, if not destroyed, was held in abeyance. . . . They even had the strength to abstain from a 'love of bonnet.'" "Picture Number 2," however, was painted in different colors. The Ladies Aid Societies had fallen by the wayside; "the self-sacrifice has vanished; wives and maidens now labor only to exempt husband and lovers from the perils of service, to secure them a position in some *life insurance department*, or among the *Buttermilk Rangers*. The love of country has become another term for the love of self." Women had re-turned to their love of finery, getting luxuries from blockade runners or even buying them for themselves and bringing them back into the Confederacy under flag of truce. Women, particularly those in the cities, were falling prey to a rise in general licentiousness and moral corruption, spreading gossip and associating with men of "insufficient rank." All of these vices threatened not just the moral health of the new Confederate nation but its very physical independence as well. In order for the Confederacy to fulfill its destiny as a godly nation, its female spiritual guardians needed to be above reproach. To be virtuous was to be patriotic, and vice versa—the two were ideally in-distinguishable.[24]

Readers of the *Montgomery Advertiser* were not about to let Micare's criti-cisms go unanswered. Three days later, the paper published "The Women and the War, Picture No. 3," written by "Une Mere," who argued that women were no less patriotic than they had been at the beginning of the war. Rather, "circumstances have rendered it necessary for them to labor more assidu-ously at home, to keep the wants, the actual necessities of their families supplied." Une Mere made an explicitly class-based argument, speaking for those women whose families were struggling to make ends meet. Women who sought positions close to home for their husbands, Une Mere argued, were not doing so for selfish and unpatriotic reasons but out of a desperate need to have men provide for their families. The good and patriotic women of Montgomery had done as much as they could, giving up blankets and car-pets to keep soldiers warm, but they had an equal responsibility to provide for their children and "keep them decent." She continued:

> We, thus situated, are debarred the pleasure of *giving* as those who have accumulated money during the war, can do. . . . Those lady friends of ours who have no such cares, who can leave their homes daily and soothe the suffering soldiers, making them grateful for the little attentions they offer, have no greater desire to do good or exhibit patriotism than have we. Their field of action is different, but Heaven has made it so. The dis-tinction is marked, not from the dying out of patriotism in our hearts, but from the tide of circumstances, which the wisest did not foresee at the beginning of our struggle.

Rather than spend their time and energy sniping at one another, Une Mere seemed to argue, women would better serve the cause by making whatever contributions they could.[25]

Une Mere's ringing defense of Confederate women provoked still another

"Making Clothes for the Boys in the Army." In this etching by Adalbert Volck (part of his Confederate War Etchings series), women are hard at work spinning and sewing for the soldiers. In reality, many women struggled to live up to such a selfless ideal. Collection of The New-York Historical Society.

response a few days later. This final "Picture" was submitted by "Suzette," who claimed to be the wife of a captain in the Confederate army. Suzette praised Micare's first picture as an accurate depiction of the "enthusiastic events of ever-memorable '61" in Montgomery. She was less enamored of Picture No. 2; while she agreed with its depiction of "deplorable" truths, she felt that Micare's "indignant strictures" were too harsh. As for Picture No. 3, Suzette seconded Une Mere's defense of patriotic women who were nevertheless forced to put their families ahead of service to the cause. She, however, took issue with the dismissive nod Une Mere gave to the "sewing women" and "presumed" to "hang picture No. 4" in their name. Many of these sewing women were the wives of soldiers or refugees, trying to earn enough money to survive. Suzette blamed the decline in female virtue noted by Micare on the speculators, extortioners, and blockade runners, "whose wives outdress the Empress Eugenie." Such vulgar displays could only inspire gossip and anger, while poor women were forced to "forsake 'virtue and chastity'" to keep from starving. Suzette closed by challenging Micare to "devote a chapter to the 'Lords of Creation' for their especial benefit, thereby doing her country more service than in bringing out in such bold characters the faults of her own sex."[26] The discussion did not end there. While Micare appears not to have spoken in her own defense, Une Mere penned a letter to the editor of the *Advertiser*, assuring Suzette that she meant no offense by her remarks. She had nothing but sympathy for the women of the working class, and "she is never forgetful of the sorrow-stricken and afflicted." With that, the exchange of letters and pictures appears to have vanished from the *Advertiser*'s pages, leaving the women of Montgomery publicly, if not privately, in agreement.[27]

Whether these three authors were actually women or not, we have no way of knowing. What is significant is that they presented themselves as women—all loyal to the Confederacy, all trying to do their patriotic duty. These three authors consciously and publicly drew distinctions between women behaving in appropriately Confederate ways and women who lacked virtue, and, consequently, lacked patriotism. Une Mere and Suzette consciously set the mass of Confederate women apart from the elite women who had the luxury of time to serve the soldiers, and they argued forcefully that all women (with the exception of those associated with speculators and extortioners) should be praised for the contributions they made to the war effort, however small they might appear in the grand scheme of things. At the same time, they also demanded recognition of women's rights to put their families first, to provide for and protect their own before the nation, thus illuminating the constant tension between public and private good. Sometimes they were one and the same, sometimes not.

Another example of the press using a woman to appeal to other women's patriotism appeared in early 1865. A newspaper clipping from February introduces "some earnest, eloquent words of pleading" from the well-known Southern author, Augusta Jane Evans. The presumably male author of the introductory passage made no attempt to hide the strategy behind Evans's appeal, explaining that "no man would dare intimate that the ladies are in these hours of gloom and peril given to follies and vanity; but one of their own sex, who writes so heartfully as she has acted so nobly, will surely be listened to and perchance heeded."[28] Augusta Evans was certainly a good choice of messenger to spread words of encouragement. A staunch secessionist, her popularity as an author took off in 1864 with the publication of her third novel, *Macaria; or, Altars of Sacrifice*. The book was dedicated to "The Army of the Southern Confederacy," and told the story of two women's self-sacrificing devotion to the Confederate cause. It was immensely popular, selling over 20,000 copies in the Confederacy, and it was also well-received in the North. Her address "To the Ladies" drew on these same themes.[29]

Evans joined the chorus condemning Confederate women for their frivolity and "mirth and reckless revelry" even as "every passing breeze chants the requiem of dying heroes, and is burdened with the lamentations of stricken wives and wailing orphans." She was shocked and horrified at the possibility that Southern women could be so lacking in not only patriotism but basic humanity that they would "thread the airy mazes of the dance while the matchless champions of freedom are shivering in bloody trenches, or lying stark in frozen fields of glory." Evans appealed to Confederate women as mothers, wives, and sisters, asking them how they could "waltz across the graves" of their "darling dead" and begging them to be sympathetic to their less fortunate neighbors who had lost loved ones. She threatened them, warning that their frivolity outraged "the nation's holy dead." God would bring down punishment upon the Confederacy: "Woe to that wretched land, whose insensate women seek only amusements during the bloody drama of revolution!" Evans concluded with an appeal to women's inherent goodness and nobility, asking them to resist "the encroaching tide of demoralization, to check the increasing and corrupting traffic in foreign luxuries and trifles; to popularize only Confederate articles of dress; to arouse the people to a realization of their imminent peril and to rekindle and fan the fires of patriotic devotion on every household sitar." Women held the future of the Confederacy in their hands, Evans claimed, promising, "You have but to will the success of our cause, and under the blessing of heaven it will be speedily accomplished." Evans's language shows the ways in which elements of Confederate identity interlocked—female virtue, male honor, and God's favor were all parts of the whole.[30]

"OUR WHOLE WORLD IS DEMORALIZED — TURNED TOPSY-TURVEY"

Confederate men and women could not always live up to the patriotic demands of sacrifice and devotion to the cause. Selflessness does not come naturally to many people, and years of war and deprivation chipped away at Confederate willingness to share with others who struggled. They complained about being forced to support refugees in areas already stretched to the brink of starvation, about having provisions impressed to feed the armies when they had little enough to spare at home, about both state and national governments. Both men and women grew accustomed to suffering without necessarily being uplifted by it; their hearts grew hard, and they came to resent their sacrifices. Men shirked and deserted, and women let them. With all of this, however, Confederates still wished they could do better and be better. They tried to convince themselves and each other to live up to their ideals, even as they failed to do so.

The problem of refugees sometimes divided Confederates against one another. The ideal was of a nation united, absorbing those less fortunate and sharing with each other, protecting the women and children forced to flee. Many Confederates opened their homes and larders to friends, relatives, and even strangers. Other times the reality was much different, as refugees arrived in areas already suffering from shortages of food and housing. A woman complained about the refugees flooding into Hancock County, Mississippi: "I don't know what will become of all this people that is come to this poor part of the country, there was nothing to eat for them that was already here, and these that came bring nothing with them they will be sure to starve." A letter from "Mary Ann" to the editors of the *Southern Field and Fireside* asked, "What do you think of refugees and how do you think they should be treated?" S. Atkinson, the paper's literary editor, answered by describing several types of refugees. Those fleeing the destruction of their homes or from occupied cities like New Orleans or Nashville should be treated sympathetically and helped in any way possible. But "those spiritless drones, or money-loving shop keepers and speculators who have skulked away from threatened points, to avoid military duty and the dangers of the war, while they fatten on the spoils of illicit or heartless extortion," deserved only contempt. Refugees who sought to protect their pocketbooks, rather than their persons, did not deserve assistance. Suspicion and hostility naturally resulted from Confederates' questioning each others' motives.[31]

Kate Stone, herself a refugee from Louisiana living in Texas, commented on the growing tensions between natives and newcomers. She reported a rumor spread during the summer of 1863 that Louisiana, Missouri, Mississippi, and Tennessee had applied for readmission to the United States. "Of course, we know it is a base fabrication," she wrote, "but many of the natives believe it firmly. They will believe anything against Louisiana." The feeling was mutual, as Stone and her family frequently complained about their Texas neighbors. Kate Cumming commented that "the refugees are very clannish" in Montgomery, but she had nothing but praise for one woman who had been forced to leave New Orleans as a "registered enemy to the United States." She and her family were living "refugee-style" in two rooms, but she was "an enthusiastic southerner, and seems to glory in living as she does."[32]

Confederates feared that such sniping between refugees and their hosts was symptomatic of a broader problem within their society. While on the one hand they argued that the trials of war would uplift and perfect them, creating a new and virtuous nation, on the other hand they feared that the years of hardship and disappointment were taking a toll on Southern character. The signs of demoralization, it seemed, were everywhere. One woman tending her wounded son in a Richmond hospital was horrified to find that "they bury the dead like animals, without any religious service & without clothes *almost* if not entirely. They say the Confederacy cannot afford to lose the clothes." She was not the only Confederate to remark with horror on changed attitudes toward death. "People do not mourn their dead as they used to," Kate Stone observed in Tyler, Texas. "Everyone seems to live only in the present—just from day to day—otherwise I fancy many would go crazy." A resident of New Orleans lamented that "this terrible war seems almost to disorder the ties of kindred. The newspapers are full of details of fights & the names of the killed & wounded. All personal sympathy appears to have been swallowed up for the time being by the momentous fate of thousands and I really believe that the death of Genl. Scott or Lincoln or Jeff Davis could be forgotten in a week."[33]

The treatment of the living seemed little better. From Augusta, Eliza Smith warned her daughters that "men & women are robbed in these streets daily, also in the cars. Clothes stolen out of the tubs & off of the ironing table. Our whole world is demoralized—turned topsy turvey." Mary Chesnut described a grisly evening in Columbia where one of the guests, a soldier recuperating from typhoid fever, did his imitations of dead soldiers' expressions. "Can the hardening process of war go further than that?" she asked. A more sensitive officer expressed concern with what he thought years of war was doing to soldiers' spirits. "No one can know anything of the guile of this world without having been in the army three years in a Revolution. God grant that present depravity may not survive the army and the Revolution," he told his wife, concluding optimistically, "but I doubt not there is much purity and truth, also." Confederates feared that the war to show their superiority was in fact destroying their virtue.[34]

The war gradually became commonplace, something in the background of Confederates' consciousness as they tried to escape its horrors. Mary Chesnut marveled at her ability to block out the sounds of nearby fighting while reading a George Eliot novel and wondered if she could be "the same poor soul who fell on her knees and prayed and wept and fainted as the first guns boomed from Fort Sumter." Emma LeConte was similarly impressed by her own equanimity while making preparations to abandon Columbia in January 1865. "How callous our hearts have grown," she reflected. "Two years ago with what despairing agony I would have looked upon the prospect before us, and now I only feel a dull heart pain. . . . We seem sunk in an apathy." Lancelot Blackford was appalled by the facade of normality he found in besieged Petersburg: "I saw ladies and gentlemen, but mostly ladies alone promenading as though nothing was the matter, and little children playing on the side-walks in blissful unconsciousness or unconcern."[35] Those who participated in promenades and parties believed that they needed these small gestures to maintain their own sanity in the face of incomprehensible suffering and fear. Those who condemned could not understand how the war that dominated their own lives could be ignored—even momentarily—by others.

Nowhere was this dichotomy between suffering and socializing more apparent than in Richmond. As the capital city, it was filled with politicians and their families, many of whom sought entertainment in each others' company. Mary Chesnut was one of the leading figures in this Richmond social set, and her diary is filled with descriptions of parties, salons, concerts, rides, and other entertainments. Her husband, however, disapproved and frequently "denounced" his wife and her friends "for being so disippated." He repeatedly chastised her for making merry in town while a war raged in the countryside and complained that she lacked "proper feeling" for the times. For her part, Chesnut had been accustomed to such a social whirl in prewar Washington and was unwilling to live a life without intellectual and social stimulation.[36]

Visitors to Richmond were repeatedly struck by the opportunities for entertainment. Sallie Bird described the city to a friend in Athens, Georgia: "There has been and still is considerable depression here, and yet people have dances and weddings, and bands serenade (delightfully too), and ladies dress and walk the streets as if there was no war." Lancelot Blackford's brother, Lewis, "never knew Richmond so pleasant" despite the war and the blockade, commenting that "the entertainments are not expensive but they are well attended and much enjoyed." Isaac Read described the city in detail in a letter, finding "a good deal of expense in living and dress, mainly among a class that like obscene birds and beasts have grown fat on the war; & a plentiful lack of superior men in the several legislative bodies. With these & some other abatements one, like myself subject to despondency, can find something to encourage him even in this extreme hour." But Read was pleased to report that Richmonders for the most part did not share his melancholy. Rather, "everyone seemed aware of our condition & no wise disposed to disguise or underrate its difficulties."[37]

The debate over socializing in Richmond was repeated in cities and towns across the Confederacy. One Louisiana soldier was appalled by the nightly balls and parties in Mobile and shocked that no one else seemed to mind: "I tell the young ladies that it is contrary to my profession to attend parties, particularly while the war is going on, that I do not think it is right to give and attend parties now. They say that it would be of little use for them to grieve over the troubles of our unfortunate country but they and I are pleased to differ in opinion." Furthermore, he reported, "I think *all* the *uggly* women of our Confederacy have assembled in this city." While Kate Cumming, a Mobile native, would probably have disagreed with his assessment of her sisters, she did find in early 1865 that "Mobile is gayer than ever; it seems as if the people have become reckless." Kate Stone offered some explanation of the fatalism seizing Confederates around the nation: "I did not think two months ago I would ever dance or care to talk nonsense again. But one grows callous to suffering and death. We can live only in the present, only from day to day. We cannot bear to think of the past and so dread the future." Now living in South Carolina, Mary Chesnut heard the news of Sherman taking Savannah and despaired of her own reaction: "We care for none of these things. We eat, drink, laugh, dance, in lightness of heart!!!"[38] Lightness of heart, or denial of the inevitable? Historians have read this to be a withdrawal of support for the Confederacy. But all people at one time or another put self-interest above the collective good. To do so does not necessarily translate into a lack of patriotism, or a desire to see the Confederacy fail.[39]

"TO GO OR NOT TO GO, THAT IS THE QUESTION"

The tension between the personal and the national becomes especially visible when looking at conscription, shirking, and desertion—interrelated issues that fostered deep divisions not only between Confederates and their government but between soldiers and civilians, and even among different groups of soldiers themselves. Men who had volunteered early for the army, swept up by an initial burst of patriotism and sense of duty, had little use for the able-bodied who stayed home, saving themselves. Some women joined the volunteers in condemning the stay-at-homes; others encouraged their sons, husbands, and brothers to remain with them for reasons of both economics and protection. The Confederate government and the Confederate press kept up a barrage of requests for soldiers, appealing to manhood, patriotism, duty, and honor. At the same time, however, the number of exemptions provided in the various conscription acts, especially the first, was staggering. This problem was only compounded by various supplemental state actions, especially in Georgia and North Carolina, which kept even more men from joining the ranks. A draft was particularly problematic in a country dedicated to preserving individual liberty at all costs. The Confederacy was founded on the rhetoric of slavery and liberty, and forcing men into service for an unspecified term seemed to many to be too close to the former. The issue of service was an issue of loyalty—the question was: to whom?[40]

Conscripts, substitutes, and shirkers—men who either took advantage of exemptions, hired substitutes, or secured positions in local home guards—were generally treated with the same scorn reserved for the other enemies of the Confederate war effort, the speculators and extortioners. "Since the war began over 74,000 substitutes have been placed in the Army, in many cases by men who soon made up their substitution fee off the families of soldiers," the *Montgomery Advertiser* reported in November 1863, thus explicitly linking substitution and "extortion" or profiteering. James Henley Thornwell tried to appeal to shirkers' sense of duty by attacking their notions of class privileges, explaining that "the man who stands back from the ranks in these perilous times, because he is unwilling to serve his country as a private soldier, who loves his ease more than liberty, his luxuries more than his honor, that man is a dead fly in our precious ointment." The author of "The Duties of the Hour" also alluded to the class conflict lurking beneath the surface of shirking and exemptions when he commented that "a poor farmer, dragged from home, where he leaves ten or a dozen little ones to combat with poverty, passing on his way to the field of slaughter, sees such crowds of well dressed men whose coats and pants are worth thousands out of service; his love of Confederate liberty vanishes into smoke." Thus the language of white liberty and slavery pervaded conscription just as it had secession.[41]

An article in the Richmond *Whig* tried to appeal to republican sensibilities, cautioning that "the fear of getting killed or wounded threatens to reduce us all to slavery. . . . A little less fright and more common sense—we will not say patriotism—may compose these difficulties and show us a pathway out of the bog in which we have fallen." Confederates had to make the rhetoric of white republicanism real. If all white men were equal citizens (a key tenet of antebellum herrenvolk democracy), they had to be equal when it was time to make sacrifices as well. To that end, the Augusta *Daily Constitutionalist* proposed that all able-bodied men should be enrolled for three months, with no exemptions or substitutions, except for those deemed absolutely essential to home business. While acknowledging that such a mass mobilization would be difficult for the people at home, the author opined that it would be less onerous than life under Yankee domination. "It is independence or an honorable death, on one hand—chains, and slavery, and degradation, on the other. Who can hesitate a moment as to his choice?" he asked. "Will we not rather all die free men than live all slaves, and with such a master?"[42]

In a speech before the Confederate Senate, Albert Gallatin Brown of Mississippi addressed a series of resolutions calling for similar actions. The first would put every white male in the Confederate States capable of bearing arms into military service; the second proposed a repeal of all substitution and exemption laws; the third would authorize the president to force all men "claiming and receiving foreign protection" to decide within sixty days to either take up arms or leave the Confederacy; and the fourth would detail the military for civil pursuits only when absolutely needed with reference to "competency alone."[43] Brown justified all of these measures on the grounds of military necessity. He believed that an all-out assault on the Yankees, using as many men as possible, would provide the final victory that had thus far eluded the Confederates and thought that a general conscription would provided the needed manpower. He had nothing but scorn for men who hired substitutes, complaining that "if [the] twenty thousand men in the army of Virginia who had furnished substitutes had been at Gettysburg, Philadelphia would have been ours in a week." Brown recognized the impact the situation on the homefront had on soldiers' morale, and he railed against the men who had received exemptions to stay home and raise foodstuffs and were then charging soldiers' wives exorbitant prices. The exempt had not acted in good faith and consequently should no longer remain protected. The government had a moral and a strategic obligation to take care of soldiers' families, as Brown explained: "We had the power to take husband and father from his home and force him into the army; and where you found the power to do that, I find the power to feed and clothe his dependent wife and children. It is not in human nature, Mr. President, for any soldier's heart to grow and swell with the fires of genuine patriotism, if he knows that his wife is shivering in the cold and his children are crying for bread." Brown had the utmost faith in the patriotism of most Confederate men, but he believed the government had an obligation to make the "laggards" do their duty as well. Once every Confederate pulled his own weight, Brown argued, the war would swiftly come to its conclusion.[44]

Women were frequently asked to bring their influence and powers of persuasion to bear on men—first to encourage them to enlist and later to keep them from deserting.[45] An "Appeal from Women," included in Jackson's *Southern Women of the Second American Revolution*, was an example of the latter. The "Women of the South" who signed the piece began in a typically self-deprecating fashion, casting men as their "natural protectors" and themselves as "weak and timid." These women shared men's desire for the war to be over, but they recognized that the only way for the war to end would be for every able-bodied man to join the army. And despite the fact that women needed men as their protectors, and longed to keep their loved ones near them, they urged men to fight, for "your lives cease to be dear to us when you fail to provide us a country that we can be proud of, and when we can no longer reverence your honor, your patriotism and your courage." They promised love and respect to any fighting man, even the "poor private in rags," and to ignore cowards and laggards, and they promised to never counsel dishonor and desertion; rather, "we will still try to do our duty; labor for, assist, relieve and encourage our brave defenders; and though our hearts are torn; though we are bereft of our dearest ones, we will never say 'hold! it is enough!' till the last vile foe shall bite the dust, or is driven from our soil, and our country proudly takes her place among the nations of the earth."[46]

These women were not alone in promising to scorn the men who stayed behind. The *Southern Field and Fireside*'s weekly "Gossip with Readers and Correspondents" column printed this question from "Emma" in September 1863: "Do you think able-bodied young men who have not been in the army deserve the respect of the young ladies?" Literary editor S. A. Atkinson offered a considered response, suggesting that those men who were kept out for medical reasons or because they were performing government service were perfectly respectable. As for the "skulkers," however, "the ladies cannot better serve the cause then to manifest a contempt for the pusillanimous conduct of all such persons." The ladies were only too happy to oblige, and they heaped opprobrium not only on the men who took advantage of exemptions or hired substitutes but on the men in the Home Guard as well. The resolutely single Sarah Morgan wrote, "There is only one set who take better care for their safety than married women; and that set is composed exclusively of the 'Home' Guard." Gertrude Thomas took issue with the "indiscriminate praise" the Confederate press heaped upon all military organizations: "The idea of praising militia and local troops in the same eulogistic strain as the volunteer organizations! It wars with my idea of justice—for certainly this was not their *first* call and they went because they were compelled to." Mrs. Allen S. Izard conceded that although she "had no heroism," she could tolerate no such weakness in the opposite sex, explaining, "I [should] hate a *man* who would flinch, even from martyrdom for his Country."[47]

The late arrivals were no more popular in camp then they were at home. In his diary, John C. Murray of the Crescent Artillery repeatedly complained about being forced to associate with conscripts. "Several conscripts have arrived in camp, for the purpose of becoming members of *Ours*. The boys don't like conscripts. There will be trouble with these fellows," he wrote on 7 February 1864. The trouble was not long in coming, and Murray appears to have been in the thick of it, for his entry for 9 February reads: "Promoted to Sergeantship this morning. Reduced to the ranks for refusing to mess with conscripts." Murray felt that by being forced to associate with conscripts, his commanding officers were not treating him, and the rest of the original volunteers, with the respect due to patriots defending their country. They were heroes; the conscripts were not.[48]

When all else failed, Confederates turned to humor and satire to goad men into service. "Achilles Hoppleggs, Esq.," the hero of an occasional feature in the *Southern Field and Fireside*, wished "to entreat all men in these Confederate States of America not to be a conscript. If you are not quick enough to get a '*posish*' that will secure you from conscription, go like a man and volunteer, for if you don't you will spend many a sleepless night in tears." "To go or not to go, that is the question," wrote "Exempt" in a take-off on Hamlet's soliloquy.

> Whether it pays best to suffer pestering
> by idle girls and garrulous old women,
> Or to take up arms against a host of Yankees
> And by opposing get killed.—

Exempt actually made a rather convincing case for staying home, citing the need to take care of his "babes" and "Mary," and worrying "would patriotism pay my debts, when dead." Even worse was the thought of another man doing his "huggin" with Mary, frightful enough to make him want to stay home:

'Specially as I am mad with nobody.
Shells and bullets make cowards of us all,
And blamed my skin of snortin' steeds,
And pomp and circumstance of war
Are to be compared with feather beds
And Mary by my side.

Despite the fact that the poem seems to justify staying home, it seems unlikely that it was meant to be taken at face value. It would have been out of character for the *Montgomery Advertiser*, the newspaper in which it appeared, to publish such a blatant appeal to self-interest. Rather, the choice of the pseudonym "Exempt," given the scorn with which stay-at-homes were treated, indicates that this should be read as a litany of feeble and self-serving excuses, an exaggeration showing how wrong, how cowardly, it would be to shirk one's duty.[49]

Just a few weeks earlier, the *Montgomery Advertiser* printed another poem, this one titled the "Croaker's Dialogue." It consisted of two sections, the first full of complaints, and the second, a soldier's response. The "croaker," a common term for a complainer both in and out of the army, fretted that "Johnston will not turn / And force the Yanks to fight." He has lost confidence in his leaders, in Johnston, and in himself:

The Yankees have the upper hand,
And ours—a gone case.
What shall I do? I do not know
What course to be pursuing:
The Yankees come, my cotton gone—
I'm ruined, ruined, ruined.

Oh, we are ruined—I can see
It all before me plain;
My money gone, my friends all fled,
I call them back in vain.

The soldier's response made quick work of the croaker's complaints by expressing faith in Johnston and the army. He then turned angrily on the croaker:

Whipped did you say? No *you* are whipped.
Your country is forgotten;
You'd sell your dearest right on earth

If you could save your cotton,
You'd mortgage principle, everything—
You'd let religion tumble,
Forget your birthright, God and all,
So you might turn and grumble.
Such men as *you* will whip the South,
If you're not stopped in season;

Confederates told themselves they would not and could not lose the war on the battlefield. They could lose only by giving up, by quitting, and by betraying one another. This poem, and others like it, return again and again to the ideology of suffering that was so much a part of Confederate culture. The individual Confederate soldier was more than up to the task of fighting the Yankees, but what he, and the army and the nation, lacked was a population truly willing to give everything they had to the cause. If soldiers could fight without worrying about their families suffering at home, the end of the war would come swiftly. The problem was not with the soldiers but with the hypocritical profiteers, who sought to enrich themselves at their nation's expense and were inevitably the loudest grumblers as well.

Shame on you, for your croaking words,
Although your head is hoary.
I'd dare to strike you as you stand,
You speculating tory.

This poem told Confederates to keep their fears and worries to themselves.[50]

Another attack on shirkers came in the form of a fourteen-page illustrated poem titled "Special Service Hero! Self-Detailed" and published in Richmond in 1863. "Special Service Hero" professed to sing the praises of the "heroes valour hath not proved," that is, to mock the men who took exemptions and stayed home, spending their time drinking and carousing. The Special Service Hero is a bejeweled dandy, whose costly baubles are:

Spoils not in battle won by strike of sword,
But trophies Infamy would shame to hoard;
Spoils torn by guile or force from some frail fair,
To swell the importance of our hero's air.

He is portrayed as an ungentlemanly womanizer, debauched and insolent, part and parcel of the corruption and vice swirling around wartime Richmond. When a woman is trapped on the sidewalk, unable to navigate an "odious puddle," the hero and his cronies are "exultant o'er her plight," rejoicing at the opportunity to glimpse an ankle. The hero strolls about town, taking advantage of the free lunch offered in bars and congregating with other loafers to hear the latest war news. There the hero makes a speech, decrying the rumors that fill the papers, and is applauded by his fellow shirkers. At the same time as the crowd is hailing him, a "crippled" soldier, "war-worn and battle-shattered," dressed in rags of poverty, limps by, a crutch in place of the leg "left upon a gloomy field / Where thousands bled and died but none would yield." The crowd ignores him, "worse than an alien in his native land":

> Pass on, O cripple! on, and disappear—
> Wants, wounds and misery find no favor here.
> Had every wound a thousand tongues to speak,
> And every want a thousand hands to seek,
> Relief from present ill, sympathy for past,
> The hands would palsy, tongues grow dumb at last,
> Long ere they would unlock the purse or heart
> Of any in this throng.

"Special Service Hero! Self-Detailed" is laced with palpable anger, at both the men who stayed home and the general public, men and women, who accepted the shirkers' cowardice. This split in Confederate society was the subject of great consternation, as it not only damaged Confederates' sense of loyalty to each other but was also evidence of their straying from God's will, which would surely result in disastrous consequences.[51]

Arguably an even greater problem than shirking was that of desertion. Solid numbers are difficult to come by, for many deserters would either rejoin their own regiments or be conscripted again into the army, but one commonly cited figure places the number at about 104,000, or 13 percent of the Confederate army.[52] This figure is somewhat deceptive, however, as desertion really became a problem late in the war, during the difficult winter of 1864–65. Desertion perfectly exemplified the tension between national commitment and self-interest with which so many Confederates struggled. Soldiers in the field were horrified by the carnage they saw on the battlefields, weary of marching with woefully inadequate rations, clothing, and supplies, and worried about families left unprotected at home. Civilians with family in the army experienced conflicting emotions—they were proud of their soldiers' sacrifices, especially in the early years, but they worried about both the soldiers' and their own safety and survival.

SPECIAL SERVICE HERO!

SELF--DETAILED.

BY THE AUTHOR OF "THE ROSE OF SHENANDOAH."

RICMOND, VA.,
PUBLISHED FOR THE AUTHOR,
1863.

PRICE, ONE DOLLAR.

"Special Service Hero! Self-Detailed." This 1863 illustrated poem attacked able-bodied men for shirking their duties to the Confederacy. Virginia Historical Society.

Annette Koch, at home on her plantation in southern Mississippi, worried constantly about her son Elers, a soldier in the army. "Oh don't I wish this war was over, it makes me mader and mader every day," she wrote to her husband in New Orleans in May 1863. "If we only had poor Elers home with us, it makes me miserable to think he has to stay whether he will or not, or be a deserter." She struggled with her own feelings, worrying equally about Elers's physical and moral well being. "I almost wish Elers would desert and come home," she confessed but continued, "too, then again I would hate to have him be a deserter, but they have such hard times and there is so many that have come home that it looks like it is no shame, but that they do just right." In a letter written several weeks later, she was no closer to a decision, wondering, "Can I tell him to desert. No as much as I long for him I cannot tell him to desert. He is our child and I hope he will always be what is honest and upright." Ultimately, social concern for appearances and for her son's honor outweighed Annette Koch's own selfish desires.[53]

Not everyone was as concerned with notions of duty and propriety as was Annette Koch. Kate Cumming asked a doctor why one of the men under her care had deserted, and "he answered, nothing would have made him except an earnest appeal from his wife, and that the women were the cause of nearly all the desertions." Confederate brigadier general J. Johnston Pettigrew wrote to North Carolina governor Zebulon B. Vance and enclosed two letters encouraging men to desert. He complained that North Carolina troops were receiving such letters every day and that many men were, in fact, leaving the ranks. Pettigrew blamed the letters on the climate of public opinion in North Carolina that opposed the war and the Confederate government, inspired by several newspapers and members of the state legislature: "They utter nothing but declamations calculated and intended to make us dissatisfied, not only with the Confederate government, but with the Confederate cause; to impress us with the hopelessness of the struggle, and thus to unnerve us, preparatory to submission." Pettigrew was careful to tell Vance that he believed that the majority of North Carolinians were still loyal to the Confederate cause, and that he was "equally convinced that when the war is over and our true soldiers return to their homes, there will be a bitter day of reckoning, with the enemies behind us. But that is not sufficient for the present." Soldiers were being told that they could desert "with impunity," that militia officers at home were not doing their duty and that they would not have to work. Even worse, "the rascals" were not going home to work but instead formed bands of thieves and raiders, "inflicting double injury upon their country" and "demoralizing" the men left in the field "to an extent you can scarcely conceive." Pettigrew closed by asking Vance to use his influence in the state to "reform matters," for "it is absolutely necessary to bring the public opinion again to the condition of patriotically and manfully meeting those trials, which every people struggling for independence must meet, and so far as the army is concerned, the best way to accomplish this, is to convince them, that a man who [illegible word] deserts them in the face of the enemy will be met at home with scorn and then returned to [illegible] punishment."[54]

It was no coincidence that both Koch and Pettigrew couched their discussions of desertion in the language of honor. To desert meant to abandon one's post, to shirk one's patriotic duty, and to set one's own interests above those of the regiment and the nation. Clem Watson explained his position succinctly in a letter to his wife, telling her, "It is useless to think of my leaving the army as long as I can be of service to my country in the field. Honor and every sense of patriotism and duty to my country forbid it." Watson was discouraged by the selfishness he saw throughout the ranks, and was particularly troubled by those men who deserted from his company to join regiments stationed near their families in Louisiana. He shared their anxieties about their families, but, he asserted, "a man's private misfortunes, his personal wrongs, his individual suffering can never justify him in leaving his post in the time of need." Watson angrily suggested that "their conduct deserves the contempt of mankind and their fate should be a disgraceful termination of their unworthy lives."[55]

Desertion wreaked havoc on unit cohesion, and often the advocates of harsh punishment were none other than the deserters' former compatriots. Abandonment of one's fellow men was unforgivable. "Mr. Arnold has *deserted* and disgraced himself for ever," Gustave Cook told his wife. Henry Fortson mentioned that two men deserted to the enemy the night before he wrote his letter. Surprisingly, he preferred that they desert to the enemy, as opposed to returning to Georgia in a gang. "I hope they will catch them, and shaft them to a stake, shooting is almost too good for such: fight four years, then desert, never do," he wrote, adding, "I am proud to say none of [company] B has deserted lately." Lancelot Blackford, clerk of a military court attached to Longstreet's corps, noted approvingly in early 1864 that the court "seems beginning now to appreciate for the first time the paramount importance of a stern discipline to keep the army up, and are inflicting penalties somewhat adequate for the oft-repeated offenses of 'Absence without Leave' and 'Desertion.'" A few weeks later, he told his mother that, within the preceding fortnight, his court had sentenced four or five men to death for desertion. Blackford had no qualms about the severity of the punishment, explaining, "Desertion *must* be put down if it costs the life of every tenth or fifth man in the army."[56]

As Confederates struggled with the sacrifices demanded of them, their private interests came into conflict with the public good. They wanted to be worthy of the promise of their new nation, but they could not always do it. Even as they acted in ways that hurt their new nation, Confederates professed their love for it. They wanted the war to end, but they wanted it to end in victory, even as they did little to help it. As the war dragged on, they longed for peace, but not at the expense of honor.

Interlude

Only Not a Victory

The summer of 1863 has long been seen as the turning point of the war. The double Union victories at Gettysburg and Vicksburg in July, the fact that the Confederacy never again controlled the Mississippi or crossed the Potomac, the eloquence of Lincoln at Gettysburg in November have all conspired to make this *the* moment when the war hung in the balance. Or did it? For the problem with this Gettysburg-centric view of the war is that it fails to take into account the fact that the war itself lasted for almost two more years. If the war was over, why did Confederates keep fighting? They kept fighting because they would not let themselves believe that they had been beaten. The summer of 1863 reveals the myriad ways Confederates worked—and they worked very hard—at convincing themselves and each other that they were still winning the war, that independence was still within their grasp.[1]

The stories of the battle of Gettysburg and the end of the siege of Vicksburg have been often told, and their supposed impact on morale and the course of the war have become fixtures of our cultural understanding of the war.[2] This is especially true where Gettysburg is concerned, for, with hindsight, it has been transformed into not just the literal high-water mark of the Confederacy but the figurative one as well.[3] Quite simply, for Confederates, the defeat at Gettysburg was not the crushing blow that we have come to believe that it was. At the time, no one, Union or Confederate, knew that the fight in Pennsylvania would be the so-called high-water mark of the Confederacy, and they understood Gettysburg in a much more ambiguous light. Confederates saw the battle as one of many—true, they had hoped for a great campaign that would have resulted in the capture of a major Northern city, even perhaps of Washington itself—but they had suffered defeats before. They took pride in the audacity of bringing the war to the North and in Lee's being able to live off the Pennsylvania countryside, granting a few weeks of relief to Virginia. The *Southern Field and Fireside* chastised its readers for allowing themselves to become upset, reminding them that "we expected Gen. Lee to perform impossibilities, and because our extraordinary expectations have not been realized, we are not satisfied with the result." The *Richmond Examiner* took a similar stance, explaining that "the result was not a defeat, it was not a loss; it was only not a victory, not one of the most brilliant triumphs ever recorded." Gettysburg represented a disappointment of expectations, not a failure.[4]

Much as Confederates sought to minimize the impact of the defeat at Gettysburg, so, too, did newspapers try to limit the psychological effects of losing Vicksburg and Port Hudson. The *Richmond Examiner* tried to calm a crisis-prone populace by asking, "What military advantage have we lost by the fall of Vicksburg? The South has held that place for a year chiefly from pride." The author minimized any lasting effects, claiming that the Confederacy "has a bloody nose and a black eye—but it was never sounder in mind and limb than it is at this moment." Other writers looked at the circumstances surrounding the fall of Vicksburg. Because the surrender was negotiated, argued the *Southern Recorder*, it could not "be regarded by the enemy as a complete and victorious triumph. At least it does not carry with it that prestige which an unconditional conquest by assault would have given it." It was a fine distinction. Or, as the *Charleston Mercury* put it, the Yankees did not succeed "by their valor or skill in arms." Rather, they had to starve out the Confederate garrison, which allowed Southern boosters to maintain their belief that Yankee soldiers were still no match for Confederates on the battlefield.[5]

And the events of the rest of the summer of 1863 seemed to bear out this thinking. Confederates were quite interested in the news of the New York City draft riots, seeing them as evidence of the unjustness of the Yankee cause and the lack of support among Northerners for the war, the Lincoln government, and emancipation. Headlines trumpeted "Glorious News from the North," and the rioting seemed a vindication of pre-Gettysburg ideas about Union morale. Since Gettysburg had no mitigating effect on antidraft sentiment, Confederates implied, it could not have been a great Northern victory after all. If the Northern people were already so sick of the war, and the Southerners still so willing to pursue it, it would come speedily to an end.[6] Furthermore, Meade's failure to pursue Lee's army had greatly displeased Lincoln, and Meade himself had no other substantial successes. Thus, in mid-August 1863 one Confederate soldier could conclude that "there seems to be a lull in the storm of war. The great depression our people labored under, after the fall of Vicksburg and Port Hudson, was uncalled for. The Battle of Gettysburg so disabled Meade, that he is unable to resume the offensive."[7]

Public encouragement and optimism were not always sufficient to keep Confederates from expressing their worries. Josiah Gorgas was overcome by one of his periodic (though temporary) bouts of melancholy when he lamented, "It seems incredible that human power could effect such a change in so brief a space. Yesterday we rode on the pinnacle of success—to-day absolute ruin seems to be our portion. The Confederacy totters to its destruction." A professor at the University of Virginia felt "oppressed" by the "news of the day" and the "gloom" pervading his community "in consequence of tidings received of so many of our 'unreturning brave.'"[8]

Some Confederates, both publicly and privately, expressed their frustration with the state of events by criticizing either military figures or the Davis government. In Columbia, Mrs. Robert Smith blamed the loss of Vicksburg and Port Hudson on President Davis's poor choice of appointments, complaining, "I am afraid we have not men fit for such trying times." One such political general was John C. Pemberton, the commander at Vicksburg. In the same letter, Mrs. Smith also complained about Lee's decision to invade Pennsylvania, asking what he had to show for it. The *Mercury* raised much the same question in "Aggressive War," arguing that Lee's invasion was ill-timed and that the country would have been better served by concentrating all of its military efforts on holding Vicksburg and the war in the West. "It is impossible for an invasion to have been more foolish and disastrous. It was opportune neither in time, nor circumstances. We must pay the penalty and redeem our errors like men," charged the *Mercury*, which then went on to argue that such redemption could only be achieved by shifting back to a purely defensive focus.[9]

Lee felt keenly the criticisms leveled at him in papers like the *Richmond Examiner* and the *Charleston Mercury* and in August 1863 offered Davis his resignation. Fearful that the Confederate people and his troops were losing confidence in him, Lee explained, "I cannot even accomplish what I myself desire," adding, "how can I fulfill the expectations of others?" Davis refused to accept it, telling Lee that "our country could not bear to lose you," and a few months later he publicly expressed his confidence in the general. In an official "Resolution of Thanks," Davis commended the Army of Northern Virginia and its commanders on their "great and signal victories." A long list of their "masterly and glorious achievements" followed, including the expected Seven Days, Second Manassas, Fredericksburg and Chancellorsville, and the unexpected Gettysburg. Clearly, for Confederates, anything short of annihilation could be scored a victory. Self-deception, yes, but self-deception with real political salience.[10]

Ordinary Confederates shared Davis's faith in Robert E. Lee. Margaret Wight wrote in her diary in late July (before Lee actually made his offer) that "a rumor has reached us that Gen. Lee had resigned. Of all misfortunes that could have happened to us *this* is the greatest." To her great relief, Wight wrote the following day: "Gen Lee has *not* resigned and as long as so good and great a man has charge of our army in Virginia we will not despair." Andy Heirs, a member of the Washington Light Infantry, believed deeply in the abilities of his army. "The Army of Northern VA., must be the savior of our country, must support the crop of trials with which she has become involved and afflicted. . . . I believe it to be the bright destiny of this army to achieve our countries independence." Lee and his army could still deliver the Confederacy.[11]

With the passage of time, soldiers' spirits rebounded from the defeats of early summer. In August 1863, Lancelot Blackford sought to reassure his mother that soldiers were not giving up the fight: "The *morale* of the army is from all accounts that reach us from the rear far better than that of the people at home, in view of the present dark aspect of our affairs." In fact, he continued, "it is declared that the chief source of depression, when any exists, among the troops, is the intelligence of faint-heartedness, and in some sections base 'caving-in' that reach them from home." Here is a perfect example of the close relationship between home and battlefield, the two-way flow of information. Blackford exhibited a bit of Virginia chauvinism at this point, claiming that the problems of morale existed "chiefly among the Alabama and Mississippi troops," who had never been known for their "gallantry & conduct." He did, however, single out for praise a meeting of North Carolina troops at which they declared their dedication to the Confederate army in the face of Unionist newspaper proclamations back home. Edgeworth Bird, in camp near U. S. Ford, Virginia, brooked no talk of surrender. "Any man who advocates reconstruction should be hung to the nearest tree," he told his wife, Sallie. "Disband our armies, and mind never dreamed of such a scene as the South would soon represent: murder, rapine, conflagration. But Poh! They can never subdue us, and our people are staunch." Andy Heirs, an Illinois native, felt deeply the importance of soldier's loyalty to their cause and to each other:

What would be the result, what would be the fate of our country, if the soldiers of our army were as desponding, as void of hope and determination, as are the croakers in our towns and cities, who, more than anything else depress the spirits of the people outside the army and enervate the cause throughout the land? . . . No matter how dangerous how destructive the conflict, the soldiers of this army, even while mourning the loss of comrades are not dispirited! Relying on each other and upon their leaders, knowing the danger of defeat to other country, the glory and honor of success, they know their strength, and with it are supported with invincible determination which the armies of the world could not intimidate. . . . Notwithstanding our Southern reverses, the prospects of the Confederacy still are bright.[12]

Soldiers hoped that evidence of their own good spirits would prevent those at home from faltering.

In his resignation, Lee made reference to the importance of the citizenry to the cause and in so doing unwittingly reflected a shift in the language of defeat. As he reminded Davis: "We must expect reverses, even defeats. They are sent to teach us wisdom and prudence, to call forth greater energies, and to prevent our falling into greater disasters. Our people have only to be true and united to bear manfully the misfortunes incident to war, and all will come right in the end."[13] This showed the combination of Confederate fatalism and optimism at work: defeats were lessons, not signs that the cause was wrong. Lee's assessment of the role of civilians resonated strongly with Davis, as it echoed some of the latter's official pronouncements. On 25 July, Davis made one of his periodic proclamations for a national day of fasting, humiliation, and prayer, set for 21 August. He urged his citizenry to "unite in supplication" and ask God for his favor and protection. It was time, Davis reminded Southerners, for self-examination of hearts and consciences. Early military successes had made them self-confident; and "love of lucre" had "eaten like a gangrene into the very heart of the land." The Lord was chastening the South, and its duty was to "receive in humble thankfulness the lesson which He has taught in our recent reverses."[14]

At the same time that Confederates put forth a public image of a brave and steadfast people who were certain of their eventual victory and would brook no backsliding, they could not help unconsciously revealing fears and anxieties. How else to explain the news of a strange phenomenon that appeared in the western part of Virginia in late September? According to reports in the *Staunton Spectator*, several residents of Greenbrier County described seeing a spectral column of thousands of men, dressed only in white, "without arms and knapsacks," marching across a field for over an hour.

A different account featured the white-robed men, but had them following behind mysterious white bundles. The figures were described as "marching north or northwest, right thro' the mountains." The eyewitnesses, a "truthful" man, several "respectable" ladies, a "youth nearly grown," and a "servant girl," were all described as being above reproach. Clearly, this was a sign, but of what seemed unclear. Was it, as one correspondent mused, "a good or a bad omen to the cause we are defending with all our energies," and did it portend "peace or a longer continuance of this bloody struggle, or is mere delusion, who can say?"

Staunton Spectator editor Richard Mauzy took a stab at interpretation, and his explanation reveals very clearly what weighed heavily on his, and presumably his readers', minds. He did not see these white-robed men as ghosts, or as symbols of fighting men per se. Rather, Mauzy used this omen to make a political point, charging that the white bundles were, in fact, cotton bales, the very bales being sold illegally to the North by "the weak-kneed secessionists of Mississippi." Mauzy then vented his deep anger toward the hypocrisy he perceived emanating from farther South: "The figures of men marching North at a rapid pace in the scanty garb described, represent that these traitorous cotton sellers should be reduced in their dress to a cotton shirt fastened on their 'tight hides' by a plaster of tar, and be made to march North at a 'double quick.'" These men, he charged, were the worst kinds of cowards, the sort who "before the war, were so willing to spill their 'last drop of blood,' but since the war have shown an unconquerable dread of spilling the 'first drop.'" By construing this apparition not as a sign of defeats or victories to come but rather as a critique of shirking within the Confederacy, Mauzy seemed to be reminding his readers that the key to their independence lay within: the Confederacy would not be beaten by the North, only by itself.[15]

3 Enemies Like an Avalanche

Yankees, Slaves, and Confederate Identity

As the Confederacy willed itself into being, it faced a variety of challenges. Confederates created their identity under constant assault, and that identity was ever changing. As many new nations do, they defined themselves in opposition to others. Yankees and slaves, in particular, threatened Confederates' sense of self in different ways, forcing them to think about the meaning of loyalty and, in the case of slaves at the end of the war, the meaning of the Confederacy itself. Confederates in areas under occupation found themselves angry or repulsed by Union soldiers but often drawn into relationships with them—whether out of necessity or circumstance—that complicated feelings of loyalty. Could one take the oath of allegiance to the Union yet still remain Confederate? Many people thought so. Confederates also convinced themselves that their slaves were a source of national strength, not, as we know, a force eating away at the Confederacy from within. But by the end of the war, a significant population of Confederates believed that their slaves could be another kind of asset, that they could help Confederates militarily. For these people, the Confederacy had transcended its origins as a slaveholders' republic.[1]

"THEY EXASPERATE BUT DO NOT SUBDUE"

"The enemy like an avalanche has spread over our whole country. Disregarding all rights, social, religious, and political," complained Zillah Haynie Brandon, an Alabama woman, in 1864. Such callous disregard for Southern rights, Confederates believed, was not a function of war but its very cause. Many white Southerners felt certain that the sanctimonious Yankees wanted only to exploit the South's agricultural riches and turn its residents into second-class citizens. The North's concerns, Confederates believed, were less about the ideals of Union and more about the realities of production and exploitation. Brandon confided to her diary that "the North has long run the vast machine of our government, drained our treasury and now to glean us out of all our toils they plow our valleys, mountains, cities and even the dark waters are turned out of their course that they may engulf all their hellish passion craves." An essay titled "War" in the *Southern Field and Fireside* condemned the Union for inaugurating the war, charging hypocrisy: "Under the magic words of liberty and union they sought to hide their groveling worship of mammon."[2]

Francis Williamson Smith, serving in the Confederate army in Virginia, saw "no peace & no prospect of peace," condemning the North as "narrow minded" and antidemocratic. Like many of his compatriots, Smith attributed the conflict to "the apparent difference of interest between the agriculturalist, & the merchant, & manufacturer." He went on, however, to blame the U.S. government for exacerbating rather than ameliorating the tensions. The war that engulfed the Confederate States was not their fault; they were the victims, not the instigators.[3]

This fear of being subjugated by the North, this image of Northerners as villains bent on "enslaving" the South, echoes throughout the writings, public and private, of Confederates. Demonized even before war broke out, Northerners were increasingly characterized as "Huns" and "barbarians." Emma LeConte, in Columbia, South Carolina, called them "vandals" and "fiends incarnate." In Camden, Arkansas, John W. Brown complained about the Union division, "in other words rogues, robbers, and vagabonds," occupying his neighborhood. William R. Smith doubted the Yankees' Christianity, and Gertrude Thomas was struck by the "repulsive" appearance of Northern prisoners of war.[4]

Far from scoffing at this seemingly unworthy foe, however, Confederates feared them. The presence of Northern troops became a nationalist rallying point. Stories of Yankee brutality were legion in personal correspondence and became staples of journalism and oratory. Civilians were unaccustomed to confronting their enemies at home, and they responded angrily to Union attempts to break their spirit.[5] Josiah Gorgas marveled at the reported cruelties of Union troops and wondered, "Has war ever been carried on like this before, among civilized people?" Gorgas doubted, however, that their mistreatment would break Confederates' spirit, noting that the Union soldiers "exasperate but do not subdue." Months later, he again reflected in his journal that "the war has now assumed that phase in which no mercy can be shown to the enemy. He burns, robs, murders, & ravishes & this is to be met only by killing all."[6] Revenge, too, was a powerful motivating factor, and Confederates who had frequent contact with Union troops, or whose families were in the path of armies, had ample provocation. After witnessing the devastation wrought by Union troops in Mississippi, Clem Watson of the Sixteenth Louisiana Infantry prayed for the strength "to inflict that punishment upon our fiendish foes that their acts so richly deserve."[7]

The damage inflicted by the Yankees, writers warned, would be nothing compared to the horrors should the Confederacy be conquered. The *Richmond Examiner* published a long, two-part analysis of what subjugation meant. Northern rule would lead to utter domination, every town garrisoned with "Yankee guards . . . every court with Yankee judges; every church with Yankee preachers." The Confederates would become like the Irish or the Poles, a people crushed under their inferiors, even their churches subject to political controls.[8] If Confederate men did not rally to the cause, an article in the *Southern Field and Fireside* predicted, they could expect to see their wives, daughters, and mothers working as maids for Yankee generals' wives; their sons forced to serve in the Yankee army, fighting the French in Mexico; their children forced to learn abolitionism in school while being taught to detest Lee, Jackson, and Beauregard. Southerners would be forced to "adopt an Anti-Slavery Bible and an Anti-Slavery God; to welcome Free Love as a new dispensation." Finally, and worst of all, they would see their proud heritage erased and be forced "to forget that ladies and gentlemen existed."[9]

"Are we, the proud and boastful people of the South, dumb cattle to be worked with yokes upon our necks?" asked another writer. Through a series of rhetorical questions, the author struck at Confederate men's fears of a world where gender roles were ignored and Confederate women were forced into degrading servitude: "Are our mothers, who gave us suck, to be made cooks for Yankee matrons? Are our wives, the mothers of our little ones, the bone of our bone and the flesh of our flesh, to be made washerwomen for itinerant butchers and libertines? Are our sisters, into whose sweet arms we dreamed all our childhood dreams, and who gave us when we left them to fight this war, the holiest kisses ever given upon earth, to be made chambermaids for Yankee harlots?" Losing the war would not only mean losing political independence; it would mean the end of the Southern social structure. The conquered Confederates would become no better than their own slaves, subject to the arbitrary whims of their Northern masters. Such a dishonorable predicament was surely a fate worse than death Implicit in all of these prophecies was a racial component, tapping into the same exaggerated visions of black rule that the secession commissioners and fire-eaters had expressed in 1860–61.[10]

This powerful rhetoric was not limited to public speech; privately Confederates expressed many of the same fears. Lise Mitchell, a teenage niece of Jefferson Davis, wondered if a just God would "let the Yankees subjugate our beloved country." Echoing racialized rhetoric, she worried about being "enslaved" by Northerners to the point that "we would scarce dare assert ourselves over our own." An Augusta woman confessed that "the idea of Yankee, wh[ich] means Negro, rule, withers my heart and paralyzes my will." The possibility that in defeat the Confederate world might be turned upside down, with Southerners' former slaves on top, was almost too horrible to contemplate. Others were inspired to proclamations of defiance, vowing to destroy the Confederacy before they allowed it to become subject to Northern rule. A New Orleans man asked a Northern friend to tell his people that "Lincoln may occupy Southern territory, but that territory will be a desert, a vast cemetery, with not a man, not a woman, not a child, nor a four-footed animal."[11]

"SOMETIMES THE BLUE DEVILS WILL INTRUDE"

The truth of life under occupation, increasing numbers of Confederates discovered, did not live up to its apocalyptic billing. How could it? This was not to say that interactions between Yankees and Confederates were not sometimes frightening, especially when they came in the form of raids, both authorized and extralegal. Blue-garbed men, heavily armed, burst into homes generally populated by women and perhaps a few young boys or old men. They took food and clothing from people who could ill-afford to lose it, stole valuables and family heirlooms, and sometimes terrorized the inhabitants for sport, destroying what they could not take and occasionally setting places afire.

Confederate letters and diaries are filled with stories of women terrorized and property devastated. One such account can stand for many. In a letter to a friend, Mrs. L. P. Lewis of Monroe County, Virginia, tried to describe "the horrors and the outrages we have passed thro' in this valley." She lost everything: "I have not in the whole house *one single* thing that was ever given to me as a token of affection or remembrance." But Lewis refused to allow her enemies to get the better of her. Rather, she explained, "I actually forgot my losses in the indignation of outraged feeling, and the remembrance of the insult to God and to human nature.—I had read sensation novels & police trials, & many a learned discussion about human depravity, but never till I saw that compendium of human villainy, Genl. Hunter, had I any distinct idea of what that favourite Puritan dogma meant." By 1864, the Union was following an explicit policy of bringing the "hard hand of war" to civilians.[12] Designed to break the spirit and will of the Southern population, such policies appeared not to have the desired effect on Mrs. Lewis. Although she admitted that she sometimes felt "a sense of utter bereavement," she refused to allow herself to become depressed. Instead, she assured her friend that she and her family were "cheerful & full of high hope—neither 'humbled' nor 'subjugated'; but ready & willing to work & to suffer unto the end." Her daughters, presumably grown-up, asked Lewis and her husband to leave their "plundered home" for the duration of the war, but Lewis refused, describing her feelings in words that demonstrated her profound commitment to the cause of Confederate independence:

> Honour & duty require that I shall stick to my own shelter while I have one. I shall stay with it, like the defenders of Fort Sumpter no matter what the ruin. I shall stand by the Flag of *Home*, & like a true Indian will die by the graves of my ancestors. I do not mean to try to do more than live, till God gives us better days. I shall not tempt enemies nor distress friends by taxing their generosity for even the least thing I can do without. I am neither afraid nor ashamed to be poor. Why should—I wish to appear other than I am? and why seek rest & ease at the expense of others, even of a good child?

Lewis and her family had absorbed the lessons of Confederate citizenship and were determined to live by them. Having lost their material possessions, they were determined to hold onto what little remained to them—their good name and their self-respect. Confederates believed they came from "better stock" than Northerners; the war gave them an opportunity to prove their mettle and with it their fitness for independence.[13]

As difficult, dangerous, and frightening as it might be to endure a raid, at least the period of terror was finite. Although the house might be in shambles, its occupants broken in spirit if not body, sooner or later the hated Yankees would leave. Living in an area under occupation, however, afforded no such relief, and Confederates in that situation expressed both depression and disgust. The sight of "the Stars and Stripes floating on every hill" around his home in occupied Arkansas "brought up mingled emotions of sorrow and despondency" in John Brown. Sally Armstrong, whose home was surrounded by a Union encampment, reacted by withdrawing. She confided in her diary, "I destroy all the time I can sleeping, hoping by so doing the time of the Yankee's stay will be shortened." She was especially troubled when soldiers came to her house seeking companionship, and she complained bitterly, "I wish the Yankees would not take it on themselves to come over here to be entertained, for I really dislike them so I can't bear to talk."[14] In Columbia, South Carolina, Emma LeConte found herself "sink[ing] into a dull apathy," even as the sight of Union soldiers in control of her beloved city stirred up feelings of "horror and hatred, loathing and disgust." Emma Walton, living under occupation in New Orleans, reassured her father, "We are all very well indeed, and as a general thing, in excellent spirits, sometimes the *blue devils* will intrude, and annoy us, but we will not *submit* to them."[15]

Many Confederates reacted viscerally to their encounters with the enemy, describing feelings of physical revulsion. Cloe Whittle described the dilemma she faced as she tried to leave Norfolk in October 1863. "A very long step had to be taken to get on the cars & I did not fancy being almost taken in the arms of the Yankees or jerked up as I saw some common people getting up." Fortunately, her father was there to assist her. She had not been so lucky a few months earlier, when she had to ask a U.S. Army officer to help her get a package from a relative in the North. Despite being forced to rely on the Union lieutenant, Whittle could not bring herself to actually touch the man, noting that when they were introduced, "I put on my gloves and filled my hands with my parasol that I might not have to shake hands with him."[16]

It was easy to express revulsion and unhappiness in the pages of a letter or journal, but many Confederates went further, standing up to the Yankees with whom they came in contact. Newspapers and books served up a steady diet of inspirational stories about women, and even children, fighting back. In one such example, Union sentinels in New Orleans reportedly picked up a small boy and tried to force him to "Hurrah for Lincoln." He resisted, and the soldiers held him over the canal, threatening, "'Hurrah for Lincoln, or we'll drop you in.' 'Drop and be damned' said the little rebel; and, with a shout, they set him down, saying he was rebel pluck to the backbone." The moral of this story was clear: even savage Yankees could be made to respect Confederate rights, if these rights were defended courageously. Emma LeConte related a similar story, illustrating the virtues of acting "with quiet dignity": While "pillaging" the house of a lady, a soldier asked if "they had not humbled her pride *now*. 'No indeed,' she said, 'nor can you ever.' 'You *fear* us anyway.' 'No,' she said. 'By G—, but you *shall* fear me now,' and he cocked his pistol and put it to her head. 'Are you afraid now?' She folded her arms and, looking him steadily in the eye, said contemptuously, 'No.' He dropped his pistol, and with an expression of admiration, left her." Confederate women's emotional strength could protect them even when they were physically at risk. Indeed, LeConte later related that the Yankee occupiers "concurred in unqualified admiration for the pluck and dignity of the Columbia women. . . . They did not think they could ever conquer the South if the men were animated by the same spirit as the women of South Carolina." This was another example of the idealization of Confederate womanhood. Standing up to the Yankees was as much a virtue as wearing homespun or sending off a son to fight.[17]

Hoping that their gender would afford them some protection from Yankee soldiers, Confederate women channeled their anger and fear into defiance. And if they were mistreated, they would have more evidence of the inhumanity of Yankees, more reason to hate them and to inspire men to fight on. Pauline DeCaradeuc joined her family in South Carolina in making preparations for the arrival of Yankees in 1864 and related proudly that "all here think that in the event of their coming I would be quite cool, I think & hope I would be." Like DeCaradeuc, Kate Cumming praised the virtues of silence, reminding herself that "we much oftener lower ourselves by insulting language than the people whom we abuse." Mittie Bond, however, approvingly recorded a neighbor's behavior: "Mrs. Maxwell . . . talked pretty saucy to the Feds and told them she wished 'the Yankees as far in Hell as a pigeon could fly.' They asked her for some cornbread she hadn't any bread for them, she had plenty of bread but it was all for the Confederates for her brothers and friends. They were very mad with her." Mad, but it appears from Bond's account that Mrs. Maxwell suffered no punishment for her defiance, saved, perhaps, by her gender. Another story illustrates the fears of Confederates regarding Yankee transgressions against women despite the protection of femininity. A refugee family in Richmond described some "incidents of the abominable treatment" they had received at the hands of the Yankees. In the worst example, one of the little girls said that "she had been offered a five dollar gold piece by a Yankee officer, if he would let him kiss her, which she indignantly refused." Confederates could expect no more from the Yankees, and no less from their own children.[18]

It was easy for most Confederates to hate the anonymous Union invaders, easy to demonize them, easy to dismiss them as inferior. It was much harder for those Southerners with family ties to the North, who were forced to negotiate between competing loyalties. Lancelot Blackford reported with great relief that a refugee who had met his Uncle James in New Jersey described him as "the most rabid Southerner she has seen in Dixie or out of it." According to this woman, Blackford's uncle, tired of life in "Yankeedom," was "talking very strongly of going with his whole family in October to Europe to remain until the war is over." Fleeing to the North or being trapped there by the outbreak of war was one thing; actively supporting the Union cause was a very different matter. Kate Stone described a neighbor in Texas with a Northern-born wife whose five sons were all living in the North. "It is strange that he could raise five sons in the South to love the North better than their own native land," she reflected, and continued tartly, "Let us hope he is satisfied with them, as no one else is. All have a hearty contempt for them. What a disgrace to belong to that family."[19]

Even more troubling for Confederates were those women who chose to marry Northerners, especially when those men were officers in the Union army. This romantic rejection of Confederate men, in direct contradiction to the many public appeals for Confederate women to save themselves for soldiers, provoked family disagreements and social conflicts. Kate Cumming told of a dinner she attended with several cavalrymen and a young woman from Louisiana, Miss Womack. The men told Womack of a friend from home who had married a Union general. As Cumming recalled: "They were all a good deal annoyed that this lady had lowered herself in such a manner. I told Miss Womack that no Alabama girl would be guilty of such a disgraceful act. She replied, that the girl was so ugly that no Confederate would marry her." Making cruel comments at the expense of an acquaintance was one thing, but what to do if the culprit was a member of one's own family? Cloe Whittle found herself faced with a troubling dilemma. Her cousin had become engaged to a Union army officer before the war began. The man had been stationed in the Pacific but had now arrived in Charleston for the wedding, and Whittle had to decide whether or not to attend. Although she was quite upset to see him wearing his uniform inside the family's home, she did ultimately decide to take part in the festivities. Her heart was not fully in the proceedings, and as she watched her cousin leaving "to take up her sojourn among the Yankees," Whittle predicted that "she will find her situation not very pleasant for all she looks so happy now." Confederates had drawn the lines of difference between themselves and Northerners so starkly that they believed the two could never be reunited.[20]

Another Confederate woman who felt torn between her loyalty to the Confederacy and her relationships with Northerners was Mahala Perkins Harding Eggleston Roach, a widow living in Vicksburg. By the time the surviving volume of her journal commences in late 1864, life under Union occupation appeared to have settled into a comfortable routine. Roach's diary is full of accounts of socializing, card-playing, and eggnog-drinking, frequently with Federal officers. She liked many of them, as shown in this entry from October 1864: "*Gen. Hawkins* called to see us this afternoon! I am much pleased with him tho he *is* a *negro officer* and a Yankee! hitherto two of the crowning hating pieces of creation, but now Col. Brinkerhoff, & Gen. Hawkins make the fifth (only) gentlemen we know in the Y. service!" She later defended Hawkins, a white man, explaining that "I like Gen. H. if he *is* a 'nigger officer' that abomination to southern eyes! he is a *gentleman* and has proved himself a *friend* to us." She also struck up a very close friendship with the wife of the commanding Union general, Napoleon J. T. Dana.[21]

Roach was alone in her family in socializing with Yankees. She had a son in the Confederate army, and her mother, Mrs. Eggleston, was such a staunch Confederate that she was actually expelled from Vicksburg by General Dana. Dana banished five women: four for being "Rebel sympathizers, mail carriers and smugglers," and the fifth, Eggleston, for being a "general busybody with rebel interests, rebel philanthropist, mail receiver, carrier of smuggled funds to prisoners in jail, &c. &c." Eggleston spent the duration of the war elsewhere in the area and was not permitted to return until the late spring of 1865. Roach was fortunate that her friendship with General Dana's wife afforded her some protection; Mrs. Dana was able to secure permission for the rest of the family to remain in their home. She tried several times to persuade Generals Dana and Hawkins to allow her mother to return, without success. Although one might expect such harsh treatment to color her impressions of the Union soldiers, Roach continued to socialize with officers. In late February 1865, she was disappointed to learn that the 124th Illinois Regiment was ordered to leave Vicksburg, noting, "I am really sorry for while we have Federal troops here I would like to have these." She was particularly sorry to part with a Mr. Durley, as "he has been a true friend to us, tho' in an enemy's guise!" Roach appears to have been untroubled by her divided life, and there is no hint of reproach from anyone else reported in her diary. Her life shows just how complicated were the decisions made by Confederates when they were faced with their enemies.[22]

"GUILTY, OR NOT GUILTY OF PERJURY"

Facing their opponents at close quarters forced Confederates to make personal decisions with political and ideological implications. They walked a tightrope between loyalty to their new nation and instincts of self-preservation. Should they overtly snub Federal troops and risk being punished for their defiance? Should they take the path of social accommodation and risk social censure from their Southern neighbors? Many factors influenced the choices Confederates made, including their gender, their age, their social position, and their prewar connections to the North.

The hardest decision Confederates within enemy lines were forced to make involved taking the oath of allegiance to the United States. Debates over the propriety of taking the oath, which, of course, involved a repudiation of the Confederacy, consumed Confederates who agonized over this conflict between self-interest and self-respect. Many Confederates who took the oath justified their actions to themselves and others by arguing that an oath taken under coercion was not binding and could therefore be violated with impunity. Much as children cross their fingers to negate a promise, Confederate oath-takers held their breath and put thoughts of perjury and dishonor out of their heads in order to tolerate an intolerable predicament.[23]

In New Orleans, Union general Benjamin Butler increased his unpopularity by forcing Confederates in the city either to take the oath or to register themselves as enemies of the United States. This demand prompted Louisiana congressman John Perkins to introduce resolutions in the Confederate Congress commending the loyalty of those "true men and women of the Confederacy" who refused to take the oath. Perkins's resolution, in turn, prompted the Reverend Benjamin Palmer to publish a lengthy treatise on the "Duties and Obligations" of citizens falling within enemy lines, with particular reference to the question of the oath. Palmer was most concerned with those Confederates who chose to take the oath and hoped that it was not too late, in February 1863, "to rouse those who are involved in this dire calamity to retrieve their lost position, and to wipe off the dishonor which must else cleave to them forever." Palmer divided the oath-takers into two groups: the first, "those who were never true to our cause," were fortunately "inconsiderable both as to numbers and influence," and the second group was composed of "those who in their secret hearts, are still loyal to the Confederacy, and have taken the oath under constraint, regarding it as one of the necessities of war." Palmer devoted very little space to the former, whom he considered traitors. It was the latter group, however, who Palmer sought to disabuse of the notion that taking a false oath hurt no one.[24]

Palmer believed that these false oaths caused profound harm to the Confederate spirit, both collectively and individually. Each oath-taker dishonored him or herself and showed contempt for God by bearing false witness. Furthermore, by permitting, and even praising, the notion that a false oath could ever be permissible, Confederates contributed to a weakening of the rule of law in their society. People who took the oath publicly while privately professing their loyalty to the Confederacy were no better than the Yankees who had once sworn to uphold the Constitution and then betrayed the Southern states, provoking the war. "Are our people willing to walk in the footsteps of our foes?" Palmer asked. "Can it ever be lawful for men to place themselves in that condition of disability where their simple word can never be accepted as the gauge of truth?" He worried, too, that these newly sworn citizens of the United States might be forced to take up arms against their Southern brethren.[25]

Palmer's greatest lament was that the oath-takers sabotaged themselves and their supposed patriotism. He argued that they should have risked their life and property for the cause, taking the courageous stand of registering as aliens. They would then have been protected by the rules of war, which could only demand "actual submission to military supremacy." Such a principled stand would have worked in New Orleans, Palmer believed, for "wherever else in the Confederacy the enemy has been stoutly defied, with all his bluster, he has been compelled to yield a reluctant acquiescence in the moral code established by civilized nations for the regulation of war." Even worse, Palmer saw oath-taking as a repudiation of Confederate patriotism, a conversion of it into "an affair of simple contract," where the people swore to uphold the Confederacy only so long as it could protect them. Once the Confederacy was unable to do so, as in a captured city, "like traders in the market, they bargain with another party, purchasing protection with loyalty." Palmer begged his readers not to fall into this trap, to do as much for the Confederacy as did the soldiers in the field, that is, to risk their lives and property in return for their honor as Confederates. He urged anyone who had taken the oath to do the right thing and make a "bold and manly retraction" in order to preserve the Confederacy.[26]

While Palmer had lived in New Orleans for a time, he wrote his pamphlet from the relative security of Columbia, South Carolina. It was, perhaps, easier for him to condemn the actions of people living in frightening and confusing times when he himself was able to avoid having to decide whether or not to take the oath. Certainly, it was not a decision made lightly, and the psychological tactic Palmer condemned was one that gave many people some security. Sarah Morgan's family was faced with a difficult choice in March 1863. Both she and her mother were in poor health, but their place in East Feliciana Parish was threatened by the assaults on Port Hudson. They would have preferred to remain elsewhere in the Confederacy, going so far as to have one of Sarah's brothers search for lodging in Augusta, Georgia, but finally decided that the best course would be to go to New Orleans and live with Sarah's half-brother, a Unionist who had already pledged his allegiance to the United States.[27] Upon finally arriving in New Orleans, the Morgans were compelled to take the oath before entering the city. Sarah, "half-crying, . . . prayed breathlessly for the boys and the Confederacy" while the oath was being read. Her reaction once it was over surprised her, for, she wrote, "strange to say, I experienced no change. I prayed as hard as ever for the boys and our country, and felt no nasty or disagreeable feeling which would have announced the process of turning Yankee." Her initial composure did not prevent her from continuing to worry about the consequences of her false oath. "Guilty, or not guilty of Perjury?" she wondered, and then consoled herself, "according to the law of God in the abstract, and of nations, Yes; according to my conscience, Jeff Davis, and the peculiar position I was placed in, No." Furthermore, she promised herself that should the Confederates retake New Orleans she would "break their sham oath without hesitation, on the first opportunity." She already broke it every day in her heart, by praying for the Confederacy and her brothers in the army.[28]

Many Confederates, like Morgan, saw the oath in purely pragmatic terms. Robert Andrews Wilkinson wrote his mother the day after he was captured along with the rest of the Vicksburg garrison. Wilkinson was being paroled, and he wanted his family to secure their safety as well, so he urged them if they could to "get to New Orleans [to] take the oath for God's sake if necessary." (His mother had already refused to take the oath once and been banished from the city.) Margaret Wight hoped that her son-in-law, who was captured during a raid on his home, would agree to take the oath, as it was the only way he would be able to return and care for her daughter. Even Union officials sometimes recognized the ulterior motives inherent in oath-taking. One anecdote told of a "secesh" woman who hoped that by taking the oath enthusiastically she might secure a position in a girls school in New Orleans. General Butler threw her out of his office in disgust, saying, "I have never seen the woman in the South yet who would take the oath of allegiance, or even hear of it, unless they had an object to gain in it."[29]

There were still people in the Confederacy who would have made Reverend Palmer proud, who categorically refused to take the oath and condemned those who did. Alfred Smith, a prisoner in Camp Douglas, Illinois, explained his predicament in a letter to a friend: "I should like to go to work in the shop but I cannot do it for I would have to take the oath and that I cannot do. You know that my father and mother are both in the south and then again if I was to take the oath it would not do for me to show my face in the south any more." Cloe Whittle in South Carolina missed her father

"Taking the Oath and Drawing Rations." 1865. This statue sympathetically portrays Confederates (and their slaves) taking the oath in order to draw Union rations. Many Confederates convinced themselves that oaths taken out of necessity or under duress were not necessarily binding. Smithsonian American Art Museum, Washington, D.C./Art Resource, N.Y.

back in Norfolk terribly and wished that she could be with him to "do the thousand little things an attentive daughter can do to contribute to a families comfort." She could not, however, see any way of rejoining him, for, she wrote, "I cannot believe it to be my duty to take the oath to go to him & I do not know how it can be avoided." Mahala Roach, trying to secure permission for her mother to return to Vicksburg, lamented, "'[General] Dana would permit Mother to return to Vicksburg if she would take the oath of allegiance'! This is equivalent to saying she shall not come *at all*, for Dana knows she cannot take the oath!" It is noteworthy that Roach's mother "cannot" as opposed to "will not" take the oath—submission was simply not an option, despite the discomfort that a principled stand might engender.[30]

Confederates sometimes echoed Palmer and condemned their fellow citizens for losing faith and taking the oath. "Have any more of my female acquaintances taken the oath?" asked a soldier. "Well I am sorry for them, but I supposed they considered [Louisiana] lost forever and they forgotten by all their friends in the army." Gustave Breaux was not so understanding when he raged against the "large number of men without principle guided solely by cringing interest" who "rushed to take the infamous Yankee oath of allegiance." He was pleased to note that their treachery did not afford any real protection, "that such degrading acts do not relieve the actors from being plundered and ruined by those to whom they cringe, any more than other citizens who are more manly."[31]

Arkansas planter John Brown expressed a combination of disappointment and understanding toward his neighbors who had taken the oath in April 1864, noting that they had believed "that by so doing they would obtain protection for their families and something to eat." A few months later, though, he was "stirred up" by an anonymous newspaper report that insinuated he had taken the oath. Brown retaliated, explaining in his diary, "[I] felt myself called upon to make a public denial of the Report of my having taken the oath of allegiance to the U. S. . . . I did not notice the slanderous publication before alluded to (under a fictitious name[)] but fully met the matter as far as it related to me. I think I was fortunate in the management of and diction of the publication. The vile slanderer, who ever he may be, is I think left out in the cold." For Brown, who had actually opposed secession and filled his diaries with complaints about the Richmond government, being called a turncoat was an unacceptable assault on his dignity.[32]

Confederates' choice of words to discuss the oath of allegiance shows how bound up it was with ideas of honor and gender. Patriotism was manly, although in a unique way: women could be patriotic without "unsexing" themselves. To succumb to the Yankees was to exhibit a weakness that was undesirable and unseemly in a virtuous and dedicated people, regardless of gender.

"OUR IDEAL IS A PRO-SLAVERY REPUBLIC"

Slavery was inextricably linked to Confederate nationalism, just as it had been inextricably linked with Southern society and identity for hundreds of years. Despite the fact that the vast majority of white Southerners did not own slaves, the Confederacy was emphatically a slaveholders' republic. Slavery for Confederates was about security both economically and socially. In a slave society where race was the marker of freedom, all white men, from the poorest tenant farmer on up the social ladder, benefited. The Southern states seceded to protect slavery from perceived Northern encroachment; the Confederacy was explicitly founded to preserve it. The initial secession conventions, where men voted to leave the Union, often focused on slavery as a dividing force. According to one Alabama delegate, slavery was simply "the cause of secession"; the governor of Arkansas reminded his fellow conventioneers that the peculiar institution was "now upon its trial before you." An Augusta, Georgia, newspaper put it most succinctly in November 1861, not two weeks after Lincoln had been elected: "Our ideal is a PRO-SLAVERY REPUBLIC."[33] In *Apostles of Disunion*, historian Charles Dew elegantly uses the words of the Southern secession commissioners (men sent from the lower South states that had already seceded to the upper South conventions) to show the centrality of slavery to both secession and the new nation that these states would found. These commissioners, some fifty in all, spread the gospel that only independence could protect Southerners from three things: "the looming specter of racial equality," "the prospect of race war," and, finally, "racial amalgamation." They painted an apocalyptic picture of what remaining in a Republican-controlled Union would mean to the "Southern way of life."[34]

The choice was a stark one, and the answer came both in the form of secession and in the shape of the Confederacy itself. Confederates enshrined slavery in their Constitution, decreeing that no federal laws denying "the right of property in negro slaves" could be passed and promising that such slave property would be ever portable (that slaves could be taken into free territories with no danger of emancipation). While the U.S. Constitution avoids the word "slave" whenever possible, the Confederates did not fear to use it. They did, however, ban the international slave trade, primarily in a bid to attract the more moderate states of the upper South and border region. The editors of the *Charleston Mercury*, one of the Confederacy's most conservative and emphatically proslavery newspapers, were so concerned that slavery continue to hold pride of place in the new Confederacy that they cautioned against allowing nonslaveholding states to join the new nation (a moot point, as it turned out).[35]

Once the war had begun, Confederates continued to embrace slavery. If slavery was what distinguished North from South, Union from Confederacy, than slavery was the key to the Confederacy's mission. Slavery and white supremacy tied the disparate strands of Confederate identity—race, honor, religion—together. God had chosen the Confederates to protect and uplift the slaves; or, as Bishop Stephen Elliott, one of the Confederacy's leading divines, put it, "We do not place our cause upon its highest level . . . until we grasp the idea that God has made us the guardians and champions of a people whom he is preparing for his own purposes and against whom the whole world is banded." As long as Confederates carried out this mission, they would be favored. "I am looking to the poor despised slaves," Elliott explained, "as the source of our security, because I firmly believe God will not permit his purposes to be overthrown or his arrangements to be interfered with."[36] Elliott seemed unaware of the irony inherent in this remark, for slaves would prove to be, as in fact they had always been, a threat to their masters' security.[37] But Elliot also succinctly expressed the ways in which slavery and the fortunes of the Confederacy were tied together: "The great revolution through which we are passing certainly turns upon this point of slavery, and our future destiny is bound up with it."[38]

Other Confederates saw in slavery a different form of security—one more material than spiritual. The *Charleston Mercury* repeatedly made the case that slavery was not a weakness but a strength. In the most utilitarian sense, Confederates were well aware that slave labor freed up white men to fight and that without slaves the Confederate economy would founder. An 1864 editorial proudly proclaimed that "without our slaves, a constituent of our wealth and power, we could not have maintained our armies in the field, and without those armies we could not have preserved the sources of our subsistence." While that was true, and this fact formed the basis of Union contraband and emancipation policy, it also ignored the reality that by this late in the war, slaves were not the faithful helpers that Confederates wanted them to be.[39]

Slavery, and the ways in which it was believed to elevate white men, was also integral to the Confederate sense of mission. As the *Mercury* explained in the aptly titled editorial "The Effect of Nobility of Race and the Sense of Honor of the South," slavery was not only beneficial to blacks (using the old proslavery argument of paternalistic uplift), but it helped whites as well, by bringing out "those qualities fitted for predominance." Slavery allowed for Confederate liberty, this editorial explained, for it allowed whites to develop their "higher characteristics," specifically because "authority and the exercise of command tend strongly to engender self-respect, dignity, decision of character, and the feeling of self-reliant power." Confederates wanted to believe they possessed these character traits, and they needed their slaves to make that possible. Too, the *Mercury* was careful to point out (perhaps aiming its argument directly at its nonslaveholding readers), because slaves occupied the lowest rungs of the social ladder, all whites felt a kinship and shared status: "A spirit of manly pride is cultivated, and the sentiment of honor is everywhere seen and felt as the grand pervading principle of the Southern people." Rather than drive a wedge between the classes, Confederates wanted to believe, slavery would bind them together.[40]

"THE FREEMEN OF THE COUNTRY ARE NOT DEPENDENT ON THEIR SLAVES"

If the Confederacy was dedicated to the protection of slavery, what would happen if slavery were challenged in some way? A powerful aspect of the proslavery argument was a paternalistic rejection of black manhood and masculinity. Black men could not be soldiers because they were not seen as men. Confederates were also (perhaps rightfully) fearful that putting weapons in the hands of their slaves might result in them being turned not against the Yankees but against their masters. To allow slaves to fight would be to threaten Confederate security in frightening, almost unimaginable ways. And yet, by the end of the war, this is exactly what many Confederates were prepared to do.

In the Union, from the moment that the war began, many free blacks clamored to be allowed to serve in the military. They wanted to show their patriotism and prove themselves worthy of the rights of citizenship to a Northern population that saw them as worthless people destined for the bottom rung of the social ladder. David Demus, a native Pennsylvanian who served in the all-black Fifty-fourth Massachusetts believed that if it had not been for the black troops, the war would last another ten years. He also thought it "plane to see" that if the black soldiers had not fought then black people would not be in a position to claim full citizenship. He considered "us Colard Men" the cause of "this ofel [awful] Rebelon."[41] The Lincoln administration, ever mindful of appeasing the slaveholding border states that had remained in the Union, initially resisted black enlistment. By the end of 1862, however, individual generals in some occupied areas (South Carolina, Louisiana, Kansas) had begun to raise black regiments, and by early 1863, the Union army had launched an official recruitment drive. The War Department officially established its Bureau of Colored Troops in May 1863, and, ultimately, over 180,000 black men wore Union blue, the vast majority of them (80 percent) former slaves. Though African American soldiers were subject to discrimination in assignments, treatment, promotion, and pay, by the end of the war, most Northerners had come to an at least grudging acceptance of their presence in the Union ranks. Certainly the courage and commitment displayed by black troops at places like Fort Wagner and Port Hudson helped nudge Northerners toward a more favorable opinion.

From the Confederate perspective, any attempt to grant manhood to blacks was a threat to the Confederacy. Or, as the *Charleston Mercury* complained when it was confronted by the men of the Fifty-fourth Massachusetts in 1863, "Our slaves are to be made our equals in our own country, fighting against us."[42] That was, of course, an unacceptable challenge to Confederate identity and honor, and Confederates displayed their fear and anger in vengeful ways. Confederate soldiers refused to treat black troops by the rules of war. In some instances, captured black troops were sold into slavery and their white officers were charged with fomenting insurrection, a capital crime. More often, however, Confederates simply refused to take black prisoners at all, massacring them instead. In one example, Confederate troops under the command of General Nathan Bedford Forrest (later a founder of the Ku Klux Klan) not only shot black defenders at Fort Pillow, Tennessee, but also set wounded men on fire and buried wounded men alive. In retaliation, black Union troops, often using "remember Fort Pillow" as their rallying cry, refused on occasion to take Confederates prisoner. It was the "Apostles of Disunion's" dreaded race war come to life.[43]

If Confederates found the sight of armed black men fighting for their freedom under the banner of the United States such an unbearable specter that it had to be essentially erased through violence, what about the situation closer to home? What would happen if slaves were to fight for the Confederates? Just as white Southerners understood the implications that enlistment had for black manhood and citizenship, so too did they recognize the manpower advantage that black troops conferred on the Union. At the same time, they also realized that the nearly four million slaves in the

Confederacy were a source of strength, albeit one that would fade away. From the start of the war, slaveholders drew on their slaves to serve the cause—unofficially as personal servants to wealthy men, officially as impressed labor building fortifications, repairing railroads, and manufacturing ordnance and as teamsters. This use of slaves as support staff away from the front lines (and without weapons) seemed to be an extension of their antebellum role: slaves as helpers, freeing up their masters for the glorious work of war. That these slaves were being forced to aid the cause of their continued enslavement seems not to have occurred to their masters.

There were a few examples of African Americans taking a more active (and voluntary) role in serving the Confederacy, through the free black Native Guard units in Louisiana and South Carolina, not coincidentally the two states with the largest and wealthiest free black populations. These Native Guards were used for local defense, not combat, and were not welcomed with open arms by the Confederate high command. The motives of the Guards themselves were likely pragmatic: the free blacks who had prospered in the prewar South had done so by seeking favor with local whites and assuring them of their loyalty. Some of them had owned slaves themselves. By offering their services to the new Confederacy they were demonstrating that they could be trusted and counted upon, that they knew their place and would not use the excuse of war to challenge it. Not, at least, until they were sure their military service would keep them safe. After the Union took control of New Orleans in the spring of 1862, for example, many of the Native Guard switched sides, and two regiments fought with the Union at Port Hudson the following year.[44]

For the first two years of the war, Confederates seemed to be winning, and their slaveholders' republic did seem—to them—to be favored by God. But, at the same time, Confederates increasingly faced a manpower shortage in their armies. War weariness had set in, making it harder and harder to recruit, and the Confederate draft was of only limited success. As the war ground on into its third year, some Confederates began to discuss utilizing slaves in a more formal way.[45] In early 1864, General Patrick Cleburne, a commander in the Army of Tennessee proposed "that we immediately commence training a large reserve of the most courageous of our slaves, and further that we guarantee freedom within a reasonable time to every slave in the South who shall remain true to the Confederacy in this war." Cleburne justified his suggestions on the basis of numbers, explaining simply, "We can only get a sufficiency [of troops] by making the negro share the danger and hardships of war." What was so radical about Cleburne's proposal at the time was not just that he was suggesting putting arms in the hands of slaves. It was the open acknowledgment of the fact that slaves wanted to be free. A key tenet of the proslavery argument before the war, and of the Confederate raison d'être, was that slavery uplifted blacks and that the paternalistic system meant that blacks were both contented and faithful. While individuals might have thought, in their darkest thoughts in the middle of the night, that perhaps their slaves weren't happy being slaves, no one was to speak of this aloud. It was too dangerous.[46]

Yet here was Cleburne's plan, endorsed by about a dozen of his fellow officers. It was eventually forwarded on to Jefferson Davis himself, who promptly ordered it suppressed, fearing the outcry it would provoke should it become public. Joe Johnston, the commanding general of the Army of Tennessee gave the order to Cleburne and added some choice comments of his own, warning his subordinate that constitutionally no such action could be taken, and, furthermore, "such views can only jeopard among the States and people unity and harmony, when for successful co-operation and the achievement of independence both are essential."[47] In essence, Johnston was arguing that the Confederacy required unanimity—of purpose, of commitment, and especially on slavery—to survive. Davis, already unpopular, facing a population increasingly divided along class lines, could not afford to bring that fissure out into the open. The sticking point was always emancipation: how could slaves be asked to fight for Confederate freedom without being granted it themselves? And to emancipate slaves, for any reason, was to call into question one of the very foundations of Confederate identity.

In January 1864, the course of the war still seemed uncertain and either side still could have won. But as the Confederacy faced mounting losses of territory and men and an associated plunge in morale during the summer and fall of 1864, debate over the proposal to arm slaves began in earnest. Backed by both Jefferson Davis and the Confederate cabinet and eventually Robert E. Lee, the proposal forced Confederates to confront the question of what, exactly, they were fighting for. The varied answers, and the degree to which people felt that the Confederacy had transcended its origins as a slaveholders republic show the complexities of national identity in crisis.

On 7 November 1864, Jefferson Davis sent a message to the Confederate Congress in which he called for the employment of slaves in a variety of noncombatant positions, while leaving open the possibility that "should the alternative ever be presented of subjugation or of the employment of the slave as a soldier, there seems no reason to doubt what should then be our decision." In so doing, Davis made explicit the great contradiction of slavery, for he acknowledged that slaves were not just property with whom they could do as they chose but people as well. As such, they could not be expected to work hard for a cause that would result in their permanent enslavement, and thus Davis also suggested that any slave employed in the army should be made eligible for a form of gradual, compensated emancipation.[48]

Predictably, Davis's suggestion met with scornful, even angry, opposition. By suggesting that at some point in the future the Confederacy should think about turning to slave soldiers, Davis had brought to the surface simmering questions about the meaning of the Confederacy. Could a nation born out of the desire to defend slavery at any cost survive emancipation, even emancipation on its own terms? Davis and the other supporters of arming slaves argued that, in fact, they were protecting the peculiar institution. Emancipate a few slaves in order to win the war, they claimed, and preserve slavery intact for others. Let the Confederacy be destroyed, and slavery would be lost forever. As an added benefit, support for any level of emancipation demonstrated to foreign nations and wavering yeomen that this was not a war exclusively to preserve the property of a wealthy few. Indeed, rumors still flew that this demonstration of Confederate determination to avoid "subjugation" would be just the thing to inspire British or French intervention.[49]

Essentially, supporters of arming slaves were making a pragmatic argument: the Confederacy was dying of a manpower shortage, and slaves could alleviate it. For many Southerners, the meaning of their new nation had changed. Protection of slavery was no longer their paramount concern. But to other Confederates, particularly those in the Deep South, such a suggestion was anathema, tantamount to an admission of defeat. The Savannah, Georgia, *News* refused to publish any letters about the possibility of placing slaves in the army, on the grounds that such a question was not proper for a "newspaper discussion." Gertrude Thomas, a wealthy Georgia slaveholder, perfectly understood the contradictions inherent in putting slaves in the army: first, doing so "clearly betrays the weakness of our force," and, second, it was "strangely inconsistent, the idea of our offering to a Negro the rich boon—the priceless reward of freedom to aid us in keeping in bondage a large portion of his brethren, when by joining the Yankees he will instantly gain the very reward which Mr. Davis offers to him after a certain amount of labor rendered and danger incurred."[50]

The *Charleston Mercury*, a perennial critic of Davis, warned ominously that "the freemen of the country are not dependent on slaves," and should they not work out their own "redemption," they would become "the slaves of their slaves." Raising the issue of white liberty was a classic piece of pro-slavery rhetoric. The *Mercury* filled its pages with criticism of the proposal in November, providing a clear example of the proslavery aspects of Confederate identity. In an editorial titled "The Employment of Slaves," the paper hearkened back to Bishop Elliott's proclamation that slavery was a source of strength to the Confederates, not a weakness. It cautioned its readers that should slavery not be "the best condition for the negroes amongst us . . . and manumission be a desirable improvement . . . which they may obtain as a reward for service—then the justification heretofore set up for holding them as slaves is false and unfounded. . . . We cannot believe that a policy as inconsistent, unsound and suicidal can meet the sanction of any respectable body of Southern men." In essence, if the only way slaves could be induced to fight was to promise emancipation, then the argument that slaves were happy with their lot was wrong. And if that notion, crucial to the culture of paternalism, was wrong, what did white Southerners have left to believe in?[51]

Rather than allow themselves to answer that question, the *Mercury* stayed on the offensive, hurling invective at anyone who dared support arming slaves. The paper's comments on the topic in early 1865 made clear that it believed support for arming slaves was tantamount to giving up on the war and the Confederacy itself. It repeatedly derided supporters of the plan as "mad," calling the proposal the work of "panic-stricken men . . . desperate, destructive, utterly hopeless." The *Mercury* struck at the honor of those men who would put slaves in the army, calling them "unmanly" cowards. South Carolina, proclaimed the *Mercury*, fought "for our system of civilization—not for buncomb or for JEFF DAVIS," adding, "we are free men, and we choose to fight for ourselves—we want no slaves to fight for us. Skulkers, money lenders, money makers, and blood-suckers, alone will tolerate the idea." But not good Confederates. Elsewhere, they warned, the only men talking about sending blacks into the ranks were men who were "afraid to fight. . . . But the brave soldier who is fighting for the supremacy of his race will have none of it—no none of it. He wants no Hayti here—no St. Domingo—no mongrels here—no miscegenation with his blood." This is the same kind of apocalyptic language used four years earlier to inspire secession—emancipate any slaves, and chaos and racial mixing will follow.[52]

In perhaps the strangest statement published on the issue of arming slaves, the *Mercury* charged Robert E. Lee (who had not yet made his views public but was privately known to be a supporter) with being a Federalist—like Alexander Hamilton—someone who had always evidenced a "profound disbelief in the institution of slavery." This comparison was drawn in contrast to South Carolina's great Democratic/states' rights standard-bearer John C. Calhoun, and the paper put the question starkly as "JOHN C. CAL-HOUN VS. DANIEL WEBSTER and ROBERT E. LEE." Choose the latter, and the "fungus corollaries" of Federalism would reign; choose the former and allow Confederates "to stand by the political doctrines of their lives, to assert their power, and to uphold the entire integrity of their institutions, upon which rests both their political power, and their material prosperity and industry of everything."[53] The *Mercury* was nothing if not consistent. For them, the Confederacy ever was and ever would be about the protection of slavery. Any crack in the façade would bring down the whole.

South Carolinians had long indulged in the luxury of radicalism. Elsewhere, opinion was more sensitive to the contingencies of wartime. Virginians had borne the brunt of war and were perhaps more willing to think creatively about strategies for achieving peace. And it is important to remember that this debate took place in the context of a desire for independence, not surrender. Joseph Waddell, a Staunton, Virginia, editor, spoke for many Confederates when he confided in his diary, "I greatly prefer independence without slavery, to submission with it, and would be glad enough to get rid of it if I could see any way of disposing of the negroes without giving them up to barbarism or annihilation." But how could that be accomplished? In his own way, Waddell feared emancipation as much as the *Mercury*.[54]

A different Virginian moved the debate along in February 1865. Robert E. Lee finally entered the public discourse over this issue with a letter that shifted public, and congressional, opinion squarely to the side of enlistments. In his letter to Congressman Barksdale, reprinted in newspapers throughout the Confederacy, Lee explained that the measure was "not only expedient but necessary." He went on to answer another question, one familiar to Northern black soldiers as well: would blacks make good soldiers? Lee felt that they would, explaining, "I think we could do at least as well with them as the enemy, and he attaches great importance to their assistance." Lee cited slaves' physical strength and "habits of obedience" as reason to believe that they would serve well, especially if they were induced to service through promised freedom. He went even further, suggesting that a draft of slaves would be unnecessary and counterproductive, preferring instead to call for slave volunteers, a measure more likely to "bring out the best class."[55]

Lee's letter was reprinted around the Confederacy with approving comments, and it inspired more serious, more public discussion of the future of Confederate slavery. Confederates who believed that the Confederacy stood for immutable principles tended to oppose the plan, whereas those who had come to see independence as an end in itself were willing to contemplate the prospect of slaves at war. A soldier in the Eleventh Virginia told of Robert E. Lee taking a vote among the troops on the "negro bill" to enlist slaves: "I am ashamed to say it was near a unit in the regiment[;] only six men in Company B voted against it[,] Morton Ward Cardwell Clark Clorance and myself. I think we have disgraced ourselves and besides I think we are whipped[;] the idea of having negroes fighting to enslave their offspring is mor than redicalous."[56]

Those Confederates who were willing to win at any cost accepted the inevitability of arming slaves and took comfort in the fact that their beloved Robert E. Lee was a staunch supporter of the plan. David Schenck, a slave-holding North Carolina lawyer, thought that "the most intelligent of our people advocate the plan, but the 'Peace agitators' and factionists in ever quarter are urging objections against it." Schenck scoffed at the opponents' arguments that to arm slaves would be "to give up the 'casus belli' the principle for which we contend," adding that they "forget in their theory of honor that it is our only and last resort and that the crisis demands speedy relief." Schenck was not, however, willing to go so far as the "Extreme party, led by the Richmond Enquirer," which purportedly proposed emancipating all the slaves in order to form an alliance with England and France.[57]

Following the failure of the peace mission in early February and the attendant realization that there was no chance for a negotiated end to the war, the Confederacy actually enjoyed one last burst of martial spirit, one last gasp of the old bravado that had characterized the early years of the war. The *Richmond Enquirer* boldly declared that the enlistment of slaves not only would strengthen the armies, "without doing the least injury to the institution of slavery," but would also increase discipline among white troops. The soldiers of the Fifty-sixth Virginia unanimously declared, "If the public exigencies required that any number of our male slaves be enlisted in the military service in order to the [*sic*] successful resistance to our enemies and the maintenance of the integrity of our government we are willing to make those concessions to their false and unenlightened notions of the blessings of liberty, and to offer to those, and those only who fight in our cause, perpetual freedom as a boon for fidelity of service and loyalty to the South." These Virginians subscribed to one of slavery's perennial misconceptions—that slaves did not know what was best for them, that not all of them wanted to be free. Somehow, Confederates wanted to believe that they still controlled the survival of slavery, that they could free some slaves to fight in order to keep others in bondage. In this, they demonstrated a willful ignorance of their slaves' inner lives.[58]

In late February, citizens of Augusta County, Virginia, held a mass meeting at which they both condemned "the course of the United States in proposing to tear away the last vestige of our rights as a condition of peace" and expressed their support of arming slaves. The citizens of Augusta echoed David Schenck's faith in Lee, concluding simply, "We shall not stop to discuss abstract questions, but will cheerfully give our servants, as we have our sons, to our country." What was left unspoken, though one can hardly believe un-thought, was that the lives of their slaves were not the Virginians to give.[59] Joseph Waddell seemed to understand. He saw talk of enlisting slaves as "a concession of despair" rather than the "virtue of necessity" that Robert E. Lee would have had Confederates believe. For Waddell, however, the most problematic issue was not the abolition of slavery per se but the upheaval that would surely accompany emancipation. Already, he noted, Augusta's slaves, the very ones that his fellow whites were eager to give to the Confederate cause, had heard of the enlistment plan and were "greatly troubled," and he "shudder[ed] at the prospect" of wartime emancipation.[60]

As it turned out, Confederates came to the decision to arm slaves too late to save themselves. The Confederate Congress passed a bill authorizing the recruitment of black soldiers, who would be compensated with some form of emancipation, to be more fully defined later on, once the Confederacy had won the war. Though not to universal acclaim, "Congress it seems has passed a law to put Slaves into our Army—a move which proves our desperation," John Brown recorded in his journal. "It is virtually giving up the principles upon which we went to War. And I fear besides it will be a failure." David Schenck was more optimistic, noting that "Gen'l Lee has great faith in their efficacy, and many persons look to the measure with great hope." A company of black soldiers was hastily recruited in Richmond, and their drilling was reported in the cities' newspapers with somewhat patronizing praise for their military aptitude. But within days Richmond itself was evacuated. Reports placed some of these African Americans at a rearguard action a few days later or building earthworks. But they do not appear on the surrender rolls—the only blacks who do were the cooks, teamsters, and musicians who had served throughout the war.[61]

What does this all mean? Was the movement to arm Confederate slaves nothing but desperation? Or did it signify a shift in the meaning of the Confederacy for many people? If the Confederacy was supposed to have died from failures of will and nationalism, on which side of the argument does this turn of events fall? I believe that the willingness of Confederates to arm their slaves, thus bringing into life their greatest fear, shows the depth of their attachment to their nation. Born in slavery, the Confederacy had become about more than that for many people. It had become a viable alternative to life within the United States, one in which slavery was no longer the only marker of differentiation. National identity, loyalty, and patriotism were ever changing during the war, and we do Confederates a disservice when we hold them to a fixed standard. This turn of events also brings into sharp relief the degree of white self-delusion that lay at the heart of slavery. The *Charleston Mercury* was remarkably clear-eyed about the motives of those slaves who would enlist in the army, predicting that "out of the two hundred thousand muskets placed in their hands, one hundred and fifty thousand at least will be presented by him to the enemy."[62] But few others seem to have voiced anything beyond a naive optimism that blacks would gladly give up their lives for the promise of freedom. What they failed to realize was that their slaves were, by this point in the war, well aware that they had other options, and they were taking advantage of them. Confederates would never have the chance to free their slaves because their slaves were freeing themselves.

Interlude

Peace (with Independence Always)

As they had for three years, Confederates acted on their perceptions of events much more than on what we, with the benefit of hindsight, would deem reality. For as long as they possibly could, they cast defeats and retreats in a positive light. Confederates had no vocabulary for defeat, no way to fit it into their ideology of God-sanctioned nationhood, and at no time was this dissonance more visible than in the final months of the war.[1] Between September 1864 and January 1865, between the fall of Atlanta and the months after Lincoln's reelection, Confederates became progressively less sure of their future independence. At the same time, however, they still publicly tried to keep spirits up, attempting to construct a world where the war was prolonged, not ending. To us this seems an exercise in self-deception and denial, but it was deception with real political consequences. Confederates refused to admit that the war was drawing to a close because they didn't want to believe it.

With hindsight, and of course knowing its impact on the Northern election of 1864, we believe that Atlanta was a fatal blow to the Confederacy.[2] But Confederates themselves, especially those who could not allow themselves to see defeat, sought to convince themselves that the loss of Atlanta was, as Gettysburg had been, a setback, a disappointment. It would not end the war, only prolong it. Sallie Bird's sanguine description of the loss of Atlanta as "a great disaster, but not irretrievable," was a typical response. Kate Cumming heard that "few regret the loss of the city itself, not even Georgians, as they say it was the most wicked place in the world." Gustave Breaux took a balanced look at the situation and decided that "beyond the actual loss of territory, which is immaterial in actual, & the moral effect on the northern people, which the loss of Atlanta, magnified as it is into a huge victory, (and by the by just at this moment, a serious effect to us)[,] the evacuation of the city by Gen. Hood does not affect vitally the status of the Confederacy." This comment is a perfect example of the intellectual gymnastics Southerners engaged in during the prolonged endgame of the war—what mattered from a defeat if not the loss of territory or the impact on the enemy's morale? But rather than address the fundamental illogic of this view, Breaux turned instead to a traditional platitude: that defeat was good for the Confederacy because it would "only incite our devoted people to greater efforts to recover from the blow." The unspoken question remained, however: how many more blows could the weakened Confederacy absorb?[3]

During the early fall, Confederates seemed to be of two minds regarding their future. The coming Northern elections still provided some hope to which they could cling. Lincoln might not be reelected; Grant was still stymied outside of Petersburg. At the same time, however, Confederates could not avoid the dismal reality staring them in the face: the victories they had seemed so sure of in the spring had failed to materialize over the summer. They were edgy and emotional, searching for signs yet always trying to maintain some equanimity. "Was it ominous that I should find my pen split when I took it up to write tonight?" asked Gertrude Thomas. "Shall I dare hope that this new Journal which I am commencing will record Peace, an independent Southern Confederacy?" Margaret Wight was struck by "the gloom" that seemed "cast over every one just now, even the most hopeful," as rumors spread that Grant was preparing for another assault. Hearing that Macon and Augusta were made vulnerable to Sherman, Mary Chesnut lamented, "We are going to be wiped off the face of the earth."[4]

Another troubling rumor centered on an emerging peace movement within the Confederate government. On 29 September, in a public letter to Jefferson Davis, South Carolina congressman William Boyce warned that the nation was sinking into "military despotism" and called for an immediate armistice and a joint convention of Northern and Southern states to negotiate a settlement. Supporters of Boyce included the Georgians Alexander Stephens, Joe Brown, and Robert Toombs, none of whom enjoyed good relations with Davis. The letter was not well-received by the Confederate public, who saw it as little more than submission inappropriate to Southern manhood.[5] Nevertheless, Boyce's letter, coupled with the clear demoralization witnessed in Georgia, signaled troublesome questions of morale ahead. Josiah Gorgas noted with displeasure that "the reports from Georgia represent the people as very despondent & ready to make terms with the enemy." Whether the rumor about a peace movement (or one that had Stephens et al. meeting with Sherman) was true or false mattered little. What was important was that the rumors were "*believed* & shows the state of the country." Cloe Whittle heard the same rumor, and that, coupled with the factionalism reported from Richmond, prompted an angry diatribe against any such "reconstruction" schemes. "Peace! Rather wash the knife than such peace. It seems to me that all that is needed to ruin us [would] be for God to take President Davis out of the world, when Stevens [would] succeed him."[6]

Gertrude Thomas "sigh[ed] and yearn[ed] for Peace, honourable Peace—." This notion of an honorable peace is an important one, for peace had a specific meaning to Confederates. It meant independence, not merely a cessation of hostilities. And, frequently, as noted above, it meant peace through arms, not through negotiation. "How I long for peace (with independence always)," sighed one war-weary writer, who found herself so "sick and weary of life" and the hardships of war that she would "be willing and glad to leave children and all and lie down and die." But not so willing as to accept peace without freedom. Thomas had a more limited understanding of peace when she yearned for "honourable Peace." Her husband had just been called up to fight under General Hood in a campaign to retake Atlanta, and Thomas found herself torn by the divided loyalties to family and nation that plagued Confederates: "It would be a brilliant thing to recapture Atlanta. I wish it could be done. I wish Mr. Thomas could be engaged in the fight if he could escape safely, but he *might not* and then what? Am I willing to give my husband to gain Atlanta for the Confederacy? No, No, No, a thousand times No!"[7]

On 8 November 1864, Northern voters went to the polls and overwhelmingly reelected Abraham Lincoln. Confederate hopes were dashed.[8] Now they faced four more years of the man they hated, the man who they believed was dedicated, with every fiber of his being, to their destruction. "There is no use disguising the fact that our subjugation is popular at the north," complained Josiah Gorgas, "& that the war must go on until this hope is crushed out & replaced by desire for peace at any cost." "This is a dark hour in our country's history," reflected Gertrude Thomas. "The Union candidates at the North are elected and peace, blessed peace as far away as ever," lamented Kate Stone. An Alabama woman recorded the news and added, "Anguish fills the soul of many a mother and orphans are crying for a home & bread."[9]

Even as they despaired, Confederates tried to make the best of their situation. Just as they perceived military defeats as only setbacks, rarely as losses, so, too, did they convince themselves that Lincoln's reelection meant only a prolonging of the war, not its end. "From the heavy guns fired at the fort recently I presume 'Our royal Master Lincoln,['] is re-elected," wrote a Mississippi woman, continuing, "Much joy to him & his northern slaves—We await the events of the next four months, with deepest interest.—Alas that our great country should be leaping into such an abyss of infamy. But with you dear friend I am opined, The South will nobly triumph." Some Confederates went so far as to argue that the election results would actually help the Confederacy. An Arkansas planter said he was "at a loss" to determine whether a Lincoln or McClellan victory would have been better for the South, for "it was but War or Reconstruction any way," adding that "no Government erected by the Democrats could have been permanent." In the end he concluded that he did not "know that it matters much with us which may be elected." In a similar vein, one Northern-born soldier in Butler's brigade confidently assured his parents that "Lincoln's Reelection is considered by most thinking men as the best thing that could happen for the Confederate States." He was the devil, they knew, and they were "ready & willing to fight them for as long as it may continue agreeable to them. I see Mr. L. calls for a million more men. We can confidently promise his subjects to furnish them with the same 'settlement' as we have so generously done to their predecessors, a grave, not too deep, in Southern soil." Such bravado seemed little more than empty words, however.[10]

Privately, Confederates fretted over increased loss of territory, as when David Schenck mourned the loss of Fort Fisher, and therefore of Wilmington, the Confederacy's last port, calling it "the crowning disaster" and an undeniably "alarming crisis." Publicly, they were repeatedly told that losing land to the Yankees would not have an effect on the ultimate outcome of the war. So the *Southern Field and Fireside* of 21 January minimized Fort Fisher, arguing that it would "by no means cast the die of our cause." The editors called for a shift in attitude: "Let our people stop overestimating our disasters; let them cease underestimating our victories, and let us stand amid this hurricane of war like a brave people—let us stand without trembling, *we will not fall*." They encouraged their people to work together, "to man the ship," and to ride out the storm by putting their trust in a higher power. "Let us be calm, confident, and unalterable determined, and the Good Father who holds the destiny of nations in His hand will defend the right and bear us through the struggle."[11]

Senator William S. Oldham gave his speech "The State of the Country" on 30 January 1865, in support of several Texas resolutions "concerning Peace, Reconstruction, and Independence."[12] Oldham conceded that "there is a depression of spirit amongst many of our people," but he blamed it on disappointed hopes, not "any well-grounded apprehension or distrust of our final success." He scoffed at the notion that loss of territory would mean loss of the war. Although Atlanta, Savannah, and Fort Fisher had been taken, although Hood's army had been driven from Tennessee, "'all is not lost, honor is not lost,' liberty and independence are not lost, while we have the spirit to defend them." Even the loss of Richmond would not prove fatal, he asserted, for the tremendous force required to hold the Confederate capital would weaken Yankee forces elsewhere. For Oldham, the Confederacy was being stripped down to its essential attributes. It was not just a geographical space but rather a way of life, a set of precepts, that could not be extinguished by external forces. If Confederates could remain true to themselves, to the reasons they left the Union in the first place, no reunion would be necessary.[13]

Peace without independence would be a betrayal of everything the Confederacy had stood for, and Oldham attacked the manliness of those who would accept it: "Can any man but a conquered coward consent to reunite with them? Can any man but a traitor at heart to his country, to her institutions and the liberty of her people advocate such a reunion?" And Northerners could not be trusted to treat Confederates fairly if they willingly rejoined the Union. Confederates would always be a conquered people and would be treated accordingly. To Oldham's mind, a negotiated settlement would be far worse than outright conquest, for at least the latter would preserve Confederate honor. For Oldham, the road to peace "is enfiladed by hostile armies, hedged by glittering bayonets, and slippery with blood; but it leads them to the temple where liberty sits enthroned." Confederates needed to walk down that road together.[14]

4 Blue-Black Is Our Horizon

The End of the War

The Confederate struggle for statehood came to an abrupt end in the early spring of 1865, but Confederates' sense of national identity would prove more flexible and resilient. For four years, Confederate armies had been able to hold off the Union; for four years, Confederate civilians had believed that they could work together, overcome obstacles, and build a nation. But setback piled onto setback in 1865, and by the time Grant's army broke through the Petersburg lines, there seemed to be no way to put a good face on the subsequent loss of the capital, the president being forced to flee into the Confederate interior, and the crushing of Lee's army. Confederates, particularly those far away from Virginia, had scarcely been able to comprehend the loss of Richmond when the news of Lee's surrender at Appomattox arrived. Shock, horror, and disbelief greeted the news. The sheer emotionalism of Confederates' response to the end of the war gives the lie to the notion that Confederates had lost their sense of national allegiance.

During the spring and summer of 1865, Confederates confronted the new realities of their lives. The Confederacy had ceased to exist, yet it continued to exert a hold over its citizens' emotions and activities. The national identity forged through the war, the sense that Confederates were a distinct population, outlasted the state apparatus. Confederates negotiated new boundaries between themselves and the occupying army, between civilians and former soldiers, between their Confederate past and their indeterminate future. They only knew how to create a nation; they had no experience with dismantling one. They were no longer Confederates, but they were not yet sure of who they would be. Could they be Americans? Should they be Americans? Could they return to their prewar sense of themselves as Southerners, or had the war fundamentally changed regional identities? In those first weeks following the surrenders in Virginia and North Carolina, Confederates tried to comprehend how they had lost the war even as they tried to make some sort of peace and accommodation with their present. Some resolved to fight on, no matter the costs, while others tried to make the best of their new lot in life. Their struggle would last for years.

"ALL IS OVER AND GOD HELP THE POOR SOUTH"

When the end came, it came quickly. The news of the evacuation of Petersburg and Richmond traveled with varying speed through the Confederacy.[1] The first to hear, of course, were the citizens of Richmond and its environs, whose dismay at losing their capital was increased by their concern for their own safety and security. Many families lost everything in the fire that consumed downtown Richmond, while others had to contend with Union foraging and raiding parties. Old habits of denial died hard, even in the face of such seemingly insurmountable odds, and Confederates like Harriet Caperton tried to "bear [her] sorrow bravely" and accept it as God's way of chastising his transgressing people. She kept herself occupied by trying to "have the house cleaning done before the Yankees come in. *Then* I must go to work, and show the enemy and *traitors* that with all their success they can never break the spirit of southern women." Caperton thought the fall of Richmond was the "crisis of the revolution," but she assured her correspondent that the Confederates would "rise" to the occasion and expel the invaders.[2]

In Henrico County, Emma Mordecai, her sister-in-law, and her niece busied themselves while waiting for the arrival of the Yankees by hiding their valuables. What they couldn't hide they simply left in trunks, with keys in the locks "to prevent their being *broken* open." Then they waited, trying, like Caperton, to maintain the appearance of normalcy. "I again dressed myself with care," she wrote to family in North Carolina, "and we sat down in the chamber to our knitting—the usual work of Confederate women, but now, Alas! we should have no army to work for." Mordecai was eventually visited by Yankees, but her family got off comparatively easily. They had a horse stolen but were not subjected to wholesale thievery and destruction.[3]

Mordecai's neighbor, Fanny Young, was not so fortunate. The fire in Richmond consumed her husband's office and law books, along with their "carpets, china, glass," and, perhaps most important, six barrels of flour. Their home in Henrico was searched by African American troops, who forced Mr. Young at gunpoint to show them where the family silver was hidden. They stole it, along with other of the Youngs' possessions, but returned the silver a few hours later—it was only plate, not solid, and therefore not worth keeping. Its return was cold comfort to the Youngs. Mordecai described Mr.

Young as "almost erased" by the confrontation with black troops. His wife, Fanny, made no mention of her husband's emotional state since she had more practical concerns: "We have no money, no silverware, no arms, no provisions, & nothing but our ragged clothes! . . . I dare not look to the future; I leave it all to God."[4]

Those Confederates who were removed from the fighting had worried less about their families and more about the fate of the nation. Past reactions to defeat were a good predictor of present attitudes. In Arkansas, John W. Brown called the loss of Richmond "the hardest blow yet," news that left him "dull, and almost lifeless." "Richmond has fallen—and I have no heart to write about it," Mary Chesnut moaned. "They are too many for us," she continued. "Blue-black is our horizon." Kate Cumming, always more of an optimist than Chesnut, took the news in her customary stride. She adopted the (unrealistic) position that the loss of the capital need not mean the loss of the war, explaining that "we shall never have peace until the enemy has possession of all our large towns, and then they will see that they have work still before them to conquer the South."[5] In this assessment, Cummings was, unwittingly or not, echoing the words of Jefferson Davis's last official proclamation, made 4 April from Danville. The president on the run urged the people to enter a "new" phase of the war, essentially the guerrilla war that Lee would reject a few days later. The loss of territory was, Davis argued, a positive thing for the Confederacy: "Relieved from the necessity of guarding cities and particular points, important but not vital to our defense, with an army free to move from point to point and strike in detail detachments and garrisons of the enemy, operating on the interior of our own country, where supplies are more accessible, and where the foe will be far removed from his own base and cut off from all succor in case of reverse, nothing is now needed to render our triumph certain but the exhibition of our own unquenchable resolve. Let us but will it and we are free." The meaning of the Confederacy continued to shrink, first as it rejected slavery as an essential aspect, now as it no longer needed to occupy a real geographic space. Such constriction—admittedly born out of desperation and denial—nevertheless can be seen to foreshadow some of the flexibility of postwar Southern identity. Just as territory could be abandoned, so, too, could be aspects of national feeling without threatening the whole.[6]

It was easier for a Kate Cumming or even a Jefferson Davis to construct a world in which retreats could lead to victory. Soldiers, especially those in Lee's army had a different perspective and a different set of choices. For them, the choice to remain Confederate was a stark one, and they could vote with their feet. Some deserted as they fled the lines at Petersburg, others on the outskirts of Appomattox, others stuck it out through the surrender itself. William Lyne Wilson, a member of the Twelfth Virginia Cavalry's "Laurel Brigade," was already over the Appomattox River when he learned of the complete evacuation of the Petersburg trenches and the fall of Richmond. "Words cannot fathom the depth and breadth of my soul's anguish at this unexpected news," he wrote on 2 April. "Where shall we turn our fugitive footsteps? What city of refuge shall open its hospitable gates for us?"[7]

Wilson spent the next few days, as so many of his fellow soldiers did, trying to rejoin his command, rounding up stragglers, and trying to sort out fact from rumor. He saw Davis and his cabinet pass by on their train to Danville, a sight that did little to lift his fearful spirits. The only bright spot in those few days was the generous hospitality that civilians offered "the fugitive soldiers." Even as civilians realized that the army could no longer protect them from the Yankees, "their devotion to their country grows brighter and no disaster alienates their affection from the war-scarred veterans whose unsurpassed valor has hitherto been so successful." This observation does not appear to have been wishful thinking on Wilson's part—Confederates seemed never to express bitterness toward individual soldiers (a foreshadowing of postwar rhetoric).[8]

Sergeant J. E. Whitehorne, of Company F, Twelfth Virginia Cavalry, embarked on a journey similar to Wilson's. The retreat from Petersburg left Whitehorne "almost demoralized," feeling that he "would rather die than live." Whitehorne had no delusions on 2 April about the significance of Lee's retreat, as he confided in his diary—begun just three days earlier: "If we, the Army of Northern Virginia, are defeated, all is lost. We must bow in submission." But his spirits had lifted by the following day, and Whitehorne and his men had "resolved to fight them to the bitter end," despite the troops being "almost naked" and having very little food. Whitehorne worried about the army's state of mind as it pushed farther back into Virginia, believing that men were "breaking after four years of strain. This retreat is doing terrible things to our minds." But Whitehorne remained strong, "ready for more marching or fighting." By 8 April, Whitehorne and his men were in Buckingham County, within hearing distance of the firing at Appomattox.[9]

On the morning of 9 April, after a Confederate attempt to break through the Union lines failed, Robert E. Lee realized that the time had come to surrender. He rejected completely the idea of turning his army into a guerrilla force, believing that it would swiftly degenerate into bands of marauders, resulting only in more years of fighting, desolation, and death, not independence. The story of the surrender is well-known: the two generals met in an atmosphere of mutual respect, both for each other and for each other's armies. Grant offered extremely generous terms, allowing the Southern soldiers to keep their horses and mules and bring them home to "put in a crop." The Confederates were allowed to surrender with their honor intact; there would be no disrespectful imprisonment of men or officers. The announcement that the war had ended for these men sparked rejoicing in the Northern ranks, misery in the Confederates'.[10]

"Oh des irae! How shall I record the recurrences of today!" wrote a horrified William Wilson. "The proud Army of Northern Virginia with all its glorious history ceases to exist." Wilson could "not dwell" on the "sad tale" of the surrender, as he decided to join several other soldiers in trying to escape to Lynchburg, thus avoiding the humiliation of personally surrendering to the enemy. He succeeded in reaching Lynchburg, only to be greeted by a scene of "inexpressible" gloom and disarray. Wilson, like the rest of his fellow soldiers, was undecided about his next move. Many of his companions spoke of trying to join the "Southern Army," meaning Johnston's forces in North Carolina, but Wilson opted against it, believing that "it is idle to go to Johnston—His days are numbered. . . . I shall return to the Valley and await developments there." As far as Wilson was concerned, "it is impossible to prolong the struggle on this side of the Mississippi. The Army of Gen. Lee was the bulwark of the Confederacy, disasters came thick and fast elsewhere, yet she proudly rolled back the tide which so often dashed against her. But as an organization she shall never more exist to fight the battles of freedom. Henceforth and forever she will live only in the memory of her glorious valor and patriotic devotion." In deserting the army, Wilson was bowing to the reality of the situation; the Army of Northern Virginia had clearly ceased to function, and so it seemed had the Confederacy.[11]

J. E. Whitchorne reacted with a combination of "thunderstruck" horror and shame at the news of the surrender. "Sad is a poor word to describe how I feel," he lamented. "I have a feeling we are not being true or loyal to our countless comrades who gave up their lives during this four years. What would Jackson, or Stuart, or—any of them say about us? It is humiliating in the extreme." Whitehorne described officers crying and privates who "broke down and wept like little children" at their fate. Unlike Wilson, however, Whitehorne chose to stay with his regiment and go through with actually surrendering and receiving his parole. The few days of waiting seemed to soften the blow for Whitehorne, for the "remarkably respectful" treatment that he and his fellow Confederates received from Union officers reminded him that "after all, I never hated any one Yankee. I hated the spirit that was sending them to invade the south." On 12 April, Whitehorne received his parole, and he started for home the following day. Although the memory of "the tragedy at Appomattox" continued "to hurt like an open wound," Whitehorne's last entry was hopeful, full of talk about putting in a crop and the reopening of churches and the Masonic Lodge at home in Brunswick County, Virginia. He even planned to help start a Confederate veterans organization as a way to keep the nation alive.[12]

Kena King Chapman, a second lieutenant in the Nineteenth Virginia Battalion, Crutchfield's Artillery Brigade, described the surrender as "*the saddest day of my life*." He not only remained with his brigade to receive his parole but, as the most senior officer remaining, was charged with making lists of the men present at the surrender. His work notwithstanding, Chapman reported that "the opinion seems to prevail that the war is ended but I cannot think so—there is life in the old land yet—and I cannot believe that the southern people are subjugated." Chapman took his parole and made his way first to Richmond, where he again remarked on the endurance of the Southern cause: "The Yanks seem to be very desirous to get us all out of this place and I believe I share their anxiety. The 'guerrilla' Mosby seems to hang over these Yankees like some frightful nightmare, and they seem to suspect every man as belonging to his command." As he continued toward his home in Smithfield, Virginia, Chapman was galled to be returning as a paroled prisoner, but he vowed to "submit *for the present* hoping always that the tide will again turn in our favor."[13]

Chapman, Whitehorne, and Wilson represent a spectrum of soldiers' reactions to the surrender, a spectrum replicated among civilians. Some Confederates immediately understood that the Confederacy had no hope of surviving with its president on the run and its finest army defeated. A Southern woman who had been living in New York described herself as "completely overwhelmed," having always said that she "would never lose faith until Genl. Robert E. Lee surrendered." That having happened, she went on, "all is over and God help the poor South. . . . If I could only leave the Country and never see it again." Margaret Wight also feared for the future, but she went on to disavow the past: "What is our condition now? Virginia particularly—lands laid waste and desolate—mills, barns burnt & dwelling homes, servants gone, nearly all the horses taken, Confederate money nothing but waste paper and but one in a hundred with *specie*. No prospect of making anything or going any where and all this for nothing—*nothing*." Emma Mordecai's emotions ranged from "agony" to resignation as she contemplated the news with her weeping niece and sister-in-law. Mordecai claimed to have "given up all hope" after the fall of Richmond, so the surrender itself was no great shock to her. Nevertheless, she confided, "I felt terrified as to what the consequences might be, and my fears absorbed my grief. I felt utterly miserable — that the earth might open & swallow us all up was the only wish I could form." Gradually, though, Mordecai came to comfort herself with the notion that the surrender was God's will, "that in thus [surrendering] we were not humbled before our foes but before God."[14]

Many other Confederates remained defiant in their despair, unwilling to admit that they had been fully beaten. Sarah Morgan recorded the surrender in her journal, adding proudly, "Every body cried, but I would not, satisfied that God will still save us, even though all should apparently be lost." Peace held no appeal for this young woman, not so long as it meant reunion with the enemy. "Let us leave our land and emigrate to any desert spot of the earth," she continued angrily, "rather than return to the Union, even as it Was!" Edwin Fay, far from the action in Louisiana, did something few of his countrymen did — he directed his anger not toward the Yankees or even toward God, but toward Robert E. Lee. Fay blamed Lee for surrendering, or, as he put it, having "sold the Confederacy." Fay's concern for himself and for his nation seemed inextricably tied: according to his logic, "I firmly believe the Confederacy will gain its independence but it will be when *every man* is forced by Yankee tyranny to take up arms. I cannot wait for that time but must just as soon as I am released from the Army . . . hasten out of the Country." So while the Confederacy could be saved, Fay would not be the one to save it. He felt, as he had throughout the war, that he had done his share. He wanted the nation saved, just not to save it himself.[15]

"NO ONE BELIEVES IT, THOUGH IT MAY POSSIBLY BE TRUE"

Confederates who wanted to keep believing that their nation could survive had ample reasons to do so. News had never traveled with great speed or accuracy in the Confederacy, and the fighting in 1864 and 1865 only exacerbated the problem. This problem was not limited to the far-flung corners of the South. Even in Virginia, rumors spread faster than news, and since the rumors were generally more upbeat than the reality, they were often believed. William Nalle, a teenager in Culpeper, Virginia, recorded several rumors in his diary, illustrating their power over public opinion. On 6 April, Nalle reported not only that Lee's army had fallen back toward Danville but also that "France had recognized our independence." While initially dismissive, having "heard it a hundred times before," Nalle returned to these tales a week later. On the thirteenth, Nalle "heard that the Yankees had surrounded our forces at Lynchburg and compelled about eight thousand of them to surrender & but heard they didn't get gen. Lee." A conversation the following day with his cousin and other paroled soldiers did not fully resolve the story: "They said the yankees took gen. Lee also. Which if it be true is a deuced finishing blow to our cause for gen. Lee is not only the greatest general in the Confederacy but in the whole World and without gen. Lee if the French or English don't hurry, and reinforce us & intervene, the yankees will get the upper hand by having ten to one." In this passage and others like it, Nalle encapsulated the combination of false hopes and real despair that Confederates felt in this time of upheaval.[16]

The rumors became progressively more outlandish, and Nalle continued his cautiously optimistic stance. On the seventeenth, he wrote that he "heard the French had set in to help us and had retaken New Orleans but thats too good to be true." He found more convincing the news that Lincoln had been in Richmond for a week, "making conciliatory speeches" and proposing that "if our state would go back into the Union there should be no forfeiture or confiscation of property whatever and we should be restored to our old rights." Nalle clearly thought that the Confederacy was still viable, for he scoffed at the offer: "Our old rights indeed[;] what more rights does a fellow want than he has now. Mr. Lincoln has done very well but I think we had better not go back."[17]

Of all the rumors reported by William Nalle, the ones about French involvement appear to have been most prevalent throughout the Confederacy during April 1865. A soldier in Louisiana heard of the French arrival in Mexico from a supposedly unimpeachable source—a fellow soldier's brother in Paris. Charles Hutson reported a rumor that France had recognized the Confederacy, adding, "of course no one believes it, though it may possibly be true." Back home in Orangeburg, South Carolina, Hutson's younger sister received confirmation of Lincoln's death and the armistice on 24 April, but the next day she heard "the very pleasant news that France had recognized us and sent out ships which had sunk some of the Yankee gunboats and taken New Orleans from the old wretches." Her next entry, dated 26 April, was equally upbeat, as she recorded the following "good news" (albeit inaccurate): "Seward is dead, all the Yankee papers in mourning, and everybody seems to believe the news about French recognition." In Griffin, Georgia, on 22 April, Kate Cumming heard that not only France but also England, Spain, and Austria had recognized the Confederacy and that Lincoln had been assassinated, Seward wounded, and an armistice signed. Georgians seemed unwilling or unable to separate the true from the false, however, as "none of our people believe any of the rumors, thinking them as mythical as the surrender of General Lee's army. They look upon it as a plot to deceive the people." Four days later, one rumor at least had been confirmed, as Cumming celebrated: "We have just heard that the French fleet has had a battle with the Federal fleet and whipped it and taken New Orleans. All are much rejoiced. There really is an armistice."[18]

In the same letter that described her preparations for the Yankees, Harriet Caperton asked, "Do you believe in the French treaty? *I hope.*" Confederates tended to "hope" rather than to "believe." That is, they knew in their hearts that the cheering stories they repeated were most likely false, but they couldn't keep from wanting them to be true. If a rumor allowed one to think that the Confederate nation still existed, that delusion was preferable to the grim reality of defeat. And as long as the worst rumors — those reporting the surrender or capture of armies — remained unconfirmed, why not trust the good news rather than the bad?[19]

Confederates wanted to believe that France had finally intervened because it was a way for them to keep their nation alive. Similarly, rumors about military victories and Jefferson Davis's whereabouts let Confederates delay thinking about what a loss might mean to them. Thus a woman in Virginia lamented that she heard nothing "except the most extravagant reports first on one side and then on the other, such as Lee's surrender, to the capture of half of Grant's Army." A soldier in Sumpter County, Alabama, told his wife even more "glorious news," having heard that "Genl. R. E. Lee has had a great Battle with Genl. Grant and had killed a great number of Yankeys, and that Grant had asked for an armistice to which Lee had agreed, and that since the death of Lincoln, one hundred thousand of Grants army had deserted: also that Genls. Johnson and Beauregard had whipped Sherman badly." The news was read to the troops and was "generally believed by officers," but this soldier confessed to having doubts about its accuracy. Nevertheless, he hoped it was true.[20]

While no one appeared to doubt that Richmond had fallen into Union hands, Jefferson Davis's extended flight provoked plenty of speculation about his plans for reconstituting the Confederate government elsewhere in the South. Kate Cumming heard that Atlanta or Macon was to become the new capital, but she couldn't see how that would happen, given that "we have no army in either place, and the enemy is now all around us, and our railroads torn up in every direction." It so "puzzled" her that she decided to "give over thinking about it, and await the issue." One frequent explanation that provided Confederates with a focus for their enduring nationalist dreams was that Davis was heading west, toward the comparative security of the Trans-Mississippi. The hope, as expressed by a niece of Davis's, was that Davis would "take command of the army and yet achieve our independence." Pauline DeCaradeuc also believed that Davis had gone west to "try and rally, and continue the war, every man is a traitor & coward who doesn't go with him, & fight to the death to keep us from this disgraceful reunion." As long as Davis and other men fought on, DeCaradeuc refused to believe that the cause was lost, for "so far we are only outnumbered."[21]

Confederates had one last hope on which to cling as they adjusted to the news of Lee's surrender. Along with the rumors of foreign intervention and Davis rallying troops anew in the Trans-Mississippi came tales of victory in North Carolina. In Texas, Kate Stone heard that Johnston had 125,000 men at Augusta, Georgia, prepared to "make a gallant fight." Margaret Wight reported "cheering news" on 14 April, having learned "from Yankee authority" that "Gen Johns[t]on (who did not surrender) has whipped Sherman badly and taken much ammunition & many wagons!" Her journal entry for the following day acknowledged that the rumor was untrue. Fanny Wight was more realistic when she reflected, "Where [Gen.] Johns[t]on is I don't know, but I scarcely think when Lee surrenders his noble army that Johns[t]on will keep up his—I suppose the war is well over." Right she was, for on 26 April, Johnston and Sherman agreed to surrender terms that duplicated those at Appomattox. The war had effectively ended.

"THE MAN WE HATE HAS MET HIS PROPER FATE"

One other rumor, more surprising than any other, reached Confederate ears during late April. The news of Lincoln's assassination, only five days after the surrender at Appomattox, threw Confederates into even greater confusion. On the one hand, most Confederates hated Lincoln with a passion, using him as a symbol of all that was wrong with the Yankees—their fanaticism, their bloodthirstiness, their irrationality—but on the other hand, Confederates rightly feared that they would be blamed for the murder. Too, they justifiably worried that Lincoln's successor, Andrew Johnson, frequently derided as "the tailor" from Tennessee and reviled as a turncoat, might not be so generous toward the South as Lincoln undeniably had been. Those Confederates who were glad that Lincoln was dead dared not express their glee in public; those people who smarted at the public displays of mourning crepe and badges did so in silence. To do anything else might be to invite true repression from the occupying army. The response to Lincoln's assassination shows the ways in which Confederates began reshaping their identity with an eye toward reunification as the war drew to a close.[22]

Privately, and especially in the pages of personal journals, some Confederates were not so circumspect. "Hurrah! Old Abe Lincoln has been assassinated!" exulted Emma LeConte. "It may be abstractly wrong to be so jubilant, but I just can't help it." Although LeConte realized that Lincoln's death would not change the fact that the Confederacy had ceased to exist as an independent state, she could not help but feel, if not glad, then somewhat satisfied: "The first feeling I had when the news was announced was simply gratified revenge. The man we hate has met his proper fate." Indeed, it appears that her scorn for Lincoln was only exceeded by her distaste for Johnson. Kate Stone was similarly gladdened by the death of Lincoln and the attack on Seward (who was also rumored to have died), which provided her a bright spot amid the gloom that followed the surrender. She could not "be sorry for their fate. They deserve it. They have reaped their just reward." She reserved her concern for the attackers, John Wilkes Booth and Lewis Paine, "earnestly" hoping that "our two avengers may escape to the South where they will meet with a warm welcome." A few days later, having learned Booth's fate, she reflected sadly, "Many a true heart at the South weeps for his death." Not so for Lincoln; Stone was "glad he is not alive to rejoice in our humiliation and insult us by his jokes." A Louisiana cavalryman shared her admiration for the conspirators, telling his wife that they were "the heroes of the Confederate revolution" and proposing that their next son be named Booth. "Assassination is by no means a favorite amusement of mine," wrote a North Carolina woman, "but I think sometimes that it is a pity that Boothe's crazy fit did not last a little longer."[23]

Other Confederates were saddened by the assassination, believing that no matter how much they might have disliked Lincoln, he did not deserve to die. Sarah Morgan, long torn between her own love of the Confederacy and her half-brother's Unionism, considered Lincoln's assassination completely unjustifiable. "Where does patriotism end," she wondered, "and murder begin?" A Richmonder thought that the "murder of Lincoln was an infamous, diabolical, nay a hell-born crime, that the American name can never be proud of." He claimed to have found no disagreement in Richmond, where "all regret it," although Kena Chapman painted a slightly different picture. "Poor 'old abe' the 'Ape' was buried to-day and all yankeedom is of course in mourning—Richmond of course included," he wrote on the nineteenth. "The 'Johnnies' in this place do not seem to grieve tho' as if their hearts would break." William Nalle confided in his journal that he was "very sorry" to hear of Lincoln's death, "for though he was our enemy still from all I hear he must have been a most excellent, good hearted kind man." The passage was lightly crossed out, whether by Nalle or someone else is unknown and relatively unimportant. More significant is the fact that unqualified praise of Lincoln was unacceptable, even in the most private of places.[24]

Most Confederates fell somewhere in the middle, their dismay prompted more by fearful self-interest than by any real regard for Lincoln. Margaret Wight feared that the attacks on Lincoln marked "the beginning of a 'reign of terror,'" although she worried more that her newly emancipated servants were "in a state of perfect insubordination." The assassination, she predicted, "will cause us much sorrow. . . . They seemed from policy inclined to be lenient to us but now we have nothing to expect but the hardest terms." A Louisiana woman was shocked by the news, writing, "What is to result from it to us? No one knows. It may be only the beginning of trouble." In Arkansas, John W. Brown feared that "this bloody catastrophe . . . will only bring new and aggravated troubles upon the Southern people."[25]

A Danville, Virginia, man thought the assassination "a great calamity to the nation," not least because he thought it set a bad "precedent" for the future of republican government. "And I think it was a bad exchange anyhow for the South," he continued, "for Lincoln had no personal feelings to govern him that Johnson will. Though I hope Johnson will rise above personal animosity and take into consideration the welfare of the Republic." This was a common fear among Southerners, for Johnson was almost uniformly reviled. David Schenck considered the assassination "politically disastrous, as old Abe with all his apeishness, was a kind hearted man and disposed to treat us generously and mercifully. I am sincerely sorry he was killed. The South too feels specially galled at the power of Andy Johnson, who as a renegade, demagogue and drunkard is peculiarly intolerable to them." A Georgia woman perfectly encapsulated Southern regrets when she confided in her diary, "The South has lost its best friend. Had he lived, Mr. Davis our Southern President had never been treated as he will probably be doomed to be under existing circumstances." Confederates were extremely aware of the political situation that awaited them and worried about being in the best possible position. At the same time, such awareness means that expressions of sadness at Lincoln's death were not necessarily indicative of a lack of Confederate patriotism.[26]

Perhaps concern for future treatment at the hands of the occupiers motivated those Confederates who took part in the public displays of grief that occurred throughout the South. Most, if not all, of these commemorations were mandated by occupying Union officers, following orders from Washington that a national day of mourning be observed. Buildings were draped in black crepe, and black-bordered announcements were printed and distributed. Mahala Roach, the Vicksburg woman who had socialized with Union officers throughout the war, described her town's commemoration: "There was a meeting held at the Court House today. Bells tolled, stores closed. Flags at half mast—badges of mourning worn, and hung from almost every house. *We* gave black badges to more than twenty colored soldiers." While Roach appeared to be an eager and sincere participant in the mourning, other Confederates may have acted with more self-interested motives. Sarah Morgan charged many New Orleans residents with flagrant hypocrisy, complaining that "the more violently 'secesh' the inmates, the more thankful they are for Lincoln's death, the more profusely the houses are decked with the emblems of woe. They all look to me like 'not sorry for him, but dreadfully grieved to be forced to this demonstration.' Men who hated Lincoln with all their souls, under terror of confiscation and imprisonment which they *understand* is the alternative, tie black crape from every practicable knob and point, to save their homes." [27]

Southern preachers were also ordered to offer up prayers and sermons for the martyred president. The preachers of the first group of such sermons, made immediately following the assassination, tended to abhor the murder while denying that Southerners as a group had any role in the killing and avoiding all but the most general praise for Lincoln himself. Andrew Johnson later ordered a national day of mourning and prayer for 1 June, at which time ministers were expected to eulogize Lincoln. Many Southerners chose not to attend these enforced homages; others resisted as best they could. In Emma LeConte's church, the minister recited the prayer for Lincoln, but the entire congregation refused to bless it with a closing "Amen." One Richmond minister confronted with only five or six congregants reputedly dismissed them as follows: "My friends, we have been ordered to meet here by those in authority for humiliation and prayer on account of the death of Lincoln. Having met, we will now be dismissed with the doxology: 'Praise God from whom all blessings flow.'" [28]

Another Richmond clergyman, John Lansing Burrows of the First Baptist Church, took his charge more seriously, delivering a discourse on Lincoln and Southern nationalism. Burrows began by telling his listeners (who presumably included both Southerners and Northerners) that Southern Christians had a pious duty to abhor Lincoln's murder. They joined the nation in mourning; they sympathized with those who suffered. Yet it was "not becoming" for Southerners to "press forward as special eulogists of Mr. Lincoln," given that they had long opposed him and his beliefs. To pretend otherwise was to leave themselves open to charges of hypocrisy. The Southern people, Burrows continued, accepted that they lost the war, accepted that "a centralized nationality" has triumphed over the doctrine of state sovereignty. That said, Southerners "cannot yield all manliness and self-respect, and consistency and conscience" by pretending to approve of that result.[29]

Burrows then turned his attention to the torrent of blame pouring out from the North toward the South, particularly condemning the Northern religious press for fostering such hatred. Neither slavery nor the Confederacy killed Lincoln. Furthermore, "private, skulking assassination" was never "encouraged or excused by the popular sentiment or spirit" in the South. Simply put, assassination was not honorable and therefore Southerners would not have condoned it. Nor was Booth even really a Southerner, having been a native of Maryland. Indeed, Burrows concluded, Lincoln's assassination was more than just a crime against the United States; it was "not only morally, but politically . . . *a stupendous crime against the South*" since it denied Southerners Lincoln's benevolence and angered the Northern people. Confederates, at least those disposed to make the best of their situation, seized upon Lincoln's death as an opportunity to push for reunion, to show their good faith, and to call for leniency. In this respect, mourning for Lincoln represents one of the first of many redefinitions of Southern identity after the war. As the war ended, Confederates gave up the idea of the Confederacy as territory. Now, as the Confederacy itself ceased to exist, certain aspects of identity could be jettisoned.[30]

"HAD WE NOT BETTER MAKE THE BEST TERMS THAT WE CAN?"

For most Americans, and many Confederates, too, Lincoln's assassination marked the symbolic end of the war. But armies remained in the field until May, and soldiers were sometimes least willing to accept that their war was over. Officers sometimes urged their men to fight on, surrenders notwithstanding. Confederate brigadier general Thomas Munford, despite having dismissed his men at Lynchburg on 9 April, prepared a week later to recall his cavalrymen and lead them to Johnston's army. In his special orders of 21 April, Munford reminded his soldiers that "one disaster, however serious, cannot crush the spirit of Virginians and make them tamely submit to their enemies." The orders reminded men of their promise to avenge the deaths of their fellow Confederates and urged all men at home, men more numerous than those who surrendered at Appomattox, to rally once more to their cause and their president. Munford made a special appeal to the men of his brigade, telling them that "the eyes of your Virginia, now bleeding at every pore, turns with special interest to you. Will you desert her at her sorest need?" Munford was certain that they would not. General Sam Jones in Florida made a similar call to men on 28 April, comparing the surrender of Lee's army to the surrender of Vicksburg in 1863. Just as the Confederacy had "rallied" from that disaster, so, too, would it endure the surrender of Lee's army. Jones seized on rumors of armistice talks and used them to spur patriotism, explaining, "It is not only the imperative duty, but to the interest of every man in the Confederacy, to stand firm and true and present a bold and defiant front to our enemies. Such a course will strengthen our government and aid in securing an honorable peace." In both cases, reality overtook defiance: Johnston's army surrendered before Munford could bring his men, and, with that, resistance collapsed. More so than their generals, ordinary soldiers knew when their time in the army was over.[31]

William Wilson made two significant choices in the upheaval that followed Lee's surrender: he chose to escape to Lynchburg rather than surrender to the Yankees, and he chose to leave the army entirely. Unlike other of his companions, Wilson had no desire to keep fighting, to prolong a war that was, as far as he was concerned, over. Indeed, the swiftness of this realization that the war was over and it was time to go home mirrored nothing so much as Southerners' swift shift from American to Confederate identity four years earlier. That decisions are quickly made does not mean they are not made based on deeply held convictions. While some soldiers spoke of trying to reach either Johnston's army or the Confederate forces in the Trans-Mississippi, Wilson returned home to the Shenandoah Valley.

Charles Hutson, a soldier in Johnston's army, faced many of the same choices as Wilson. When he heard of Lee's surrender, Hutson laid out two possible strategies for the Army of Tennessee and the Confederacy. First, they could take up positions to the east, west, and south of the Blue Ridge, drawing supplies from eastern Kentucky, eastern Tennessee, north Georgia, northern South Carolina, and western Virginia. They would then wait for the Union army to appear, "massing to receive it, and striking it heavily when it draws near, pursuing it hotly through the great reach of country between it and the seacoast, until utter annihilation is the result." Or, they could march west to the Mississippi River and concentrate forces in Arkansas, Missouri, Louisiana, and Texas. From that base, Confederates could cross into Ohio, sweep east into the North and on to Washington, "living on the country as we pass through and leaving a desert behind us. That course would secure peace on *our* terms very promptly, especially if we carry negro troops with us." As far as Hutson was concerned, "nothing less than total ruin" could ever shake his confidence in his army. As they marched through Raleigh, he found that the ladies of the town shared his feelings, for though "they expected to be in the enemy's lines with a few days time," they were "hopeful for our cause and expressed great confidence in Joe Johnston." Their spirit left him "much pleased."[32]

The news of Lee's surrender and the demise of the Confederate government left Hutson "sick at heart" but determined to "bear our fate manfully and keep ever ready to renew the struggle when the right moment comes." For Hutson, that meant deciding whether or not he and some friends should escape and strike out for Texas. He felt that he could not live under Yankee rule and deplored the anticipated choice between taking the oath of allegiance or spending his life in prison. Hutson feared that under Northern occupation, life for white Southerners would be intolerable: "The passport system will be rigidly kept up, spies and every feature of despotic rule will be vogue, and life at such a rate will be hateful and a burden." As Hutson weighed his options, several seemed attractive. Echoing the rumors about French involvement, he predicted that Mexican emperor Maximilian would soon invade and take over Texas, Louisiana, and the rest of the Trans-Mississippi department. He suggested that his family emigrate to Costa Rica as soon as they could raise the money. But by the next day, Hutson's plans had changed; he was no longer escaping to Texas. An armistice had been declared between Johnston's and Sherman's armies, and Johnston was (falsely) rumored to have "no intention of surrendering his army." Too, the rumors of European intervention had infiltrated the army, for Hutson heard that a French fleet lay in Mobile Bay, as well as that Lincoln had been assassinated—in this version by a Virginia soldier. Those rumors cheered Hutson, but the following did not: "The worst report, because it involves shame and dishonor is that a treaty is on foot for a general amnesty, gradual emancipation, and reconstruction." So horrible was that for Hutson to contemplate that he vowed, "If this is consented to by S. C., I abjure my allegiance to her and will emigrate." Hutson rejected a plan to join a proposed partisan force in South Carolina, holding out again for Texas.[33]

Jared Sanders, of the Lovell Rifles (Company B, Twenty-sixth Louisiana

Infantry), grew increasingly "nervous" as he waited for news of the East to reach him while he was encamped in Nachitoches Parish. On 11 and 12 May, he poured out his conflicted emotions in a letter to his sweetheart, telling her that even as he wrote, a delegation of Union officers was negotiating the surrender of General Edmund Kirby Smith's forces. Sanders realized that, given the state of the Confederacy, "our armies captured, our President fleeing for his life and the victorious legions of the enemy marching for our subjugation," only "the hands of Divine Providence" could deliver them to independence. Sanders, however, was unwilling to go quietly, suggesting that the remaining soldiers break up into smaller parties to carry on "a partizan warfare, as did Sumpter and Marion of the old revolution." A "disorganized resistance," rather than resulting in increased hardship for Confederates, would make their country "a dead weight" on the Union, "requiring huge armies to keep it in any sort of subjection, & not returning one dime to the possessor." Sanders was confident that continued fighting would eventually force the Yankees east of the Mississippi. Too, he had obviously heard the same rumors of foreign action that had spread throughout the South, for he added encouragingly that "recognition and armed intervention will come immediately—it has been promised and everything now tends that way."[34]

Sanders's worst fears came to pass later that day, for when he resumed his letter, he reported the terms of surrender as he understood them: Confederate soldiers would be disfranchised, Confederate property confiscated, and commissioned officers exiled. His initial reaction was angry and defiant:

> Oh horrors! Can any man with warm southern blood coursing through his veins think for one moment of submission to such ignominy! No! we cannot, will not yield! and we draw encouragement & confidence in our final success from history, from the rise of Grecian republics—from the foundation of the Dutch Republic—Holland contested for eighty years & at last won her independence from the Spaniards, overcoming obstacles greater ten fold than those we now have to meet and our fathers forced recognition from the haughty invincible Britons—we finally must succeed if we fight it to the Last—

But by the end of his letter, Sanders appeared more resigned. He seemed to sense that few of his fellow soldiers were inclined to continue the war, and although he thought them "unworthy of their liberty" for preferring to live under Yankee rule, he accepted that "if the people are not willing to make every sacrifice, our fate is inevitable, and you will hear of *submission* before this reaches you. God avert this direst of national calamities."[35]

Although many soldiers, like Sanders, found the various surrender terms offered to be disgraceful or dishonorable, most believed they had no choice. General James Longstreet defended the Appomattox surrender in a public letter, explaining that the army submitted because it was surrounded and the generals wanted to avoid "a great and useless sacrifice of human life. . . . It was never intended to give up the Confederate cause with the Army of Northern Virginia." Accepting that the war was over, argued a Louisianian, did not mean that a person was "lacking in patriotism." Given the situation, with an enemy already flush with victory, whose superior numbers would eventually crush the demoralized Confederate armies, "had we not better make the best terms that we can, procrastination will only work pain and distress upon the people." Men were not the only ones who would suffer under a prolonged conflict, for the fighting and devastation would hurt women and children as well, "and why destroy them without a prospect of equivalent results?" This writer, even as he advocated surrender, took pains to make it clear that he was "as far from yielding the issues upon which the War has been fought as any man." He was simply a realist, urging that Confederates "take a national and common sense view of the condition, [and] if the future presents the remotest glimmering of hope, then let us pursue it." If it did not, then they needed to determine what the "next best" strategy would be, and follow that instead, being careful "not [to] destroy everything because we can't save everything."[36]

The slow transmission of news and information contributed to Confederates' ability to delay believing that the war had come to an end. Thus even after the last man had surrendered, Confederates in outlying areas still thought that the war could go on. On 28 April, Kate Stone reflected that Lee's surrender was "a crushing blow hard to recover from" but hoped that "maybe after a few days we can rally for another stand." She seemed more upset by the defeated attitudes of the people around her than by the news itself, and she lamented that she herself could not join the fight against the enemy, complaining that "most seem to think it useless to struggle longer, now that we are subjugated. I say 'Never, never, though we perish in the track of their endeavor!' Words, idle words. What can poor weak women do?" Two weeks later, even Stone seemed to realize that the Confederacy could not long survive, but she raged against its fate: "*conquered, submission, subjugation* are words that burn into my heart, and yet I feel that we are doomed to know them in all their bitterness. The war is rushing rapidly to a disastrous close. Another month and our Confederacy will be a nation no longer, but we will be slaves, yes slaves, of the Yankee Government."[37]

As upset as Confederate soldiers and civilians were by the end of the war, none of their anger was turned against their soldiers. From the first, the surrenders of the armies were not perceived as having been due to any shortcomings among the fighting men—shortcomings in the government or the ranks of generals, perhaps—but not of the soldiers. The chorus of a song titled "Lee's Surrender" expressed deep sympathy for the soldier who "yielded up Virginia his pride" and continued in the second verse:

You did your part well noble band
Outnumbered yet brave and true you stood
Determined to battle for the land
Of the noble, the brave and the good.

There was only sadness, not shame, in their surrender.[38]

Furthermore, soldiers were heroes for having fought so long against a more numerous and better-equipped foe, and they were often accorded hero's welcomes. One Louisiana soldier described traveling through St. Martinsville and New Iberia as "pleasant moments" that "will for ever be agreeably remembered by all True Southerners present." The soldiers were welcomed effusively: "Cheers, Banquets, Hurrahs, Flags, Banners, cakes and other niceties were literally showered upon us when we marched through most places. The Ladies and *Some* of the men of this lower country are not yet cowed—we found much more patriotism down here then I ever dreamed there was left in the whole of the State." Soldiers who returned to Halifax County, North Carolina, were treated to a dinner hosted by local notables, complete with flowery speeches singing the praises of their heroic and honorable patriotism.[39]

"OUR SYMPATHIES GO OUT FOR JEFF DAVIS"

More than perhaps any other Confederate, Jefferson Davis resisted accepting that the Confederacy had ceased to exist. On the night of 2 April, as Richmond fell around them, Davis, his family, and several cabinet members and their families departed the capital by train headed for Danville. They remained there, in the "last capital of the Confederacy," until the news of Lee's surrender reached them. On the night of 10 April, the Davis party again boarded a train and headed farther south into North Carolina, stopping first at Greensboro and eventually reaching Charlotte. On the 25th, Davis sent orders to Joe Johnston, asking him to disband his army and make arrangements to rendezvous later and commence a partisan struggle against the

Yankees. Johnston was then to report to Davis. Realizing the utter futility of such a strategy, Johnston refused, and surrendered his army a few days later. Davis continued to flee farther south into Georgia, hoping ultimately to make his way into the Trans-Mississippi and then rally the people for a new assault against the North. In early May, Andrew Johnson, angry about the assassination of Lincoln, offered a $100,000 reward for the arrest of the Confederate president.[40]

In refusing to surrender, Davis took a stand for the Confederate nation, and his citizens responded with newfound respect and admiration for him. Except for an early burst of enthusiasm following his inauguration and the beginning of the war, Davis had never enjoyed the same popularity as his generals, particularly Lee and Jackson. His decision to replace the popular Joe Johnston with John Bell Hood in the midst of the Atlanta campaigns during 1864 did nothing to increase his standing with a public that had already grown frustrated by some of his shortcomings as an executive. Nevertheless, most Confederates still felt a degree of loyalty to Davis as an embodiment of the nation, and that loyalty transmuted into fervent affection during the spring of 1865. As Confederates themselves surrendered and came under occupation, the image of their uncowed president, bravely clinging to his freedom, gave them a focus for their continuing desire for independence. They prayed for him in church, even as they were being asked to pray for the spirit of Lincoln. "My womanly sympathies go out for Jeff Davis," Gertrude Thomas professed, "and I do hope and pray that he will escape. Not to save my right arm would I betray him if I knew where he was and yet I was beginning to think him despotic." Kate Cumming similarly feared that the reward being offered might tempt "some of our men . . . to betray him for love of gain." She was angry with Davis's critics, appalled that he was being unfairly blamed for Lincoln's assassination. A North Carolina woman seconded Cumming, arguing that it was "a likely story indeed that any high minded Southerners would stoop to such means to rid himself of such an unworthy foe. President Davis conspiring against Lincoln indeed! Abe need not flatter himself so much."[41]

As it turned out, Davis was not betrayed by Southerners, but he was captured on 10 May in southern Georgia. Soldiers of the Fourth Michigan Cavalry cornered him and then, allegedly, caught him fleeing disguised in some type of woman's garb. Although Northerners seized on the image of "Jeff Davis in Petticoats" as an opportunity to portray the South as not just conquered but emasculated, in all likelihood he was simply wearing a shawl or cloak.[42] He was taken first to Savannah, and he eventually spent two years

THE LAST DITCH OF THE CHIVALRY, OR A PRESIDENT IN PETTICOATS.

"The Last Ditch of the Chivalry." This satirical image portrays Davis, disguised as a woman, fleeing his captors. White Southerners saw such images as attacks on their masculinity and honor. Library of Congress.

in prison at Fortress Monroe, Virginia. Captured and transported through the South in chains, Jefferson Davis provided Southerners with their own martyred president, a counterpoint to the North's Lincoln. Gertrude Thomas was horrified to see him taken through Augusta, calling his treatment "the crowning point, the climax of our downfall." She was quite cognizant, too, of the powerful symbolism of their president being made a prisoner and thought that "the United States made a great mistake in having Davis carried through the Southern States in this way. It will prove a triumphal procession to him for even those persons at the South who were becoming disaffected towards him will have their sympathies aroused and a manly emotion of regret for him will be experienced." A companion of Mary Chesnut's thought that the Yankees, no matter how vehement their rhetoric, would not hang him: "Not they—too cute for that. They won't have his blood crying to heaven against them and make him a martyr on the scaffold, like Charles I, for us to worship down here forever." Another friend, this one a clergyman, was horrified by demands that he pray for Andrew Johnson, crying out, "Pray for people when I wish they were dead? . . . No—never. I will pray for President Davis till I die. I will do it to my last gasp. My chief is a prisoner, but I am proud of him still. He is a spectacle to gods and men. He will bear himself as a soldier, a patriot, a statesman, a Christian gentleman. He is the martyr of our cause." Chesnut's only reply to this outburst was her tears.[43]

The capture of Jefferson Davis unequivocally brought the war to a close for Confederates. The final western surrenders in late May were nothing more than an epilogue, for the story of the Confederate state had already ended. Pauline DeCaradeuc realized that she could no longer "delude" herself into thinking that the Confederacy might somehow come back. She had nothing but sympathy for Davis, "the purest patriot, the greatest statesman and wisest administrator that ever lived," and wished that she could "die to save him from sorrow, and the humiliations which are to be heaped upon his great soul." DeCaradeuc, who had not mentioned Davis at all in her wartime entries, now could not contain her feelings for the "immortal President." Later in the summer, she recorded an instance in which she and a suitor got into an argument over Davis. Her companion requested that she allow him to change her opinion, and she acquiesced, "but all he or anyone else can say, will only increase my admiration for the greatest man of the age."[44]

White Southerners truly faced a world turned upside down. The collapse of the Confederacy took away a fundamental focus of Southern identity. For four years, Southerners had been "Confederates," their own nation. While the state and military apparatus were rapidly dismantled, the emotional hold that independent nationhood had over people was not so easily broken. During the spring and summer of 1865, former Confederates began the process of negotiating a new identity for themselves, one that would allow them to honor their Confederate past while securing the benefits of American citizenship. Paramount among these benefits were the protection of property, the right to vote, and the right of white Southerners to determine the postwar South's racial order. That concern underlay almost all the struggles over Southern identity during Reconstruction.

Reconstruction

5 Nursing the Embers

Race and Politics during Reconstruction

As the shock of defeat wore into a sense of angry resignation, white Southerners turned to more personal concerns—rebuilding their lives, farms, or businesses, adjusting to the deaths of loved ones and friends, coming to terms with emancipation and new relationships with African Americans. Although these issues of household economy and family relationship might seem personal or individual, collectively they had national salience. As whites rebuilt their lives, they rebuilt their communal identity as well. They had spent four years defining themselves in opposition to the North; now most realized that economic and social control, especially of the freedmen, could best be found by rejoining the Union, preferably on the same terms of political citizenship as before the war. But to demand the rights of political citizenship, specifically voting for white males, was not to reject all aspects of Confederate nationalism. Southern whites wanted to have their cake and eat it, too: they self-consciously held onto aspects of their Confederate past, in the process transforming Southern identity.

The politics of Reconstruction were, of course, deeply racialized. White Southerners had lost not only their nation with the collapse of the Confederacy but their slaves as well. That loss had real material consequences for slaveholders as they struggled to rebuild economic lives without slave labor. The loss had more complex psychological resonances as well: slaveholders felt betrayed by their slaves, whom they believed were faithful; whites were deeply angry to see the freedmen living as free people, moving about, asserting their rights; and, finally, whites were frightened that their long-prophesied "race war" might come to pass, that their former slaves might rise up in justifiable anger and exact revenge. If slavery, with its attendant associations of security and stability, had seemed essential to the Confederacy, what would replace it in the limbo of Reconstruction? If protection of slavery had been reason to leave the Union, what rationale might inspire reunion? The answer was white supremacy. White supremacy, whether implicitly or explicitly, drove much of the ways in which white Southerners negotiated the boundaries of identity during this period of flux.[1]

By far the greatest shock facing white Southerners, especially members of the elite, came with the end of slavery. Slavery had been the scaffolding upon which whites had constructed their hierarchical view of the world. For generations, whites had used the demons of "race war" and racial mixing, of whites victimized by the same sort of mistreatment they had meted out to their own slaves, as a means of controlling dissent. Fear mingled with venomous anger as well. Emancipation not only freed slaves from forced labor but freed them from the social strictures of false affection and deference as well. Suddenly the mask of paternalism dropped away, and whites were confronted with the reality that their faithful, loving "servants" did not care about them at all, felt no allegiance and no need to stay.[2]

Letters and diaries during the spring and summer of 1865 are filled with a mixture of self-pity and anger regarding the difficulties whites had in either persuading their slaves to work or finding replacements for those who left. Emma Mordecai's slaves in Henrico County, Virginia, began asserting themselves right after Richmond fell into Union hands, and she found herself increasingly frustrated by their unwillingness to work or leave. "To have to submit to the Yankees is bad enough," she complained in mid-April, "but to submit to negro children is a little worse. They will, I hope, get ready to go soon." Her seeming willingness to have her slaves depart changed quickly a few weeks later, when she discovered them packing: "They will now begin to find out how easy their life as *slaves* has been, & to feel the slavery of their freedom." Her bitter response was typical. A Texas woman whined about her challenges, lamenting, "My baby was sick and I scarcely able to walk and my negroes were all ready to leave me after all my kindnesses to them. It makes me have no kind feeling for them. I have been too indulgent and too kind and thereby the fault." White Southerners continued to deny that blacks had any agency of their own.[3]

The diary of Staunton, Virginia, newspaper editor Joseph Waddell is full of references to emancipation during May and June 1865. He begins by expressing surprise at the number of African Americans who left town with departing Union troops, remarking that "there were negroes of all ages, and some who, I thought, had too much family pride or attachment to go off with the Yankees." Like many whites, Waddell attributed this leave-taking to black simplicity—"poor wretches, they seem possessed with mania"— or trickery by the Union—"miserable creatures! miserable government!"— rather than to considered decision making. Waddell couched his dismay at emancipation and his anger at Northerners in the language of concern for slaves, repeatedly describing "poor negroes" and worrying that they faced a future of "distress and ruin." He had, he wrote repeatedly, long opposed slavery and favored some form of gradual emancipation. Waddell, and many white Southerners like him, genuinely mourned the passing of close relationships between master and slave, seeing in the new contract system of labor a harshness that he believed slavery had mitigated. But he also worried for himself: "The whole social fabrick will be destroyed and the negroes be the chief sufferers. That a great change has taken place and will ultimately be consummated in the institutions of slavery; no one doubts; but laws must be enacted to regulate the new state of affairs, and the negroes, in the mean while, kept under some control, or universal ruin will result. This, however, is probably what the Yankee nation desires to accomplish— destroy us and the negroes together." Southern whites seemed unable to imagine a world without slavery to keep the "social fabric" of caste and race knit together.[4]

This view is also an example of white Southerners' sense of themselves as the true victims of Reconstruction. Every manifestation of black freedom— choosing a name, traveling freely, negotiating for better labor terms, keeping women and children out of the labor force—was seen as an assault on white prerogatives and another example of the unfairness of this new world. One woman wrote from her plantation near Pendleton, South Carolina, to complain bitterly about the new labor contracts, adding, "I used to be proud of my name, I have ceased to be so. I fear it will no longer [be] spotless, as the two meanest negroes on the place have appropriated it." Nothing, it seemed to the planter elite, was sacred. And each slight was seen as intentional humiliation. In an angry letter, Benjamin Huger vented his spleen about emancipation, summing up the feelings of many whites: "We hoped that when peace came, vengeance would have been satisfied & hatred glutted, but it is not so. . . . The whole labor system subverted, every relation in Society violated & destroyed, & all of this done by a *proclamation!*"[5]

A satirical piece in the *Hinds County (Miss.) Gazette* in 1866 showed the depths of the resentment whites felt toward black freedom. Purporting to be a series of amendments to the Civil Rights Act, it listed various "penalties upon those who refuse to recognize 'Cuffee' as abolitionism thinks he should be recognized." These supposed "crimes" began with interactions in the street—refusing to give way on the sidewalk or tip one's hat to a freedman—but built up to infractions like "believing that you are as good as a negro, five hundred dollars and three years imprisonment; . . . refusing to marry one, imprisonment for life, and the confiscation of your property" and culminating in "refusing your daughter to any buck that wants her, to be hung by the thumbs until dead, and have your wife and children turned out on the highway to starve." White Southerners were unwilling to let go of the rhetoric that had sustained them during secession and war, the idea that a straight line ran from black equality to assaults on white womanhood.[6]

This sense of victimization that ex-Confederates felt, however misplaced or irrational, had real political import, because it governed the ways they responded to Reconstruction. Southern whites resented the mistreatment they felt they were receiving at the hands of the Union, and that in turn gave them a sense of political entitlement. They resented black freedom and saw it as a challenge to white liberty and honor. Therefore, it needed to be quashed. This element of angry self-pity that white Southerners felt gave them the justifications they needed to keep themselves from full reabsorption into the Union. Losing the war, and with it the dream of independent nationhood, seemed to be punishment enough.

As former Confederates negotiated the limits of their evolving relationship with the United States, they found themselves most frustrated by the political arena. Some former Confederates publicly professed their loyalty to the United States and their desire to put the past behind them, while others clung to their anger and bitterness, continuing to proclaim the validity of their belief in states' rights. These two strains of defiance and accommodation coexisted in the Reconstruction South. Each strategy was couched in the same terms of doing what was best for the region and its people; each was exquisitely sensitive to the idea of preserving the idea of Southern distinctiveness. One group claimed to be taking the path of least resistance; the other thought resistance still honorable.

With the passage of time, ex-Confederates grew accustomed to their gradual reincorporation within the American nation. That is not to say that they were necessarily happy about the demise of the independent Confederacy or their anomalous position within the American Union, but that they had accepted the results of the war. They were quick to (at least publicly) concede their defeat and pledge their willingness to submit to the federal government, the better to regain political power. Longing for Southern independence had by 1867 and 1868 given way to calls for equal treatment by the federal government. Jefferson Davis had finally been released from prison, symbolically freeing all ex-Confederates from their shackles. White Southerners were less interested in forming their own nation and more concerned with preserving elements of Southern distinctiveness within the larger

United States. To this end, they resented measures that they saw as punitive or mean-spirited. The Radicals became the enemy, an enemy as much
hated as the Yankee soldiers of wartime. The disfranchisement of Southern
whites in 1867 and the simultaneous enfranchisement of African Americans
was an unacceptable affront to whites' honor, striking as it did at the heart
of their ideology of racial supremacy. White Southerners responded bitterly
and vengefully, often physically assaulting and even killing black voters and
politicians in an attempt to seize control again. In this we can see aspects of
the guerrilla war that Confederates rejected in 1865.

"NOT ONLY BROKEN DOWN IN FORTUNE BUT CRUSHED IN SPIRIT"

Former Confederates, according to Whitelaw Reid, a reporter who toured
the South during the summer and fall of 1865, ran the gamut of emotions,
first expressing "baffled rage," then "actual anguish," and finally "bewilder-
ment and helplessness."[7] An Arkansas woman's miserable words encapsulated the region's dislocation: "Where shall I begin? What must I first say to
you now? Events, thoughts & feelings, hopes & fears, pains & griefs, rush
into my mind & heart in such innumerable bursts 'tis almost impossible for
a pen, so insufficient & unpracticed as mine, to portray them." Former Confederates had no idea what their future might hold, in terms of civil rights,
legal position, or property claims. In losing the war, they had lost their
sense of self. They were no longer Confederates but were not yet Americans
either.[8]

Many people initially retreated within themselves. One South Carolina
matron lamented that "one feels too much to talk" and supposed that "all of
us are Volcanoes with a crust outside & the only way of judging the secret
fires consuming others is to look within ourselves." The power of this image
comes from its expression of barely controlled violence, violence that would
erupt with disturbing frequency in the next few years. Emma LeConte apologized for neglecting her diary for two weeks in May, explaining that it was
too painful, her thoughts and words too wicked, and vowed to try to "keep
back the expression of what fills my heart and thoughts." Similarly, Mary
Chesnut also chose not to write, "not for want of something to say, but from
a loathing of all I see and hear. Why dwell upon it?" "I could not write, in
fact could not for some time open my mouth to any one [I] felt so badly
about our national affairs. The result of the hard contests left such a heavy
weight upon my heart," wrote a Texan to his mother, explaining a long gap in

his correspondence. Any reminder of the war was painful. Kate Stone found herself "sicken[ed]" by the sound of war songs like "All Quiet on the Potomac Tonight." She could not "bear to think of it all" and thought it "best not to waken bitter memories by familiar heartfelt songs."[9]

Englishman Robert Ferguson described a "stupefaction" that reigned over Charleston during the summer of 1865, a sense of profound malaise that had descended over the city's white residents. A Richmonder described the Virginians around him as "very much impoverished and for the most part not only broken down in fortune but crushed in spirit." Another white Southerner bemoaned life in his "wrecked country, surrounded by our oppressors and looking almost hopelessly for better days." The physical devastation wreaked in the South was bad enough, "but the ruin went farther yet. Our souls were scorched & scathed in the furnace." Physical ruins could be rebuilt, but former Confederates feared they might not be able to rebuild themselves and would be relegated to a permanent second-class status.[10] A once wealthy South Carolinian was saddened by his loss of money and slaves but found "the most painful thing is I can't any longer send my boys to school." He reiterated his complaint more pointedly in a later letter, this time lamenting that "the only education the children are getting is that of being servants." This seemed to be the crux of his anxiety, that in a world without slavery, distinctions of class would become meaningless.[11]

A sort of defiance coexisted with misery in 1865, with the anger rather swiftly overshadowing despair. Anger was politically more powerful, more dangerous to reconstruction as well. Whites were not always circumspect about their continuing identification with the Confederacy. Gertrude Thomas described hearing three drunken men pass by her home. "'I told him I was a rebel,'" one proclaimed, "'I am a rebel now, will be for twenty years, will be for fifty years, will be forever, hip hurra'—'Bully for you' cried the other and with shouts they proceeded up the street." Thomas was shocked by her reaction to the men. Once she might have been horrified by such a vulgar display and would not have shared the sentiment. This time, she reported, "I felt my face flush, my eyes filled with tears and in my heart I echoed the sentiment. Last week I would not have done it—Now I could not help it." Kate Cumming experienced a similar disturbance as she made her way home to Mobile. While spending the night in West Point, Georgia, "some of the *rebels* kept up great noise all night, singing 'Dixie,' and hurrahing for Jeff. Davis." Cumming was not so receptive as was Thomas and "thought they would have to be informed that they were '*whipped*,' as they did not seem to be aware of that fact." The following day, Cumming and her party needed to be ferried across a creek, as the bridge had been destroyed. The owner would only accept Confederate money as payment (not a very sound financial decision), prompting one of Cumming's companions to say that "he felt like giving three cheers for the Confederacy, as there still seemed to be a spot of it left."[12]

Such pockets of loyalty existed throughout the defeated Confederacy. Whitelaw Reid saw Confederate soldiers welcomed with open arms in both Savannah and New Orleans and in the latter city found a swift resurgence of expressions of Southern pride, as "the returning Rebel soldiers seemed to have called into active utterance all the hostility to Northerners that for nearly four years had lain latent." Indeed, Reid was surprised by the depth of sympathy white Southerners, and members of the upper class in particular, felt for the vanquished fighting men. They were still seen as patriots, "defeated, but not disgraced." Some people went even further, proclaiming allegiance not only to the soldiers but to the endurance of the cause. One South Carolina man warned the reporter that "the race of arms-bearing men in South Carolina is not extinct." Even more disturbing was Reid's story of a Union officer who while searching through some "Rebel" papers discovered a torpedo set to go off if the papers were disturbed. Fortunately, he found the booby-trap in time, but the incident prompted Reid to remark, "The spirit of unconquerable hate, after the battle was fought and lost, could hardly go further."[13]

During the war, Confederates concerned with preserving their links to the patriotism of the American Revolution continued to celebrate holidays like Washington's birthday and the Fourth of July. But in the postemancipation South, July Fourth quickly took on a new meaning. This holiday that had once been the province of whites became a day of celebration for the freedmen, much to the disgust of ex-Confederates. A day in celebration of the conquering Union was bad enough, but one accompanied by African American public jubilation was impossible to endure. Emma LeConte described the day with distaste, noting that "the white people shut themselves within doors and the darkies had the day to themselves—they and the Yankees." "Ah, how differently we are to spend this day from what we [are] used to," mused a Georgia woman. "We used to hail it with joy as a day of feasting and gladness, now it is almost the saddest day we have ever witnessed. The flag of the enemy is to be flaunted in Athens today, almost every negro in the whole county has gone to see the sight."[14]

During the war, Confederates living in areas under occupation were forced to come to terms with Yankees in their midst; after the war, almost all white Southerners were confronted by their former foes. Part of redefining one's relationship to the Union as a whole involved redefining relationships with individual Northerners. In the immediate aftermath of the war, men and women made personal choices and individual decisions about where to draw the line. Some chose to react angrily to the invaders, actively snubbing them or (less commonly) expressing anger to their faces. Others tried to take the high road of indifference and neglect. But many Confederates found themselves drawn into employment arrangements, or forced to rely on charity from the Freedmen's Bureau, or involved in romantic relationships. Reunion was not so simple, and in forming personal bonds—willingly or not—white Southerners began to reshape their individual and, ultimately, their collective identities.

Many people, and especially women, strove to express nothing but disdain for their former foes. Kate Cumming was not surprised when an acquaintance told her of several quarrels between Confederate and Federal soldiers on the trains to Atlanta. Her solution, as she advised her friend and everyone else she came in contact with, was "to treat them with perfect indifference, as we were in their power, and none but *cowards* would taunt a fallen foe. If we quarreled with them, we put ourselves on their level." Cumming was concerned not only with preventing quarrels but also with maintaining what she believed to be appropriate standards of behavior. White Southern superiority had not ultimately been proven on the battlefield, but it could be shown on the streets of cities and towns. Cumming, on her way home to Mobile, had been distressed by rumors that Mobilians, particularly the women, had welcomed the Union occupiers with open arms, and she was pleased to note when she arrived that "there are but two or three ladies who have countenanced the enemy in any way, and now their old friends will have nothing to say to them." The majority of Mobile's ladies took "no more notice of the Federal officers than if they were invisible," much to the Union officers' dismay. Cumming happily reported that even "the color blue is wholly ignored." She even overheard a little girl "crying bitterly because her mother was going to put a blue ribbon on her hat. She said the Yankees might take her for one of them."[15]

Like Mobile's women, Emma LeConte also hoped to avoid the soldiers garrisoning Columbia, which was a bit more difficult as many of them were encamped across the street from her home. She found herself in a constant state of turmoil, overcome by "horrid feelings." Whenever possible, she stayed in the back of her house or kept the blinds drawn so as to avoid even a glimpse of her enemies, for just the "sight of a blue uniform" made her "blood boil!" One day, however, she caught a glimpse of them outside, and "before I knew it my hands were clinched, and such a feeling came into my heart as startled me and I fled upstairs away from the sight of them." LeConte could not hide at home forever, but she, like Kate Cumming, chose not to give vent in public to her private anger. She adopted a variety of strategies to telegraph her disdain, including doubling her veil when she went out and using a different exit from her property to avoid the guard stationed at the gate, and reported feeling "a little shudder" when she passed "within twenty yards of one." Like many women, she self-consciously pulled her skirts around her to avoid even her dress coming into contact with a Yankee. LeConte mocked the Yankees in Columbia for taking offense at being socially slighted by Columbians. "What do they expect?" she asked. "They invade our country, murder our people, desolate our homes, conquer us, subject us to every indignity and humiliation—and then we must offer our hands with pleasant smiles and invite them to our houses, entertain them perhaps with 'Southern hospitality'—all because sometimes they act with common decency and humanity! Are they crazy? What do they think we are made of?" For LeConte and women like her holding onto resentment and using the weapon of social sanction was the only way they could hold onto the Confederate past.[16]

Interactions with the Yankees upset Confederates. At home they could shut out their enemies, but in the public sphere of street and streetcar, contact was unavoidable and fraught with tensions. Some interactions were purely social, others were humiliating reminders that Southern whites were now a beaten people. Margaret Wight was upset about being subjected to a search before boarding a steamboat in Richmond but resolved to "keep quiet under such rule," no matter how difficult. Sarah Morgan was discomfited by an encounter with an old family friend, now a Union soldier, on the streetcar in New Orleans. As she had done on similar occasions during the war, she spoke briefly with him, electing not to make a scene by publicly snubbing him. Even as she took the high road, however, she felt ashamed and traitorous, berating herself, for "in behaving like a lady, I have forfeited my self-respect." Her self-inflicted misery was not assuaged when she returned home, for "mother was so angry with me when I told her how very, very quiet I had been! What a fierce bitter politician that meek little mother is! What astounding depths of hatred she reveals speaking of these matters!"[17]

Former Confederates were particularly troubled when forced into contact with African American troops. Black soldiers represented a dual affront—not just as occupiers but as people white Southerners had long deemed inferior. Pauline DeCaradeuc "felt every imaginable emotion upon seeing them, they who two or three months ago were our respectful slaves." Emma Mordecai first confronted African American troops at Camp Lee outside Richmond, a place she called "black and blue with well-equipped negro troops." She "walked through them majestically," never in her life as "proudly defiant" as at that moment, and, to her satisfaction, she "met with no rudeness or interruption." On her way home, however, she was stopped by a black soldier on picket, whom she described as "insolent." When she was finally allowed to pass, Mordecai could not resist commenting aloud that "they are as ill-breed as old Lincoln himself." Her interjection angered the black soldier, who again ordered her to stop, threatening to shoot her if she didn't. After some argument, she was finally allowed to continue on her way. Mordecai was "astonished" at her behavior, particularly her "coolness" as she fought with the black man. Proudly she proclaimed that she had felt only "incensed, not at all frightened."[18]

White Southerners resented the presence of Federal troops in large part because they represented the new racial order being enforced from above. Upset by the loss of their emancipated slaves' labor and deference, whites sought desperately to reassert their own racial control and superiority. Too, whites who had truly believed that slavery was a benevolent institution as concerned with moral uplift as it was with controlling labor were mystified and hurt by the depth of the freedmen's animosity toward them. Unable to accept that former slaves might have always resented, if not loathed, them, white Southerners blamed black "demoralization" on the influence of Yankee outsiders. "The Yankee privates enter your yards and kitchens without leave and with a manner indicating their total disregard of you and your property, and have the negro servants to cook or wash for them; and often sit for hours conversing with them and putting all sorts of mischief in their heads," grumbled David Schenck. A Lynchburg resident complained that "the place is alive with Yankees and free negroes" and predicted that "the latter will no doubt give us much trouble."[19]

Former Confederates had great difficulty admitting that they might need the Yankee occupiers' help. Thousands of Southerners had been displaced from their homes by battles or economic circumstances, and these refugees represented an enormous drain on the already taxed resources of Southern towns and cities. Croplands had been destroyed throughout the South as part of the Union's total war strategy of devastating Southern agriculture, and emancipation resulted in a profound shortage of African American labor in the fields. Just as the Freedmen's Bureau provided financial support and rations to former slaves, so, too, did it offer a helping hand to the former masters. Whitelaw Reid reported that during the month of May 59,000 rations were given to white residents of Mobile, while only 11,080 went to blacks. In South Carolina and Richmond, Reid found that many elite families were also willing to accept handouts from their former enemies, although not simply for reasons of subsistence: "They explained that they preferred to make 'the Washington Government' support them. It had robbed them of all they had, and now the very least it could do was to pay their expenses."[20]

While some former Confederates might have justified drawing rations as a means of "sticking it" to the Yankees, such reliance on charity was often perceived as evidence of suspect dedication to the late cause, or as indicative of a lack of honorable conviction. A Natchez, Mississippi, man complained that he couldn't understand "how some of those men whom I knew have ever lost their self-respect so much, as to have asked, or received assistance from those, on whom they could not heap sufficient abuse, when they were clothed in their grey uniform." "They should look & feel mean all their lives," he proclaimed in disgust, "yet I am told that they do not & go about as bold as a *sheep*." Emma LeConte noted that while the Yankees were issuing rations in Columbia, "they are only drawn by people in actual need or who have no self-respect." Her family fell into neither category, but by the summer of 1865, the LeContes were in bad financial shape. Her father, formerly a professor of chemistry at the South Carolina College, had gone into business with her uncle, using a flatboat to haul goods. Union general Alfred Hartwell hired the LeContes and, taking pity on their situation, offered to loan them some extra money. "Of course his offer was declined," Emma wrote indignantly. "As long as we can keep body and soul together, Father would not borrow from anybody, but to be under obligations to a *Yankee*!"[21]

Even as they regarded their conquerors with a combination of anger, revulsion, and disdain, some white Southerners found themselves admitting a grudging respect as well. Throughout the war years, Confederates had conjured up images of Armageddon to describe what Yankee rule would be like—a time of lawlessness, repression, and violence, a society where Southern women would be maids and mistresses to Yankee brutes while their men were subjugated and destroyed. The reality of occupation was much different, and relatively benign. Union soldiers largely followed their leaders' lead in being magnanimous in victory, and while they might be firm in their demands for polite treatment and in the application of laws of confiscation and emancipation, there was certainly no wholesale raping and pillaging of white Southerners—although blacks were not always so fortunate. Even Josiah Gorgas, as staunch a member of the Confederate cabinet as there ever was, found himself less than a month after he left Davis in North Carolina taking tea with Union officers at a Montgomery hotel. "The sensation is novel," he reflected "but we must get used to the presence of our late enemies, now our masters."[22]

"ALL WE WANT NOW . . ."

As congenial as individual Yankee officers might be, no one forgot that the rules that would govern the defeated South ultimately emanated from Washington. During April and May, former Confederates accepted the generous surrender terms and worried about what would happen next. "We are scattered—stunned—the remnant of heart left alive with us, filled with brotherly hate. We sit and wait until the drunken tailor who rules the U. S. A. issues a proclamation and defines our anomalous position," Mary Chesnut lamented. She mocked as "idiots" her Camden neighbors who thought that Johnson's reunification terms would be generous and who, "because they are cut off from railroads and telegrams[,] think they are to go back into the Union better off than we were before the war." She had no such hopes. "They are now parrolling our men but what the conditions will be, we cannot imagine," Margaret Wight fretted. "They can require any thing they please we are utterly powerless." James Walton, the captain of the Washington Artillery, remained in Richmond after the surrender, concerned about what the new president's policies might be. He was willing to accept some form of punishment but asked only "that I may be free to pursue the even tenor of my way, unobstructed & unmolested to be permitted to gain my livelihood in a dignified & honorable way."[23]

Gertrude Thomas reflected on 1 May that by the same time next year the South would no longer exist as an independent nation but would instead be part of the United States—"how united will depend alone upon treatment we receive from the hands of the North." Thomas, like most white Southerners, thought it would be in their interest to be "very discreet," for "the South will prove a smoldering volcano requiring little to again burst forth. Treated as members of one family—a band of brothers, *in time* we may have a common interest—but pressed too hard upon, our property taken from us—a desperate people having nothing to lose, the South may again revolt."[24] Thomas's analysis of the situation, made even while Jefferson Davis was still on the run, is important, for it shows the degree to which white Southerners wanted to believe that they were still in control of their own destiny. Although Thomas's expression might be taken as a statement of bravado, given the date on which she made it, it would prove to be all too true. She would have nothing to fear from Andrew Johnson, whose lenience shocked Northerners and Southerners.

White Southern attitudes toward the war and the North depended on the politics of the moment. Fears of Northern retribution immediately after the war were eased by Johnson's lenient plan for Reconstruction, and Southern whites quickly became his greatest champions. During the summer of 1865, a Natchez, Mississippi, writer praised Johnson for his "just and liberal" policies. In particular, this writer appreciated the fact that the provisional governor chosen by Johnson had quickly begun "filling the necessary offices, as far as practicable with the incumbents in office at the date of the secession of the state in January 1860 [sic]." This was exactly what white Southerners wanted in politics—a return to the status quo antebellum. An editorial in *Scott's Monthly* described Andrew Johnson not as the drunken tailor who so many white Southerners had derided him as during the war but as a man of "admitted sagacity and tried patriotism," an "able politician" and a "merciful magistrate" who had allowed the South to rebuild while saving face. The editors praised Johnson for standing firm against Radical pressures, conjuring up an awful vision of what would have happened had he yielded: the Southern states would have become "a festering body of death," infested by guerrillas and burdened by an "immense standing army." There could never have been peace with the South as a perpetual thorn in the side of the North. Now if Johnson could only convince Congress to follow his lead, white Southern worries would be over. "God bless our native land," the editorial concluded, "and may she always have, for her chief magistrate, one like Andrew Johnson, whose patriotism is as broad as the boundaries of the Republic."[25]

Southern whites interested in coming to some kind of understanding and accommodation with the rest of the Union made public professions of acquiescence. These might be grudging in tone, as opposed to ringingly patriotic, but they got the message across that white Southerners would not take up arms against the Union again. The residents of an Alabama county made the following proclamation in late 1865:

> Whereas, We have for four years most bravely and gallantly contended for our rights with the United States; and
> Whereas, We have been overpowered by numbers, *Resolved*, That we will, for the present; submit to the Constitution of the United States, and all laws in accordance with the same.

Northern force would be sufficient to keep white Southerners from revolting against their former foes.[26] Acknowledging that the Confederacy had lost the Civil War was a quick and relatively painless way for white Southerners to signal that they were ready for, and deserving of, equal political treatment. It was a calculated position, one that could have no bearing on wartime loyalties. White Southerners knew that the reporters flooding the South during 1865 and 1866 wrote for Northern audiences, and we can assume that to some extent they tailored their opinions to that audience. Thus a Barclaysville, North Carolina, farmer could tell John Dennett that he was in favor of "acknowledging we're whipped and asking forgiveness, and then if the United States won't take us back, why its not our fault." His desire for forgiveness notwithstanding, the farmer went on to scoff at his neighbors who claimed to have always supported the Union, sniffing, "We were all rebels together." In Charleston a few months after the war, Sidney Andrews found "very few who hesitate to frankly own that the South has been beaten." Although he also found "very few who make any special profession of Unionism," Charlestonians (or at least those willing to talk to a Northern reporter) were almost "unanimous in declaring that they have no desire but to live as good and quiet citizens under the law." In Columbia, Andrews noted, the reluctance was even more striking: "The war spirit is gone, and no fury can re-enliven it." A Meridian, Mississippi, man echoed the sentiments of Charlestonians, telling Whitelaw Reid that "the Southern people have been so soundly thrashed that just now they've got d—d few opinions of any kind. All we want now is to get back to civil government and the making of our own laws."[27] This desire was at the heart of Southern willingness to reunite with the Union.

"Yes, put them away—the old grey uniform and the torn and tattered banner of the stars and bars," urged the usually unreconstructed *Southern Opinion* in 1867, implicitly suggesting to readers that they concentrate on fighting through the legal and social systems. It was a quietly conditional sort of loyalty, however. In his testimony before the Joint Committee on Reconstruction, James D. B. De Bow claimed that the majority of Southern whites would support the Union should it become engaged in a foreign war. Former Confederates could be trusted for three reasons: because, first, they were sick of war in general; second, they recognized the overwhelming power of the federal government; and, finally, they were angry with foreign nations for not recognizing the Confederacy and therefore had no desire to aid them. Significantly, De Bow did not mention that white Southerners should have been trusted because they accepted the integrity of the Union. Perhaps he knew that such an assertion—De Bow reported on his testimony in an issue of the *Review*—would not have won him any more readers. Perhaps, too, De Bow was not yet prepared to make that final concession. It was one thing to admit that Southern whites had been beaten, another to fully reject one of the things they had been fighting for.[28]

Of De Bow's three rationales, war-weariness was the most common explanation given for white Southerners' willingness to put the past behind them. In Montgomery, Whitelaw Reid found "no indication whatever of the slightest disposition to foment another war." A young planter still believed in the right of secession but summed up the general reluctance to act on that right, asking Reid, "What's the use of your right to do a thing, if you know you'll get soundly whipped if you attempt it?" A few days after that conversation, Reid overheard another expression of war-weariness while riding a train through Alabama:

> "Mighty ha'd on po' Confeds. We're the unde' dogs in the fight. We're subjugated. I wouldn't fight no mo' for the stars and bars than for an old dish-rag."
>
> "Nor for the stars and stripes nuther," exclaimed his companion, and the sentiment elicited general approval.

A former Confederate soldier near Lynchburg explained to John Dennett that "his sympathies were with the Southern cause, and always would be, but there wouldn't be another war in behalf of it. The South was sick of fighting, and the North was too strong."[29]

Naturally, it was much simpler to counsel patience and moderation in theory than to put them into practice. White Southerners were angry with the Union leadership and the Northern people, and they gave vent to their emotions both in private and in public. While they did not act on their threats, simply making them was enough perhaps to alleviate feelings of powerlessness. Whitelaw Reid, who had spent the better part of a year on two trips around the South, seemed to understand how most Southerners felt:

> I do not mean that these people are nursing a new rebellion. For many years they will be the hardest people in the civilized world to persuade into insurrection. But they nurse the embers of the old one, and cherish its ashes. They are all Union men, in the sense that they submit, (since they can't help themselves) and want to make all they can out of their submission. But to talk of genuine Union sentiment, any affection for the Union, any intention to go one step further out of the old paths that led to the rebellion, than they are forced out is preposterous. They admit that they are whipped; but the honest ones make no pretense of loving the power that whipped them.[30]

Travelers to the South in the months and years immediately after the war frequently described the people they encountered as "sullen" or "bitter," still preserving their enmity toward Northerners, "as rebellious as ever."[31]

"Is There Any Peace in the Land?" asked the *Montgomery Advertiser* in late 1865. In the months since the war ended, the article explained, the Southern people had made many concessions, including acquiescing to emancipation and passing laws protecting the freedmen. Given their demonstration of good faith, the *Advertiser* argued, white Southerners had every right to ask for the same rights that Northerners had to determine who was qualified to vote. This was the crux of the white Southern argument after the war—in a sense it went back to ideals of honor and masculinity. White Southerners believed that they had demonstrated good faith, shown they were men of their word, and were thus entitled to "concessions" from the other side. These were not, the *Advertiser* charged, forthcoming, with the blame falling squarely on the shoulders of the Radicals, specifically Charles Sumner and Thaddeus Stephens. This attitude was the height of hypocrisy, for every supposed "concession" was negated by white Southern machinations like the Black Codes.[32]

Even as they adopted postures of submission, many whites chafed under them, concerned that they were making all the concessions. "We of the South accept as final the determination of the American people that the Union shall be perpetuated," sighed D. H. Hill, former general and the editor of *The Land We Love*. He merely wanted Republican "disunionists" to accept that determination as well, so that "the 'stars and stripes' will once more float over the South, as an ensign of protection and not of subjugation."[33]

The importance of retaining dignity pervaded Southern political discourse, and it contributed to white Southerners' anger toward the Radicals. They believed that they were making a good-faith effort toward political reunion and that they were not being given credit for their efforts. Rather, the Radicals continued to punish them, continued to treat them as wayward children, continued to reinforce their lowered status, all of which whites perceived as a blow to their personal and regional honor. "If they wish to control the South in any other way than by the bayonet, let them begin by showing us that respect which our relations to them as fellow-men, not to say our rights as fellow-citizens require," explained an author in *De Bow's Review*. "The ardent Southerner can forgive any injury to his property; but to scoff at his faith, or to assail his honor, is to commit an offense which blood alone can atone for." White Southerners were asking for a lot: the degree to which they seemed to be demanding peace on their own terms was shocking. The editors of the *Crescent Monthly* thought it "extraordinary" that so many Northerners, "friends as well as foes," continued to labor under "the hallucination that conquest by the sword carries conviction to the heart and that submission to the irresistible force must imply belief in the rectitude of the cause, in behalf of which the force was exerted. . . . If our convictions were so feeble as to be destroyed by the issue of war, our 'penitence' would be just as fickle and uncertain, and our allegiance would not be worth a bawbee." Honor dictated that Confederates continue some vestige of allegiance to their former cause, and Northerners should both understand and respect that need. The leniency of Presidential Reconstruction left Southern honor intact; Radical Reconstruction did not, and that was one of the reasons Southerners fought it so forcefully. Reconstruction politics were a discourse on loyalty, on honor, on respect, with race always an implicit, if often unspoken, corollary.[34]

"WE CAN'T BE KEPT ALWAYS IN OUR PRESENT FIX"

Reconstruction politics both upset and infuriated white Southerners, who responded with a combination of fear, misery, and defiance. "No people ever looked forward to a gloomier future than the noble, generous people of the South; and above all to be inflicted by *vile Yankees*," mourned David Schenck in September 1866. Nine months later, Schenck filled his diary with a litany of complaints about the military government, the Congressional Civil Rights Bill, and the Heroes of America. "Day by day witnesses the political, moral and social decline of our people under those baneful influences. . . . Our country which, by God, was designed to be the nursery of his church, has become 'a den of thieves' and Yankees, and the day of purgation will as surely succeed." Similarly, a Georgia woman feared that the "trying times" of 1867, with "one side trying to exercise Arbitrary measures & the other side strongly resisting," might give way to another war.[35]

White Southerners told outsiders like Whitelaw Reid and John Dennett that the South would never rise again against the United States. They painted a portrait of a beaten people, desiring only to be left alone to lick their wounds and rebuild. But when they wrote for each other, either in the form of private letters or in the pages of newspapers and regional publications, Southern whites took a slightly different tack. Rather than stress defeat and fear of Yankee might, moderates counseled their fellow whites to simply be patient when faced with unfair treatment and economic woes. The tone of these writings is ominous. "Now let us keep up a pleasant equanimity of mind under all circumstances and not be cast down by trifles," counseled an Alabama colonel. "We have well learned the lessons of toleration and will we not profit by it? Yes, and when we can stand on our feet, will we forget the law 'an eye for an eye?'" R. H. Maury used a similar argument to cheer up a despondent friend, assuring him that "we can't be kept always in our present fix—bound yet to get 'Top' again & then we will give the 'Villains the devil.'" Maury was confident that "trouble to the Yankees is ahead" and then when it came, white Southerners could capitalize on it, returning to their past national prominence. Race was implicit in this argument as well. Southerners wanted two related things: local control and national political power. While they might speak of only one at a time, the subtext was clear. In this respect, white Southerners demonstrated the degree to which they were unreconstructed.[36]

Whites upset by the Radicals were urged to keep their counsel and bide their time. They had endured hardships during the war and were encouraged to draw again on their reservoirs of patience and perseverance. J. C. Delavigne, writing in *De Bow's Review*, urged Southerners to just wait out the difficult times. "Who can doubt that a momentous political change is at hand?" he asked. "He who will have the patience to wait for it, the fortitude to endure his misfortunes, the courage to assert his rights, and a little patriotism, may expect a rich reward." The author of "Terribly in Earnest" gently suggested that Southerners change tactics and try to spend more time "looking out for good men and friends" in the North and less time "hunting up enemies and bad men." Such a shift could easily win over the Conservatives, and might even persuade the Radicals to be reasonable. Regardless, this author was confident that the Radicals would eventually destroy themselves. Thus, "in the meantime, it will be most dignified and most politic for the South to bear with quiet composure all the injustice, wrong and oppression which their terrible earnestness and malignant passions may hurry them on to inflict. Give them rope enough and they will surely hang themselves." Patience would pay off in the end, the author continued, for as soon as Federal troops were removed from the South, "they will become again watchful and efficient guardians and defenders of the liberty of the South. In the meantime, we must keep cool, evince the same fortitude under a temporary oppression that we exhibited throughout the war."[37]

Former Confederates believed they were being grievously wronged by Northerners, and the injustice of it weighed heavily on them. Northern Republicans and military governments added further insult to the injury of Confederate defeat. In the March 1866 edition of *De Bow's Review*, James D. B. De Bow emphasized that his journal was "in the path of reconstruction and order" but stressed that in his opinion "the battle for the South is hereafter *to be fought in the North*." The South had no say in its future; it threw itself on the mercy of its former enemies, and they responded cruelly. The result was a growing sense of bitterness and alienation among the planter class.[38]

White Southerners were largely unwilling to disavow their decisions to secede in 1861, refusing to admit that their desire for independence and the war itself had been mistakes. In the pages of *De Bow's Review*, the Honorable Charles Gayarré demanded that Southerners always maintain the legitimacy of their Confederate experience. "The North, therefore, must have the magnanimity to admit that great provocation had been given to us," he argued. "If denied, we ought still to contend for it, because it is the truth and if we were wrong in the mode of redress which we chose, we must never cease to maintain that we thought at the time that we were right."[39]

One of the greatest proponents of the legitimacy of Southern secession was Albert Taylor Bledsoe, and he filled the pages of his *Southern Review* with explanations and justifications.[40] He invoked the Hartford Convention to illustrate that talk of secession had not historically been the exclusive purview of the South, and he stressed the long-standing tensions between the sections, at times going back to the Whiskey Rebellion and the debates over the Northwest Ordinance of 1787. That territorial conflict, Bledsoe charged, set the tone for the future, for in it "the North manifested her lust of empire, her unhallowed desire of unchecked dominion; while the South aimed to preserve her independence in the Union." This pattern of Northern bullying and Southern compromise, Bledsoe asserted, was repeated throughout the antebellum years, until finally the South had enough. In "The Origin of the Late War," Bledsoe listed seven crises that contributed to "the conflict of 1861." They were the debates over first the Articles of Confederation and then the Constitution, the Revolution of 1801, the Missouri Compromise, the conflict over Nullification, the problem of the territory annexed during the Mexican War, and, finally, the Compromise of 1850. These longstanding constitutional conflicts, Bledsoe explained, precipitated the war, not anything else, meaning slavery, of course. Bledsoe was confident that the Southern position would eventually be vindicated, for "history teaches that the causes to which discontented communities have at the time attributed their dissatisfaction, have been generally determined by the calm and dispassionate judgment of posterity to be the correct ones."[41] In this desire to "win the peace" and in the rejection of slavery as a cause of secession or the war we can see the origins of the Lost Cause.

Just as ex-Confederates still maintained that they had done nothing wrong in seceding from the Union in 1861, basing this belief on constitutional justifications, so, too, did some continue to believe in the primacy of states' rights. In postwar Georgia, reporter Sidney Andrews noted that "the supremacy of the Constitution of the United States is formally acknowledged, but the common conversation of all classes asserts the supremacy of the State" and that "the worst feature of the political situation is that the secondary character of the authority of the general government is everywhere virtually asserted." Similarly, in South Carolina, Andrews found that "the common sentiment holds that man guilty of treason who prefers the United States to South Carolina." The loss of "war spirit" did not mean that ex-Confederates disavowed the war itself.[42]

Nor did it mean that Southern whites accepted Reconstruction, and particularly the Radicals, with any kind of grace. Indeed, white Southern hatred of the Radicals had an unmistakably racial cast—not only in its denigration of the Radicals themselves as inferior to Southerners but also in its abhorrence of Radical advocacy of black voting. Whites could generally cope with the fact of emancipation; they were far from happy about it, but they could construct explanations and rationalizations to make it palatable. The systems of tenancy and binding contracts and the strict social control of the Black Codes resulted in a rough approximation of the prewar racial order, with whites on top and blacks on the bottom. Black political participation threatened that stability, by granting blacks a role in what had been exclusively the purview of white men.[43]

"George Washington if he now lived would be less than a negro," a Charleston man bitterly complained, "and Gen. Lee has less political power at the polls than the negro boy who blacked his boots. It is a sad jumble!" David Schenck thought black suffrage the "most appalling of all alternatives" to Southern whites, "and what they would sacrifice everything to avert." In a rhetorical twist, he complained that white Southerners were "living now in a vassalage as abject as Ireland," as much subjects as their slaves had once been. This feeling of being unjustly oppressed pervaded white Southern sentiments. "There seems to be no end to the oppression we are to undergo," Josiah Gorgas complained in July 1867. "We now are wholly under military government, and that imposes *blacks* as officials over us. We have negros who swear in white people & decide on their right to vote." Even more disturbing to Gorgas were the "negro" policemen in Selma and city council aldermen in Mobile. The raising of African Americans to positions of political power heaped further insult on the disgrace of military Reconstruction. As one Virginian wrote regarding black office-holding, "If we could be spared this, we might well be content with the military rule of Schofield."[44]

A Mississippi writer expressed the commonly held view that Northerners did not really care about black suffrage but were only using it as a tool to further humiliate the South. He described black equality, or perhaps more accurately, the advocacy of it, as "a mixture of greeneyed envy and diabolical hatred of everything Southern" and referred to the federal government as "patriarchal and beneficent to the negro, but an engine of oppression to you and yours." Here again is that sense of victimization, that feeling that Southern whites were being unfairly oppressed and would therefore be justified in fighting back.

As there had been on every issue during Reconstruction, there were white Southerners whose pragmatism outweighed any emotional reactions they might have had toward black office-holding and voting. The same Virginian who had believed he could stand military oversight as long as there were no black office-holders thought black voting better than having Yankees taking control: "If the Radicals have their way with the Negro, there is great trouble ahead, but somehow we (I the writer) have more faith in the Negro than in the Yankee—he is very 'aristocratic' in his feelings and actions while the latter is a 'leveler.'" Perhaps he felt that Southern whites, who had historically believed that they had a special understanding of and even a sort of kinship with their slaves, could exert some subtle influence on the freedmen. Not surprisingly, *De Bow's Review* took by far the most utilitarian approach.

The author of "The South" urged his fellow Southerners to accept the fact that the freedmen were being granted some limited equality. Racial harmony was absolutely necessary for Southern economic progress. Too, "the first thing the South should do is not to despair. Many whites refuse to register. This is to abandon their country, and invite the worst." A better course of action would be for whites to act kindly toward blacks, for "if the South wishes to get rid of the Radicals in the Federal capital, let them become the benefactors of the blacks and the Radicals will disappear from the stage." Then, presumably, white supremacy could be reestablished unhindered.[45]

The imposition of military rule also fostered Southern resentment. "'Tis not the Union our fathers gave," charged Rosalie Miller Murphy in her poem "The Broken Idol." She continued:

Together held by force alone;
We're buried in *coercion's* grave
The glorious rights our sires won.
United pride can we e'er feel more?
Union—freedom—are now vain words of yore!

De Bow's Review took a more legalistic approach to the use of force in the South, arguing that the laws dividing the South into military districts were manifestly unconstitutional. Indeed, by granting political rights to the freedmen, Congress was itself guilty of "treason to the white race which includes treason to the white man's country, and is the greater crime." The Southern states were immediately placed under constitutional authority at the end of the war, and thus it was unjust to act as if they were still in rebellion two years later and place them under military authority. Congress, in so doing, was perpetuating a fraud upon the American people and was allowing itself to become nothing more than a Republican-controlled, illegitimate "mob."[46]

Ex-Confederates' visceral hatred of the Radicals echoed their feelings toward the Yankee invaders during the war. An 1868 article in the *Southern Home Journal* referred to the Radical Congress as a "convention of buzzards . . . destroying every political right of the people that they may glut themselves, like horrid harpies or ravenous carrion-crows, upon the bodies of the slain." The *Macon (Georgia) Telegraph* took aim not only at the Radicals but at Southern Republican scalawags, warning that "Southern-born men who have deserted their country in the hour of her distress, and joined the Radicals of the North to erect Negro governments over the Southern States, complain and whine no little about the hard names that are applied to them. As well might a man who has stolen a horse complain of being called a thief."

Just as Confederates had hearkened back to the rhetoric of the American Revolution in referring to Union soldiers as Hessians, so Reconstruction era whites turned Republicans into the Jacobins of Revolutionary France.[47]

White Southerners constantly charged the Radicals with hypocrisy, complaining that, in D. H. Hill's words, "'Twas hatred of the South and not love of the Union which made them champions of the old flag." Another former Confederate general, Jubal Early, warned in the preface to his memoirs, "The people of the United States will find that, under the pretence of 'saving the life of the nation, and upholding the old flag' they have surrendered their own liberties into the hands of that worst of all tyrants, a body of senseless fanatics." "If they would frankly say they intend to keep us down," Frances Butler Leigh complained in 1867 from her Georgia plantation, "it would be fairer than making a pretence of readmitting us to equal rights, and then trumping up stories of violence to give a show of justice to treating us as the conquered foes of the most despotic Government on earth, and by exciting the negroes to every kind of insolent lawlessness, to goad the people into acts of rebellion and resistance."[48]

Leigh's portrait of white Southerners wounded by mistreatment at the hands of an unfair federal government neatly illuminates the conflicts that would endure well beyond Reconstruction. Former Confederates wanted a return to the political status quo—whites on top, blacks on the bottom. The willingness of so many people to return to the bosom of the Union need not be seen as evidence of weak Confederate (or white Southern) nationalism; rather, it appears as a self-conscious attempt to manipulate Northerners. What Southern whites wanted after the war was over was local control—how they got that control mattered less. But the bitterness, anger, and duplicity would have lasting consequences.

Interlude

To Receive the Oath and Brand of Slave

he issue of whether to take an oath of allegiance to the United States struck at the heart of questions of self and nation in the Reconstruction South. It was an intrinsically personal decision, though one with powerful collective implications. Historians of Presidential Reconstruction in the South have tended to discuss the loyalty oath in a purely political context, as a little-debated precursor to white Southerners' voting in the elections for state constitutional conventions. But for ex-Confederates, the oath struck at the heart of their sense of themselves, for to take the oath was to explicitly and publicly sever oneself from the Confederacy and unite oneself with the Union. Although some white Southerners found it easy to take the oath, because they had been Unionists, for example, for most people the oath was more problematic. Many people who took the oath had been loyal to the Confederacy. For them the oath was an example of postwar pragmatism and calculation. If being a Confederate encompassed both a political attachment to the Confederate state (its government) and a sentimental attachment to the idea of a distinctive Southern nation or people, being a postwar Southerner meant dividing oneself into a political American and a sentimental Southerner. As they discussed the oath, white Southerners also revealed the highly gendered nature of their recreated identity, linking loyalty to ideals of honor and masculinity.[1]

Few Southerners seemed as upset by the 1865 loyalty oath as Henry Brown Richardson, a Maine native who had married a Southern woman and joined the Confederate army. In a long letter to his parents in Maine, Richardson described having "sold myself for a very inferior 'mess of pottage.'" After being paroled in Virginia, Richardson was making his way home to Louisiana after the surrender when he was taken prisoner in Tennessee and kept with several hundred men in Chattanooga. They were lined up in groups of fifty while someone from the Provost Marshal's office read the oath and told the men that taking it was entirely voluntary. Richardson and two other men refused; they were imprisoned again. "My companions were re-proaching me for having got them into a bad position, and persuading me that it was 'no use for *one man* to try to be the Confederacy,'" he explained sadly, "and so taking it all together, after a day and a half of that life, having another opportunity, I went out and worshipped the great golden image, and became a prostitute—and that is what is called taking the oath volun-tarily."[2]

Richardson thought that the Yankee tendency to forget promises made his fellow Southerners more willing to swear false oaths, but he held himself to a higher moral standard. Although the oath of allegiance to the United States could not "change the desires and emotions" of his heart, Richard-son had no intention of "disregarding it." In fact, he told his parents that his greatest objection to taking it in the first place was "that I felt that so long as a Confederate flag was flying anywhere there might be a Confederate Gov-ernment, and I could not while it existed violate my allegiance to it." "Of course," Brown added ruefully, "when there was no longer any Confeder-ate Gov't that objection ceased to exist." Despite his clear reasons for taking the oath, reasons that were shared by thousands of other ex-Confederates, Richardson could not contain his self-loathing at his perceived betrayal of the Confederate cause: "I cannot make myself appear as having played other than a very weak part or as anything better than a prostitute: I did that under the pressure of circumstances, which can never be undone and for which there is no more excuse than for a woman who loses her chastity—in fact not so much:—rape does occur sometimes, a forced oath, never."[3]

Richardson's narrative of his own oath-taking illuminates several of the ways in which the issue of the oath can be understood. He was concerned, first and foremost, with his own honor, or rather the dishonor he felt at having taken the oath.[4] He took his allegiances seriously, for he could only bring himself to take the oath when the Confederate government had ceased to exist. That the demise of the Confederate government did not fully re-lease Richardson from his sense of obligation is obvious. The other issue that Richardson raised is that of false oaths: he was unwilling to take one but believed that he was surrounded by people, North and South, who were willing. In this he was largely correct. Oath-takers often claimed that they owed their enemies nothing more than lip service. During the war, the Con-federates who found themselves taking an oath of loyalty to the Union con-soled themselves by arguing that a coerced oath was not binding. Such argu-ments continued into Reconstruction, with white Southerners keeping their hearts true, even as they professed loyalty to their former enemies. One woman proclaimed that "she would take it as a mere form forced upon her and therefore not binding on her conscience, and that she would break it as readily as she would take it."[5] Traveling journalist Sidney Andrews overheard two "typical" residents of Albany, Georgia, discussing their fates: "I have my pardon in my pocket, and have taken the oath three times," said one of them, "but I'll be d—d if I ain't as big a Rebel as I ever was!" His companion agreed, adding proudly, "That's jest my case, only I ha'n't got my pardon yet."[6]

Not all people took their oaths so lightly. Some were concerned with how false oaths might be perceived by outsiders. "Professions contrary to our faith can only degrade us in our eyes and the eyes of the world," complained an article in the *Montgomery Advertiser*. A Presbyterian minister in Georgia shared that conviction, explaining that he had not yet been able to persuade himself "to receive the oath & brand of slave from the U.S. government." He justified his refusal on biblical grounds, believing that God counseled only submission to conquerors, not sworn allegiances. A Confederate prisoner of war chose not to take the oath because he did "not at this time disire to become a citizen of the U. S." While he reserved the right to change his mind at a later date, he thought it "a wicked game to force me to take an Oath which I intend to invalidate by hereafter removing from the country."[7]

More than arguing that their oaths had been coerced, ex-Confederates took a pragmatic, almost positive approach to the oath questions. Oath-taking was about politics and political identity more than anything else. White Southerners realized that the way to regain control over their region, and by extension over African Americans, was to regain the rights of political citizenship in the United States. Consequently, many white Southerners, in both public and private writings, urged men to take the oath, regardless of the convictions in their hearts. In this construction, one could take the oath and still hate Yankees. The two were not mutually exclusive. Taking the oath was a necessary evil on the road to rebuilding.

Newspapers also appealed to pragmatism when they encouraged their readers to take the oath, even as they also condemned it as unfair and disrespectful toward the South. Indeed, the two contrasting strains of resentment and accommodation ran throughout Reconstruction writings. Authors and editors strove to preserve their Southern identity even as they sought to reestablish themselves on equal footing with the rest of the United States. The *Montgomery Advertiser*, which had frequently complained about the oath, urged its readers to demonstrate their enduring respect for law and order. Thus, "the quiet and orderly return of the people to their domestic pursuits and enterprises with such cheerful alacrity" would illustrate that Southerners could "govern themselves in peace as in war, that they can work as well as fight, that they are possessed of all the essential elements that go to make up a renowned and progressive people." Taking the oath went hand in hand with this demonstration of good faith and good citizenship. Too, if white men wanted to vote in state elections, they needed to take the oath. And white Democrats were needed as voters in order to counter the Republicans and the freedmen. In an October article titled "Qualifications for Voting," the *Advertiser* assured its readers that the oath "is one that can now be taken cheerfully." Even the usually unreconstructed *Southern Opinion* called upon its readers in 1867 to perform their duty "however disagreeable" and register to vote. That was the only way to save the South from "self-degradation."[8]

Reuban E. Wilson, a Confederate soldier, vacillated between defiance and pragmatism. Wilson had been wounded in the final days of fighting around Petersburg, necessitating the amputation of his left leg, and he was subsequently placed in a Union prisoner-of-war camp. Despite being "surrounded with Yanks," Wilson assured his aunt that he was "just as true, firm, and determined as ever," with the "fire of revenge" still burning in his eyes. Yet, even as he described his blood boiling at being a Yankee prisoner, Wilson expressed his belief that "it is the duty now of all good men to take the oath of allegiance to the U. S." His reasons were eminently practical: first, Confederates no longer had a national government to owe their loyalty; second, their state governments had been disbanded; and, finally, without taking the oath, men would not be allowed to vote, "and we should try to send good men to the legislature or convention. By sending good men to the legislature we will be able to elect good new senators to go to Washington[;] if every southern state will send two good senators we will with the aid of the democratic party (which is bound to be very strong) of the north we will be able to check the republican party in their wild scheme." Wilson was never able to take his own advice and put his plan into action, however, for shortly after his release, he was accused of murdering Unionist citizens in North Carolina and was sent to prison.[9]

Although the vast majority of Confederates decided for themselves whether they would take the oath, several thousand fell under the categories exempted from the act. These Southerners, whether because of the amount of property they owned or their roles in the Confederate government or military, were forced to apply for individual pardons. Their fate was out of their hands, and they initially had reason to suspect that Johnson would not be well-disposed toward them. Southerners had nothing to worry

Pardon granted to Mary Gilliam. Wealthy former Confederates needed a special pardon in order to vote and regain property. Women were not exempt from the requirement to swear an oath of allegiance. Gilliam Family Papers (#3593), Special Collections, University of Virginia Library.

about. By the end of September 1865, the Radicals had so infuriated Johnson that he was granting pardons liberally, at the rate of 100 per day. Altogether he granted some 13,500 pardons out of 15,000 requested, most under the thirteenth exception, that having to do with property.[10]

Officials in the Confederate government and military provided a thornier problem. Presumably they were more committed to the Confederate cause than was the average planter. Too, as formerly staunch Confederates took the oath and received pardons, Southern Unionists grew resentful. They had suffered during the war for their convictions and had expected to reap the benefits of their loyalty after the war.[11] They were not entirely wrong in their charges of hypocrisy toward Confederate officials who requested (and received) amnesty. Josiah Gorgas unhappily took the oath in August 1865 and was finally "amnestied" by a proclamation of Johnson's in September 1867. Upon receiving the news of his pardon, Gorgas still expressed hope that the battle between Johnson and the Radicals would continue "until utter chaos is produced, when we may emerge with our Confederacy as we struggled for it." Stephen Mallory, the Confederate secretary of the navy, had few qualms about trying to secure a pardon, a willingness perhaps explained by the fact that he was in prison. From his cell, Mallory sent detailed instructions to his wife about securing his pardon. He firmly believed that, "properly presented," his case would "have the favorable consideration of President Johnson," and he urged his wife to stress the moderation of his prewar congressional voting record. He had originally opposed secession, he reminded her, and had "always hoped for a means to avert war." Now he accepted emancipation and was "anxious to take the oath of allegiance" and do what he could to "evoke order from chaos & in good faith, to aid the administration to harmonize the country."[12]

Henry Richardson's choice of metaphors—prostitution and chastity—shows the extent to which questions of oath-taking and identity were bound up with issues of gender and masculinity. Ex-Confederates used the idea of a soldier's loyalty to argue for citizenship rights and home rule. Repeatedly, white Southerners (and Northern visitors) claimed that the most trustworthy Southerners were former soldiers. A soldier's word was his bond, automatically honorable, and thus when he pledged his loyalty to the United States, he could be trusted and should therefore be accorded all his rights as a citizen. "Trust without fear those men who have fought to the last for the cause which they loved, and which claimed their fidelity," a Louisianian advised President Johnson. "Trust those rebels who come to you with clean hands, and even after having deposited the keys of their loyalty on the dead body of the Southern Confederacy." A Northern-born steamboat pilot in Louisiana thought that the men around him who had fought in the Confederate army were "honest in their professions of loyalty and wish[ed] for an enduring peace," even while he believed that the "great body" of the people were "as rebellious as they were two years since." Over the course of his travels, Sidney Andrews came to much the same conclusion, finding that "the men who did the fighting are everywhere the men who most readily accept the issues of the war." These former soldiers, and especially the former privates, mourned the defeat of their armies and were "fond of showing that for this little mistake or that little accident, or that other little blunder, the Confederacy would now be a great nation," but they took their defeat "in good faith and with a determination to do their duties hereafter as ordinary citizens."[13]

Much of the Southern rhetoric of postwar reconciliation bore a particularly gendered cast. "The great danger now at the South is that the manhood, the independence, the integrity of the people will be destroyed," worried D. H. Hill in 1868, and his concern was shared by countless other Southern whites.[14] People across the spectrum of opinion turned to the language of manhood and honor to justify their positions. Advocates of resistance to Northern "oppression" and proponents of swift reconciliation each did so by appealing to persistent regional notions of duty and manliness, couching their appeals in language that was sure to resonate. They were careful always to argue against the notion, all too prevalent, that the South had somehow been "unmanned" by its defeat, that Northerners were more masculine and therefore superior to Southerners. These definitions of masculinity, or of the manly path, seemed to shift with time and situation. In the early months of Reconstruction, white Southerners still thought that they could control the process, thought that by adopting a posture of submission to Northern rule that they would quickly be brought back into the Federal union and put in charge of their own affairs. When that didn't happen, white Southerners expressed anger and bitterness over their treatment, believing themselves to be dishonored.

To call something "manly" in the South was to bestow a compliment of the highest order. A female reader praised the angrily unreconstructed *Southern Opinion* for its "fearless and manly tone," adding that she was gratified to see "that there yet remains some men in the South . . . who dare to express their true sentiments, regardless of the consequences. Would that there were more such men and more such papers!" A later issue noted how many ladies enjoyed the paper, adding that they "in this gallant region, make and rule the higher and purer popular sentiment, as well in politicks as in everything else, and they are the first to discover and condemn any lapse from what is manly, honorable, and right." That same edition praised "Wade Hampton's Manly Speech" made before the South Carolina Convention of Conservatives. Hampton's oration, the *Southern Opinion* asserted, "embodies the true spirit that should fill all high-minded men, under whatever circumstances of duress and oppression. . . . We commend it to the earnest consideration of the weak-kneed and faint-hearted among us, in the hope that they may be inspired with a new manhood by its vigorous patriotism." Josiah Gorgas was similarly inspired by Georgia senator Benjamin H. Hill's writings condemning Radical Reconstruction. "The manly 'notes on the situation' of Mr. Hill of GA. attract attention at the South, where people arc so timid that a little manliness is refreshing," Gorgas noted approvingly during the summer of 1867. In all of these instances, manliness was equated with standing up to the Northern Radicals, with taking a stand in favor of Southern rights.[15]

The question of taking the oath or asking for a pardon struck at the heart of Confederate nationalism. By repudiating loyalty to the Confederacy and swearing allegiance to the United States, Southern whites made a public declaration about their political identity. They recognized that their state, the Confederate States of America, had ceased to exist and that, like it or not, they were part of the Union. But the degree to which most whites agonized over taking this step shows that they still cared about the Confederacy. Many people split their identity after the war: politically, they could become Americans, but emotionally, in their "true hearts," they continued to remain apart, protecting their memories. Some made that division more neatly than others.

Many Southern men, like Reuban Wilson, found the manhood of conciliation deeply unsatisfying. The men who turned to violence against African Americans through individual attacks, riots, or the more organized forum of the Ku Klux Klan believed they were acting out of deep frustration with their treatment as men. The establishment of Republican state governments in 1868 seemed to show that conciliation had failed: White men had taken their oaths, given their word, and felt they had received nothing in return. Blacks in positions of political power represented an affront to Southern white manhood. It appeared that if white men wanted to regain local control over politics and race relations, they would have to fight for it. Fight they did, sparking a veritable orgy of racial-political violence. And when the dust settled in the 1870s, white Southerners had succeeded in defining for themselves their new place in the Union: as political citizens who maintained both Southern distinctiveness and white supremacy virtually unimpeded for generations.

6 To Restore Their Broken Fortunes

Reconstructing White Southern Identity

During the summer of 1865, a piece in the *Montgomery Advertiser* drew a distinction between "Young America," the "fast young man of the glorious United States," and the new "Young South," born in 1860 or 1861, "very hopeful and full of life." Young America was somewhat of a rake—he could be a dashing filibusterer or "an unmitigated vagabond and villain"—and a bit of a dandy as well. Before the war, Young South had been an upper-class man of leisure with gloved hands and stylish clothes. But he lost his fortune in the war and could now be spied on top of his wagon "with his ungloved hand holding the reins made of Southern cotton, on his head a Southern palmetto, going to market to sell his 'country produce.'" The war had strengthened and changed Young South, leaving him only the "peerless, priceless spirit of a noble manhood." His new values of hard work and determination made him a "prize of a husband" for any Southern girl. Young South was to provide the *Advertiser*'s readers, specifically former Confederate soldiers, with a model for recreating themselves and their nation: he was a man with new "faith in the dignity of labor," whose newfound "self-reliance" rescued him from the idle dissipation that would have been his lot before the war. But Young South was not to be a replica of Young America. Southern men were supposed to be better than that: "He has learnt, at last, that 'Young America' will be unpopular and unprofitable in this country now; and from the constraints which go to make up the character of Young South, we may look for a society of staunch, strong, reliable men who will be capable of bearing this section of country on to honor and prosperity. *Vive la* YOUNG SOUTH!" In essence, Young South represented the continuation of the Confederate notion of a virtuous and hardworking Southern people. Within months of the end of the war, the destruction of slavery was to be perceived as a blessing in disguise, for it allowed hard work to be treated with a new respect and dignity.[1]

"Young America and Young South" neatly encapsulates one strain of

Southern thinking about labor, patience and masculinity during the early years of Reconstruction. White Southerners told themselves repeatedly to put the past behind them and look to the future, even if that meant abandoning their self-image as an agrarian people (and certainly as a master class). In a sense, the rhetoric of economic rebuilding, which was often tinged with calls for new industrialization, worked in tandem with demands for local political control. Both were concerned with strengthening the South's position within the Union as a whole; both were concerned with preserving Southern distinctiveness, if not independence.

"WE MUST BUILD UP ANEW"

Once the initial shock of emancipation wore off, white Southerners were faced with the question of how to rebuild their economic lives. About 10,000 of them decided that they could not bear to live in the South any longer and left the region entirely, hoping to rebuild in regions where slavery was still tolerated. Exponentially more ex-Confederates dreamed of leaving, using the idea of emigration as an emotional safety valve for those who stayed behind. It gave them the illusion of control, the possibility of escape from their troubled situation.[2] But in the end, few Southern whites were either willing or able to leave, and so the majority were faced with the vexing questions of how to rebuild their lives and their region. White Southerners confronted with economic ruin, the loss of their capital in slaves, and the specter of politics being controlled by their twin bogeymen—Republicans and freedmen—could easily fall into depression. Too, Southern white men's identity had long been bound up in their sense of themselves as chivalrous and fierce fighting men, a self-image dashed with the loss of the war. Add depression to a culture that, because of slavery, had long devalued both agricultural and industrial labor, and it appeared that the South might never be able to lift itself out of its economic and spiritual doldrums.[3]

Recognizing this, white Southerners both publicly and privately exhorted their fellow countrymen to get to work rebuilding their region. They put aside politics for the time being, adopting the attitude that material and economic strength would eventually lead to a reestablishment of political power. Borrowing language from wartime cries to "Cheer Up and Work," white Southerners redefined their notions of manhood to include hard physical labor. By rebuilding Southern agriculture and developing industry at home they would show the world that they were a worthy people—virtuous and hardworking. If they could not prove their strength through national independence, they could do it by making their region even stronger than the North. James D. B. De Bow traveled around the South in late 1865 and described his findings in the February 1866 issue of his *Review*. With great pride he reported that "everywhere we found the people rallying from their recent discomfiture and taking hold with true masculine grip of whatever might offer to restore their broken fortunes, and a spirit of enterprise was waking up in quarters which were least expected." De Bow was most pleased to see that men who had been born to lives of luxury were now working uncomplainingly at hard physical labor: "There were few repinings. Brave and true men never waste time over the inevitable and the irretrievable." The message was clear. The best way to be a "true" Southern man was to put misery, resentments, and depression aside, and shoulder the burdens of rebuilding without complaint or nostalgia.[4]

"My old friends in Virginia are despondent & hopeless as to the future of this country," wrote one gentleman to another in January 1866. "Get rid of this feeling—a brighter day never dawned upon a people than is now breaking. . . . To believe that a country so gifted by nature with soil, climate, mineral wealth, & manufacturing facilities is to lay wasted & go to ruin is the worst reflection that can be posed upon its people." His solution was to put the population to work outside in the fields and mines. Commodore Samuel Barron's decision to return to Virginia, purchase a farm, and undertake the agricultural life met with great approval from a friend in Washington, who was "glad to hear you are willing to take hold of things and make the best of them. You may rely upon it that it is the only cause for our southern friends." A North Carolina woman made a similar point when consoling a friend: "The only encouraging thing I see in the present prospects of the South, [is] that her young men and women are so willing to *work*. There is always hope while we see patience and industry, all energy is not yet paralyzed and is not the *South* ours still?"[5]

Part of this struggle to rebuild the South necessitated letting go of political questions for the time being. Southern journals, especially *De Bow's Review*, *The Land We Love*, and, to a lesser extent (because it was less overtly concerned with politics and regional identity), the *Southern Cultivator*, frequently urged their readers to express their love for the South through labor. Their postwar sense of regional identity was bound up with questions of economic prosperity and self-sufficiency. Perhaps, too, Southern whites were biding their time: rebuilding on many fronts and rejecting dependency took many forms. A New Orleans man offered advice to a young Floridian in reduced circumstances, counseling him to go out and make his fortune, as his ancestors once had done. He thought it best to put aside the political struggle for the moment "and in the meantime work at something that will contribute to restore our material prosperity." The future promised to be a calm one, a "future, we, old and young must address ourselves to improve by labor, economy, and clear consciences." There was no point in struggling against the Radicals, not until white Southerners had the material resources to back up their threats and challenges. An editorial in *De Bow's Review* took the same approach, charging that "it is clearly in vain, now, for the Southern people to discuss political affairs." To struggle was not only futile but undignified. Yet white Southerners were not without some resources on which to draw, for they possessed "a power more potent than any and all political combinations." In the South's as yet undeveloped natural resources, rebuilt farms, factories, railroads, and developing "material wealth" lay "the power of political rehabilitation and herein *alone*." And it would not do to give up before the work was done, for "if we falter or quit the field, our subjugation below our former bondsmen is complete." This fear of subjugation, too, played a role, for whites wanted to show that they were not dependent on the freedmen to survive and prosper.[6]

An assessment of the South's "Condition and Prospects" offered by the *Southern Field and Fireside* drew much the same conclusion. Rather than lament the destruction of the slave system, this author argued that in fact the slave system was so inefficient that only the South with its abundant natural resources could have prospered under it. Given that the South was better off without slavery, "it is now not only the interest, but the imperative duty, of every true hearted Southerner, to put his hand to the plough, the axe, or whatever tool Providence may place in his path." To some extent, this argument was sour grapes—white Southerners would not have fought so fiercely to protect something that they could so easily do without—but it also demonstrated an element of flexibility or realism. Slavery was gone, and wishing could not bring it back. Former Confederates who had not lost all faith in God after the defeat seized on the idea that slavery had been a sin—not for its keeping of other humans in bondage, but because it was wasteful and destructive of the land. Thus "Bently," a Jasper County, Georgia, farmer suggested obliquely in the *Southern Cultivator*, "We must build up anew, and in such a different manner as, avoiding the unfortunate error of the past." Recognition that slavery was an evil did not translate into any sort of support of sympathy for the freedmen. Southern ideologues were talking about white—not black—labor.[7]

In the first issue of his magazine *The Land We Love*, editor and former Confedcrate general D. H. Hill argued that one of the reasons the Confederacy lost the Civil War was that its people had placed too great an emphasis on the production of statesmen rather than on industry. The antebellum North trained its young men in practical things, with an eye toward labor, productivity, and wealth, whereas in the South the focus was on classical training and "political preeminence." The very gentlemanly qualities that Southern whites had claimed made them superior to Northerners before and during the war now seemed to be impediments. White Southerners, if they wanted to re-achieve national prominence, needed to emulate the North's practicality. In an early expression of the Gilded Age "New South creed" of industrial development, Hill called on Southern men to learn to be useful, to develop agriculture, mining, and industry. Writing exactly one year after the war ended, Hill was pleased to see that the "highborn" were working with their hands, and he wanted the mechanical arts to be legitimated as school curricula. After all, Hill reasoned, "will political economy be as valuable to an impoverished people as knowledge of household economy? Will the figurative digging of Greek and Latin roots aid us in extracting the real articles from our neglected fields?"[8]

Hill was joined in these calls by other prominent Southerners, including Alexander H. H. Stuart and General John Tyler Morgan. In an 1866 speech to the Washington and Jefferson literary societies at the University of Virginia, Stuart told his audience that they had a great responsibility before them. It was up to this new generation to rebuild the defeated South, to open up new sources of wealth through mining, manufacturing, and the development of natural resources, to extend canals and railroads throughout the region. "In this peaceful field," Stuart told the young scholars, "you can achieve victories more glorious than those of war." General Morgan had similar advice for the 1868 graduating class of the Virginia Military Institute. He, too, stressed that these young men would have to take charge of the work of restoring the South, but he took a slightly more discordant tack, calling on them always to be mindful of their heritage. "Make no dishonorable truce with the men who continue to malign your country. Make no base alliance with those who assail her, that you may gain places or emoluments by the betrayal of your natural allegiance." Perhaps the difference in tone reflected differences in the political situation of the day. The 1868 graduates were clearly being warned away from voting Republican.[9]

By far the greatest booster of Southern industrial development was *De Bow's Review*, under the direction of both its original editor, James D. B. De Bow, and his successors, R. G. Barnwell and Edwin Q. Bell.[10] During Reconstruction, *De Bow's Review* walked a fine line between pro-Southern proclamations and calls for regional harmony and Northern investment, divergent positions unified by the paper's overarching procommercial ideology. In articles like "The New Era of Southern Manufactures" and "Manufactures—The South's True Remedy," its contributors argued that the South, in order to maintain her own independent and distinct character, actually needed to be more like the North. By not developing its own industrial capabilities and processing its resources and raw materials at home, the South had made a colossal blunder for which it paid with its independence. "The South will lose the most compensatory lesson of the war from which she has just emerged," warned one writer, "if she does not unlearn and discard the theory which once governed her policy, that she controlled her own prosperity in her control of cotton." Indeed, Governor Robert M. Patton of Alabama went so far as to ask white Southerners to refrain from even vacationing in the North at spots like Cape May and Saratoga, for the money spent in Northern resorts enriched only "the New England nabobs, whose whole object seems to be, to tax the cotton-planter and his hired freedmen in such a way as to degrade them to a condition worse and more intolerable than that of hewers of wood and drawers of water." It was the old argument recast: just as before the war secessionists had claimed that Northerners wanted to make slaves of them, so now were white men to be reduced to near-slaves.[11]

Regardless of whether they advocated industrial or agricultural developments, Southern boosters were faced with the same problem: how to inspire whites defeated and demoralized by the war to work hard to rebuild their region. No reader was immune from published encouragements to hard work, not even children. An article titled "Seeking a Situation," in the *Southern Boys and Girls Monthly*, tried to teach children the importance of working hard in school and preparing for a life of honest labor. "In these 'times which try men's souls,'" the piece explained, "how many there are in our fair Southern land, that were raised in affluence, who are now earnestly seeking situations, where they may, by honest industry, obtain the means of supporting life." These children's older brothers were subject to even stronger advocacy. "Time, Faith, Energy. Let these talismanic words be the motto of our young men, and we need not then despair of the fortunes of the South, nor of the welfare of this great Republic, one and indissoluble," proclaimed an editorial in *Scott's Monthly*, also aimed at lifting the spirits, and thus the productivity, of its Southern readers.[12]

During the war, Confederates had wanted to see and present themselves as a virtuous, disciplined, and hardworking people, using this image (with varying degrees of success) to spur on self-sacrificing dedication to the cause. After the war, white Southerners continued to employ similar rhetoric, praising their fellow-citizens' strength in facing adversity, the better to outlast the trials of emancipation and Reconstruction. An essay by George Fitzhugh in *De Bow's Review* asked, "Shall the Spartan Virtues of the South Survive the War?" One author argued that surviving the war had actually improved Southern whites' character, rendering "them less selfish, and according to their means, more ready to aid and assist each other." A Hanover, Virginia, man was pleased to report that "since the necessity has arisen many hands that once were soft & white are now hard & rough with daily toil & yet they are uncomplaining & ask only to be employed."[13] "Adversity is a stern school," wrote a South Carolina professor, but, he continued, "it is the gymnasium of great souls; and the awful calamities which have befallen the South may prove in the end to have been only the discipline of Providence to purify and consolidate its character, and to make it, as hitherto the ornament, so now and hereafter the support of a great nation."[14] This religious imagery clearly evoked memories of wartime sermons. White Southerners, loathe to believe that secession and the war had been a mistake, constructed a fatalistic worldview in which God had a plan for them.

Even as they praised white Southerners for being hardworking, authors expressed concern about those men who were either unwilling or unable to join in the work of rebuilding. Those considered unable, often because of the trauma of war, were to be given sympathy and charity. Those who shirked were not treated so gently. William Lee Alexander, who had moved to Texas after the war ended, had a constructive suggestion for "those poor Southern young men" who were seeking gainful employment, and he urged his aunt to tell them that there were great opportunities in Texas. He had only scorn for those who cried "'no work,'" for "we have room out here for several millions of working men. Any kind of honest labor is better than loafing or living on others. One is no man if he will idle away his life because he can't find the particular work that most pleases his mind & body." The *Field and Fireside* warned against negativity: "Seeing a knot of careless and unsuspecting young men at the street corner, the miscreant easily sows sorrow among them; 'Ill weeds always grow apace,' and the poisonous shade soon kills their energies, clouds their understandings and cumbers their minds, filling them with evil doubts and surmises and rendering them the ready propagators of the evil with which they are infected." White Southerners needed to guard against such spirit-sapping thoughts, always remembering that "in this struggle, long and severe it may be, we have everything to cheer us, everything to expect; love of country, hope for the future, the desire of individual advantage."[15]

"NORTHERN CAPITALISTS MAY FEEL SAFE IN HIS HANDS"

Few Southerners could argue with the desirability of rebuilding their home region. Developing industrial capacity, urging young men to expand their professional horizons to include manual work previously thought beneath them, and even working out a system of agricultural labor utilizing free blacks could all be understood within a framework of regional Southern identity. White Southerners in the immediate postwar period struggled over how to reconstruct their identity, as well as their region. The fortunes of the two were linked in Southern minds. For white Southerners, their sense of themselves as a separate and—in their opinion—superior people relied to a great extent on their sense of the South as a vibrant, powerful region. The question was how to regain what they saw as the South's former glory, and whether that could best be achieved through defiant independence or through pragmatic reunification with the rest of the American nation. For the South to endure as a distinctive region, and, more important, to have any hope of regaining its former leadership in the American polity, it needed to strengthen itself economically. Thus, advocating modernization and development was a way to honor one's Southern and Confederate past, not challenge it. The problem was how to do it, given Southerners' lack of capital.

While the majority of Southern whites after the war wanted nothing more than to be left alone—politically, socially, and economically—and directed nothing but bitterness and scorn toward the outsiders in their midst, a significant minority took another tack. These pragmatic and commercially minded men, typified by James D. B. De Bow, argued that for the South to rebuild politically it would have to first do so economically. And, they continued, the best way to achieve this economic reconstruction was to welcome Northern investors and immigrants and use their money to make the South whole again. Those men and women who advocated immigration were not abandoning the persistent ideal of a distinctive South; rather, they argued that by fostering industrial and agricultural development they were honoring their Confederate past. Their efforts to encourage Northern and European immigration and investment operated within an explicitly pro-Southern ideological framework. Too, their advocacy had clear racial overtones: the immigrants were to be white. This would have the dual effect of both lessening the planters' economic reliance on the freedmen and, even more important, shifting the balance of population between freedmen and whites to a more decisive white majority, thus paving the way for white political and social control. Outsiders would not exploit the South, the advocates assured their friends and neighbors. Instead, white Southerners would use Northern and European labor and knowledge to "conquer the conquerors" and once again achieve Southern regional and racial superiority. In their explanations and promotional literature, the immigration advocates revealed the emerging contours of a more open, more flexible Southern identity.

As the Union army set up its postwar military administration and as Northerners either remained in or moved to the region, opportunities arose for Southerners to work for their "late enemies." Those Southern men and women who chose to work with and for Yankees often did so reluctantly, concerned that their actions might be construed as an abandonment of their Southern sympathies. Lewis Blackford, a Lynchburg, Virginia, native, provides an example of this internal struggle to be a "good Southerner." A member of the Confederate Engineer Corps during the war, Blackford was offered a job in the Union Corps in May 1865. After some soul-searching he decided to take it, influenced no doubt by his long-standing romance with a Northern girl. Blackford was concerned, however, that by taking a paycheck from his former enemies he might somehow dishonor himself and his family. His family, with the exception of one brother, supported his decision, understanding that Blackford acted out of economic necessity. His brother Charles was "truly glad" to hear that Lewis had taken the job, telling their mother that "in this step Lewis was perfectly right—He needs employment & money & because the Fed. Govt. pays him he should not refuse to work." Charles also assured the doubting Lewis that "it is far more honourable to go to work whoever may pay for it, than to eat other men's bread in idleness—and I admire the determination you showed in at once going to work & incurring [sic] the odium which may be expressed by a very . . . foolish people, all of whom are actuated more from jealousy than any other motive." Charles was quick to add that their friends and neighbors in Lynchburg shared the family's opinion, telling Lewis that, so far as he had heard, "it has been that [you] are perfectly right. All the business men here think so and so do your friends at the university." Blackford's Union paycheck, uniform, and sweetheart—in short his public acquiescence to Northern rule—did not prevent him from complaining privately about Northerners and condemning the "Yankee character" as "utterly wicked" and depraved. He found no contradiction in hating Yankees even as he worked for them. They were a means to an end. And when his romance with the Northern woman ended, he had no reason to continue to associate with Northerners, and hoped instead to emigrate.[16]

Lewis Blackford was far from the only Southerner to make a bargain with himself and accept employment from Northerners, even while professing his loyalty to the South. Charles F. Barnes, who had been a member of the Confederate Signal Corps, found himself in Charlotte, North Carolina, at the end of the war, stranded with only four dollars to his name. The Union telegraph superintendent offered Barnes a position, which he "was constrained to accept." He found himself stationed in Wilmington, working in the "telegraphic fraternity" with one other Southerner and three Yankees. Barnes defended his decision by assuring his mother, "I made no pretense of concealing my views or former standing in relation to the U. S. Govt. & though I never mention it unless questioned, never deny that I was a *rebel*, incorrigible, & as far as sentiments are concerned, am so yet. I find I am more respected than those who have suddenly become so intensely Union & loyal."[17]

"You will doubtless be equally surprised with the rest of my friends, that I should have ever been induced to make 'Loyal East Tenn.' my home," wrote James Comfort to his brother in March 1866. Although he had spent the war years teaching in Princeton, New Jersey, Comfort still considered himself a supporter of the Confederate cause and thus felt the need to explain his somewhat peculiar circumstances. "I was laughed at, exclaimed at & remonstrated with in Va.," he continued, "but it proved to no purpose, for here I am, & have no reason, as yet, to regret my course. To East Tennessee I have come, & am living in a loyal East Tennesseean's house, teaching his loyal children—Very strange! but the only explanation I can give of it, is that my long sojourn in Yankeedom has so blunted my sensibilities, that I can swallow any amount of Loyalty without a wry face—." Comfort had grown fond of his East Tennessee pupils while they had attended his school in New Jersey, and the boys and their parents had persuaded Comfort to move to Knoxville. Comfort defended himself against charges of disloyalty by stressing the "moderate" Unionism of his employers, who, "since the war, have pursued a course of conciliation towards ex-Confederates, which has done honor to themselves & gained for them the esteem of all good citizens." Furthermore, his employers both opposed Unionist governor William Brownlow and had been mistreated by Union soldiers during the war, thus making them "all good Yankee-haters down here," a quality that Comfort appeared to both admire and encourage.[18]

In general, former Confederates seem to have forgiven their friends and neighbors for seeking employment from Northerners on the grounds that they must have needed the money. Taking a Northern paycheck was not seen as deserting one's fellow Southerners or as somehow betraying the cause. Southerners paying Northerners was not necessarily viewed the same way. Charles Barnes himself complained that, "shameful to say, the most of the old merchants here [in Wilmington, North Carolina] have employed fancy Yankee Clerks and salesmen, while numerous poor Confed's walk the streets in utter idleness, searching for work but finding none." Francis Dawson was unable to find steady work in either Richmond or Petersburg after the war because "a swarm of Yankees" had descended on the cities. The insect metaphor is noteworthy: the unwelcome visitors devouring the Southern economy.[19]

Hiring Yankees while former Confederate soldiers starved was unforgivable, as was patronizing a new, Northern-run business. "Reader, if you have a dollar to spend, be sure to spend it with our own people," charged the *Southern Opinion*'s "Signboard" feature. "Give nothing to the Yankee adventurer and sneak, who comes among us only to pocket our money. . . . Whatever you have to expend let it go to *your own people*." The *Southern Opinion*'s unreconstructed editor, H. Rives Pollard, repeatedly urged his Richmond readers to consult the paper's advertising columns before going shopping. There they would find "real Southern men who are not afraid to support or advertise in a true Southern paper." Not to patronize Southern businesses was to dishonor Confederate memory.[20]

Southerners were encouraged not only to patronize local, Southern-owned shops but also to think always of the South in any commercial transaction. In a self-serving editorial, Pollard called on Southern manufacturers to do more than just produce; they also needed to advertise if they wanted to encourage local patronage. An editorial in *The Land We Love* endorsed several Southern firms and complained that Southerners annually sent over six million dollars to Northern insurance companies. What was particularly galling was that some of these companies, D. H. Hill explained, had actively supported the Northern war effort and the "ruining" of the South. While Southerners were "magnanimous" in supporting their former enemies, they were also "very unwise," for "every dollar sent out of the South, adds to the general poverty and distress."[21]

How could the "Southern Capitalists," to borrow historian Laurence Shore's term, counter this angry rhetoric?[22] They did so by making their appeals within an explicitly pro-Southern framework, by assuring their readers and correspondents that rather than threaten Southern distinctiveness, Northern investment would help it to flourish. Don't imagine outsiders stuffing their carpetbags with Southern wealth and resources, the capitalists argued. Rather, imagine the bags filled with money and knowledge for white Southerners to exploit. The bags weren't coming to the South empty and leaving full; they were coming full, and staying. An article in the *Field and Fireside* in December 1865 promised that "we shall yet see our beloved South rising superior to every impediment," explaining that "to attain this end, we must all work; men and women, boys and girls; we must learn from our Northern neighbors, borrow from them, buy from them, bring them down here and colonize them among us." The new blood would not dilute that of conservative white Southerners, it would instead strengthen it.[23]

Not only would Southern whites be able to win over the newcomers to their cause, but only certain types of people would be encouraged to join this new enterprise. There were clear racial overtones to immigration advocacy: the immigrants were to be white, thus helping to shift the balance of population between freedmen and whites to a more decisive white majority. The outnumbered blacks could then be pushed to the fringes of society. The newcomers were integral to the notion that the reconstructed South would be for whites only. "The only hope that the South will not relapse into the condition of Jamaica and the other West India Islands, depends on fostering white labor," warned a typical piece in *De Bow's Review*. The newcomers could be either Northern or European, as long as they were young and hardworking and had the right color skin. A piece in the *Montgomery Advertiser* asked readers to encourage emigration to the South, "especially [of] laboring men, industrious men, to teach us to work as white men are taught to work in other countries." What is striking about this article is that within it lies an implicit criticism of antebellum Southern attitudes toward labor. The new Southern white man found labor honorable.[24]

A Massachusetts native felt entirely comfortable practicing law in New Orleans in early 1866. The people there, especially businessmen, accepted defeat and welcomed Northern money. "They want to see business reviving," he told John Dennett. "The whole planting community here is wishing for Northerners; they want them as partners or as capitalists; and whatever money is loaned the planters are ready to secure by a mortgage of their lands—not their crop, mind, as they used to in old times, but their land— or they will sell land to the Northerner." And willingly, too, treating Northern investors to traditional Southern hospitality. A Louisiana planter confirmed the Massachusetts native's impressions, assuring Dennett that among his class "there was not nearly so much bitterness now as there was three months ago." He scoffed at talk of Southern hostility to Northern businessmen, for "anybody could see it was for the interest of the South, that it was absolutely a necessity for her, to invite capital and enterprise from all quarters."[25]

E. C. Cabell of Florida used the pages of *De Bow's Review* to argue that the Northern and Southern people had been *taught* to hate each other. In contrast to the prevailing understanding of the differences between Southerners and Northerners, which held that the two people were organically and fundamentally different, a difference that no amount of political unification could erase, Cabell claimed that regional antipathy was artificial and unpatriotic. It was time, he charged, to forget about emigration out of the South, and therefore the United States, and work together for the common good.[26] A contributor to the *Southern Cultivator* argued that in order to rebuild, the South needed capital, not labor. And the only feasible means of acquiring this capital was for it to come from the outside. In order to attract Northerners and Europeans, white Southerners needed to be more courteous and hospitable toward outsiders. "The South is united to the North for good or evil," he chided. "Our effort to gain a separate nationality, has failed, and will not be renewed. As long as we persist in keeping ourselves *distinct* — as long as we are a *separate class* — so long will we as the weaker section, be more or less under the ban." Let go of the past, he urged. The only hope for the South was for its people to fully mingle with the Northern population, erasing distinctions of inferiority. Northern families who were well-treated in the South would report back and dispel the "slanders" that continued to flame sectional animosity. Simply by being polite, he concluded, Southern white men and "especially" women could "be of service to the desolate and distressed South."[27]

An argument that so explicitly called for unification challenged notions of Southern distinctiveness and not surprisingly provoked an angry response. M. W. Phillips, a former contributor to the *Southern Cultivator*, charged bitterly, "If we are to go on begging Northern folks to come here — if we are to promise them 'social consideration' — to fawn on them, for capital — for one, I say, let the capital rip and let the owners stay where they are." This unseemly pleading for investment was, Phillips complained, nothing less than an unacceptable affront to Southern "self-respect" and "honor." The *Southern Cultivator*'s editors, in turn, tried to moderate Phillips's anger by first defending the original contributor as a loyal and manly Southerner. They were not recommending "courting the favors of ranting radicals" but wanted only those families "disposed to be friends and neighbors" to join in the rebuilding of the South. And certainly the Northern immigrants would have to prove their social worthiness before being treated with respect, soothed the editors. "The idea of promising them 'social' equality" without it being earned "is a condescension unbecoming gentlemen." The South would have nothing to fear from exposure to the "right" kind of immigrants—that is, whites who were willing to vote alongside the Conservative Democrats. The next task was to convince those immigrants that a move South would be to their advantage.[28]

In their advertisements and promotional literature, Southern capitalists presented an idealized image of themselves and their region, both drawing on and dispelling historic stereotypes. That is, they emphasized Southern friendliness and hospitality while downplaying the recent war and the racial violence that swept across the region alongside Reconstruction. A typical advertisement in an 1866 issue of *De Bow's Review* sought to assuage immigrants' fears. It listed 100 Southern estates offered for sale by a W. T. Withers of Jackson, Mississippi, and assured readers that "Northern capitalists may feel safe in his hands." A letter to the editor of the *Montgomery Advertiser* was similarly directed at foreign readers. Minimizing any tensions between blacks and whites, he promised that "throughout the world the *Eldorado you seek is to be found in the South*." The article "Emigration South," an example of boosterism in the *Southern Cultivator*, urged "Northern and Western men, of character, means and energy" to move South to make their fortunes. Rumors of violence and resentment to the contrary, the Reconstruction South was perfectly safe—at least for "decent" people.[29]

While some of this boosterism addressed immigration regionwide, the vast majority of articles and pamphlets were about individual states, frequently written by state officials. The pages of *De Bow's Review* were filled with articles with titles such as "Alabama and Her Resources," "Florida—Past, Present, and Future," "Arkansas—Its Advantages to Immigrants," "The Inviting Fields of Arkansas," "The Wealth and Future of North Carolina," "The State of Missouri," and "The Vast Resources of Louisiana." These articles followed certain conventions, stressing their respective states' fertile soil, gentle climate, mineral wealth, timber, and general development possibilities. They were lands of opportunity, with fortunes waiting to be made by "industrious" immigrants.[30]

Both state governments and groups of private individuals sponsored publicity campaigns, drawing up promotional pamphlets designed to appeal to outsiders. "Under the recent changes in the system of labor," an 1865 flier for

SOUTHERN ESTATES IN THE MARKET.

W. T. WITHERS, of Jackson, Miss., who is one of the most reliable gentlemen in the South, and one whose statements it gives us pleasure to indorse, has issued a pamphlet containing a list of over 100 fine Southern estates which have been placed in his hands for sale. We condense from the pamphlet a few facts in regard to each estate, but full information will be furnished by Mr. Withers whenever addressed upon the subject. His references are the best in the country, and will be forwarded when desired. He proposes to purchase and sell estates, and will guarantee satisfaction. Will examine titles and prepare papers, and aid in obtaining the most satisfactory superintendents and managers for estates. Northern capitalists may feel safe in his hands.—EDITOR.

1. Plantation in Madison parish, Louisiana, 1800 acres, 1100 of which cleared and ready for cultivation. Splendid improvements; admirable for stock-raising. Price $50,000, half cash. The owner would prefer a partnership with some one having money.

2. Plantation in the same parish, 2693 acres, of which 800 well cleared and 200 more deadened. Has produced three bales to acre. Good improvements. Price $30,000; worth $140,000 before war. Half interest would be sold.

3. Plantation, Madison county, Miss., near Canton, 2600 acres, of which 1100 in cultivation. Excellent buildings, etc. House cost $22,500 in 1859. Laborers now on the place. Price $10 per acre, cash.

5. Plantation same county, five miles from Canton, 850 acres, 600 opened; good improvements. $7 per acre.

6. Plantation same county, 1450 acres, 1150 cleared and in cultivation; fine improvements; horses and other agricultural stock, and laborers on the place. Price $33,000, of which $20,000 cash.

7. Plantation in Warren county, Miss., three miles from Vicksburg, 1500 acres, 700 acres cleared. Magnificent place, secure from high water. Price $30 per acre, $15,000 cash.

8. Valley Plantation, Yazoo county, Miss., 1700 acres, of which 800 are cleared. Place now occupied by Northern lessees. Splendid estate. Price $37 per acre in instalments.

9. Plantation, Benton county, Miss., five miles from Benton, 1597 acres, 700 cleared. Price $7 per acre, nearly all cleared.

10. Plantation on Yazoo River, near Sartatia, 1800 acres, 250 in cultivation; splendid wood land; good houses. Price $12.50 per acre, cash.

11. Plantation, Sunflower county, Miss., 1090 acres, 500 cleared and deadened; good shipping point and improvements. Place now worked; $15 per acre, half cash.

12. Valley Plantation, adjoining Greenwood, on the Yazoo, Miss., 1560 acres, 450 in cultivation; fine improvements. Now rented at $10 per acre. Price $40 per acre, half cash.

14. Plantation, Sunflower county, Miss., four miles from Tallahatchie, 2700 acres, 400 cleared. $10 per acre.

15. Same county, 840 acres, half cleared. Price $40 per acre.

16. Same county, 2160 acres, 1300 cleared or deadened. Laborers on the place. Excellent stock and improvements. Price $78,500, half cash. Magnificent place.

17. Same county, 1200 acres, half cleared, and above overflow. Price $50,000, half down.

18. Plantation, thirteen miles above Yazoo City, Miss., 1640 acres, 500 cleared, and above overflow. Price $40,000, half cash.

19. Splendid estate on Yazoo, Holmes county, Miss., 3,500 acres, 1300 opened and now under cultivation; free from overflow; machinery run by steam. Excellent improvements of all kinds. Price $100,000. Laborers on the place.

21. Plantation on Tensas River, La., Madison parish, 1000 acres, 800 cleared. Sold for $60 gold before the war. Price now $30 greenbacks per acre.

22. Plantation, Carroll parish, La., 2000 acres, half cleared, good house, well drained. Price $30 per acre.

25. Plantation, Chicot county, Ark., eight miles from the Mississippi, 1400 acres, one-third cleared and improved. Price $18 per acre, cash. Prefers to sell half interest.

26. Plantation, sixteen miles from Grenada, Miss., 600 acres, one-third cleared. Price $12 per acre.

27. Plantation, nine miles from Grenada, 570 acres, 400 cleared. Price $8500, half cash.

28. Plantation, Carroll county, Miss., two miles from railroad, 1179 acres, half cleared and in cultivation. Excellent improvements. Corn and saw-mill, etc. Price $15 per acre, half cash.

29. Plantation, Carroll county, two and a half miles from Vaiden, 1840 acres, 400 cleared. Price $14 per acre.

30. Plantation, Carroll county, 800 acres, 300 cleared. Price $6 per acre.

31. Plantation, Carroll county, 1440 acres, 300 cleared. Price $5.50 per acre gold.

32. Plantation, Carroll county, near Duck Hill, 1400 acres, 600 cleared. Excellent improvements; laborers on place. Price $20 per acre.

35. Plantation, Madison county, Miss., 1120 acres, nearly all cleared. Splendid improvements. House cost $10,000 in gold. Price for place $30,000.

36. Plantation, Hinds county, Miss., 1700 acres, 600 cleared. Price $15 per acre.

37. Plantation, Hinds county, Miss., 320 acres, mostly cleared. (Sold cheap.)

40. Plantation in Hinds county, Miss., six miles west of Jackson, containing 560 acres, 350 cleared. Price $10 per acre, all cash.

This advertisement, which appeared in DeBow's Review *After the War Series, assures would-be purchasers of Southern estates that they will be welcomed with open arms. Virginia Historical Society.*

the North Carolina Land Agency explained, "it becomes the interest of proprietors to part with a portion of their real estate." The Land Agency's object, the flier continued, was to bring North Carolina's many virtues to the attention of "men of energy and capital" in order to start the state "in a career of prosperity hitherto unknown." Each pamphlet stressed the mild Southern climate, the fertility of the land, and the undeveloped natural resources. The Florida Improvement Company called Florida the "Italy of America," blessed by an excellent and healthful climate, a year-round growing season, an abundance of fish and game, and inexpensive housing. It also promised discount steamship tickets for settlers. The Southern Land Company, chartered in New York, took Western companies as its model, arguing that "the Great West is throwing out its arms and using its persuasive voice to invite and welcome the coming throng, and is reaping golden advantage from the effort. The South is far more attractive and a more desirable field" for the thousands of Europeans coming to America each year. To that end, the Southern Land Company promised to actively publicize the South's agricultural attributes and resources and, last but not least, "the kindly feeling of its people to welcome the actual settler and the capitalist."[31]

The pamphlet *Virginia: A Brief Memoir for the Information of Europeans Desirous of Emigrating to the New World* was published in both English and German, for distribution at home and abroad. Like other examples of state boosterism, it stressed the opportunity that awaited only diligent farmers, who would be sure to turn a profit whether they grew grain or tobacco. It made a special appeal for immigrants to come to the Shenandoah Valley and the Alleghenies, areas worthy of "particular interest" because "there have never been many negroes within them." The Virginia pamphlet made few references to "the late war," and then only in the context of absolving Virginia of responsibility. Virginians' "most distinguished traits are hospitality and conservative sentiments betokening a stable population, not easily drawn into revolution, except for self-preservation." Virginians got involved in the war only to defend constitutional principles, not to defend or protect slavery. Virginia hospitality had already been proven, the pamphlet asserted, by the warm welcome given to a group of exiled Poles who had settled in Spotsylvania County in 1867. They could vouch for the many advantages of moving to the South.[32]

By far the most aggressive recruiter of foreign immigrants was South Carolina, under the auspices of its state commissioner of immigration, General John A. Wagener. While his dedication might be surprising in light of the state's prewar conservatism and insularity, Wagener justified his mission on racial and political grounds. In a speech on German immigration given in May 1867, Wagener argued that immigration was more necessary than ever in order to counter South Carolina's rising free-black majority. His hope was that the new immigrants would help to transform South Carolina from a plantation state producing labor-intensive staples into one more in line with its origins: a state of small farms producing diverse crops and home manufactures, a land of virtuous yeomen. What Wagener didn't need to explain were the political and economic implications of that change: that there was no place for free blacks in his idealized Carolina.[33]

In April 1867, Wagener published *South Carolina: A Home for the Industrious Immigrant*, a pamphlet designed for foreign distribution. He began with a discussion of state history, alluding to the war only briefly and claiming that slavery had been abolished with state consent. He stressed his desire to bring "industrious" and "kindred" people to help rebuild South Carolina, urging that "although she is prostrate now, no manly men need be ashamed for himself or his descendants to participate in her future or past history." The bulk of the pamphlet was devoted to descriptions of the state's geography and climate, its abundant fish and game and mineral resources, and its burgeoning agriculture and livestock. Wagener also included some sketches of economic topics, including the cost of a farm, and discussions of commerce, railroads, taxation, and education. He closed with a section titled "Character of the People," in which he characterized South Carolina's whites as orderly, liberal, enlightened, devout, prosperous, and progressive—especially when compared to Northerners. Wagener took pains to assure possible immigrants that manual labor, admittedly undervalued in the past because of slavery, was now seen as honorable and right. Industrious men and women would be sure to prosper and be accepted by their new neighbors.[34]

In August of the same year, Wagener published a supplement to his original pamphlet, advertising over seventy-five positions and properties for sale around the state. Wagener also used the supplement's introduction as an opportunity to counter some negative publicity coming out of Western states, which he dismissed as their "regular system of abuse and detraction of the South." Wagener highlighted South Carolina's fair immigration laws, its lower land prices, even its lower crime rate when compared with Northern and Western states. Unlike the advocates of immigration in the North and West, who were presumably in the market for industrial laborers, "our only desire is an increase of a good and industrious population. Their prosperity will be our prosperity, their happiness will increase our happiness, and, therefore, any wrong perpetrated against them would be a wrong against ourselves as a community, and in possible conflict with the policy and laws of the State." Wagener described how happy and successful South Carolina's "adopted citizens" were, and how the German, Irish, and native-born lived harmoniously together. Wagener conceded that "there is but one drawback," which he "in candor and truth" could not deny: the "uncertainty" of South Carolina's political status during and after Reconstruction. But, Wagener was quick to point out, he thought that "if it shall be unsafe for the immigrant to come to the South, it will be equally unsafe for him to go to any portion of the Union; for loss of law and liberty in one section is certain to result in loss of law and liberty to all." Ultimately, Wagener was unconcerned about the current political situation, preferring instead to proclaim his "unshaken confidence in the future of America, and, above all, in the future of our beautiful and fruitful South. Let the industrious stranger come and fear not."[35]

Wagener's closing invocation of a South Carolina, and for that matter of an entire South, whose destiny was inextricably linked to that of the United States as a whole, is not the rhetoric we would expect to hear in August 1867. The Radical Republican division of the South into military districts and the enfranchisement of African Americans prompted angry and often violent responses from white Southerners. Some spoke of a renewed civil war. The Democratic elite urged white Southern men to stay away from the polls in 1867 and 1868, arguing that by so doing they would show the illegitimacy of Reconstruction. Expressions of Southern political anger filled the pages of the same periodicals that sought immigration.

This juxtaposition tells us that the relationship between white Southerners and Northerners during Reconstruction was more complicated than simply one of bitterness and resentment. In the midst of their campaigns to preserve local control of matters of race, economics, and politics, Southern whites also recognized that Northerners could be of some use to them. Debates over immigration were debates over the limits of white Southern identity, couched in the language of separation and preservation. Would outsiders threaten the elusively invoked "Southern way of life"? Not if they were chosen carefully, advocates argued, and not if they were willing to play by the white South's rules regarding racial politics. The code words are not even well-obscured: "men of character," "industrious men," "families disposed to be friends and neighbors," "kindred people." Southern white identity was flexible enough to encompass a degree of reunion, so long as it was on Southerners' terms and respected their desire to be both of and apart from the American whole. Outsiders were welcomed when they were perceived as sharing the interests of Southern whites. But those who sought to disrupt the business of rebuilding, disrupt the reestablishment of white supremacy and political control, were another story.

"A SOUND LITERATURE BASED ON SOUTHERN SENTIMENTS"

We tend to think of rebuilding in material terms, as quantifiable in dollars or bales of cotton or reconstructed homes. But white Southerners rebuilding after the war wanted to do more than just reconstruct their economic and political lives. They also worked to create a new identity for themselves as Southerners, one that took into account their time as Confederates, and they did this by trying to hold onto markers of cultural distinctiveness. Thus, the calls of Confederates during wartime to reject Yankee writings in favor of creating a distinctively national literature continue into Reconstruction. Editors of the major postwar magazines walked a fine line between professing loyalty to the United States, without which they were in danger of having their presses shut down, and proclaiming themselves as authentic voices of the South. They tried to be explicitly regional, appealing to white Southerners who wanted to preserve both their Confederate pasts and their antebellum sense of Southern distinctiveness while also maintaining a degree of openness to the North, if only to protect themselves from charges of chauvinism.[36] Thus the inaugural issue of the short-lived *Richmond Eclectic* magazine included the following editorial statement, not once, but twice: "The sections [of the magazine] will NEVER BE OF A SECTARIAN CHARACTER, but such as are equally suitable to evangelical Christians of every denomination. Nothing SECTIONAL will be admitted; at the same time nothing will appear which is out of harmony with the convictions and sentiments of SOUTHERN READERS, with reference to the interests, rights, and the institutions of the States they inhabit." In its "prospectus," the editors of the *Southern Home Journal*, a Baltimore publication, justified their sectional slant on the grounds that their paper was "strictly a literary publication of the South" and promised to avoid "everything of a political nature, to be devoted to the publication of choice Literature, Biography, History, Poetry, and the News of the day." Of course, discussions of history and the news of the day necessarily strayed into political waters, and the *Southern Home Journal* was as vocal in its denouncements of the Radicals as any of its sister papers.[37]

In his introduction to the After the War Series of *De Bow's Review*, editor James D. B. De Bow stressed the journal's "National Character" and its concern with both "the honor and Prosperity of the Country" as a whole, and especially the reconstruction of "Southern Prosperity." De Bow fervently hoped that Reconstruction would follow the Presidential plan, but he largely eschewed discussion of national politics. The *Review* would look forward, not back, arguing that what benefited the nation as a whole would benefit the South as well, and vice-versa. Pure sectionalism had no place in De Bow's ideology of commercial progress. Even the title page reflected the dual character De Bow wanted the magazine to embody, proclaiming that the *Review* was "devoted to the Restoration of the Southern States" and "the development of the Wealth and Resources of the Country." In a change from the antebellum version, which had boasted that "Cotton is King," the cover now featured the less loaded "Commerce is King."[38]

De Bow may have felt the need to stress the *Review*'s national character because it was actually published out of New York, despite having offices in Nashville.[39] His choice of printer did not go unremarked in the South. The 3 February 1866 issue of the *Field and Fireside* included a review of De Bow's first issue. Although the editors expressed happiness at its return, they could not resist a dig at some of De Bow's plans, taking issue with the magazine's support for northern immigration and investment. Even worse was that "it deals out figurated schemes of negro philanthropy with lavish profusion. Many of these free negro dishes are too large for the table. It is one thing to print these essays in New York—it is quite another thing to give the latter day African science a practical application here at the South." Race and politics could not be extricated from questions of identity.[40]

In attempting to be both pro-Southern and pro-Northern investment, the *Review* found itself being criticized from both sides—some charged it with being too Southern, others not Southern enough. A reader in Georgia "coolly" asked the editors to "stultify the past record of the REVIEW and to admit [their] treason," prompting the following indignant defense: "While in the language of the late Editor, we 'accept the results of the war in good faith and seek only to restore harmony and peace and prosperity to the country at large,' it must not be understood that we feel the slightest self-conviction of having committed what Webster defines to be the 'highest crime of a civil nature of which a man can be guilty.'" But only a few months later, the editors responded to another subscriber's complaint—this one presumably about the *Review*'s disloyalty—by explaining that the journal was "not opposed to the Government of the United States, nor does it devote its pages to matters strictly political. But there may be an honest difference of opinion between us as to what really constitutes the Government, and with regard to what questions are to be considered purely political."[41]

D. H. Hill, the editor of *The Land We Love*, also made much of his professed loyalty to the United States, even as he expressed his love of the South and the Southern people. Hill's magazine frequently juxtaposed pledges of fealty to the Federal government with nostalgic reminiscences of the Confederacy. Many of Hill's declarations of himself as a "loyal editor" were clearly tongue-in-cheek, but he genuinely believed that Southern whites needed to accept the changes being wrought by Reconstruction, "else our very name and nation will be taken away."[42] Like De Bow and his successors, Hill soon found that in his quest to please both Northerners and Southerners, he pleased no one. "This 'Land We Love' is still printed in the land its editor hates," the *Field and Fireside* observed tartly, referring to the fact that Hill used a New York printer for his first four issues.[43]

Complaints about *The Land We Love*'s Southern sympathies were more prevalent, or at least those were the ones to which Hill chose to respond in print. In 1867, the *New York Methodist* apparently charged that "the land loved by the Editor of this Magazine is not the whole United States, but only a rather troublesome section of it." Hill replied that in fact the magazine was "exceedingly national" but simply had no preference for Massachusetts, the real troublesome section. When another New York subscriber complained that the magazine was unfit for "loyal" readers, Hill mocked him, explaining that it was "reasonably loyal for rebels," who had no better examples placed before them. An article in the *Philadelphia Dispatch* claimed that *The Land We Love* was too "intensely Southern in sentiment" and that Hill "needs 'reconstructing' badly." Hill responded that he wanted nothing more than that and alluded to a two-year-old request for a pardon in his name, as well as noting his (and his magazine's) many proclamations of loyalty to the United States.[44]

H. Rives Pollard's weekly *Southern Opinion*, published in Richmond, stood in marked contrast to the self-conscious moderation of journals like *The Land We Love* and *De Bow's Review*. The brother of the well-known author and historian of the war, Edward A. Pollard, H. Rives Pollard was unapologetically unreconstructed both in his personal sentiments and in his editorial choices.[45] In the opening issue of the *Southern Opinion*, Pollard took the opportunity to explain that he had no "incendiary" motives in starting the paper and that he was willing to accept "the inexorable and irreversible decree of Fate." But, Pollard continued, his beloved South had not lost everything when it lost the war: "The South can yet preserve its moral and intellectual distinctiveness as a people, and continue to assert its well-known superiority over the North in civilization, in political scholarship, in its schools of refinement and in all standards of individual character. This superiority the war has not conquered or lowered, and the South will do right to claim and cherish it." Pollard claimed that Southerners had an absolute right to preserve "these distinctive features" of "Southern thought or Southern culture" and that their preservation would be the mission of his paper. Pollard did make a nod toward the North in "counsel[ing] submission" to the 1867 Reconstruction Bill, but he vowed never to "admit the cause of the South to be a 'crime' and brand as 'felons' and 'traitors' the gallant men" who fought for Southern independence. Honor remained paramount for Pollard.[46]

Pollard also provided a detailed reading of his paper's masthead, which he described as representing the "glory and sorrow" of the South, as it commemorated the struggle for independence. The right-hand side of the image featured a Confederate soldier's grave, visited by a grieving woman and her children, in a cemetery "thick with martyrs graves" and reminiscent of Richmond's two main Confederate resting places, Hollywood and Oakwood, in the background. The left side portrayed a raging battle, watched and sketched by the Goddess of Fame. Next to the goddess is a vignette of George Washington, along with paraphernalia representing each branch of the military. The entire image is crowned by a banner proclaiming, "My country may she always be right, but right or wrong my country." The image covered all the Lost Cause bases: praise for women's patriotism, appropriate memorialization, and explicit connections to the Founders. Interestingly, in view of Pollard's regional chauvinism, the design was executed by a Richmonder but the engraving work was done in New York.[47]

Although Pollard initially took a moderate stance toward the federal government, counseling his readers to accept the realities of Reconstruction and endorsing the district military commander, he soon took a harder line toward both the Radicals in Congress and the "carpetbaggers" in Virginia and Richmond. In August 1868, fourteen months after commencing publication, Rives reiterated his paper's mission: "We shall strike hard blows for the people and against their oppressors, whether they be native enemies or imported tyrants. Though others flinch from duty in the presence of mighty Wrong, we shall not, but continue hereafter, as in the past, to march straight forward in the thorny path of unconquerable right."[48]

The vast majority of regional periodicals, be they newspapers, literary journals, or commercial reviews, made appeals to readers based on their Southern characteristics, but the *Crescent Monthly*, a New Orleans magazine, sought explicitly to distance itself from this approach. In the "Introductory Note" to their first issue, in April 1866, the *Crescent*'s editors assured readers that, "upon its merits alone we rest all claim to patronage, without asking sympathy because it is a Southern work, without any appeal to a sectional spirit, feeling assured that it will find patrons enough on account of its own intrinsic worth." They expounded on this reluctance to trade on their Southernness in their "Editorial Notes" at the end of the issue. Remarking on the many failed Southern literary magazines, all of which "begged for public patronage on account of their being *Southern*," the editors further noted that, unfortunately, "there was no necessary connection between a Southern latitude and excellent literature."[49]

The editors of the *Crescent Monthly* acknowledged that Southern belles lettres had long lagged behind those of the North, owing to the South's less advanced commercial and industrial development. Nevertheless, they observed that before the war Virginia, Louisiana, and South Carolina had all had a thriving literary culture. Writers like Edgar Allen Poe had been able to "offset, with the superior quality of their writings, the commercial disadvantage of Southern literature." Had the editors of the many failed Southern magazines paid more attention to the quality of their efforts rather than appealing to "the mysterious potency of a parallel of latitude," they would have "done much towards establishing a literature worthy in itself, and worthy in the South." The editors of the *Crescent Monthly* were not, therefore, opposed to promoting Southern literature, per se; they only opposed promoting bad writing on the grounds that it was Southern.[50]

The editors returned to their crusade against regional mediocrity in their next issue, again stressing their explicitly national aspirations. They apologized for the rather plain appearance of their journal, as they did not have access to the better presses and more talented engravers available in the North. But what mattered was what was on the pages, not how the pages appeared. The editors also hoped to provide a political counterweight to the Republican-dominated Northern press by furnishing "a literary journal for a large class of people in the United States who hold opinions different from those expressed in the magazines published in the North. Whether true or not, a great many of our people believe that these magazines are published in the interests of a particular party." The *Crescent Monthly* editors also apologized for the "eclectic" character of their magazine, explaining that they hoped someday to fill their pages with original literature, thus proving that literature could be profitable in the South.[51]

The editors of the *Crescent Monthly* were not alone in calling for a resurgence of distinctively Southern letters; they continued a trend that had flourished during the war. The demise of Southern nationhood, they argued, need not mean the end of Southern literature. The first postwar issue of the *Field and Fireside* proudly proclaimed, "We shall go forward in the future, leaving the dead past to bury its dead, in confident expectation of seeing, ere long, a ripe fruition of the hope that Southern literature will soon assume a rank and tangible place in the world of letters, and thus render our full and acknowledged portion to the honor and stamina of our current American literature." Paul Hayne, the well-known South Carolina poet, drew readers' attention to the ever-increasing number of Southern literary magazines and papers two and a half years after the end of the war. He saw the silver lining in the cloud of Confederate defeat and military Reconstruction, explaining that "vanquished by mere brute force—shackled and deprived of the plainest privileges of freemen—with our best and ablest men reduced to a political level far beneath that which is now occupied by our former slaves—the intellect of the country, depressed in one quarter, is beginning to assert itself unmistakably in another." In short, as Southerners' independent political identity was being subsumed into the American whole, they continued to maintain a separate literary identity. Perhaps the two needed to coexist, one making the other possible.[52]

The editors of *Scott's Monthly Magazine* shared Hayne's belief in the rightness of distinctive Southern literature. After all, they reasoned, the people of the South still remained "distinct in race, separate in the true sense of nationality, . . . with manners, customs, habits, thoughts, and modes of thinking peculiar to us as a people," so why shouldn't they have a literature of their own, "founded in these essential characteristics"? White Southerners' failure to establish their own government "will not suppress their elegance of imagination, so congenial to our clime, nor deprive them of the exercise of those intellectual faculties, the product of which will be traced in the choicest fruits and flowers." Indeed, the ordeal of fighting and losing a war could only improve Southern literature, by deepening Southerners' unique experiences. "We have now had our heroic age," they proclaimed with great pride. "We have had a revolution of our own. We have a history peculiar to ourselves. . . . We have heroes and battle-fields, and feats in valor to celebrate in song. We have memories sacred to the dead, to cherish in the mournful memories of the living." Like their Scottish and Irish counterparts, these writers hoped that Southern authors would flourish after defeat. What is most important about this line of thinking is the idea that white Southerners were *essentially* different from other Americans, a distinct race. Their identity had outlasted their nation.[53]

A piece titled "Southern Literature" in the *Raleigh Progress* argued that the South needed its own writings more than ever during Reconstruction. White Southerners needed to preserve their own history in order to protect it from "the egregious vanity and arrogance and malice of New England"; they needed to write their own schoolbooks and generally create "a sound and able periodical literature based on southern sentiments." By "Southern sentiments," the author meant more than just the obvious political differences between white Southern Democrats and their Republican enemies but also the "characteristics and idiosyncrasies that gave individuality and attractiveness to southern civilization and rendered it as distinct from that of the north as day from night." This author's interest in supporting Southern writings went beyond a simple desire to preserve long-lasting cultural distinctions. In an echo of wartime proponents, he wanted Southerners to have their own writings as a means of ensuring respect from the other sections of the country, as well as from abroad. Great nations had great writing, and white Southerners still felt a need to prove that they were worthy of independence, even if they had been unable to secure it. This language of distinctiveness, often left nebulous and undefined, hearkened back to the Cavalier and Yankee myth. It was a way of showing Southern whites, and Northerners for that matter, that differences still mattered.[54]

External factors contributed to Southern calls for their homegrown literature as well. Southerners justifiably complained about their treatment at the hands of the Northern press, and they openly criticized Northern papers for their biases. Echoing the reasoning behind the 1863 founding of the Confederate Press Association (which did not survive the war), both the *Mobile Advertiser and Register* and the *Montgomery Advertiser* charged the Associated Press with being unfair to the South. They called it "a humbug" because "it does not answer the ends for which the Southern press supports it, either in the quality or the quantity or the dispatch of its intelligence, and it is a nuisance because it is evidently in the hands of political radicals, enemies to the South and its best interests." The Alabama editors suggested that Southern papers band together and form their own association, one more representative of their interests, feelings, and principles. The editors of the *Crescent Monthly* charged Northern newspapers with hypocrisy, arguing that their unfair portrayals of the South only fostered bitterness and prejudice. "It is a curious thing to notice the manner in which such papers take the Southern press to task for keeping up the asperities of section," they observed, "while their own columns are dedicated to sneers, ridicule and abuse of our people, individually or in classes."[55]

Particularly galling to Southern editors was the fact that Southerners continued to read Northern newspapers and magazines, often at the expense of their own regional publications. The *Southern Opinion* implored its subscribers to stop reading "Yankee abortions" like *Harper's* and the *New York Ledger* and confine their interests to Southern papers. In an 1868 editorial, D. H. Hill expressed frustration that "the Southern people seem determined to patronize only the pictorials of the North, which prostitute art to falsify history." Presumably Hill was referring to papers like *Frank Leslie's Illustrated Weekly* and *Harper's*. The latter was a favorite target of Hill, who considered it full of "slanders" and "trashy tales."[56]

James Gardner and the other editors of the *Field and Fireside* supported the efforts not only of Southern writers but of Southern publishers as well. In September 1866 they expressed dismay that Southern authors continued to have their books (and editors, their magazines) published and printed in New York, even though there were several good printers in the South. This criticism may have been somewhat self-serving, as the piece then launched into a defense of the *Field and Fireside*'s Augusta printers, Wm. B. Smith & Co. Regrettably, they explained, Smith & Co. were unable to offer advances to every single author who requested one, because they were still attempting to recover their prewar prosperity. But Southern authors should be patient and contribute to regional recovery by working with their neighbors.[57]

The *Field and Fireside* also criticized Northern printers for exploiting Southern readers. The editors were indignant that New York's Richardson & Co., the publishers of both Edward A. Pollard's *Lost Cause* and William Gilmore Simms's collection *War Poetry of the South*, had asked them to publish "a great puff" of a review of Simms's effort. Their real complaints, however, lay with Richardson's educational marketing efforts: "A few weeks ago, Messers. RICHARDSON & CO. announced, with a great blast of *southern* trumpets a series of *southern* school and text books, prepared by *southern* educators and designed for *southern* schools and colleges, and which the *southern* people are, of course, expected to buy in preference to all others." Although the editors of the *Field and Fireside* had great respect for the Southern authors of these texts, they believed that the effort was doomed to failure because the Northern publishers "do not understand our people. They think we are all fools—from the highest to the humblest—and that their puerile puffery and blatant *magnanimity* will humbug the *southern* people out of their senses whenever they choose to spring such miserable tactics upon us." Only a book's "paternity and manufacture" could make it truly Southern, and the editors expressed their desire for a variety of books prepared, printed, stereotyped, and bound in Southern cities. They disavowed any ulterior motives in their call for local production, explaining that they were simply

> tired and sick of this eternal cry of *southern* books, *southern* poems, *southern* novels, *southern* histories, *southern* grubbing hoes and *southern* this and *southern* that. This is the cry that ran us into war once; this is the cry that kept all of us four years in the trenches, cost us our best men and our best blood; this is the cry that brought *southern* defeat and *southern* humiliation; this is the cry that is bending our faces in the dust, to-day; and by this same cry, RICHARDSON & Co. and all of his ilk would keep our noses to the grindstone forever. We have had enough of it; and, if we are not greatly mistaken, the southern people have had enough of this feature of the books of RICHARDSON & Co.

Thus the proponents of distinctive Southern literature both during and after the war took the interesting position that such regionalism was actually destructive, but only when it came from the mouths of outsiders.[58]

The *Field and Fireside*'s dislike of the Richardson series of textbooks was not shared by fellow members of the Southern intelligentsia. Publications as disparate as *De Bow's Review* and the *Southern Cultivator* praised the series, noting that most volumes were written by Southern professors and that it was endorsed by the University of Virginia.[59] Perhaps, too, they agreed that any specifically Southern textbooks were better than none. The calls for improvements in the region's educational system that had been so prevalent during the war continued into Reconstruction.[60]

"The Yankee Attempting the Intellectual Conquest of the South," trumpeted an article in the 3 August 1867 issue of the *Southern Opinion*, upset that Southerners were allowing the "mendacious" and "untrustworthy" Yankees to educate Southern children. The article painted a frightening picture of a future of "perverted and degenerate" Yankee-schooled children, one that could only be avoided with some effort. At present, though, "having been overcome in the unequal physical contest, we lie supinely on our backs while our conquerors proceed unimpeded to a moral and intellectual conquest of vastly more consequence." It had already started, as "Radical pedagogues" had infiltrated the South through the new freedmen's schools. Currently, the Yankee taught only African Americans, but "insidiously, treacherously, more potently operative, he is whispering to our sons and daughters in all our abodes of learning. His books are broadcast through the land, and the young of the South are acquiring their first rudiments and their highest science from a polluted source. Always subtly infusing his venom in his works of instruction, the Yankee now openly poisons all the founts of learning." The first issue of concern was a Northern history book that included the false claim that Lincoln's killer had been hired by the Confederate government; but the Yankees would not stop with the mere falsification of history:

> They will make the figures of arithmetick lie, the x, y, z of algebra stands for unknown quantities of misrepresentation, and even the demonstrations of geometry serve to enforce falsehood in fact or in principle. In grammar their best syntax will be false, and their exercises in parsing will tell, not how 'Grant was a brutal butcher,' but how 'Lee was a perjured traitor;' not how 'The Southern people were patriotick and brave, but unfortunate,' but how 'Sherman made a glorious march to the sea.' In geography their slanders will pervade the whole of North America, and the remotest regions of the earth will still be enveloped in a New England atmosphere. They will leave no ingenuity untried to make their pupils believe their pernicious lies and theories.

Southerners had a duty to write their own schoolbooks and thus exclude the teachings of their "didactick enemies." Yankee teaching was worse than no teaching at all, the article swore, and "if Yankee civilization be the standard of education in the South, let us embrace ignorance for ourselves and children for all time to come."[61]

Although white Southern writers tried to make the connection between regional publications—for both children and adults—and the preservation of a distinctive identity, they often struggled to attract readers. Many readers seemed not to care about the origin of their books and journals, or maybe they tired of the constant pressure to measure up to a standard of behavior that no longer seemed relevant. Writers and editors protested the fading of white Southern identity so vehemently because they feared total absorption into the Union. White Southerners during Reconstruction found themselves in a push-pull relationship with the federal Union. Each step they took toward integration with the American whole—economically or socially— seemed to be accompanied by a counterimpulse to hold onto separation. As with politics, white Southerners seemed to arrive at a sort of utilitarian strategy of accommodation (which more cynically might be described as talking out of both sides of their mouths). Use Northern capital and labor to rebuild the South, they told each other. Then, once the South was stronger than ever, they could be cast aside once more. In this way, former Confederates were able to convince themselves that accommodation and cultural independence could coexist.

Interlude

The Vicarious Sufferer

Northern treatment of Jefferson Davis after the war transformed white Southerners' opinions of him. Whether they had liked or disliked him, thought him an inspiring executive or a petty tyrant, white Southerners were united in outrage at his plight. Davis's ignominious capture, the rumors that he had been fleeing in women's clothes, and his subsequent months in captivity at Fortress Monroe, Virginia, combined to turn him into the chief martyr to the Confederate cause. White Southerners chafed under the humiliation of his imprisonment and feared that he might be tried and executed for treason—a crime they believed he had not committed. Each day that he remained a prisoner reminded ex-Confederates of their own subject status. The imprisonment of Davis struck a disrespectful blow to white honor, serving as a constant reminder of their defeat.[1]

As early as the summer of 1865, white Southerners were calling on each other to do what they could to secure Davis's release. An article in the *Selma Times* reminded readers of the "duty" they owed Davis and suggested that petitions from each state be sent to President Johnson, requesting that Davis be released. In urging Southerners to help, the *Selma Times* chided them for "the selfishness and ungratefulness of the people of the South" in allowing him to be "punished for an offense we all committed." The people had voted for Davis, yet they were abandoning him to his Yankee captors. No one had offered to negotiate with the North on Davis's behalf, an omission that shamed Southern whites in the eyes of the world. Davis was "no more responsible for the desolation, death, and ruin of the past four years than any other prominent man—indeed, not so much as some who have their liberty—but the people are the responsible parties and should now, in obedience to the sacred duties of respect and obligation, intercede in behalf of him who is being punished for their faults, offenses, and crimes." The piece was reprinted in the *Montgomery Advertiser*, which thought it was a bit hard on Southern whites, who, after all, had just finished a war. Nevertheless, the *Advertiser*'s commentator agreed with the essential premise that "Mr. Davis is no more of a criminal than all the rest of us, and it is this which should strengthen his claim to mercy, unless it be the policy to exterminate our whole population for what was adjudged patriotism in Washington and his followers."[2]

White men and women sent petitions for clemency to Andrew Johnson.[3] In addition to petitions, Southerners circulated pamphlets aimed at keeping the people from forgetting their leader. The pamphlet "Ex-President Davis, of the Southern Confederacy, in Chains" perfectly exemplified this Southern version of "waving the bloody shirt." Ostensibly an excerpt from a letter to the secretary of war "on the subject of McKenzie's Mexican Raid," the four-page tract appears to have been designed to encourage Virginians to vote in the 1867 state election. It opened with the sensational image of Davis forcibly being shackled to the wall of his cell in Fortress Monroe, with its "dripping walls" and "cold, hard floor." This final indignity, worse than losing his country, worse than being captured, not only was directed at Davis himself but "was intended as an humiliation to the cause of the South and of State Rights." Davis was being dishonored by being treated no better than a common felon, the author, "Vindex," complained, and he was further defamed by being accused of complicity in the plot to assassinate President Lincoln. Nevertheless, these attempts to degrade Davis, and by extension the South, had failed: "Your honor, the honor of your race remains untarnished. It lives in the heart of every Southern patriot, and it is embalmed with the memory of your great men." Vindex encouraged white Southerners to resist attempts to force them to forget their leaders, to continue to sing "that beautiful and touching Southern song, which your Northern enemies fear to have sung at their public spectacles," and finally to head to the polls and regain their rightful positions. Davis thus became the symbol of white Southern resistance to Radical Republican domination.[4]

By far the best-known work about Davis's time in jail was John Craven's 1866 book, *The Prison Life of Jefferson Davis*. Craven, a U.S. Army surgeon, served as Davis's personal physician during the first seven months of his confinement at Fortress Monroe—from late May to late December 1865.[5] Although a Northerner, Craven had grown sympathetic to Davis's plight and closed his account with a plea for leniency. Craven claimed to paint a fair and objective portrait, one, in his words, "not written to gloat over the misfortunes of a fallen enemy—certainly not aiming to palliate his political or other errors; but to depict so much of him as was revealed to the Writer during a medical attendance of many months while Mr. Davis lay a prisoner in Fortress Monroe." He based his book on a diary he kept during his months of attendance and covered both Davis's failing health and his political sentiments, particularly regarding Reconstruction. In actuality, the book was written by Charles Graham Halpine, a Democratic friend of Craven's, who hoped that a sympathetic portrayal of Davis's conditions would prove to be, as Halpine wrote to Andrew Johnson, "the most powerful campaign document ever issued in this country—a document that could abate the fanaticism of the radicals . . . & strengthen & rally the conservative opinions of the country to your increased support." While the book may not have made Johnson any more popular, it did create widespread public sympathy and support for Davis, probably making it easier for him to be freed on bail and for the charges against him to be eventually dismissed.[6]

Craven's book received mixed reviews in the South. Davis himself denounced it as "fiction distorting fact" (though only in private), perhaps because it sometimes showed him as overly sentimental and emotional, crying over his predicament or shrinking in fear. But at the same time, *Prison Life* served a vital function in the remaking of Jefferson Davis from the ineffective president and architect of Confederate defeat to martyred scapegoat, beloved for his sufferings in the name of the Southern people. In *The Land We Love*, D. H. Hill praised the book and lauded Davis as the "vicarious sufferer for our whole people." A reviewer in *Scott's Monthly* appreciated the way that *Prison Life* elicited much-deserved sympathy for Davis from Southern whites. He was struck, not by the weakness that others found distasteful in Craven's portrayal, but by Davis's enduring manliness: "Conscious of no guilt, we see him, not bowed like a criminal, but bearing himself with dignity unblemished, yet, as a Christian man, submissive to that fate which a mightier than earthly hand had meted out to him." This reviewer found much to endorse in Davis's sentiments, about both "the gentler sex," whom Davis praised for their unfailing support during and after the war, and his thoughts about Reconstruction: Davis "shows such a thorough knowledge and just appreciation of our political status, that we wish his words could gain the attention of every thinking American citizen. Calm and dispassionate in his manner, he argues every point which he touches with a wisdom and logical precision which it would be well for his enemies to imitate."[7]

Not everyone was so enamored of the portrayal of a softer, more sentimental Davis in *Prison Life*. "Craven's book is a catch. It contains very little merit and a great deal of untruth," complained a review in the *Field and Fireside*, and "whatever of truth it does contain is miserably distorted and colored." The *Fireside*'s chief complaint was that Davis would never have cut so pathetic a figure as Craven portrayed. Seizing on the same passage that Vindex had used to arouse anger in the Southern people—where Craven described the president bursting "into a passionate flood of sobbing" and rocking back and forth like a child upon being shackled to the wall—the review charged that it was patently false. Davis was too much a man to cry and moan and contemplate suicide. Craven was not to be trusted, as he was trying to both humiliate the officers who removed him from his position as Davis's physician and make money off of a sensational book. Perhaps, too, the *Fireside* thought that a portrayal of their former leader as weak would reflect badly on the region as a whole. If Davis were unworthy of respect, and was only a figure to be pitied, would the same be said of the rest of the former Confederates?[8]

By May 1867, Northern interest in prosecuting Jefferson Davis had fallen off. Andrew Johnson had revealed himself to be sympathetic toward white Southerners; congressional Republicans were looking ahead to their battles over Reconstruction policy, not back to the war; many feared that Johnson would pardon Davis to get back at the Radicals. A treason trial would be no better, as it would have to be held in federal court in Virginia, where a conviction not only would have been highly unlikely but also would have allowed for arguments on the legitimacy of secession.[9]

On 11 May 1867, the Davis situation was finally resolved. A frail but still defiant Davis left his cell and boarded a steamboat bound for Richmond. Supporters cheered his passage, some weeping for joy. Richmond was full of troops and policemen when Davis arrived and was led to the same hotel rooms he had occupied in 1861 when he came to Richmond as president of the Confederacy. Rumors of a black "riot" had accompanied his release, and at least one skirmish broke out between white policemen and blacks. Policemen were stationed at black churches, and one black speaker, who had called on blacks to "hold high carnival, or do what you please," was arrested. Once again white fears of black uprising and race war proved unfounded.[10]

Jefferson Davis appeared in an integrated Richmond courthouse, before an integrated jury on 13 May. Federal judge John Underwood spoke of peace as he declared the case before him to be "bailable" and set the sum at $100,000. Eighteen men paid his bail, and Davis left the building to cheering crowds and the rebel yell. His case would never come to trial, and the charges were finally dropped in February 1869. In a powerful symbol of both irony and the degree to which Davis had become a symbolic impediment to

JEFF. D— HUNG ON A 'SOUR APPLE TREE' OR TREASON MADE ODIOUS.

"Jeff D. Hung on a Sour Apple Tree." Surprisingly, Horace Greeley, the longtime Republican, was one of the men who posted bail for Jefferson Davis. Davis, hanging from a sour apple tree, as in the wartime song, is embracing Greeley in thanks. Library of Congress.

reunion, three of the men who contributed to his bail were Northerners: Cornelius Vanderbilt, Gerrit Smith (at one time a backer of John Brown), and Republican editor Horace Greeley. By the fall of 1866, Greeley had begun to publicly support Davis, corresponding with Davis's wife, Varina, and using Davis in his campaign for sectional reunion.[11]

White Southerners rejoiced at his release, and whenever Davis visited a Southern city (though he and his wife initially went to Canada), he was hailed as a hero. George Rose (an Englishman better known as Arthur Sketchley) saw Davis in Baltimore in 1868, as the former president was surrounded by a throng of well-wishers at his hotel. "He commands the respect and sympathy of large numbers of his countrymen," he observed, "and is also much liked in Montreal, where he has been residing of late." Rose, along with many white Southerners, thought that Davis should be accorded the same heroic status as George Washington, "both being examples of the distinction between 'a wicked rebellion' and 'a glorious revolution.'"[12]

The protective impulse toward Davis that former Confederates had felt while he was in prison continued after his release. In August 1867, the *Southern Opinion* indignantly reported on the treatment that Davis had received during a recent journey through Vermont. Boys and men hooted at him, and in a twist on the image of the intemperate Southern woman, a woman who had lost a relative at Andersonville threw a rock at Davis. "Mr. Davis can afford to despise men and boys who hoot in the streets and 'ladies' (?) who 'hurl stones,'" the *Opinion* intoned. "The satisfaction for him and the rebuke for his 'swinish multitude' of insulters and persecutors is to be derived from the high regard invariably shown him by all the virtuous and intelligent classes everywhere." This was another example of Davis's, and therefore of white Southerners', perceived moral superiority to Northerners.[13]

Davis's release appeared to have finally ended the war. Henry Wirz, the commander of Andersonville Prison, would be the only man executed for his wartime role; Davis was safe from charges of either complicity in the Lincoln assassination or treason; men who had survived the war had long ago returned home to rebuild their lives and reconstruct their families. The insult of physical imprisonment had ended, another sign of the South's slow return to equality from its subjugated position. But almost four months to the day after Davis's release, the *Southern Opinion* shocked readers by reporting that a Confederate naval officer, Lt. John C. Braine, continued to "languish" in prison in New York, forgotten entirely by the Southern people. Editor H. Rives Pollard seized on the Braine case as an opportunity to chastise white Southerners for forgetting their Confederate virtues:

> Let us blush for our neglect. We might have forgotten Jefferson Davis in Fortress Monroe, too (as we have now forgotten him), had we not been reminded of him so often by curious and sensational Yankees. Too many of us have found the experiences of the past few years too much for our manhood. We are becoming timid, selfish slaves, with no sympathy for others and only bent on furthering our own private interests. We are learning to turn abruptly from the unlucky 'grey' to smile and smirk obsequiously to the triumphant 'blue.' Like a herd of deer we shun the 'stricken,' instead of humanely offering to relieve them.

Braine had first appealed for help in early July, and to Pollard's horror, only one Virginian had sent him any money. This blatant disregard of Braine's predicament disgraced and dishonored white Southerners, particularly those who "affect still to revere" the "Lost Cause." Braine's treatment also revealed the essential hypocrisy of Northerners, particularly Republicans, who had complained about the conditions in which their prisoners of war had been kept. Unlike the "ravishers, murders, and other foul criminals," with whom he was housed, Braine was not permitted to receive money through the mail or have visitors to his cell. His great crime was being a Confederate, and "though he is entitled to his freedom under the ordinary terms of parole, he has been selected as a scape-goat to glut the vengeance of Radicalism. He is called a 'pirate' and he is kept in close prison for a year in time of peace and amnesty, even after Mr. Davis (who was erroneously thought to be the last Confederate prisoner) is released." The appeal to Southern honor and sympathy appears to have worked, for the next time Braine was mentioned in the paper, it was to report his release. The last Confederate had returned.[14]

7 Who Shall Subjugate the Women?

Gender and White Southern Identity

Just as the war and its aftermath forced a redefinition of Confederate into Southern or American identity, so, too, did it challenge Southern notions of appropriate gender roles. During the war, women had expanded their sphere of sanctioned activity from the privacy of the household to the public world of nursing, charity, and work. Women took part in political discussions, urged men to enlist and fight, and resisted the Yankee invaders, all the while publicly maintaining a posture of ladylike femininity. Men were encouraged to fight through appeals to both their masculine honor and fortitude and their duty to protect white Southern womanhood. Losing the war implicitly challenged gendered notions of manhood. As men tried to resolve this blow to their honor and self-esteem, they sought to reassert control over women, both at home and in public.[1]

Southern white men and women struggled to re-accustom themselves to one another after years of being apart. Despite their being forced back into the private sphere of home and family, women continued to publicly express their distaste for Yankees. These expressions of dismay, particularly as they have come down to us filtered through the memoirs, travel accounts, and magazine and newspaper articles written by their male contemporaries, reveal the intellectual struggles engendered by Reconstruction. Men's writings about women can, and should, be read in several ways.[2] In this time of upheaval and rebuilding, women could find themselves alternately praised and chastised for the same utterances. First, men relied on these stories to perform a sort of political ventriloquism. The manhood of conciliation demanded that white Southern men censor their public disapproval of the Union for reasons of political expedience. But men also recognized that for the most part gender insulated women from Yankee reprisals, freeing them to say and act as most white Southerners felt. Thus, by publicizing stories of women snubbing Northerners, men were able to express their bitterness toward the conquering Yankees while offering assurances that their loyalty to the Union could no longer be called into question—the better to regain their confiscated property and political rights. This more public role to which women had become accustomed during the war, however, threatened men's social dominance at home. Women's vehemence could be seen as unlady-like, almost masculine, and ought to be tempered. Men, particularly those who swiftly accepted the reality of defeat and the need for the South to re-join the Union in order to rebuild itself, were quick to trivialize the politi-cal utterances of women as hysterical and inappropriate. Thus, the South-ern editors and writers who chose to highlight stories of unreconstructed women in their own work used them to enhance their own images. They recreated a landscape where men rationally discussed business and politics while women were again relegated to the domestic and emotional spheres.

"THE MOST VINDICTIVE OF HER RACE"

It became almost a cliché for postwar visitors to the South to comment on the unreconstructed nature of its white women. "The men are rather more inclined to reconstruction than the women," observed one visitor to Charles-ton after the war, a comment that was repeated in almost every travel ac-count. "The men of North Carolina may be 'subjugated,'" reporter Whitelaw Reid observed, "but who shall subjugate the women?" A visiting English-man found the bitterest hostility to the North "among the women, who have nothing to do but to stay at home and nurse their wrath." He did presume "that in the course of a few years this fierce hatred will subside into a sort of sentimental disloyalty." This image of the unrepentant Southern woman, shunning Yankee soldiers as she persisted in her Confederate rebelliousness, was a holdover from the war years when women under occupation resisted the invaders by using particularly feminine strategies. Southern men also re-marked on their women's uncowed spirit with a mixture of admiration and condescension: admiration for the women's lasting dedication to the cause, condescension for their stereotypically emotional responses.[3]

Women expressed their distaste for the Yankees in their midst in a variety of ways, ranging from silent shunning to outright insults. They continued to wear small Confederate flags on their dresses, they "cut" soldiers by re-fusing to acknowledge them on the street or in church, they gathered up their skirts when they passed a Federal soldier on the street, so as not to even brush against him. White women would cross the street or even walk down the middle of it to avoid walking underneath the U.S. flag or to pre-vent encounters with Yankee soldiers. Young women traveling on a Mississippi steamboat happily danced at night to songs like "Dixie" but "pouted angrily" when the band played "Yankee Doodle" or "The Star-Spangled Banner." An older woman told an English traveler "that she would not care to go to heaven if she thought that any Yankees would be there before her."[4] These small, almost humorous, acts of feminine resistance nevertheless served a valuable symbolic function by letting women express their anger in socially sanctioned ways.

Many women took more vocal or confrontational stands. A Union officer stationed in Liberty, Virginia, complained that women made faces at him from across the street and switched pews in church to avoid him until they were reprimanded by the minister, "and the men would be just as bad if they were not afraid to make so open a display." Just as during the war, women believed that their gender would protect them from retaliation. Although that was generally true, this same officer had little sympathy for a group of women in Liberty who were taken to task for their behavior. These women had made a practice of jumping up from their porch and running into the house, banging the door behind them, every time that Union soldiers walked down the street. Frequently the women would begin to play a "rebel tune" on the piano, further upsetting the soldiers. On the night that they began singing "Farewell forever to the star-spangled banner, / No more shall it wave o'er the land of the free," the soldiers had enough and began throwing rocks at the house, which finally quieted the women. In nearby Lynchburg, an old woman trying to draw rations from the Union army was asked if "it was true that she had stood upon the bridge one day a little while before and cursed the Yankees." Realizing that she wasn't going to get any more support from the soldiers, she said "yes" and "went away declaring that she wanted no more Yankee rations, and that she still had sons left to fight for the Confederacy if ever there should be another war."[5]

Railroad cars and stagecoaches provided another point of contentious interaction between Southern women and Northern men. Sidney Andrews, on the train from Charleston to Orangeburg, South Carolina, was snubbed by a young woman who refused to speak to him because he was a Yankee, although she later apologized for her rudeness. Andrews fared no better in Orangeburg, where he was turned away from a boardinghouse for the same crime. Women on the train between Macon and Columbus, Georgia, surprised John Dennett with their "outspoken" dislike of Federal soldiers. In one relatively benign instance, a woman looked out the window to see two Confederate soldiers on crutches next to several Union soldiers. "It makes my heart ache," she murmured, "to see our poor wounded Confederates.

And look at those creatures in blue mixing with them!" Later in the trip, Dennett noticed that three Southern women were sitting together, across the aisle from two Union soldiers, who "were compelled to hear much loud talk about the 'miserable Yanks' who had stolen the corn and meat of such a person, or who were the probable destroyers of this or that building by the roadside 'when they made one of their brave raids.'"[6]

Insulting or snubbing strangers was one thing, but Southern white women also scorned acquaintances. Charles Barnes, in Wilmington, North Carolina, described the town as a place where "the ladies keep very quiet and are seldom seen out of doors, and then they go hurriedly & deeply veiled." Even when home, Wilmington's women avoided Northerners, for Barnes also told of a Union officer calling on a young lady whom he had known "intimately" before the war. The officer was told that she was not home, even though he had seen her at the window as he approached the house. She simply wanted nothing to do with him. Another traveler related an anecdote about a woman from Kentucky engaged in relief work in Raleigh. She would bring her brother, a Federal officer, around as an escort, "but as at the sight of the obnoxious uniform the ladies used all to bounce out of the room, she was obliged to leave him outside while she went in to do her business."[7]

Resentment of both the persons and the symbols of Union occupation was not limited simply to adult women; as they had done during the war, mothers passed on their bitterness to the children. "I hate the Yankees, and I bring up my children to hate them too," a woman told reporter Henry Deedes. Having had met other such women, Deedes observed, "I am very certain she is not the most vindictive of her race." Sidney Andrews judged that "Mothers yet teach their children hate of the North," a realization prompted by his asking "a bright-eyed girl of half a dozen years . . . whose girl she was" and her prompt reply: "A Rebel mother's girl." An English reporter had a similar experience in Richmond when he asked a twelve-year-old girl to point out Jefferson Davis's house. "She answered the question, and then, judging us to be Northerners, added, drawing herself up half defiantly— 'He's *my* President, and the greatest man in the world!'" No childish gesture was too trivial to go unnoticed or uncorrected. A Wilmington woman was overheard sharply reprimanding her son for singing a snatch of "The Union Forever," and a woman in a Mobile boardinghouse quieted her fussy child "by threatening to leave it and let the Yankees catch it." A well-dressed Richmond matron called her misbehaving little boy a "Unionist." The lad challenged his mother, crying, "I ain't a Unionist," prompting his mother to reconsider: "No, I'm sure you're not. If you were I'd disinherit you sure, and so would the captain."[8]

The vast majority of white Southern women must have acquiesced in silence. Yet their stories were not held up as a public example. Indeed, only part of the story of Southern female intransigence was about their unwillingness to be reconstructed; part also involved their dedication to the war itself. Both Southern and Northern men praised Southern women for their unwillingness to give up, even in the face of certain defeat. "It was admitted by the enemy from their experience," wrote the author of "Memories of the War" in *De Bow's Review*, "that the men of the South might be conquered, but the women, *never*." An editor sharing a stagecoach with Sidney Andrews in October 1865 assured the Northerner that "the war would have closed two years ago but for the women of the South."[9] Such assertions complimented Southern women even as they cast a somewhat unflattering light on Southern men, implying that they lacked steadfast commitment. They also frankly falsified the war experience itself—certainly not all women were as steadfast as they had been portrayed, but former Confederates were loathe to admit such contradictions to themselves. At the same time, however, these flowery compliments were often delivered with an edge of implicit criticism—women were so dedicated as to be irrational, especially once the war had ended. "Where the men were Rebels after the Mississippi pattern of earnestness," Whitelaw Reid observed, "some new word must be discovered to define the extent of the hatred the women bore the Yankee Government. Such mild titles as 'Rebel,' failed to meet the case." A man returning from Mississippi to Maine in March 1866 complained to John Dennett that "at one time they [Southern men] were decent, comparatively. 'We're whipped,' you'd hear 'em say—'fightin's played.' But after the women folks got hold of them the men gave up all that, and now men and women were about alike—more disloyal than they were in '60."[10]

Southern white women were not alone in their hatred of the Yankees; only more open about it than men. Among men, a powerful undercurrent of bitterness and resentment ran beneath a surface veneer of polite chilliness. Jeremiah Morton angrily confided his resentment of "the Yankee nation" to a friend, explaining, "Whilst I *humble* myself before *God*, I am *erect* before *them*."[11] A sense of having been personally wronged only added to some people's hatred. A former soldier wrote to his cousin on the anniversary of his brother's death at the battle of Franklin, reflecting, "I could bear our National Misfortunes with more composure if Ben had lived through the war, but as implacable as my hate for the whole Yankee race was before, it is much more so now, and I sometimes shudder to think of the feelings I have towards them." Henry Haywood was upset that the Union general occupying his family's home in Raleigh refused to vacate the premises until his grandfather was pardoned. He found it painful to walk by the house and see Yankees taking his furniture and wondered about the ability of time to heal wounds. For his part, he felt that it would only increase "*if possible* the hatred I already feel. I do not wish I never hope to 'love my enemies' but this is a bitter and never ending subject with me so I will stop just here and so many thousands have so much more to feel bitterly toward them than I have. Father thinks though that all this has caused Mother's illness—we avoid the subject it excites her so—how can I feel otherwise than *bitterly*." He seemed unable to stop the anger from spilling forth.[12]

Hatred of Yankees was more than just a personal opinion to be kept to oneself; many white Southerners were upset to see neighbors making friendly overtures toward Northerners. In this, too, we can see echoes of wartime debates over relations with Union soldiers. A resident of Bayou Boeuf, Louisiana, confirmed that "the bitterest hatred exists among the people here towards the north. . . . All is bitter, bitter hatred tenfold worse than ever before and I can assure you they have great cause for it." He clearly shared his neighbors' opinions, for he asked his parents to tell his sister "when she writes me to please be very particular what she says in regard to the war and never speak of the 'noble' Federal soldiers. There were several phrases in her letter as well as in yours that I skiped over in reading them to Frank." An article in the *Southern Opinion* declared, "We are positively disgusted, sickened, by the nauseous and fulsome protestations of humble fealty and intense affection towards the United States, made by men among us who ought to have better taste, if not more manly principle." What made such professions of attachment to the Union so repugnant to the *Southern Opinion*'s unreconstructed editor, H. Rives Pollard, was the fact that Virginia was "*attached* to the North—by bayonet!" A former Confederate soldier admitted to John Trowbridge that not only did he believe that the South had been wrong and the North right "about the war" but he also had shared his revelations with his friends and neighbors. They were not so enlightened, and they denounced him as "a Yankee, the worst name they can give." This former Confederate was so disturbed by his treatment at home that he moved to Harrisburg, Pennsylvania, where he was free from such prejudices.[13]

Northerners were certainly aware of the prejudices against them. While an officer with the Freedmen's Bureau in Greenville, South Carolina, John

W. De Forest took a stroll around town every afternoon. "I walked alone," he recalled; "no young man would like to be seen in my company; the Southerner so forgetting himself would not be smiled upon by woman." De Forest minimized the depth of anti-Yankee feeling, however, believing the bitterness to be nothing more than "a fashion set by the aristocracy."[14] On his travels through the South, John Dennett was amused to be frequently "taken for a Southerner," although always from a different state. "When I am known to be a Northern man," however, he added, "sometimes I am made to feel that my company is not desired and sometimes there is amiable talk and argument." Such social ostracism was commonly remarked on by outsiders and was something that Southerners who were hoping to encourage immigration and development fought against. It was not surprising that white Southerners still smarting from their defeat and still influenced by years of anti-Northern propaganda would want nothing to do with their perceived conquerors. "We don't wish to associate with them," a South Carolinian told Dennett. "I suppose it would be more Christian to forgive them, and to let all vindictiveness die out, but we can never forget how they have treated us." William Huger was pleased to report to his mother in October 1865 that the spring promised a gay social season in Charleston, but he also confessed that he was concerned that Yankees, who were the only ones with money, might be included. "If that be the case," he declared, "I *won't* see the inside of a ballroom. It becomes necessary for us to see something of them in a business capacity but I don't feel that it has become necessary for us to invite them to our houses." The lines of demarcation between Southerner and Northerner needed to remain clearly drawn. Indeed, a writer in the *Vicksburg Times* was shocked that Northerners could even complain about their "social isolation," asking, "What right have *they* to expect courtesy from the people they outrage? What claims have they upon us, save only for our scorn, detestation, and hatred?"[15]

The line between social isolation and involvement with neighbors was an ever-shifting boundary. Proximity and personality often combined to determine actions, and Southerners were governed by many different influences. Gertrude Thomas was out in her carriage one day in September 1866 when she was stopped by a Union soldier asking for a ride and something to eat. Thomas curtly refused him but had second thoughts, relented, and gave the man food from her lunch basket. "I justified myself still farther afterwards by explaining that what I refused *the Yankee* I gave to *the man*." Riding a train through Tennessee crowded with former planters and Union soldiers, John Kennaway was "immensely struck by the good feeling existing between both parties, each seeming to have forgotten the deadly strife in which they had so lately taken part. . . . Many were the battles fought over again, many a 'whipping' on both sides admitted and accounted for."[16]

Part of what made it easier for white Southerners to accept Northerners was the simple passage of time: as the overt scars of war vanished from the landscape, as families were reunited and began to recover economically, there seemed to be less reason to hold on to general anger. Too, as white Southerners realized that for the most part the occupying army meant them no harm and, indeed, largely left Southern whites alone to work out labor relations for themselves, they began to soften. Finally, as Southerners saw that not all Northerners agreed with the Radical Republicans, it was not as easy to demonize a whole "race." A young woman in Staunton, Virginia, was assured by a cousin in Illinois that "the southern people have very many hearts in the north that beat in unison with them." An article in the usually virulently anti-Yankee *Southern Opinion* sought to clarify the paper's stance, explaining that it bore no prejudice against Northern men in general, for it recognized that many Northerners still valued liberty and republican (as opposed to Republican) government. Those men were welcome in the South, just not those of a more radical bent. In "The Return of Good Feeling," an article in the December 1867 issue of *De Bow's Review*, George Fitzhugh defended white Southerners' initially "cold and reserved" reception of Northerners as only "natural," given the war's bloodshed and the subsequent embarrassment of occupation. Indeed, "any other course would have justly exposed us to the charge of fawning, cringing hypocrisy, and to the contempt of those from whom we sought by sycophancy and submissiveness to curry favor." But the recent midterm elections had changed everything by showing that the Northern people as a whole did not favor the Radicals' "negro rule." As Northerners and Southerners came together in opinions about race, Fitzhugh continued, they might be able to come together as a people as well.[17]

There were, however, limits to how far such reconciliation should go. Romance between Northerners and Southerners, and specifically between Northern men and Southern women (a convention in the literature of the 1860s and 1870s), posed a problem for Southerners.[18] Given the rhetoric of heritage and racial purity that had so shaped white Southern identity, the threat of intermarriage seemed a real one, for it would dilute and perhaps sully the "true Southern blood" that still coursed through ex-Confederate veins. Too, by literally embracing Union soldiers, women were granting social acceptance to the same men who had killed their fathers and brothers, who had destroyed their countryside, and who now stood over them as occupiers.

A Little Rock woman gleefully reported the latest scandal to a male friend visiting New York: "*Ellie Merrick* struck great & melancholy astonishment into the hearts of all her friends two weeks since by *eloping* with a *federal officer*. She has always been one of those *violent rebels* who could not condescend to be even *polite* to *our enemies*. Both she & her sister indeed the whole family, have often compromised their dignity & ladyhood in their bitter abuse of *federals*." While on the one hand professing sympathy for the "poor child," who had surely made a mistake, she was also struck by Ellie Merrick's deception, for "she played a *double game* most adroitly; she certainly had more deceit & duplicity in her composition than I gave her credit for." The greatest disgrace fell on the girl's family, variously described as "mortified," "inconsolable," and threatening to never forgive their wayward daughter. What was Merrick's real crime? Marrying a Northerner? Or being a hypocrite? The letter-writer's outrage seems to be related to the same issues of loyalty and trustworthiness faced by men. Being too quick to either reject or accept Northerners made one suspect. In another letter, the Little Rock woman reminded her friend that romantic prohibitions should apply to both sexes. "Take care that some of those bright *northern beauties* don't *captivate* that *little susceptible article commonly known* as a *heart*," she warned. "We would not welcome you with a *northern* bride half so warmly in the clime of your adoption."[19]

Women who came of marriageable age during and immediately after the war, like the unfortunate Miss Merrick, found themselves in a difficult position. Two hundred and fifty-eight thousand Southern men had died during the war, decimating the marriageable-age population. Young white women had been deprived of many of the rituals of courtship and fun during the war, and it was understandable that loyalty to a national dream might pale beside the opportunity to dance and flirt. A widely published poem, penned by a "Mississippi Lady," sought to defend women who chose marriage to a Northerner over the possibility of spinsterhood:

"I never will marry a 'Yank'" she said,
　　And I believe she really meant it;
But alas! when her rebel lover was dead,
　　Why then she began to repent it.

For "rebs" were scarce in her town, you know,
　　While Yankee officers were plenty,

And who likes to be without a beau,
    When on the shady side of twenty?

So she shed a tear for her lover's loss,
    And heaved a sigh for her country's glory,
But she gave her head a coquettish toss,
    While she heard that Yankee Colonel's story.

Ah! ever thus since first the world began,
    Tho' woman was fair, yet oft she was frail,
And even that "lord of creation"—a man,
    May still be won, by a flatterer's tale.

So a mighty change of feeling came o'er her,
    Yet blame her not, nor with harshness chide,
For had she the *choice of the world* before her,
    I doubt if she had been a *Yankee's* bride.[20]

The poem well captures the tensions faced by these young women. On the one hand, it seems to be mocking women for their fickleness and frailty, the ease by which they could be taken in by handsome officers. But the final stanza puts a different cast on the entire poem, and by extension on Southern women's plight, by asking for understanding, explaining their choices away as a matter purely of circumstance, not free will. Women who married Yankees were not, in this construction, abandoning their former Confederate nation; they were simply subsuming their patriotism, making the only decisions they could.

Women did profess to prefer Confederates. A Staunton, Virginia, girl described her ideal beau to a friend. First he should be handsome, then intelligent, and ideally "have a little money." Most important, she "would like him to be a whole-hearted Rebel, ready at any time to whip the Radicals. But 'beggars are not to be choosers' but he must not be a Yankee by birth or principle." Even in matters of the heart, the politics of race and Reconstruction intruded. The article "An Opening for Destitute Young Men" in the *Southern Opinion* proposed a tongue-in-cheek solution to two pressing problems: first, there were too many men of "genteel birth" who were unwilling to take jobs as artisans or farmers, believing such work to be "below them," and, second, there were too many young "Rebellas" in need of male companionship and society. The solution: young men should immediately organize the "Territorial Escort Association." Naturally, only men of "high moral character and irreproachable manners" would be permitted to join, whereas "the buzzes of Blue-tail Flies will be unheeded, and none of that fraternity shall be allowed to enter the service, as it is a strictly Southern institution." The article further suggested that the association's uniform be "neat but gaudy—grey in colour, to suit the taste of your fair employers— minus the buttons for policy's sake." Should the plan be adopted, "Rebellas who heretofore have made nuns of themselves for lack of escorts can now enjoy society, while penniless men of high position may earn a livelihood, cheered by the humanizing influence of women."[21]

White women were also chastised for neglecting the soldiers who had survived the war. A brief essay penned by a Madge Rutledge in the *Field and Fireside* recalled how eagerly Southern women of all classes sent the men of their communities off to war. A year after the war had ended, however, elite women seemed to look down on the poor, illiterate soldiers who had fought for their protection and complained that they were so unrefined that ladies cannot "take any pleasure in them." Rutledge cast romance in the language of loyalty and patriotism, cautioning her female readers that if they truly loved the South as much as they claimed, they would not run away to Europe to rid themselves of Yankees but would stay. And it was not proper for women to speak out in anger: "Yes, if you will spend more time teaching our poor soldiers, you would prove the truth of your patriotism, and convince your country of your undying love far more than by your insatiate abuse of *Yankees, Radicals*, and the *ubiquitous cuffy*."[22] Southern white women during Reconstruction, it seemed, could not win. Chastised for their disloyalty to the cause, they were also ridiculed for being overly loyal. Yet men and women both recognized that there was often utility in speaking with a feminine voice.

POLITICAL VENTRILOQUISM

"Dear Mister Editors of the Southern Home Journal," began a letter in that Baltimore newspaper's inaugural issue in November 1867. "I got your perlite letter last week a asking of me to write to you and tell the news down here in this 'Deistrick,' so called—and went right straight and jined a sewing society, besides making my old men take to going to lodge meetings again, that I might hear all as was a going; for I don't know which is the best place to pick up news—a sewing society where no gentlemen is admitted, or a mason's lodge where no ladies is allowed." So opened the first of six "Letter[s] from Betsey Bittersweet" that graced the pages of the weekly *South-*

ern Home Journal in late 1867 and early 1868. This first paragraph—with its vernacular prose, oblique criticism of Radical Reconstruction, and satirical recognition of men and women's separate realms—introduced many of the themes that ran through these humorous columns. Supposedly the correspondence of a North Carolina woman, Betsey's letters mixed discussions of Reconstruction politics with domestic complaints about shifting racial and social relations within postemancipation households.[23] This mixture of humorous political and domestic complaints, written in the voice of a middle-class white Southern woman, could also be found in "Florence Fay Arrows," a column that appeared for several months in another regional weekly, the *Field and Fireside*. Like Betsey Bittersweet, Florence Fay relied on exaggerated humor and convoluted phrasings to express her social and political critiques, although, fortunately for the modern reader, she rarely used dialect. Compared to Betsey Bittersweet's writings, Florence Fay's messages tended to mock Northerners less and criticize Southerners more. Her writings stressed the plight of the common white Southerner, and she frequently sent her arrows flying in the direction of the intellectually and socially pretentious "small fry" or "mushroom aristocracy."[24]

Betsey Bittersweet's and Florence Fay's columns can be read on several levels. They each criticized the Union government and Union soldiers, complaining about white Southerners' political disfranchisement. Thus they provided an outlet for white Southern bitterness and resentment toward the Republican Party, the Freedmen's Bureau, and the freedmen themselves. The ladies' sharp tongues were not, however, limited to outsiders. To varying degrees, both Betsey and Florence turned their wit on themselves, addressing the behavior of white Southern women as well. They rebuked Northern women (and implicitly their Southern sisters) for demanding the vote; they warned against the dangers of overt flirtatiousness; and they condemned women who were more interested in matters outside the home than the comfort of those within.

In critiquing women's behavior, writers like Betsey Bittersweet and Florence Fay sought a resolution to the "crisis in gender" that had arisen out of the Civil War. Their complaints about black voting or Radical policies served as a sort of "political ventriloquism." By publicizing stories of women snubbing Northerners or publishing a woman's critical writings, men were able to express their bitterness toward the conquering Yankees while at the same time offering assurances that male loyalty to the Union could no longer be called into question—the better to regain their confiscated property and political rights. At the same time, however, women were also being told to cease their political activities and turn to the work of reconstructing hearth and home—men could handle the politics. By reconstructing notions of appropriate femininity, white Southern women allowed themselves and white Southern men to feel secure in their redefined postwar regional and gender identities.

Although there were enough similarities between the two columns to make analyzing them together both logical and useful, they were quite different in both tone and format. Betsey Bittersweet's letters were more explicitly concerned with politics, perhaps a function of the tumultuous months in which they were written. Every letter addressed political and racial tensions, and several dealt with North Carolina's Radical Reconstruction constitutional convention. Betsey also freely mocked African Americans for wanting to vote and women for wanting to move beyond their traditional place within the home and family. The letters were all written in dialect with frequent misspellings and malapropisms, all of which located them squarely in the tradition of the Southwestern humorists, Northern characters like Artemus Ward, and Betsey's extraordinarily popular regional counterpart, Bill Arp.[25] Florence Fay's columns were less predictable. About half of them had to do with social topics, whether in the form of diatribes against snuff-dipping or saloon-keeping or mocking attacks on social pretensions. Those that dealt with politics criticized both Yankees and ex-Confederates. Too, when Florence Fay turned to political matters, she was more likely to complain about their effects on ordinary people in the form of economic hardships than to condemn black voting or white disfranchisement.[26]

Betsey Bittersweet began her correspondence with the editors of the *Southern Home Journal* by expressing her sympathies for "the ex-queen of the United States," Mary Todd Lincoln. Betsey reported on a rumor that the "Radikills" (referred to in other letters as the "Redy-to-kills") were skimping on their financial support for Mrs. Lincoln, forcing her to sell off her old clothes. Betsey was shocked to discover that the widow's pension totaled only seventeen hundred dollars a year, remarking that the "republic's is ongrateful and that's a fact. Why that aint more'n twice as much as some private widows lives on, and to expect a public one to be satisfied with it is jest like them Radikills." This sarcasm was typical of her writings. Betsey told her husband that if she were in a similar position, rather than resort to selling her old clothes, she would pen an exposé of the situation, and "get it worked up into sich a book as the Democratick papers would pay me well for." She spun a series of potential titles for her serialized work:

One week I'd come out with a story called "The four S's, or the Secret Story of the Sable Set—Seward, Sumner, Stanton, and Stevens;" and the next I'd give the sequel to it, and call it "One Queen of Diamonds versus Four Knaves of Spades." And if that did'n't do the business, next week I'd come out with "The Loyal League, or Lace and Loot," and follow that with "The Black Cashmere, or the Blanket Contract," or the "Long Red Shawl, or Last Radikill Shift," or "The True History of the Public Pocket Handkerchief, and the Pocket it came out of, told by the Pocket it went into." And then I'd collect 'em all in a book, and call it "Rampant Radikill Revelations," or "The Public Washing of the Loyal Lincoln League Linen," and my fortune would be made.

Betsey uses her femininity to express her criticisms of the Radicals in two ways. First, rather than address their political policies directly, she attacks them obliquely through the figure of Mary Todd Lincoln, though it would be a mistake to think that Betsey had any great sympathy for the martyred president's wife. Then she couches her criticism of the Radicals through a female form, that of titles for sentimental romances, the very sort that graced the pages of the *Southern Home Journal* itself.[27]

Just as Betsey looked back at the Civil War to make her political points, so, too, did Florence Fay. For example, when she addressed the question of "Patriotism" in January 1866, she charged that, despite "the vast amount of Patriotism there is at the present day between the two oceans . . . you can't always tell the genuine from the spurious article from the cut of the cloth." You can't tell a patriot from a *port-monnaie*, she reflected ruefully, "until you find the latter convenience suddenly wrenched from your hand, on the principal thoroughfare, leaving a piece of the chain around your victimised finger, by something in blue breeches and army cap; and you look after the said breeches and cap as they widen the distance between you and them, with astonishing rapidity, and think what a surprising quantity of *Patriotism* must have got under those breeches and cap to give the fingers of that flying something the itch, and butter its heels." In effect, patriotism was nothing more than an excuse to steal from the common people.[28]

Florence Fay devoted most of her essay to a mocking assessment of patriotism—by which she meant Unionism, a recognition of North Carolina's divided population, perhaps—over the past few years, under both the Confederacy and Reconstruction. Regarding the former, she described patriotism calling at your house, asking if you have a husband in the "rebel" army. You feed it, and it goes off without paying, "and you look at Patriotism's back as it goes over the sill, and hope that it may always keep its toes in the present direction. Then you turn the bolts in the locks of your doors, and open your upper windows and when Patriotism makes you another call, there's nobody home but your poodle, whose little but loud mouth tells the news to patriotism through the keyhole." Implicit in this picture was a real resentment of the ways in which white Southern civilians had been treated at the hands of both their enemy invaders and their own Confederate government, a resentment that continued unabated into peacetime. As she explained:

> Patriotism had wide-awake eyes and cautious feet. It crept about between two days and very carefully and commendably choked old hens and young porkers, lest they should lay "secesh" eggs in the morning and utter a "rebel" squeak at day break, and so commit treason against the flag.
>
> Patriotism claimed orchards and gardens as its own, by right of conquest—it made "dumplins and things" of the fruit, and very properly cut down the trees to cook 'em with.
>
> Everything was *patriotic*; from the little nigger with both hands full of stolen candy, whistling "I wish I was in Dixie, hoo-ray!" *down* to the larger and lighter complexioned animal in blue and brass, singing musically, "We'll be gay and happy, too-hie!"

Patriotism, Florence Fay argued, was not for Southern whites to feel. All patriotism, in the form of loyalty to the Union, had ever given them was hardship and deprivation. Patriotism was money-grubbing and selfish. "Patriotism looked handsome and well until it put its industrious hands into its Uncle's pocket, in its anxiety to protect its purse, and got its fingers so pinched it disfigured its face. May the Lord bless Patriotism to the full extent of its merits, and keep its dear hands out of Uncle Sam's and his daughters['] pockets, and its precious feet away from poultry yards and pig pens."[29]

Florence Fay's oblique yet humorous indictment of patriotism reflected white Southerners' disconnection from the rhetoric of postwar American nationalism. But, because the anger came in the voice of a woman, it was softened and made less threatening. Florence Fay also took aim at the Yankees themselves, specifically the "Blue Devil or politely speaking, bonnie *Blue Beëlzebub*!": the Northern officers who persisted in flirting with Southern women. She painted the Federals as leering lechers, unwilling to take no for an answer. "If you say to Blue Beëlzebub, 'get thee behind me satan,'" Florence Fay warned her female readers, "and succeed in pushing him from before your eyes, he'll bend over your shoulder and whisper in your ear; such and so pertinacious is a Blue Devil!" Florence Fay, protected by her

lightly mocking tone, seized the opportunity to impugn not only the occupiers' present motives (that of seducing Southern women) but their past
performance: "Blue Devils are brave dogs, and 'die in the last ditch' with
the Prince of Orange, when battling with an inferiour force; but pusillanimous puppies in combat with equal numbers, and wheel suddenly and run
rapidly from a bold and well-panoplied adversary, with delicately dropped
oars and slender narrative modestly dangling between their posterior pro-
pellers." In short, a fair fight would send the "Blue Devils" running away
with their tails between their legs. While a male newspaper editor or author might have feared such an outright insult to the occupiers, the masks
of humor and gender protected Florence Fay.[30]

Florence Fay directed her ire against white northerners and Union soldiers, with African Americans almost entirely absent from her columns. The
same could not be said for the more critical, more acerbic Betsey Bittersweet, who reported several nasty practical jokes at the freedmen's expense.
In one instance, she described a new "Yankee invention" that had supposedly been keeping the freedmen from "stealing the corn and cotton from
out'n the fields." What was this miraculous invention? Nothing less than
fertilizer made from the bones of Union soldiers found on Southern battlefields, according to Betsey's cousin Jane. It worked, according to Betsey, by
playing on black fears of being "hanted." At the same time, she was also
able to get in a not so subtle dig at purported Yankee barbarity.[31] In a different letter, she told of how her husband tricked a group of African American
men on their way to vote by convincing them that if they deposited their
Radical tickets in the ballot box, they would no longer have proof of their
registration and have "nothing to show for your mule and forty acres." Better
they should drop Conservative tickets in the box and hold onto their Radical ones. By using this image of the foolish freedmen, a staple of postwar
white Southern (and nationally Democratic) rhetoric, Betsey signaled her
essential conservatism. While the medium of a woman taking on a public
political stance though newspaper commentary might be new, the message
of racial, gender, and political hierarchies was not.

In the same letter, Betsey went on to complain about something even
more ridiculous in her eyes: the spectacle of her female cook asking for time
off: "'To forge all the notes in the county.' 'To register all the votes, you
mean, don't you?' ses I. 'Well,' ses she, 'and there aint much difference between the two.' 'No,' ses I, 'there aint, but what's the need of your going?
You cant vote, 'cause you are a woman, and you might as well stay and git
dinner.' But she 'lowed she was'nt going to do no sich thing. 'I'm as black

as eny body,' ses she, 'and I knows my rights and am a gwine to the court-house after 'em.'" The cook then comes to Betsey to ask for a basket in which to bring her franchise home. When asked if she knew what she was going after, what the franchise was, the woman replied: "Well not 'zactly Miss Betsey, but that there Northern gentlemen as spoke 'tother day, sed as how God A'mighty had give us niggers the 'lective franchise, same as he gave the children of Israel manna in the dessert; he sed we was brought out of the land of bondage by Marse Moses-Lincoln, and now we was to taste the good things in store for us; and in course he's gwine to give us something good to eat better'n them rations of hard tack and salt beef they's been putting us off with till things get settled." In Betsey's eyes, black women were fool-ish to overstep their bounds and expect something that was denied to white women. Too, this anecdote highlighted the belief that African Americans had no idea what the franchise was, that they were simply sheep being led about by Northerners. Betsey's final complaint was that, while her cook was off getting the franchise, she had to do her work, and get her dinner. This highlighted the persistent white Southern complaint that emancipation had resulted in an erosion of ladylike prerogatives.[32]

Three of the six "Letters from Betsey Bittersweet" dealt with the most pressing political question of the winter of 1867–68: North Carolina's con-stitutional convention. Betsey first traveled to the capital to hear William Holden and Zebulon Vance speak. She was quite partial to the latter, whom she described as having "nothing provisional 'bout him." Indeed, Betsey claimed that his speech warning the freedmen that they would never rule the South was so inspiring that it moved a group of Union soldiers watch-ing the proceedings to jump out of their seats and yell out: "Give it to 'em Guv'nor, give it to'em; this is the white man's country, and while bagonetts and bullets is to be got, niggers shan't rule it." Thus, this section of her letter does double duty: it endorses Zeb Vance's defiance while turning the Union occupiers into buffoons, no better than the freedmen who feared fertilizer.[33]

Betsey began her next letter by endorsing a sermon written by John Quincy Adams II, in which he argues that the Radicals have gone to far. But she quickly turned her attention to a letter written by Union general Thomas Ewing, in which he likened the Southern states to "magazines, full of pow-der and percushon caps." According to Betsey, "Southern wimen is like per-cushion caps, not much harm in 'em by themselves, tho ther's a good deal of noise ef you set 'em off. But jest attach 'em to a gun that's loaded and primed, and they'll do some mischief when they explode, I kin tell you. Let the sweet, harmless critters alone, Mr. Home Journal, for making their men folk shoot true, when they do go off, and vote to suit them." She then takes issue with Ewing, who believed that the only way to keep the magazines from exploding was to guard them: "I kin tell him, and you too, that packed in these magazines along of the powder and the percushion caps, is ever so many brimstone matches, and squirming around among all this here ammunition is a passel of political rats that quit the Confederate ship when she was about to sink, and being disappointed in gitting of a nibble at the big Union cheese, theys now a doing of ther best to light the matches, explode the powder, and blow things up in spite of the bagonets [bayonets]." She advised both Adams and Ewing to "invent a Yankee rat-trap, something like a Sherman's Wringer, you know," and catch all of the "rats" who are encouraging the blacks to listen to speeches rather than work in the fields. After that, "we may make a crop, which will allow the Yankees to make money out'n the South once more; and that will do more toards quieting of them and reconstructing things ginerally, than any gospel that kin be preached or pistel that kin be fired."[34] Betsey's letter carries serious political messages: a demand for home rule, a warning that politicians North and South were jeopardizing the fragile stability of the Reconstruction South, and a bitter recognition that all most people cared about was profits. But, related in a humorous way, and by a woman, the words seemed less ominous, less threatening than they would have had they come from a man.

Betsey then wrote from the "so-called" North Carolina Constitutional Convention in Raleigh, mocking all of the delegates, but especially the newly enfranchised African Americans and the Radical Republicans. "And I can tell you, Mister Home Journal," she explained, "that the fight lays between the Conservatives and the niggers, for the white Radicals in this convention aint got sense enough even to be the puppets of the X. P. G., Mr. W. Holden, and the niggers have, and is accordingly elevated to that dignified position." Much of her letter was devoted to her desire to witness and report on the convention herself, "and not be dependent on no 'irresponsible stripling'" for her information. But, as a white woman, she presumably would not be permitted to sit in the observers' gallery. Betsey's solution was to disguise herself "in a short-tailed dress, with a red wig on, and the hair all skewered in the top of my head, with a little hat the size of a saucer stuck on in front and a pair of green specks stuck on." By adding a false nose and a blue veil, she had transformed herself into "a nigger marm on her travels, anxious to hear the debates in a convention of the wisdom, learning, and ability of North Car'liner. The Southerners will be glad if I am satisfied with listening and don't want to take a part; and as for the Radikils, they will think, no matter what I do, its all for the glory of God and to make money." In this instance of political ventriloquism, it was precisely Betsey's femininity that allowed her to cross boundaries, though always in the service of the conservative white South.[35]

The "Letter from Betsey Bittersweet" and "Florence Fay Arrows" columns also allowed white men to resolve some of the more personal or domestic "cris[es] in gender" that engulfed the South after the Civil War. Several historians have suggested convincingly that, as the war drew to its bitter conclusion, the defeated Southern soldiers, bred in a patriarchal, honor-bound society, felt emasculated by their loss.[36] Their manhood and valor had been tested and had fallen short on the battlefield. Consequently, they would need to be reasserted at home. One of the many reconstructions Southern whites faced after the war involved that of male-female relations, and one of the mediums in which this took place was the press. By presenting themselves as practical and conciliatory and women as intemperate and hysterical, men sought to reconstruct the divisions between the public and the domestic, the rational and the emotional.

This use of a woman's voice and figure could have other meanings, for not only did Betsey take aim at Reconstruction politics, but (along with Florence Fay) she also addressed social relations and appropriate female behavior. Clearly, Betsey thought it inappropriate, if not completely ridiculous, for her cook to seek the franchise. But what of *her* political interests, *her* trips to the capital and convention? Betsey justified her actions carefully and in so doing delineated the boundaries of acceptable female behavior. Betsey freely admitted that she usually went to visit her cousin Jane in Raleigh when "there's anything a stirring at the Capital," even though she thought "as a general rule politics and petticoats is too p's as oughten to be in the same pod." What made her behavior acceptable was that it wasn't her fault. Rather, the blame lay with the Union and the Radicals, "sense they've turned our men into wimen—or tried to do it by disfranchising of 'em—we wimen, who was always counted politically with the niggers, you know, is got demoralized, and has gone into politics like Senator Pool did into the Confederate service, 'jest to embarrass things.'" With this throwaway line at the beginning of a letter, Betsey neatly encapsulated the fears and resentments of ex-Confederate men. Their world had been turned upside down with black voting, imposed from the outside, and the next threat to stability could only come from one place: from women exercising the franchise. This was not an entirely irrational fear on the part of North Carolina's men, for the very convention that Betsey supposedly attended, along with others throughout the South, put in place new property rights for married women, and others saw proposals (voted down) for white female suffrage.[37]

Betsey was careful, however, not to go too far, and she pointedly condemned Northern women for wanting to vote. As Betsey saw it, "What does a woman want to vote for, when at the very least she can always, if she understands her rights, make at least one man vote as she pleases?" Women had plenty of rights already: "a right to our own way, when we can git it without a row in the family; and a smart woman kin always do that, if she goes the right way to work. And we've a right to pat and pet and coax our men folks, now a pulling of the right rein, then a twitch of the left, and then holding both of 'em sorter easy but firm; like you do sperited horses, till you can turn 'em any way you want to, and make 'em think all the time they're agoing of ther own way instead of yours." By expressing concern over women taking too public and political a role, Betsey argued for a return to antebellum gender conventions. At the same time, though, she realized that, for many women, such a retrenchment would be impossible: "But I ain't of opinion that she has a right to be a man, or even pretend she's one; and ef she is obliged to wear the britches for the good of the family, her skirts ought to be long enuf to hide 'em." If a woman had to take charge for the sake of her family, and many women did, she needed to do so in a way that preserved her man's virile image.[38]

Like Florence Fay complaining about the high cost of patriotism and its tendency to result in extra work for white women, Betsey Bittersweet also expressed her dismay with the shape of postwar Southern race relations. In the same letter in which she mocked her cook for seeking the franchise (and leaving her to get the family's dinner), Betsey complained that the Freedmen's Bureau had been invented "jest to make Southern ladies have to do their own work, like Northern ones does, so as they would by their cute contrivances." These contrivances to which Betsey referred included "Union Washing Mashins" and "Sherman's Wringers." In a letter dated 1 January 1868, she complained about Christmas, lamenting how much work it was for the mistress of the house without slaves to assist in the preparations, noting that "it was a very good thing in the old time when we had servants and money and could keep it like ladies and gentlemen, but it don't suit these times." She proposed a radical solution: "While we are a reconstructing, I vote to reconstruct Christmas, and appint that hereafter it shall fall on the twenty-ninth day of February instead of on the twenty-fifth day of December. Thanksgiving belongs to the Yankees, fourth of July to the niggers, and Christmas ought to belong to the white folks." By adopting the persona of the overworked Southern lady, Betsey was able to voice white complaints about the changes in public ritual that had accompanied Reconstruction.[39]

Florence Fay was less concerned with explicitly resolving the crisis in gender by removing women from the public and political sphere and more interested in defining appropriate and ladylike behavior for her female readers. She spoke out against snuff-dipping by women—and by men; she mocked flirtatious "wee women," who attend church for the sole purpose of catching men's attention. The wee woman at home was no better, posing and posturing, "afraid to be natural, lest she should not appear womanly." By puncturing pretensions, Florence Fay told women to retrench. The overt flirtatiousness of the war years was inappropriate for peacetime; women were no longer to take the lead, in either public or private.[40]

Although she frowned at flirtations, Florence Fay was not opposed to marriage. Indeed, in one column she provided advice (to both men and women) on choosing a mate, in the process painting a picture of desirable postwar Southern gender behavior. Women were cautioned against "a masculine" who drank with his friends, who attended church either too frequently or not often enough, who "squirt[ed] great sluices of tobacco juice," or who was prone to jealousy. "Take it for granted," Florence Fay advised, "if your *lover* is an *imp*, your *husband* will be the *d*—!" Men were given even more specific advice in choosing a proper lady. The ideal bride should not be overly interested in fashion, lest she lead them into the poorhouse while she continued "flirting around to theaters, operas, etc., with popinjays and *patriots* during your imprisonment." Nor should men choose a woman who constantly scolded the servants, for a bad mistress would never make a good wife. "You may learn a woman's worth from a domestic's tongue more certainly than you can get the truth from Robert Tomes' 'History of the great American Rebellion' or General Big Failure Butler's 'reports.'" Finally, men were warned against choosing a woman "who clamors loudly for equality with man, and thinks said equality consists in the right of poking bits of paper into the ballot box on election days—tricked out in trowsers, a short frock and shingled hair. Marry her and she'll make you feel as cheap as the famous tower at Bermuda Hundred [that] was sold, if you are a southern man. Marry her and if you are a 'foreigner' she'll help you vote southern plantations into small farms for contrabands and 'furrin squatters.'" In this last advice, Florence Fay closes the circle, neatly linking the personal and political. Even marriage for whites in the postwar South had public consequences. A good wife was one who stayed home, and a good wife was one who endorsed a return to the antebellum political status quo. A politicized wife, one who sought the franchise, was no better than a Yankee.[41]

Although the "Letters from Betsey Bittersweet" and "Florence Fay Arrows" columns shared much in terms of both tone and content, they appear to have been aimed at different audiences. Betsey's letters—with their more overtly political content, their use of feminine disguises, and their more vernacular language, in the tradition of the (male) Southwestern humorists— seem to have been written for men. Women, including at times Betsey herself, are clear objects of ridicule. The letters are not really concerned with delineating the boundaries of appropriate female behavior, or at least not for white women. Class, too, is important in the Betsey letters. Betsey is presented as somewhere between lower and middle class, not so well-bred as to speak properly or have several servants, but not so badly off as to be entirely without domestic help or other resources. While one could imagine elite men chuckling over her malapropisms, it is difficult to imagine what lessons upper-class women might take from her adventures. Florence Fay, on the other hand, occupies a more indeterminate class position. She is much more concerned with limiting roles and opportunities for women, reminding them to stay away from men, cautioning them against appearing too forward or flirtatious. At the same time, some of her writings, as in the Blue Devil column, were every bit as coarse and earthy as Betsey's.

In the end, we can never be sure what readers took away from these columns. Did they take the advice to heart, or were these writings simply amusing diversions? Politically, Betsey was clearly preaching to the choir in the disgust she felt toward both the Radicals and the freedmen. Women could do little with Betsey's suggestions and examples. Florence's advice might have been taken more to heart, though plenty of women continued to flirt with Union soldiers and white Southern men alike. These columns broke no new ground in their content. But their form, the charade that they were written by lower-class women, is provocative, and perhaps indicative of subtle shifts in gender norms. After all, the masquerade could only work when women could be writers, when women could take stances on both national and household politics. In this respect, perhaps Betsey and Florence were more subversive than their authors intended. But that would be a limited victory. Political ventriloquism succeeded all too well at limiting the roles and utterances of white Southern women during Reconstruction. It would be decades before they would be taken seriously.

"From the beginning of the struggle the sympathies and interests of the gentler sex were all enlisted on the side of resistance," claimed the author of "The Women of the Confederacy," one section of the ongoing Memories of the War series in *De Bow's Review*. "If they saw, they did not shun the peril, and their cheeks were not seen to blanch when its hour came. All through the long train of events the constancy and fervor of the women of the South never once waned. They cheered the heroic and lashed the laggard, and never, until the cause went down, had they time for regrets or tears."[42] Such glowing praise for Southern white women's heroic dedication could have been published at any time during the war itself, and it continued to be a staple of postwar writings and reflection. White Southern women appeared in two guises in print: either as the unreconstructed rebel, tossing her skirts at the Yankee invaders, or as the selfless embodiment of virtue and republican motherhood, bearing up bravely under hardships. Both images sought to fit postwar women into circumscribed roles. While the unreconstructed woman was both praised and patronized, the heroic woman was held up as a feminine ideal.[43]

The praise for Southern white women was so flowery that it leads one to wonder what male editors and publishers got out of it. Perhaps it was used as a form of ventriloquism directed not at outsiders but within, at a population of men who despaired. Part of what made the picture of women's wartime heroism so striking was the challenge it posed to antebellum notions of femininity and propriety. As the author of "The Women of the Confederacy" explained, before the war, Southern women were (ideally) "removed from rude contact with the world and elevated as a kind of household deity," and "it was commonly thought that when the stern alarms of war were sounded, and danger lurked in every retreat, the women of the South would shrink back in terror and dismay!" To their great credit, the writer continued, women more than surpassed expectations, and he praised "delicately reared and fragile women" for their uncomplaining acceptance of toil, both at home and in hospitals, all in the service of their country.[44]

Postwar evocations of white women's wartime service came in many forms. In addition to publishing articles and reminiscences like "The Women of the Confederacy," journals and newspapers sometimes reprinted wartime poems, like "The Belle of the Blue Cockade," by A. J. Requier. Requier paid homage to the good Southern maid "Who stands up for the flag, / And outflanks the blockade!" by wearing homespun and generally resisting the enemy. The noted South Carolina poet William Gilmore Simms went so far as to dedicate his *War Poetry of the South* to the women of the South, "who have lost a cause but made a triumph." In 1866, novelist John Esten Cooke issued a prospectus for a history of Southern women, "a full and reliable record of the noble actions of Southern women—their charities, self-sacrifice, and heroic devotion and courage during the tragic scenes of the late war." Cooke requested that people send him any anecdotes, statistics, and incidents they might possess, in the name of preserving for future generations "these exhibitions of a grand devotion—as much the pride and glory of the South, as the courage of her sons upon the field." Cooke assured future contributors that modesty or a sense of humility need not prevent them from adding their stories, for "no sentiment of false pride, it is hoped, will operate to with hold the required particulars. They are no longer personal but have passed into the domain of history." Public recognition of heroic women was needed for the greater good of the South.[45]

White Southern women were praised not only for their wartime devotion to the cause but also for their continued willingness to work at the task of rebuilding, even when white men had given up. "Southern manhood, overcome, wounded, manacled reclines for succor and comfort on their bosoms," extolled the *Southern Opinion*, "and they who cheered the warriors to the fight and whose smiles were ever the reward of valor, will not be forgetful of their duty to their country in the present hour of distress and adversity." Both during and after the war, Southern women were often compared to Spartan women for their willingness to sacrifice for a higher cause. A year after the war ended, the editors of the *Field and Fireside* argued that young Southern women needed to be trained in the household arts, all in the name of making them more healthy and virtuous. This was not to say that men were complaining about women's morality, however, for they quickly added that "God never gave to the men of Sparta, nor to the men of any age or country, mothers, wives, and daughters possessed of more sublime heroism, more indomitable will and spirit of uncomplaining sacrifice, than He has given to the women of the south."[46]

Noble, but not always above reproach. In another invocation of "Spartan virtues," an author complained about women's interest in new clothes, an interest understandable after four years of homespun and made-over dresses. Such vanity was not, however, a judicious use of resources. "It will require ten times as much of moral courage to cut loose from the dominion of fashion as it did to secede from and fight the multitudinous North," he chided. While this might have had a grain of truth in it, at the same time, women were still taking pride in their resourcefulness. Eliza Middleton Huger Smith, a wealthy South Carolina widow, described the "country knit socks" and "stout leather country made" shoes, "such as we gave our house sevts." that her daughters were still wearing several months after the war ended. But, she added, "do not pity Belle & Annie for their coarse garments, they are sweet & lady-like in spite of them, cheerful & contented, the sunshine of my life."[47]

Even as women were being implicitly praised for their unreconstructed ways, they were also being cautioned against overstepping the bounds of propriety. Attacking the Yankees was fine, but when a woman like Fanny Downing could write a poem berating Southern men for being unwilling to labor, a poem that included the following stanza, it was time to do something.

> Let Southern woman's red lips curl,
> And barbed shafts of satire hurl
> At men, who should, except for shame
> To womanhood, bear woman's name!
> We love not cowards, let it be
> Danger, or duty, which they flee![48]

For each approvingly related tale, there was another told with an attitude of superiority on the editor's part, often in the same magazine, if not the same issue. The praise for unreconstructed women could be a double-edged sword—useful when the women's ire was directed at Yankees, problematic when directed at Southern men.

Thus, when a "Virginia lady" wrote to *The Land We Love* asking "at what time [did] our 'late enemies' become late," editor D. H. Hill responded in feigned amazement: "What a question to propound to a loyal Editor in District No. 2!" Hill reminded the woman that Southern whites needed to take the moral high ground. Similarly, he counseled another female subscriber concerned about how to treat "our late enemies," telling her that "it is a safe rule to recognize the gentleman and man of honor wherever found, of whatever creed, sect, or nation."[49] Women needed to understand that war was like a business negotiation or a game: you fought your hardest while it was going on, but then you needed to be gracious in defeat (or victory) and put the battles behind you.

Women were both subtly patronized and overtly put back in their places at home, out of the realm of political discourse. By publishing an editorial mocking Lucy Stone and other Northern women who petitioned Congress for suffrage, the editors of the *Field and Fireside* sent a clear message to their female readers. The editorial scoffed at the suffragist's rationale for being given the franchise—that since African Americans were being given the vote, so, too, should it be granted to white women—declaring that "these 'women' surely *are* men, for no woman would ever have designed to aspire to negro equality."[50] At the same time as the *Fireside*'s editors wanted to keep women away from the ballot box, they had no objections to using them as typesetters for the paper itself. They justified continued female employment, which had been acceptable during wartime, on utilitarian grounds, explaining that since so many women had been left without male protectors by the war, the *Fireside* was doing them a service. Work was not inherently unladylike; just as men might find it necessary to work for Northerners, so, too, might women need to support themselves.[51]

The least controversial public roles for women could be found in the Southern postwar culture of memorialization.[52] Written homages to the Confederate dead were ubiquitous in the postwar South. Whitelaw Reid in Richmond in November of 1865 remarked on how "curious" it was "to see with what avidity the Virginians gulp down the praises of their heroic dead," concluding that they did so, "since it is no longer so safe to extol the deeds of the pardoned or pardon-seeking survivors." Frank Alfriend, the onetime editor of the *Southern Literary Messenger*, provided an appealing justification to Southerners when he explained that, "if we are not permitted to mourn over our failure to establish a separate nationality, . . . still there can be no sin of disloyalty, no offense of treason, that there are memories of our struggle still dear to the southern heart." Mourning the dead was thus a socially and politically acceptable way to mourn the Confederacy itself.[53]

Public homages to the Confederate dead allowed white Southerners not only to mourn the actual friends and relatives who had lost their lives in the war but also to spur on reconstruction from within. "We have no need, Sirs: to be ashamed of our dead," preached the author of "The Duty of the Hour."[54] "Let us see to it that *they* be not ashamed of us." The dead were flexible and could be invoked for all occasions. *Scott's Monthly Magazine*, a postwar Atlanta literary journal, published a two-part remembrance of "The Departed Heroes and Patriots of Macon," in early 1868. The essay combined justifications for secession and war with sketches of several of Macon's "honored dead," all in the name of preserving their "splendid achievements" for posterity. As the author explained, "the principles they died to save are not dead, but sleeping beneath a black mass of ignorance and prejudice." White Southerners had a duty to remember the soldiers who had died, not only to honor their memories, but to preserve historical truths and preserve the possibility of a distinctly Southern future.[55]

White women's involvement in memorializing and decorating graves received universal support in the South. This was a public, quasi-political arena in which women were not only permitted, but encouraged, to express their opinions, and indeed go so far as to tell men what to do. Women used the printing press and the newspapers to rally their "sisters" to the cause of remembrance. Fanny Downing, a well-known poet and the president of the Ladies Association for the Fitting up of Stonewall Jackson Cemetery in Winchester published her "Address to the Women of the South," which was sold for ten cents a copy, with the proceeds going to the cemetery. "Southern women!" she exhorted, "let us remember that we belong to that sex which was last at the cross, first at the grave. . . . Let us now go, hand in hand, to the graves of our country's sons, and as we go let our energies be aroused and our hearts be thrilled by this thought: *It is the least thing we can do for our soldiers.*"[56]

Mrs. Charles J. Williams, secretary of the Columbus (Georgia) Memorial Association, sent a letter to the *Columbus Times* in March 1866 asking that a special day be set aside to honor the Confederate dead. Signed "A Southern Woman," the letter described how "the ladies" had been "engaged in the sad but pleasant duty of ornamenting and improving" the Confederate section of the city cemetery. But, without having a day set aside for decoration and contemplation, they felt that their work would be "unfinished": "We cannot raise monumental shafts and inscribe thereon their many deeds of heroism, but we can keep alive the memory of the debt we owe them by dedicating, at least one day in each year, to embellishing their humble graves with flowers." Williams proposed that 26 April, the anniversary of the final surrender of Confederate armies, as the day to be set aside and "observed, from the Potomac to the Rio Grande, and be handed down through time as a religious custom of the South." Williams likened the various soldiers' graves to a "Southern Mecca," to which the South's "sorrowing women, like pilgrims, may annually bring their grateful hearts and floral offerings." She also asked for male participation in this ritual, calling on orators to make eloquent eulogies for "the unburied dead," presumably those men left behind on battlefields like the Wilderness. Williams closed her appeal with a plea for Northern understanding, first by stressing the honor inherent in dying for a cause, whatever that cause might have been. Southern men "died for their country. Whether their country had or had not the right to demand that sacrifice, is no longer a question of discussion. We leave that for nations to decide in the future." What was important was that the nobility of their deaths could never be denied. Finally, Williams took her plea directly to the Radicals themselves: "Legislative enactment may not be made to do honor to their memories, but the veriest radical that ever traced his genealogy back to the deck of the Mayflower, could not refuse us the simple privilege of paying honor to those who died defending the life, honor, and happiness of the Southern women." By making Decoration Day about the protection of women, Williams tried to depoliticize a fundamentally political event.[57]

In its 21 April 1866 edition, the *East Feliciana (Louisiana) Patriot* announced that, as was scheduled to happen around the South, the local ladies would "repair to the cemetery for the purpose of bedecking the graves of the gallant dead of the CSA." The paper complimented the upcoming "lovely and sacred tribute of affection" but reminded women that their obligations were not solely limited to their local cemeteries. "Let none be forgotten for they are all heroes," added the article. "For those who sleep beneath the sod of Virginia, Tennessee, Georgia and Alabama weave a wreath and hang it up in a remembrance of them. The recording angel will make a note of it, and you will be happier for having done so." The appointed memorial day did not pass as smoothly as the men and women of East Feliciana Parish might have hoped. According to one young participant, the local Union troops prevented the minister from making his speech and then tried to stop the girls from laying their wreathes. "There was a man standing by," she wrote, "and said if I had the power of somebody I did not hear who I would turn you back where you came from. I thought to myself if you would turn *me* back you would never do it again, but we all passed along and placed the wreathes on the graves." In this instance, standing up to authority was not perceived as unfeminine or inappropriate. Interestingly, the newspaper made no mention of the tensions when it described the proceedings two days later.[58]

From all corners of the South, men praised women for their displays of devotion to the memory of the Confederate dead and therefore to the Confederacy itself. James De Bow found the various tributes "touching and beautiful" and quoted from the speeches made at the Memphis ceremonies in his June 1866 editorial.[59] The women of Richmond threw themselves into the work of memorialization with a competitive vengeance. First the ladies of Church Hill organized and set to work beautifying the graves at Oakwood Cemetery. Not to be outdone, the ladies of Shockoe Hill followed their sisters' example, turning their attentions to Hollywood Cemetery. "There is also a Hebrew association to which we all belong," explained the vice president of the Shockoe group—"for many a brave confederate rests in our Jewish burying ground." She described the ceremonies at Hollywood on Decoration Day: "The enthusiasm was universal. God blessed us & sent one of the loveliest days that ever there are on earth." The three associations were united in their common purpose: "to be able as long as we or our descendants exist to keep green and beautiful the resting places of our glorious Confederate dead."[60]

Beyond memorialization and decoration, these ladies associations took up a related cause—that of bringing Confederate soldiers' remains from their original battlefield graves home to be reinterred in proper cemeteries. White women made appeals for donations in newspapers and in private, using both prose and poetry to get their message out. In November 1867, Mrs. Green of the Georgia Memorial Association wrote to the *Southern Opinion*, a great proponent of the reburials, to express her fears that "a *great many* of *our* brave, true soldiers have been taken to Chattanooga as *unknown Yankees.'*" This sort of mix-up should provide the impetus for Confederates to remove their dead from the battlefields "and shrine them in cemeteries where they would be safe from desecration, and protected from a promiscuous mingling with the remains of their enemies." This concern for the mingling of remains was not limited to Georgians. An English visitor to New Orleans and the nearby Jacksonville Cemetery was shocked to discover that "it is in contemplation to remove the bodies of the Confederate soldiers to another spot, their relatives deeming it a disgrace that they should lie amongst the Yankees." The taint of Yankeehood thus endured beyond the grave.[61]

The Ladies Memorial Association of Fredericksburg received the attention of the Lost Cause poet Father Abram Ryan, who personally composed several stanzas to encourage them in their efforts. Ryan's poem read in part:

> Gather the sacred dust
>   Of the warriors tried and true,
> Who love the Flag of our nations trust,
> And fell in a cause as great as just,
>   And died for me and you
>
> Gather the corpses strewn
>   O'er many a battle plain—
> From many a grave that lies so lone
> Without a name and without a stone—
>   Gather the Southern slain.

And the dead shall meet the dead,
  While the living o'er them weep;
For the men whom Lee and Stonewall led,
And the hearts that once together bled,
  Should now together sleep.

The poem was published in broadside form and may have been sold as a fund-raiser. Certainly its sentimental appeal could be counted on to stir Southern hearts, and possibly pocketbooks. Associations held fairs as well. Sallie Badger Hoke, a young North Carolina girl, described the excitement at a fair to benefit the Stonewall Cemetery in Charlotte. "There was a little doll baby two feet high, dressed in Confederate uniform, he had his canteen, gun, even a little Confederate silk flag! it cost twenty five dollars and whoever got it was to give it to Gen. Jackson's little daughter."[62]

Memorial associations were associated with battlefields throughout the South, including Manassas, Marietta, and Resaca. In July 1867, the *Southern Opinion* made a plea to collect the men who had died in Maryland at Sharpsburg. Apparently there was a plan to collect at least the South Carolinians and transport them back to their native state, which prompted calls for other states to do the same. "Virginia should gather to her bosom all her honored dead," chided the article. "They wished to 'live and die in Dixie,' and dying *for* Dixie, they should at least be sepulchered in her soil." The problem of the dead left behind at Antietam became even more acute in September of that year when the Federal cemetery there was dedicated, with no mention made of the Confederate dead. The slight against white Southerners could not be left unnoticed and unchallenged. "Shall they lie there forever in oblivion? Shall their unmarked graves be leveled with common dust without any fit memorial of their patriotism, fortitude, and daring?" What made the lack of recognition even worse was that the Confederates had been "the victors on this field of Antietam or Sharpsburg" (a debatable interpretation). More important was the way in which burial reflected on Southern honor: "We for whom they fought and died should see to it that their heroic relics are shrined to everlasting respect and honour by testimonials of our love and gratitude not inferior to those already given to their defeated antagonists."[63]

Once re-interments were under way, there was no guarantee that they would proceed smoothly. On 3 February 1867, Josiah Gorgas noted that "a thrill of indignation has run thro' the Southern people on learning that honors to the dead hero Albert Sidney Johnston were forbidden at Galveston

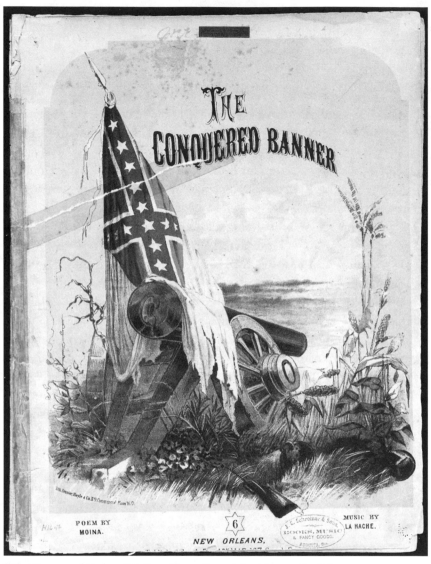

"The Conquered Banner." Father Abram Ryan is best known for this song, a melancholy call for Confederates to "furl their banner" and rejoin the Union. Library of Congress.

by Gen. [Charles] Griffin. On appeal to Gen. Sheridan by the Mayor he confirmed Griffin's action in language far more wounding than was the order of Gen. G." Johnston had actually died at Shiloh in 1862, but arrangements had been made for his remains to be re-interred in Austin, Texas. His body was transported first to Galveston, where several of his "comrades" requested permission from the Federal authorities to conduct a funeral procession through town. As Gorgas reported, permission was denied, although several thousand mourners did file past his coffin displayed on the Galveston wharf. Gorgas, true to his postwar spirit of resignation, refused to be too downcast by the slight, concluding, "No matter, we are conquered and must bear with our fate, *val victus* [woe to the vanquished]."[64]

The degree to which white Southerners wanted separation between the sections even after death extended not only to who was buried in cemeteries but to what marked their graves as well. The *Southern Opinion* indignantly reported that a Bridgeport, Connecticut, firm had been hired to create a monument for the Ladies Memorial Association of King George's County, Virginia: "We can only express our regret that the ladies concerned should have sought to obtain a monument for dead Confederates from living *Yankees*! Our own everlasting hills should have furnished the stone, and the hands of sympathetick workmen should have shaped and inscribed it." This episode provided one of the few instances in which criticism was leveled at women for their memorial activities. Indeed, it provided the author, presumably editor H. Rives Pollard, the opportunity to subtly patronize women, implying that they were perhaps ill-equipped to make business decisions. "But the deed is done," the article continued. "We know that these ladies have only endeavoured to procure the handsomest monument possible with the means at their command, and though they have erred, as we think, their errour (as women's errours always are) is of the head and not of the heart."[65]

In characterizing women as sincere in matters of the heart and, implicitly, men as experts in the realm of the head, Pollard neatly encapsulated the ways in which Southern whites understood gender identity. By 1868, men had successfully resolved the war-induced crisis in gender and were rightfully back as the heads of their households, too busy with the public worlds of business and politics to worry about keeping the fires of animosity burning. Women, at least as men understood it, were returned to the private sphere of emotion and family. The public role they could have, as preservers of Confederate memory, would be carefully circumscribed by men. Mourning the dead was laudable; outbursts of resentment or hatred toward Yankees were more problematic, lest the women turn on Southern men next. Reconstructing notions of appropriate masculinity and femininity allowed Southerners to feel secure in their redefined Southern identity.

CONCLUSION

In March 1867, David Schenck, a thirty-two-year-old lawyer in Lincolnton, North Carolina, sat down with his diary, wrote the heading "Stevens Bill for Reconstruction (so called)," and proceeded to record "the chronicle of a nation's and a peoples degradation, and of myself as one of that unfortunate body politic." Schenck raged against the dual ignominy of being placed under military government and the disfranchising "of Southern patriots and conferring on the negro the elective suffrage." For Schenck, as for most white Southerners, the simultaneous enfranchisement of African Americans and disfranchisement of former Confederates was an insult of the highest order. It "debases me politically beneath my former slave," Schenck lamented, and he ominously predicted that "the effect of this will be to create a deadly feud between the races, and give rise to scenes of violence and disorder which will make society miserable: for the white race will not suffer this outrage without bloody resentments and if it cannot be done by force it will be done by assassinations and secret means of revenge."[1]

Schenck's reaction to the imposition of Radical Reconstruction encapsulated many whites' feelings. Schenck used the language of honor to express his dismay. Disfranchisement "degraded" him, and the elevation of African Americans to positions of political primacy struck at his sense of order, and, indeed, at his sense of self. White Southerners like David Schenck built and rebuilt their identities between 1861 and 1868: first as proud Confederates, then as defeated but still defiant Southerners. One of the few constants for them in these years of upheaval was their inborn and indestructible sense of racial superiority. While they swiftly accepted the loss of slavery, Southerners had no intention of giving up their politically, socially, and economically privileged position. Although Radical Reconstruction threatened this foundation of postwar Southern identity, white Southerners reacted to this insult not by threatening secession but by protesting the loss of their rights as Americans. White Southerners thus took the high road, charging the Radicals with crimes against the Constitution, but they also turned (as Schenck had predicted) to extralegal racial violence in order to reassert control. These two strategies would ultimately allow Southern whites to win the peace, to achieve political reunification with the rights and privileges of

American citizenship while still holding on to a separate and quasi-ethnic social and cultural identity.[2]

David Schenck was shocked by the "marvellous spectacle" presented by the North Carolina Republican Convention that met in Raleigh in late March 1867. Blacks and whites "all met on an equality," and to Schenck and men like him "it seems very abhorrent, and as was natural to suppose our people of dignity either sighed or cursed as their morality allowed." Rather than act out in anger, Schenck adopted the strategy of biding his time as far as black voting was concerned, confident that white Democratic Southerners would be able to "direct" their former slaves "for the good of the country." He took the long view, hoping that "the Radicals have given us the club with which we will be able to beat them hereafter." In his writings we can see the deep hostility toward the national government that characterized Southern politics for generations.[3]

White Southerners like Schenck debated whether to stay away from the polls in 1867 and 1868. They found black voting repellent and were angry about white disfranchisement. A Quitman, Texas, man wondered about the political situation back home in North Carolina, and observed that African Americans were "away ahead of the white people in registering here." In Houston, black juries were common, "as the Yankees can't find white men enough for the purpose that can or will swallow the Oath required." George Anderson Mercer called the November 1867 election in Savannah a "solemn farce," describing "crowds of ignorant negroes from the country" coming into town and being "marched up to the polls by their Radical leaders" to vote: "It was a sad sight to every contemplative or humane man to see these ignorant semi-savages clothed with a power which rightfully belongs only to the wise and good, and to reflect how terrible, at no distant day, must be the consequences of the greatest of all political crimes and blunders—that of subjecting, in the name of liberty, all the wealth and virtue of the land, to the control of its pauperism, ignorance and vice." White Southerners appeared ready to let this sad state of affairs come to pass, for Mercer noted that almost all white men stayed away from the polls, "eschewing altogether any participation in this outrage upon the Constitution, and true liberty itself—and permitting the whole responsibility for the political crimes committed to rest upon its authors and their supple instruments." In short, white Southerners washed their hands of the political cataclysm that they thought was sure to follow close on the heels of black voting.[4]

Josiah Gorgas worried that because more blacks than whites had registered to vote in 1867, control of his local government (in Alabama) would fall into black hands: "It is impossible to predict the consequences a year may bring forth. The land South may again be deluged in blood." The *Southern Opinion* was extremely vocal in its opposition of black voting, seeing Northern advocacy of it as nothing more than an attempt to wreak vengeance on the South. It, too, threatened the worst: "The Southern country is gradually, but unmistakably, it seems to us, approaching that condition whence the antagonism between the opposite races must culminate and assume some desperate shape. . . . The white men of the South, stripped of almost every other right, have not yet parted with their right of self defence, which is part of Southern character; and where black outlaws, whose insolence keeps pace with Radical legislation, intrude upon this sacred domain, they must expect, as they will certainly receive, retribution, sudden and terrible."[5]

A resident of Hinds County, Mississippi, took a cynically calculated view of the voting question. In the article "Registration and Reconstruction," he presented white (Democratic) Mississippians with a choice between the proverbial rock of continued military rule and the hard place of black voting. Vote in favor of a state convention, he explained, and the new constitution would "place the political and civil power and authority of Mississippi forever in the hands of the negro race"; oppose it and remain under the thumb of the Radicals. He warned presciently against the fallacy of thinking that whites could control back voters and called for whites to band together in opposition to the convention. That strategy had two benefits: first, it would prevent black suffrage; second, the federal government would be forced to remove military governments, which they could not afford to keep in place forever. Sooner or later, they would be removed, and then "the wholesale ruin" of Mississippi would be avoided. It was the same strategy of biding one's time, of waiting patiently, that Southerners had been advocating since the end of the war.[6]

In fact, elections around the country in 1867 and 1868 seemed to bear out some of this hopefulness, as the Democrats began to regain power in states like California and Maine. In the results of the various 1867 contests, *De Bow's Review* found "conclusive evidence of a speedier return to good feeling and amicable relations between the sections, than could reasonably have been expected under all the aggravated circumstances of sectional alienation." In the interests of reconciliation, white Southerners needed to believe that not all Northerners were their enemies, that the majority of Northern people were also tired of the Radicals. This bit of good news encouraged Southerners to adopt somewhat of a "wait and see attitude," encouraged them to take the long view. If only they could be, in the words of the *Charleston Mercury*, "patient, firm, and hopeful," their "deliverance" would eventually arrive.[7]

"Let every man at the South of the white race remember that American politics now rests upon one grand, central overruling idea and that is the equality of universal humanity before the law," read an essay in *De Bow's Review* during the summer of 1867. While their Radical opponents might use the principle of equality to elevate the freedmen, white Southerners, the essay counseled, would be well advised to "seize this great principle as essential to their own internal repose, and inscribe it on their own banners and they will thus become the van of progress, and will conquer their conquerors, by seizing upon the secret of their victory, and appropriating it to their own use." Southern whites needed to get back into the game of politics, by swallowing their pride, taking the test oath, and becoming involved in their state constitutional conventions. "The Southern people are so apt at depicting themselves prostrate, and lying supinely on their backs, it is no wonder that they never see the sun, new[ly] arisen, just gilding the mountain tops," complained a tart article on "public apathy" in the 13 July 1867 *Southern Opinion*. The only way to defeat the Radicals, it argued, in contrast to the writer from Hinds County, was to triumph over apathy and register to vote.[8]

In January 1868, an "immense meeting" of white men in Dallas County, Alabama, adopted a series of resolutions in response to the new state constitution. The document is revealing in the ways in which it shows white Southerners self-consciously casting themselves as Americans and using the language of constitutionality to make their point. But it also shows the degree to which white supremacy during Reconstruction was governed by increasingly irrational fears. The resolutions begin by reasserting the men's pledged loyalty to the United States, "submission to the results of the late war," and desire to "see the Union restored to its integrity throughout the South." From that starting point, establishing that these men were loyal Americans with seemingly no ulterior motives, they went on to proclaim simply that "the Government of the United States is a white man's Government." Even as they made this open statement of white supremacy, declaring blacks unfit for public office, they also again carefully couched their resolutions in the language of civic equality, declaring that they supported equal legal protections for blacks. It seems, however, that this profession of fairness was nothing more than words, for the bulk of the document is dedicated to expressing outrage at the new constitution, for its enfranchisement of blacks and its allowing of black office-holding and the like. But the measured tones of the first resolutions give way to hysteria that echoes nothing more than the language of the 1861 secession commissioners: The constitution's "adoption will be a move backward from religion and civilization to superstition and barbarism; from the constitution and laws to anarchy and despotism; from the high auspices of the caucasion to the low prestige of the African. Its policy will make Alabama and the other Southern States African provinces." Just as it had been during the secession winter, this was language calculated to whip whites into a fever pitch, calculated to unite them together against the racial bogeyman. But always white Southerners proclaimed themselves the victims, in this case drawing attention to their suffering at the hands of carpetbaggers and to their fears about meetings of armed black men in the county—never mentioning, of course, that these meetings were in self-defense against white vigilantism. For these men, resistance to Radical Reconstruction and black voting was justified.[9]

David Schenck faced a similar struggle over North Carolina's new constitution, and he lamented the "unenviable" political position in which he found himself. The campaigns for and against ratification were bitter, "all decencies of debate are discarded, and social relations are broken up," and Schenck still tried to remain aloof from them. Perhaps he had read the letter to subscribers in the March 1868 *De Bow's Review* in which William M. Burwell stressed Southern loyalty to the Union and promised that Southern whites would "accord to the emancipated negro all the legal rights to which his new relations entitle him. This will be done in good faith and with perfect sincerity. We will also keep faithfully the renewed allegiance pledged to the federal Constitution. We have neither motive nor purpose of disunion. We are satisfied that the South can best work out its temporal salvation under the Union." This could only be done, Burwell stressed, if Southerners, meaning white Southern men, were assured their former place at the head of the state; they, not the freedmen, needed to hold political power. Burwell reiterated his convictions several months later, when he reminded his readers that "we deem the preservation of this American Union the first element of Southern prosperity. . . . Under and by virtue of the Union justly administered, we look forward to see the South adopt all the means of modern progress, and assume its proper relation to other States and nations, on the basis of wealth, numbers and intelligence." A "justly administered" Union would be one that only enfranchised whites, of course. The road to eventual Southern prosperity lay through political accommodation—within limits.[10]

David Schenck approached the problem of the Radical state constitution pragmatically. He thought it "our best policy to take the Constitution as the best we can do and then elect the best men to execute it." To his chagrin, Schenck's moderate views were "generally disapproved" by his friends, and he felt keenly the sting of social disapproval. Not so keenly, though, that he would abandon his belief that Southern Democrats, by submitting for the time being, would eventually triumph. "Negro suffrage, odious as it is," he wrote in his diary, "may be controlled by the white majority of forty thousand in North Carolina, and we can get the control of our state matters in our own hands. . . . It is not then policy to take the matter into our own hands—Let us accept the Constitution and elect good men to exterminate its evils by a wise administration."[11]

For every Southern white man who agreed with Schenck's judicious approach, there was another who advocated violence to reassert political and social control over the freedmen. Race riots broke out in towns and cities around the South, the worst in Norfolk, Memphis, and New Orleans, as white Southern frustration with their lack of political power overflowed into campaigns of terror against African Americans. The Ku Klux Klan was founded in Tennessee in 1866 and spread throughout the South as former Confederates sought to block the passage of new state constitutions in 1868. Dedicated to reversing the social and political changes brought by Reconstruction, the Klan sought to undermine state governments, destroy the Republican Party in the South, reestablish control over black labor, and restore white supremacy. Klansmen targeted both white and black Republicans for vengeance, but African Americans bore the brunt of the violence. Of the black members of 1867–68 state constitutional conventions, as many as one in ten were attacked and at least seven were murdered. The violence would only increase throughout the late 1860s and early 1870s, until the federal government made a concerted legislative effort to bring it under control in 1872. That this level of violence could coexist with white Southerners' public postures of acquiescence shows the hidden anger burning within former Confederates. They would cede their political power to the United States, but it would be done on their terms.[12]

While not turning to violence himself, Schenck did abandon his posture of political neutrality during the 1868 presidential election. He campaigned actively for the Conservative Democrats, making speeches throughout the North Carolina Piedmont. "The contest in this state is fast narrowing down to a division of races—Negroes, Carpet bag Yankees and office seekers on one side and Respectable decent white men on the other," he recorded. Schenck feared that the campaign might devolve into a "war of races," and he noted both the Camilla, Georgia, and Opelousas, Louisiana, riots in his diary.[13] Schenck blamed the racial violence on African Americans themselves, charging that they "incite riots, so they can use it as evidence of a rebellious design against us at the North to effect the election. . . . This is the result of Radical legislation and Radical revenge and the end is not yet—It has only begun—Revolution must and will follow."[14]

Schenck was upset, though not necessarily surprised, at Grant's election in November 1868, but he consoled himself with the good showing the Conservatives made in his home county. Schenck also took comfort in having remained faithful to his convictions. "Thank God I have been true to my race and color," he wrote on 21 November 1868. "Race and color" are two words that seem synonymous, but they were clearly different for Schenck. In opposing the Radicals, Schenck was motivated by more than just white supremacy—his color. Schenck thought that he was being true to his race as well, to the Southern people. Southerners, he believed, were a people apart before the war, they were independent during the war, and they would be different after it.

By the end of 1868, the outlines of postwar white Southern identity had been drawn. While Southern whites wanted to be part of the American state, having full rights of political and economic participation, they self-consciously maintained an emotional and cultural connection to their Confederate past. During the war, Confederates wanted to be patriotic, wanted to live up to the idealized rhetoric of nationalism and sacrifice that surrounded them. Sometimes, however, heart and head conflicted. Individuals were selfish, sometimes shirked their duty, sometimes socialized with and even married their enemies. But even as Confederates acted in ways that hurt their cause, they still longed for victory. War-weariness should not be conflated with a withdrawal of support for the Confederacy as a whole. After the war, white Southerners faced a similar tension between the emotional and the pragmatic. Although they recognized that the Confederate state had ceased to exist, they still believed that they made up a distinct nation, a distinct population. Whatever accommodations they reached with the Union would have to take that distinctiveness into account. The compromise Southern whites worked out for themselves was to cede their political independence while continuing to preserve a distinctive social and cultural identity, becoming a quasi-ethnic minority. Once they decided to take the oath and become American citizens again, they wanted to be treated as equals by the North. The continuing military presence in the South served as an upsetting reminder that Northerners were not taking Southerners at their word. White Southerners felt that they were doubly victimized: first by Presidential, then by Radical, Reconstruction. This perceived slight led them to grow bitter and resentful, venting their wrath through extralegal means.

Public accommodation and private defiance frequently coexisted, and the two strains of Southern identity need to be understood in tandem. Men and women defined and redefined the limits of acceptable behavior. Expanded public roles for women that went unchallenged during the stress of wartime were reassessed during Reconstruction. The sexes returned, though not always happily, to what Southerners largely believed were their appropriate spheres: men to the realm of politics and business, women to the realm of emotions and family. Women were given a special public role as keepers of the Confederate flame through their memorial activities. White Southerners seemed to have arrived at a level of comfort with the Yankees in their midst, even welcoming them in the name of development and progress. The numbers of Southerners who preferred to start over in a new land dwindled, and many of the first wave of émigrés returned home, disillusioned. With the exception of the Radicals, who would eventually lose power, Northerners appeared largely content with political reunification, doing little to prevent white Southerners from proclaiming and preserving their distinctiveness. Soon, in a bid for reunion, they would even leave race relations up to Southern whites.

The shards of the shattered nation would remain sharp for generations. White Southern identity was shaped by the wartime experience, whether in the form of Ulrich Bonnell Phillips's "central theme" or C. Vann Woodward's exploration of Southern history's ironies and burdens. Resentment toward the Republican Party and a federal government perceived as hostile to the South persisted well into the twentieth century. The resurgence of a form of Confederate/Southern identity after World War II, exemplified by a resurgence of interest in flying the Confederate battle flag and intensified by the civil rights movement, demonstrated that white Southern identity was still problematic, for both the region and the nation as a whole.

The fact that white Southerners could be both Southern and American, could—as I recently saw on a truck—fly both the Confederate and the American flags, shows us that national identity is not an either-or proposition. People can be many things at one time, and the relative weight that they give to each identity can shift with time and circumstance. People could support the Confederacy and urge family members to desert; they could take oaths of loyalty to the Union and then work to sabotage its laws. So often identity is seen in black and white, but for Confederates, it was a kaleidoscope of gray.

NOTES

Abbreviations

Duke Manuscript Department, William R. Perkins Library, Duke University, Durham, N.C.

GLC Gilder Lehrman Collection, Pierpont Morgan Library, New York, N.Y.

HNOC Historic New Orleans Collection, New Orleans, La.

LOC Library of Congress

LSU Louisiana and Lower Mississippi Valley Collections, Louisiana State University Libraries, Baton Rouge, La.

OR *War of the Rebellion: Official Records of the Union and Confederate Armies*, 128 vols. (Washington: Government Printing Office, 1880–1901)

SHC Southern Historical Collection, University of North Carolina Library, Chapel Hill, N.C.

Tulane Manuscript Department, Howard-Tilton Memorial Library, Tulane University, New Orleans, La.

UVA Manuscript Department, Alderman Library, University of Virginia, Charlottesville, Va.

VHS Virginia Historical Society, Richmond, Va.

Introduction

1. Alon Confino, *The Nation as a Local Metaphor: Württemberg, Imperial Germany, and National Memory, 1871–1918* (Chapel Hill: University of North Carolina Press, 1997); Partha Chatterjee, *The Nation and Its Fragments: Colonial and Postcolonial Histories* (Princeton: Princeton University Press, 1993).

2. In his 1995 article "An Exception to Most of the Rules: What Made American Nationalism Different in the Mid-Nineteenth Century?" Peter Parish blames the relative dearth of scholarship on American nationalism on the Eurocentric bent of most scholars of nationalism. Too, most of their theories were derived with reference to European and postcolonial states, generating models into which the United States fits awkwardly if at all. Ironically, while providing a good overview of the emergence of America as a nation state, Parish all but ignores the South and the Confederate States of America. The piece appeared in *Prologue: The Journal of the National Archives* 27 (Fall 1995): 219–29. Two recent works on American nationalism in the Civil War era are Susan-Mary Grant, *North over South: Northern Nationalism and American Identity in the Antebellum Era* (Lawrence: University Press of Kansas, 2000), and Melinda Lawson, *Patriot Fires: Forging a New American Nationalism in the Civil War North* (Lawrence: University Press of Kansas, 2002).

3. Wilbur Zelinsky, *Nation into State: The Shifting Symbolic Foundation of American Nationalism* (Chapel Hill: University of North Carolina Press, 1988), 4–5; Richard

Handler, *Nationalism and the Politics of Culture in Quebec* (Madison: University of Wisconsin Press, 1988), 6–7.

4. While historians, most notably John McCardell in *The Idea of a Southern Nation: Southern Nationalists and Southern Nationalism, 1830–1860* (New York: W. W. Norton & Company, 1979), have argued that Southern nationalism had its ideological roots in the nullification crisis of the 1830s, I contend that there was no Southern nationalism without an actual nation—the Confederacy. Prior to secession, the vast majority of Southerners, including many who went on to positions of great prominence in the Confederacy, were better characterized as sectionalists, believers in differences between the North and the South but not willing to act on those differences. For two classic works on antebellum Southern sectionalism, see Charles S. Sydnor, *The Development of Southern Sectionalism, 1819–1848*, History of the South, vol. 5 (Baton Rouge: Louisiana State University Press, 1948), and Avery O. Craven, *The Growth of Southern Nationalism, 1848–1861*, History of the South, vol. 6 (Baton Rouge: Louisiana State University Press, 1953).

5. The notion of an imagined nation or community comes from the work of Benedict Anderson, who argues that all nations are fundamentally imagined because they are too physically large for each member to actually know all the other members. See his *Imagined Communities: Reflections on the Origin and Spread of Nationalism*, rev. ed. (New York: Verso, 1991), 6–7.

6. On the connections between culture and nationalism, see Handler, *Nationalism and the Politics of Culture in Quebec*, 36–39, 50–51; and Eric Hobsbawm's introduction to Eric Hobsbawm and Terence Ranger, eds., *The Invention of Tradition* (Cambridge: Cambridge University Press, 1983), 9, 13; on the specific importance of print culture, see Anderson, *Imagined Communities*, 25, 35, 61–64.

7. David Morris Potter, *The South and the Sectional Conflict* (Baton Rouge: Louisiana State University Press, 1968).

8. A cursory glance at the titles of several books and articles bears out this view. A few examples are Paul D. Escott's *After Secession: Jefferson Davis and the Failure of Confederate Nationalism* (Baton Rouge: Louisiana State University Press, 1978) and his similarly titled essay "The Failure of Confederate Nationalism: The Old South's Class System in the Crucible of War," in Harry P. Owens and James J. Cooke, eds. *The Old South in the Crucible of War* (Jackson: University Press of Mississippi, 1983), 15–28; Lawrence N. Powell and Michael S. Wayne, "Self-Interest and the Decline of Confederate Nationalism," in Owens and Cooke, eds., *Old South*, 29–46; and George Rable, *Civil Wars: Women and the Crisis of Southern Nationalism* (Urbana: University of Illinois Press, 1989). See also Richard Beringer, Herman Hattaway, Archer Jones, and William N. Still Jr., *Why the South Lost the Civil War* (Athens: University of Georgia Press, 1986).

9. Historians have sought to explain, in the words of Beringer et al., "why the South lost the Civil War." Did it, as one historian has suggested, die of democracy? Can the blame be placed at the feet of the leadership, particularly Jefferson Davis? Was it a casualty of class conflict, or did women, no longer protected by the patriarchy, withdraw their crucial support? Historians who have asked these questions have tended to find that the Confederacy failed to secure its independence because

it failed to secure the loyalty of its people. This "loss of will thesis," best exemplified in Paul Escott's *After Secession* and in Beringer et al., *Why the South Lost*, argues that Confederate nationalism was built on a shallow foundation of superficial difference from U.S. nationalism. Therefore, it was by definition unable to inspire citizens and too weak to sustain the Confederate war effort. While Escott places the greatest blame on class conflict between yeomen and planters, and Beringer et al. cite religious fatalism as a contribution to Confederate defeatism, they agree that the Confederate government was weak and ineffective. In his other writings as well, especially "Southern Yeomen and the Confederacy," *South Atlantic Quarterly* 77 (Spring 1978): 146–58, and "Failure of Confederate Nationalism," Escott blames much of Confederate defeat on class conflict in the Confederacy, as exemplified by the cry that "its a rich man's war and a poor man's fight." While it is true that Southern yeomen and poor whites appear to have had no class interest in a war fought to perpetuate slavery, they had other reasons for which to fight, most notably the need to defend themselves against Northern invasion. Furthermore, they were as subject to nationalist exhortations as anyone else.

10. George Rable, *The Confederate Republic: A Revolution Against Politics* (Chapel Hill: University of North Carolina Press, 1994).

11. Drew Gilpin Faust, *The Creation of Confederate Nationalism: Ideology and Identity in the Civil War South* (Baton Rouge: Louisiana State University Press, 1988).

12. Drew Gilpin Faust, *Mothers of Invention: Women of the Slaveholding South in the American Civil War* (Chapel Hill: University of North Carolina Press, 1996); "Altars of Sacrifice: Confederate Women and the Narratives of War," *Journal of American History* 76 (March 1990): 1200–1228. Faust argues that women initially upheld the Confederacy and played an integral part in creating and promulgating its ideology of patriotic sacrifice, only to become frustrated when the patriarchal social structure of the Confederate South could not protect them from the depredations of war and the destruction of their social order. Thus, Confederate women rejected self-sacrifice, withdrew their support from the Confederate state, and helped bring about the end of the war. I believe that women held onto their attachment to the Confederacy, both materially and emotionally, until the end of the war.

13. In *The Confederate War* (Cambridge: Harvard University Press, 1997), Gary Gallagher does much to integrate the study of the battlefield with that of the homefront. He suggests that historians might profitably ask a different question about Confederate nationalism. Rather than "work backwards from Appomattox" (p. 3), Gallagher challenges the loss-of-will thesis, claiming that the correct question is not why the Confederacy lost, but how it was able to keep fighting for so long. He calls on historians to examine more closely the majority of the Confederate population who were not disaffected. The main thrust of his argument is that the army—specifically Lee's Army of Northern Virginia—not the government in Richmond, became the focus of Confederate nationalism. Like Gallagher, I have chosen to focus not on the reasons that the Confederacy might have failed to endure as a nation but on the ideas and emotions that bound Confederates together, regardless of class, gender, or geography.

14. James L. Roark, *Masters without Slaves: Southern Planters in the Civil War and*

Reconstruction (New York: W. W. Norton & Co., 1977), 95–105. On p. 98, Roark writes that "American patriotism and Southern nationalism were potent sentiments in the South, but they rarely dislodged planters from their primary commitment to slavery."

15. Michael Perman, *Reunion without Compromise: The South and Reconstruction, 1865–1868* (Cambridge: Cambridge University Press, 1973); Dan T. Carter, *When the War Was Over: The Failure of Self-Reconstruction in the South, 1865–1867* (Baton Rouge: Louisiana State University Press, 1985). Perman and Carter examine the politics of Presidential Reconstruction from the perspective of the white Southern political leadership. Perman argues that former Confederate politicians resisted even the more moderate policies of Andrew Johnson, relying instead on a combination of outright resistance and tactical acquiescence in order to dictate as much as possible the terms of their reunification. This Southern intransigence, Perman asserts, cloaked as it might have been in the language of submission, ultimately doomed moderate Reconstruction, paving the way for the Radicals that followed. Although Carter also focuses primarily on the leaders within the various Southern state legislatures, he describes them as constructive, creative pragmatists who tried to make the best of their situation as a conquered people. Above all, according to Carter, these whiggish leaders were "distinctly conservative," especially about race. A somewhat different perspective on the plight of the Southern elite can be found in Steven Hahn's article "Class and State in Postemancipation Societies: Southern Planters in Comparative Perspective," *American Historical Review* 95 (February 1990): 75–98. Hahn compares the experiences of Southern planters to those of the Brazilian slaveowners and the Prussian Junkers, and finds that the Southerners did regain national political power fairly rapidly. They were, however, excluded from the most elite positions (president, Speaker of the House, Supreme Court), for at least a generation. The former Confederates, Hahn concludes, were able to maintain local dominance without a national power base (pp. 92–98).

16. Charles Reagan Wilson, *Baptized in Blood: The Religion of the Lost Cause, 1865–1920* (Athens: University of Georgia Press, 1980); Gaines M. Foster, *Ghosts of the Confederacy: Defeat, the Lost Cause, and the Emergence of the New South* (New York: Oxford University Press, 1987); Nina Silber, *The Romance of Reunion: Northerners and the South, 1865–1900* (Chapel Hill: University of North Carolina Press, 1993). An integral component of the myth of the Lost Cause was a sense if not of nationalism then of distinct (white) Southern identity, and Charles Reagan Wilson, Gaines Foster and Nina Silber have each illuminated different facets of that myth. In *Baptized in Blood*, Wilson borrows from Clifford Geertz's theories on the social function of "civil religion," arguing that the many symbols, myths, rituals, and organization that made up the theology of the Lost Cause gave meaning to Confederate memories. In *Ghosts of the Confederacy*, Foster looks at the people who controlled Confederate memorial organizations and the ways in which they shaped memories of the war. He also argues that the Lost Cause itself not only facilitated the boosterism and economic expansion of the New South but also contributed to the spirit of reunion and reconciliation that prevailed around the turn of the century. Nina Silber's *Romance of Reunion* nicely complements Foster in that she looks at the late-nineteenth-century South from the Northern point of view. Where Wilson used religion, and Foster used

memory, Silber uses gender as an explanatory lens and finds that Northerners viewed reunion in sentimentalized, romantic ways.

Chapter One

1. The most detailed history of the Montgomery Convention is William C. Davis, *"A Government of Our Own": The Making of the Confederacy* (New York: Free Press, 1994). See also Emory M. Thomas, *The Confederate Nation: 1861–1865* (New York: Harper Torchbooks, 1979), 44–66, 71–81; and George C. Rable, *The Confederate Republic: A Revolution against Politics* (Chapel Hill: University of North Carolina Press, 1994), 64–70.

2. See Daniel W. Crofts, *Reluctant Confederates: Upper South Unionists in the Secession Crisis* (Chapel Hill: University of North Carolina Press, 1989), and William W. Freehling, *The South vs. the South: How Anti-Confederate Southerners Shaped the Course of the Civil War* (New York: Oxford University Press, 2001).

3. Benedict R. Anderson, *Imagined Communities: Reflections on the Origin and Spread of Nationalism*, rev. ed. (London: Verso, 1991), 35–36, 76–80. For an account of American newspaper-reading habits, see Thomas C. Leonard, *News for All: America's Coming-of-Age with the Press* (New York: Oxford University Press, 1995), particularly 31–33.

4. For my purposes, "newspapers" are published on at least a weekly basis while "journals" appear monthly or bimonthly. This distinction is not based on content: many newspapers cited here are primarily literary or agricultural in orientation, while some journals, for example *De Bow's Review*, were explicitly economic and political in nature.

5. Carl R. Osthaus, *Partisans of the Southern Press: Editorial Spokesmen of the Nineteenth Century* (Lexington: University Press of Kentucky, 1994), 1–10; Edwin Emery, *The Press and America: An Interpretive History of the Mass Media* (Englewood Cliffs: Prentice-Hall, 1972), 252; Frank Luther Mott, *American Journalism: A History of Newspapers in the United States through 250 Years, 1690 to 1940* (New York: Macmillan Company, 1941), 362–64.

6. Quintus C. Wilson, "The Confederate Press Association: A Pioneer News Agency," *Journalism Quarterly* 26 (June 1949): 160–66; Sidney Kobre, *Development of American Journalism* (Dubuque, Iowa: Wm. C. Brown Company, 1968), 332–33; Emery, *Press and America*, 250–51; James M. Perry, *A Bohemian Brigade: The Civil War Correspondents—Mostly Rough, Sometimes Ready* (New York: John Wiley & Sons, 2000). Perry points out in his introduction that much less (in fact very little) is known about Southern correspondents than their Northern counterparts.

7. Historian Steven Stowe has written about the ways in which the antebellum planter elite used formal and ritualized language to shape their social order, communal identity, and ideology. See his *Intimacy and Power in the Old South: Ritual in the Lives of the Planters* (Baltimore: Johns Hopkins University Press, 1987), 1–4.

8. Mary Chesnut, *Mary Chesnut's Civil War*, ed. C. Vann Woodward (New Haven: Yale University Press, 1981), 25 November 1864, 676; Nancy Emerson Diary, 8 July 1864, UVA. On women's journals as a literary genre, see Michael O'Brien, ed., *An Evening When Alone: Four Journals of Single Women in the South, 1827–1867* (Char-

lottesville: University Press of Virginia, 1993), 2–3. On the use of private sources to gauge ideology or "popular thought," see Randall C. Jimerson, *The Private Civil War: Popular Thought during the Sectional Conflict* (Baton Rouge: Louisiana State University Press, 1988), 1–7.

9. Davis, *"Government of Our Own,"* 103.

10. On Confederate nation-building and the use of a Revolutionary myth of origin, see Emory M. Thomas, *The Confederacy as a Revolutionary Experience* (Englewood Cliffs: Prentice-Hall, 1971), 1–2, 44–46; Drew Gilpin Faust, *The Creation of Confederate Nationalism: Ideology and Identity in the Civil War South* (Baton Rouge: Louisiana State University Press, 1988), 3–15; and Charles Royster, *The Destructive War: William Tecumseh Sherman, Stonewall Jackson, and the Americans* (New York: Alfred A. Knopf, 1991), 144–47, 153–54, 175–76. On the connections between culture and nationalism in general, see Richard Handler, *Nationalism and the Politics of Culture in Quebec* (Madison: University of Wisconsin Press, 1988), 17–19, 36–39, 50–51; and Eric Hobsbawm's introduction to Eric Hobsbawm and Terence Ranger, eds., *The Invention of Tradition* (Cambridge: Cambridge University Press, 1983), 9, 13; on the specific importance of print culture, see Anderson, *Imagined Communities*, 25, 35, 61–64.

11. This observation shows that, contrary to John McCardell's views in *The Idea of a Southern Nation: Southern Nationalists and Southern Nationalism, 1830–1860* (New York: W. W. Norton & Company, 1979), Confederate nationalism was not the logical culmination of antebellum nationalist and sectionalist rhetoric.

12. Confederates were not alone in hearkening back to the American Revolution. Northerners, especially Abraham Lincoln, also drew on the symbolism of the Revolutionary War as they rallied to keep the Union together. Like Confederates, Northerners and Southern Unionists had been taught the heroic stories, and they, too, believed themselves to be the heirs of "Revolutionary sires." Yankees, too, drew on tales of Revolutionary fortitude to maintain support for the war. The war to save the Union was a war to keep the Founders' Revolutionary creation alive. Northerners saw secession not as an honorable revolution but as an illegitimate rebellion, one that threatened American liberty and freedom. Like their Confederate counterparts, Union soldiers believed that they were children fighting to preserve their fathers' legacies. Only the legacies differed: for Unionists the Revolution had created an enduring nation, one to be preserved at all costs, whereas for Confederates the war had been about the preservation of liberty from despotic encroachment. The latter, Confederates believed, was the very situation in which they once again found themselves. See Randall C. Jimerson, *The Private Civil War: Popular Thought during the Sectional Conflict* (Baton Rouge: Louisiana State University Press, 1988), 32–35; James M. McPherson, *For Cause and Comrades: Why Men Fought in the Civil War* (New York: Oxford University Press, 1997), 18–19, 104, 110–13; Royster, *Destructive War*, 147–56. On Southern Unionists using Revolutionary rhetoric, see Richard Nelson Current, *Lincoln's Loyalists: Union Soldiers from the Confederacy* (Boston: Northeastern University Press, 1992), 145–47. On Abraham Lincoln's use of this rhetoric, see James M. McPherson, *Abraham Lincoln and the Second American Revolution* (New York: Oxford University Press, 1991), esp. chs. 1 and 2. For other examples of this rhetoric, see

"Proclamation of Governor Curtin," *New York Herald*, 16 June 1863, and "Blessings in Disguise—The Benefits of This War," *New York Herald*, 16 November 1864.

13. "The Day and the Hour," *Richmond Enquirer*, June 7, 1861.

14. Jefferson Davis, "Inaugural Address of the President of the Provisional Government," 18 February 1861, in James D. Richardson, ed., *The Messages and Papers of Jefferson Davis and the Confederacy* (New York: Chelsea House Publishers, 1966), 1:36.

15. "Too Much Nationality," *Southern Monthly* 1 (October 1861): 87; "Philosophy of the Revolution," ibid., 1 (January 1862): 321; "Twin Bigotries," *The Age* 1 (February 1864): 81–82; Edward A. Pollard, *The First Year of the War* (Richmond: West and Johnston, 1862), 8.

16. Henry St. Paul, *Our Home and Foreign Policy* (Mobile: Printed at the Office of the Daily Register and Advertiser, 1863), 3–5. For other examples, see Rev. William A. Hall, *The Historic Significance of the Southern Revolution* (Petersburg: A. F. Crutchfield & Co., 1864), 18–20; and "The Puritan and the Cavalier," an extract from the *London Times*, reprinted in the *Southern Cultivator* 21 (March–April 1863): 53. The definitive study of this idea is William Robert Taylor's *Cavalier and Yankee: The Old South and the American National Character* (New York: Harper & Row, 1969). Taylor uses literary sources to illuminate the growth of this myth in the antebellum South. See pp. 15–22, 327–39. See also Bertram Wyatt-Brown, *The Shaping of Southern Culture: Honor, Grace, and War, 1760s–1880s* (Chapel Hill: University of North Carolina Press, 2001), 179–80, 280–81.

17. St. Paul, *Our Home and Foreign Policy*, 5.

18. A South Carolinian, *The Confederate "Respice Finem,"* (Mobile: S. H. Goetzel & Co., 1863), 5–7.

19. Hall, *Historic Significance*, 12 (italics in original); "Speech of Rev. Dr. Palmer," *Montgomery Advertiser* 5 May 1864, 1; Richard E. Beringer, Herman Hattaway, Archer Jones, and William N. Still Jr., in *Why the South Lost the Civil War* (Athens: University of Georgia Press, 1986), 82–102, and Drew Gilpin Faust, in *Creation of Confederate Nationalism*, 22–40, argue for the centrality of religion to Confederate nationalism. Initially, Christianity functioned as a "civil religion," legitimating the Confederate nation as the Confederate people believed that they were God's chosen.

20. Hall, *Historic Significance*, 44, 39 (italics in the original); James Henley Thornwell, *Our Danger and Our Duty* (Raleigh: Raleigh Register Steam Power Press, 1863), 5–6. For a brief biographical sketch of Thornwell, see Michael O'Brien, ed., *All Clever Men Who Make Their Way: Critical Discourse in the Old South* (Athens: University of Georgia Press, 1992), 420–21. Benjamin Palmer also wrote a biography of Thornwell: *The Life and Letters of James Henley Thornwell, D.D.* (Richmond: Whittet & Shapperson, 1875).

21. William Meade, *Address on the Day of Fasting and Prayer Appointed by the President of the Confederate States, June 13, 1861; Delivered at Christ Church, Millwood, VA, by Bishop Meade Published by Request* (Richmond: Enquirer Book and Job Press, 1861), 13.

22. Fitzhugh, a Virginian, was best known for his attacks on free labor and de-

fenses of slavery in *Sociology for the South; or, The Failure of Free Labor* (1854) and *Cannibals All! or, Slaves without Masters* (1857). His writings tended to be more extreme and more sensational than those of other proslavery writers. See Eugene D. Genovese, *The World the Slaveholders Made; Two Essays in Interpretation* (New York: Pantheon Books, 1969); Harvey Wish, *George Fitzhugh, Conservative of the Old South* (Charlottesville: University Press of Virginia, 1938); and Harvey Wish, *George Fitzhugh, Propagandist of the Old South* (Baton Rouge: Louisiana State University Press, 1943).

23. George Fitzhugh, "The Revolutions of 1776 and 1861 Contrasted," *Southern Literary Messenger* (November and December 1863), 718–24.

24. On the question of constitutionality, see Don E. Fehrenbacher, "The Confederacy as a Constitutional System," *Constitutions and Constitutionalism in the Slaveholding South*, Mercer University Lamar Memorial Lectures No. 31 (Athens: University of Georgia Press, 1989), 62; Rable, *Confederate Republic*, 46–49; and Royster, *Destructive War*, 173–77. On the ways in which Confederates, particularly Jefferson Davis, downplayed the importance of slavery in their construction of national identity, see Paul D. Escott, *After Secession: Jefferson Davis and the Failure of Confederate Nationalism* (Baton Rouge: Louisiana State University Press, 1978), 35–38. In her essay "'God Will Not Be Mocked': Confederate Nationalism and Slavery Reform," *in Creation of Confederate Nationalism* (58–81), Drew Gilpin Faust argues that slavery was a cornerstone of Confederate nationalism but one that would eventually prove detrimental to it by opening up public discourse on the institution itself. I argue that Confederates rarely discussed the institution, accepting it as a given in their society even as they sought to de-emphasize its importance in the eyes of other nations.

25. For a mention of Tories in relation to East Tennessee loyalists, see Lancelot Minor Blackford to Mrs. William M. Blackford, 20 November 1863, Blackford Family Letters. vol. 2, UVA; for North Carolina Tories, see "The Other Side of the Picture," *Raleigh Register*, 6 August 1862. For instances of "Hessians," see "Country, Home and Liberty" and "Chivalrous C.S.A.," Wake Forest Broadside Poetry Collection website, <http://www.wfu.edu/Library/rarebook/>.

26. On the endurance and importance of the Revolutionary War to nineteenth-century American political culture, see David Waldstreicher, *In the Midst of Perpetual Fetes: The Making of American Nationalism, 1776–1820* (Chapel Hill: University of North Carolina Press, 1997), and Michael Kammen, *A Season of Youth: The American Revolution and the Historical Imagination* (New York: Alfred A. Knopf, 1978).

27. "Rebel Poetry: The Stars and Bars" and "The Southern Yankee Doodle," Wake Forest Broadside Poetry Collection; "The New Yankee Doodle," in *The Stonewall Song Book: Being a Collection of Patriotic, Sentimental and Comic Songs*, 11th ed., enl. (Richmond: West and Johnston, 1865), 29.

28. For a discussion of George Washington's character and the reasons he was such a popular figure, see Gordon S. Wood, "The Greatness of George Washington," *Virginia Quarterly Review* 68 (Spring 1992): 189–207; Barry Schwartz, *George Washington: The Making of an American Symbol* (New York: Free Press, 1987); and Kammen, *Season of Youth*, 42, 47–48.

29. Jefferson Davis, "Inaugural Address," 22 February 1862, in Richardson, ed.,

Messages and Papers, 1:183. For Jefferson Davis as a second Washington, see "Song of the South! Gen. Jeff Davis," Wake Forest Broadside Poetry Collection; for an analogy between the two leaders, see "Some Words to Croakers," *Southern Punch*, 14 November 1863. David Waldstreicher (*In the Midst of Perpetual Fetes*, 112–13, 129, 214–15) has traced this association of political speeches with Washington's birthday to its origins as a Federalist tactic in the 1790s. It fast became a convention for all political parties. Lee, as Richard B. McCaslin has shown, had been self-consciously modeling himself on Washington since childhood. See *Lee in the Shadow of Washington* (Baton Rouge: Louisiana State University Press, 2001).

30. "Our Flag and Seal," *Southern Illustrated News*, 12 March 1863.

31. J. C. W., "The South," *Southern Monthly* 1 (November 1861): 212; John R. Thompson, "A Poem for the Times," *Raleigh Register*, 22 May 1861; Henry Timrod, "Carolina," in William F. Shepperson, ed., *War Songs of the South. Edited by "Bohemian," Correspondent Richmond Dispatch* (Richmond: West and Johnston, 1862), 87–90. Many of the poems and songs Shepperson collected had appeared previously in newspapers such as the *Richmond Dispatch*, the *Richmond Enquirer*, and the *Columbus (Georgia) Times*. Similarly, newspapers also reprinted poems from various published collections.

32. Frank Ticknor, "The Spirit of '76 — The Old Rifleman," from the *Richmond Dispatch*, in Shepperson, ed., *War Songs of the South*, 57–58; John W. Overall, "Seventy-Six and Sixty-One," from the *Georgia Crusader*, in Shepperson, ed., *War Songs of the South*, 62–63; "The Spirit of '60," from the *Columbus Times* in Shepperson, ed., *War Songs of the South*, 58–59; "Flag Presentation," *Raleigh Register*, 5 June 1861.

33. "To the Maryland Sons of Revolutionary Sires!" Wake Forest Broadside Poetry Collection; "A Song for 'The Maryland Line,'" *Southern Monthly* 1 (January 1862): 351.

34. "Never Say Die," *Montgomery Mail*, 18 January 1862, reprinted in Henry W. R. Jackson, *Historical Register and Confederates Assistant to National Independence* (Augusta, Ga.: Office of the Constitutionalist, 1862), 37; "Our Cause & Our Course," *Charleston Mercury*, 17 July 1863; letter to the editor of the *Montgomery Advertiser*, 8 August 1864; "Lessons of Encouragement," in Jackson, *Historical Register*, 20; reprinted in *Southern Field and Fireside*, 28 February 1863.

35. On the use of metaphors of pollution and death in fostering nationalism, see Handler, *Nationalism and the Politics of Culture*, 47–50.

36. "The Brutality of the Enemy," *Southern Field and Fireside*, 28 March 1863, 100; Emma LeConte, *When the World Ended: The Diary of Emma LeConte*, ed. Earl Schenck Miers (New York: Oxford University Press, 1957), 31 December 1864, 4; William R. Smith to Jeremiah Morton, 20 January 1863, Morton-Halsey Papers, box 1, UVA; A Son to his Mother, July 7, 1862, Valley of the Shadow website, <http://valley.vcdh.virginia.edu/lettersp2.html>.

37. "The Different Kinds of Soldiers," *Staunton Spectator*, May 14, 1861.

38. For the connection between honor and patriotism, see Bertram Wyatt-Brown, *Southern Honor: Ethics and Behavior in the Old South* (New York: Oxford University Press, 1982), 112–13. Historian LeeAnn Whites (*The Civil War as a Crisis in Gender: Augusta 1860–1890* [Athens: University of Georgia Press, 1995], 2, 12) has gone so far

as to frame the Civil War as a high-stakes conflict over notions of "manhood," and the Confederacy as an explicitly patriarchal republic.

39. "The War of Independence," *De Bow's Review* 34 (July–August 1864): 50; "Exemptions and Other Matters," *Southern Cultivator* 23 (February 1865): 20–21; Gustave Arvilien Breaux Diary, 17 January 1864, Tulane.

40. Kate Cumming, *Kate: The Journal of a Confederate Nurse*, edited by Richard Barksdale Harwell (Baton Rouge: Louisiana State University Press, 1959), 31 December 1864, 247; Thornwell, *Our Danger and Our Duty*, 15; Zillah Haynie Brandon Diary, 22 August 1863 and 14 June 1864, *American Women's Diaries Microfilm, Segment II: Southern Women*, reel 3, frames 349, 363.

41. Ella Gertrude Clanton Thomas, *The Secret Eye: The Journal of Ella Gertrude Clanton Thomas, 1848–1889*, ed. Virginia Ingraham Burr (Chapel Hill: University of North Carolina Press, 1990), 7 October 1862, 211. Thomas then answered her own questions: "Perhaps when we are reduced to poverty we may by the spur of adversity be led to throw aside the indolence which is the bane of a Southern people and develop what latent talent may exist among us."

42. "From Death to Life," *Magnolia Weekly*, 26 March 1864, 204. For a brief but thorough discussion of the *Magnolia* see Carlton P. Brooks, "The *Magnolia*: A Literary Magazine for the Confederacy," *Virginia Cavalcade* 32 (Spring 1983): 150–55.

43. *Southern Field and Fireside*, 5 November 1864, 7 and 19 March 1864, 4; Ray Morris Atchison, "Southern Literary Magazines, 1865–1887" (Ph.D. dissertation, Duke University, 1956), 19–20; Bertram Holland Flanders, *Early Georgia Magazines: Literary Periodicals to 1865* (Athens: University of Georgia Press, 1944), 136–48.

44. "Seasonable Reflections," *Southern Field and Fireside*, 3 January 1863, 4; "Southern Literature," ibid., 4 April 1863, 110.

45. "Literature for the South," ibid., 20 June 1863, 159; "An Appeal to Our Friends and the Public," ibid., 19 November 1864, 4.

46. "Southern Literature," ibid., 4 April 1863, 110; "Yankee War Literature," ibid., 3 December 1864, 4; see also "To the Litterateurs of the South," ibid., 4 November 1864, 4. This sort of romance was a staple of postwar Northern writings. See Nina Silber, *The Romance of Reunion: Northerners and the South, 1865–1900* (Chapel Hill: University of North Carolina Press, 1993), 39–65.

47. "The Press Convention," *Southern Field and Fireside*, 21 November 1864, 4; "Book Publishing in the South," ibid., 2 January 1864, 4. The classic study of shortages in the wartime Confederacy is Mary Elizabeth Massey, *Ersatz in the Confederacy: Shortages and Substitutes on the Southern Homefront*, with a new introduction by Barbara L. Bellows (Columbia: University of South Carolina Press, 1993); see also William Blair, *Virginia's Private War: Feeding Body and Soul in the Confederacy, 1861–65* (New York: Oxford University Press, 1998), 55, 69–70, 109.

48. Southerners were much more concerned with their children's reading material than Northerners. While a few Northern schoolbooks adopted explicitly patriotic tones, the vast majority treated the war superficially, if at all. See James Marten, *The Children's Civil War* (Chapel Hill: University of North Carolina Press, 1998), 32–33, 52–61; Rable, *Confederate Republic*, 178–84; and Sarah Law Kennerly, "Confeder-

ate Juvenile Imprints: Children's Books and Periodicals Published in the Confederate States of America, 1861–1865" (Ph.D. diss., University of Michigan, 1956). Drew Faust briefly discusses linguistic issues in Confederate schoolbooks in *Creation of Confederate Nationalism*, 11.

49. "What Are We to Do for Schoolbooks?" *Southern Field and Fireside*, 4 April 1863, 108.

50. I looked at over a dozen different schoolbooks for this chapter, the majority of which were primers or spellers. The only arithmetic book I used, Abidjah Fowler's *Southern School Arithmetic or Youth's Assistant* (Richmond: West and Johnston, 1864), fit the pattern described in the text. An example of a repackaged work is Roswell Chamberlain Smith's *Louisiana English Grammar* (Shreveport: Printed at the Office of the Southwestern, 1865).

51. Rev. John Neely, *The Confederate Speller and Reader* (Augusta, Ga.: A. Bleakley, 1864), iii; advertisement in the back of M[arinda] B[ranson] Moore, *The Geographical Reader for the Dixie Children* (Raleigh: Branson, Farrar & Co., 1863).

52. See illustrations in William A. Campbell, *The Child's First Book* (Richmond: Ayres & Wade, 1864); M[arinda] B[ranson] Moore, *The Dixie Primer for the Little Folks* (Raleigh: Branson & Farrar, 1863); and Richard McAllister Smith, *The Confederate Primer* (Richmond: George L. Bidgood, 1864).

53. M[arinda] B[ranson] Moore, *The Dixie Speller* (Raleigh: Branson & Farrar, 1864), 37. Another example of this use of the Christian proslavery argument can be found in *The First Reader, for Southern Schools* (Raleigh: N.C. Christian Advocate Publishing Company, 1864), 17. On the role of proslavery thought in the Confederacy as a whole, see Faust, *Creation of Confederate Nationalism*, 71–81.

54. Moore, *Dixie Speller*, 39, 41, 83.

55. Ibid., 65, 45.

56. Campbell, *Child's First Book*, 31–32; Neely, *Confederate Speller and Reader*, 52–53.

57. Neely, *Confederate Speller and Reader*, 52; Moore, *Dixie Speller*, 23.

58. Moore, *Dixie Speller*, 23; Neely, *Confederate Speller and Reader*, 52–53; *First Reader*, 12, 20.

59. Neely, *Confederate Speller and Reader*, 135–36; Moore, *Dixie Speller*, 33.

60. Rev. K[ensey] J[ohns] Stewart, *A Geography for Beginners*, Palmetto Series (Richmond: J. W. Randolph, 1864), 40–43. A note inside the edition at the Virginia Historical Society indicates that it was actually printed in England, despite bearing a Richmond imprint. It is of much higher quality than the other schoolbooks mentioned, with color illustrations and a fold-out map. The note also indicates that the author "was arrested while holding services in St. Paul's P.E. Church, Alexandria, VA; and dragged from the edifice by an armed guard for refusing to pray for the President of the United States."

61. Moore, *Geographical Reader*, 39, 14. Moore described her book as a simplified geography for "the little folks." Its first section is a reader, the second is a geography, and the third is a series of review questions and answers in a catechism format. Some of the questions are geographical, the rest political.

62. Ibid., 9–11. Stewart's *Geography for Beginners* is much the same; he, too, argued that men were divided into "savage" and "civilized" races.

63. Moore, *Geographical Reader*, 13–15.

64. Ibid., 18–29.

65. Ibid., 39.

66. James Wesley Silver's classic *Confederate Morale and Church Propaganda* (New York: W. W. Norton and Co., 1967) focuses on the role that Southern clergymen played in encouraging both secession and loyalty to the Confederacy. Beringer et al., in *Why the South Lost* (82–102 and 336–67), take off from Silver's premise but stress the ways in which guilt over slavery and a sense of religious fatalism contributed to Confederate defeat. Drew Gilpin Faust devotes a chapter of her *Creation of Confederate Nationalism* (pp. 22–40) to the relationship between religion and republicanism in the Confederacy, in which she finds Confederates using religion to justify their new nation's often reactionary politics.

67. David Comfort to Mary J. McIntosh Cave, 21 July 1864, Comfort Family Papers, VHS; Daniel M. Pritchard to Jeremiah Morton, 30 May 1864, Morton-Halsey Papers, box 1, UVA; Sally Armstrong Diary, 1 June 1863, VHS.

68. Diary of Fannie Page Hume, 10, 18, 24 February 1862, LOC.

69. The text of each one of Davis's proclamations can be found in Richardson's *Messages and Papers* 1:103–4, 135, 217–18, 227–28, 268–69, 324–25, 328, 412–14, 563–65, 567–68. For an excellent exploration of the role of public fasts in Confederate Richmond and the creation of a "Confederate Jeremiad," see Harry S. Stout and Christopher Grasso, "Civil War, Religion, and Communications: The Case of Richmond," in *Religion and the American Civil War*, edited by Randall M. Miller, Harry S. Stout, and Charles Reagan Wilson (New York: Oxford University Press, 1998), 313–59. See also Beringer et al., *Why the South Lost*, 95–96; and W. Harrison Daniel, "Protestantism and Patriotism in the Confederacy," *Mississippi Quarterly* 24 (Spring 1971): 117–34.

70. Diary of Fannie Page Hume, 22, 19 February 1862, 13 May 1862, LOC.

71. Ibid., March 1862, 17 July 1862, 4, 13 August 1862.

72. For a discussion of the army revivals, see Drew Gilpin Faust, "Christian Soldiers: The Meaning of Revivalism in the Confederate Army," *Journal of Southern History* 53 (February 1987): 63–90; and Sidney J. Romero, *Religion in the Rebel Ranks* (Lanham, Md.: University Press of America, 1983). Two accounts written by participants in the revivals are William W. Beneath, *A Narrative of the Great Revival in the Southern Armies* (Philadelphia: Claxton, Remsen and Haffelfinger, 1877), and J. William Jones, *Christ in the Camp; or, Religion in Lee's Army* (Richmond: Johnson, 1887). Quotation is from Nancy Emerson Diary, November 19, 1864, UVA.

73. Gustave Cook to Lizzie Cook, 18 January 1863, 30 July 1863, 16 September 1864, Gustave Cook Papers, GLC.

74. Ibid., 16 September 1864; Margaret Brown Wight Diary, 26 May 1864, Wight Family Papers, VHS.

75. Chesnut, *Mary Chesnut's Civil War*, 14 December 1863, 505; Thornwell, *Our Danger and Our Duty*, 11, 13–14.

76. Zillah Haynie Brandon Diary, 21 January 1863 and 17 June 1864, *American Women's Diaries Microfilm*, reel 3, frames 341–42, 365.

77. Priscilla "Mittie" Munnikhuysen Bond Diary, 2 February 1864, LSU; Cumming, *Kate*, 29 November 1863, 174, 176; 9 March 1865, 260.

78. Faust, *Creation of Confederate Nationalism*, 26–27.

79. Proclamations on 4 September 1862, in Richardson, *Messages and Papers*, 268–69, and 27 February 1863, ibid., 328.

80. Quoted in Stout and Grasso, "Civil War, Religion, and Communications," 326–27.

81. Rev. Joseph M. Atkinson, *God the Giver of Victory and Peace. A Thanksgiving Sermon, Delivered in the Presbyterian Church, September 18, 1862*, (Raleigh, n.p.: 1862), 5–6, 8–9, 11–13. For another sermon on similar topics, see Rev. David Seth Doggett, *A Nation's Ebenezer: A Discourse Delivered in the Broad Street Methodist Church, Richmond, Virginia, Thursday, September 18, 1862: The Day of Public Thanksgiving Appointed by the President of the Confederate States* (Richmond: Enquirer Book and Job Press, 1862).

82. Rt. Rev. Stephen Elliott, D.D., *A Sermon Preached in Christ Church Savannah, on Thursday, September 18th, 1862, Being the Day Set Forth by the President of the Confederate States as a Day of Prayer and Thanksgiving, for Our Manifold Victories and Especially for the Fields of Manassas and Richmond, KY.* (Savannah: Power Press of John M. Cooper & Co., 1862), 5–6, 17–21.

83. "The Coming Fast Day," *Southern Recorder*, 18 August 1863; *Richmond Examiner*, 22 August 1863.

84. Margaret Brown Wight Diary, 27 March 1863, Wight Family Papers, VHS; Cloe Tyler Whittle Greene Diary, 21 August 1863, *American Women's Diaries Microfilm*, reel 7, frame 375. See also Margaret Brown Wight Diary, 10 March 1865, Wight Family Papers, VHS.

85. "Proclamation by the Governor of Alabama," *Montgomery Advertiser*, 5 December 1863; "Daily Union Prayer Meetings," ibid., 18 June 1864.

86. "A Specimen of Southern Devotion; or, The Prayer of a Rebel Saint," November 1862. "The Confederate Form of Prayer" and "Patriotic Prayer for the Southern Cause," both at VHS.

Interlude: A Hope Fully Authorized by the Facts

1. Lucy Rebecca Buck, *Sad Earth, Sweet Heaven: The Diary of Lucy Rebecca Buck during the War between the States, Front Royal, Virginia, December 25, 1861–April 15, 1865*, edited by William P. Buck (Birmingham: Cornerstone Press, 1973), 31 August 1862, 138.

2. General works on Confederate foreign policy include David Paul Crook, *The North, the South, and the Powers, 1861–1865* (New York: Wiley, 1974); James Morton Callahan, *The Diplomatic History of the Southern Confederacy* (1901; reprint, New York: Greenwood Press, 1968); and Frank L. Owsley, *King Cotton Diplomacy: Foreign Relations of the Confederate States of America* (Chicago: University of Chicago Press, 1959).

3. Mary Chesnut, *Mary Chesnut's Civil War*, ed. C. Vann Woodward (New Haven: Yale University Press, 1981), 286.

4. Buck, *Sad Earth, Sweet Heaven*, 22 June 1862, 108; 5 July 1862, 114; Chesnut, *Mary Chesnut's Civil War*, 16 June 1862, 387.

5. Thomas L. Brown to George M. Brown, 18 July 1863, George M. Brown Papers, Duke.

6. "The True Causes of Our Non-Recognition," *Charleston Mercury*, 19 June 1862.

7. "Intervention and Recognition" and "Self-Reliance Necessary," *Memphis Daily Appeal*, 6 August 1862; *Richmond Daily Examiner*, 8 August 1862 and 28 August 1862.

8. "Be Courageous," *Hinds County (Miss.) Gazette*, 9 July 1862.

9. Harris quoted in Glenn M. Linden and Thomas P. Pressly, *Voices from the House Divided: The United States Civil War as Personal Experience* (New York: McGraw Hill, 1995), 48; *Richmond Daily Examiner*, 18 June 1862 and 5 August 1862. The classic study of Confederate conscription is Albert Burton Moore, *Conscription and Conflict in the Confederacy* (1924; reprint, New York: Hillary House Publishers, 1963). On Confederate conscription policy, see also Emory M. Thomas, *The Confederate Nation: 1861–1865* (New York: Harper Torchbooks, 1979), 152–55, 260–61; Paul D. Escott, *After Secession: Jefferson Davis and the Failure of Confederate Nationalism* (Baton Rouge: Louisiana State University Press, 1978), 63–64, 80–88; and George C. Rable, *The Confederate Republic: A Revolution against Politics* (Chapel Hill: University of North Carolina Press, 1994), 138–43, 248–49.

10. *Hinds County (Miss.) Gazette*, 9 July 1862; "Caution," *Southern Confederacy*, 2 July 1862; Linden and Pressly, *Voices from the House Divided*, 50.

11. "Arming the Negroes," *Southern Confederacy*, 30 July 1862; *Richmond Daily Examiner*, 29 August 1862.

12. "Progress of the War," *Memphis Daily Appeal*, 29 August 1862; "The Last Great Victory," ibid., 2 September 1862.

13. *Charleston Mercury*, 2, 3, and 6 September 1862; *Richmond Daily Examiner*, 3, 4, 5 September 1862; "A Move in the Right Direction," *Memphis Daily Appeal*, 15 September 1862.

14. *Charleston Mercury*, 5 and 10 September 1862.

Chapter Two

1. "'Inquire Within,' Number I," *Southern Field and Fireside*, 14 February 1863, 52.

2. "Signs of Promise," ibid., 5 September 1863, 224; "The Moral Advantages of Public Calamities," *Southern Cultivator* 22 (February 1864): 38; "Suffering the Price of Independence," *Charleston Mercury*, 3 August 1863; *De Bow's Review* 34 (July and August 1864), 103.

3. Charles East, ed., *Sarah Morgan: The Civil War Diary of a Southern Woman* (New York: Simon and Schuster, 1991), 23 January 1863, 411; Edward Laight Wells to Thomas L. Wells, 1 December 1863, in Daniel E. Huger Smith, Alice R. Huger Smith, and Arney R. Childs, eds., *Mason-Smith Family Letters: 1860–1868* (Columbia: University of South Carolina Press, 1950), 71; Cloe Tyler Whittle Greene Diary, 22 March 1863, *American Women's Diaries Microfilm, Segment II: Southern Women*, reel 7, frame 335. On the struggles of poor women generally during the war, see Victoria Bynum,

Unruly Women: The Politics of Social and Sexual Control in the Old South (Chapel Hill: University of North Carolina Press, 1992), 111–29.

4. Eliza Middleton Huger Smith to Isabella Middleton Smith, 19 May 1863, in Smith et al. eds., *Mason-Smith Family Letters*, 42.

5. Clement S. Watson to Mary Watson, 29 June 1863, Watson Family Papers, LSU; Cleland K. Huger to Daniel Elliott Huger Smith, 21 March 1863, in Smith et al., eds., *Mason-Smith Family Letters*, 39–40.

6. Gustave Cook to Lizzie Cook, 30 July 1863, 22 October 1864, 12 January 1865, Gustave Cook Papers, GLC.

7. "The True Spirit! God Bless our Noble Women!" *Southern Cultivator* 22 (January 1864): 18; "Earth Angels," *Southern Field and Fireside*, 17 January 1863, 19; "The Mainstay of the South," *Southern Field and Fireside*, 27 August 1864. In recent years, several studies of Confederate women and the impact of gender on Confederate nationalism have appeared. See George C. Rable, *Civil Wars: Women and the Crisis of Southern Nationalism* (Urbana: University of Illinois Press, 1989); LeeAnn Whites, *The Civil War as a Crisis in Gender: Augusta, Georgia, 1860–1890* (Athens: University of Georgia Press, 1995); and Drew Gilpin Faust, *Mothers of Invention: Women of the Slaveholding South in the American Civil War* (Chapel Hill: University of North Carolina Press, 1996).

8. On lower-class women (about whom much less has been written), see Bynum, *Unruly Women*, 111–50.

9. Henry W. R. Jackson, *The Southern Women of the Second American Revolution. Our Naval Victories and Exploits of Confederate War Steamers, Capture of Yankee Gunboats, &c* (Atlanta: Intelligencer Steam Power Presses, 1863), i–iii. The first two-thirds of the book is dedicated to stories about women; in an abrupt shift, the remainder is dedicated to stories of naval war. Jackson planned to donate 25¢ of his profits per copy to a fund to establish and support schools for soldiers' orphans.

10. "A Brave Girl," in Jackson, *Southern Women*, 12–14. Such exclamations were not uncommon, especially from younger women. Sarah Morgan several times wished she were a man and therefore able to join her brothers on the battlefield. See entries for 26 July 1862, 166 and 31 July 1862, in East, ed., *Sarah Morgan*, 182–83.

11. "The Women of Winchester, Virginia," in Jackson, *Southern Women*, 12–14.

12. "A Word to Southern Girls," *Southern Field and Fireside*, 17 September 1864, 6. Unlike in the North, in the antebellum South the vast majority of teachers were men, so this recommendation implied a significant societal shift (Faust, *Mothers of Invention*, 82–88; Rable, *Civil Wars*, 129–31).

13. Cumming, *Kate*, 3 March 1864, 191; Mary Chesnut, *Mary Chesnut's Civil War*, ed. C. Vann Woodward (New Haven: Yale University Press, 1981), 29 August 1864, 641; Emma Mordecai Diary, 18 and 23 May 1864, 22, 26, *American Women's Diaries Microfilm*, reel 30.

14. "To the Soldiers' Aid Societies of the Confederate States," *Southern Field and Fireside*, 4 April 1863, 107; "Educated Woman—in Peace and War," ibid., 11 April 1863, 115.

15. "Acts of Kindness and Devotion of the Ladies of Louisville, Kentucky," in Jackson, *Southern Women*, 29.

16. "Home for Invalid Ladies . . . ," in Jackson, *Southern Women*, 34–39; "Help for the Soldier's Orphans," *Montgomery Advertiser*, 25 May 1864. On charity for soldiers' families in Augusta, see Whites, *Civil War as a Crisis in Gender*, 64–78.

17. "Deo Vindice," *Southern Field and Fireside*, 19 November 1864, 3.

18. "Resolutions" made by the Ladies of Mobile, n.d., in Dr. Noah Bennet Benedict Papers, Tulane.

19. Ibid.

20. "Southern Girls Song," *Southern Recorder*, 30 June 1863; Lancelot Minor Blackford to Mary Isabella Blackford, 14 February 1865, Blackford Family Letters, vol. 3, UVA.

21. Cloe Tyler Whittle Greene diary, 19 October 1863, *American Women's Diaries Microfilm*, reel 7, frame 431. In the interests of readability, I have taken the liberty of expanding her abbreviations, putting my replacement in brackets, e.g., cd becomes [could], wd becomes [would].

22. Ibid., frame 432.

23. Whittle felt herself unworthy of the soldiers but was still unable to look beyond their rough appearances. She could not bring herself to actually speak to them, even though she knew that she should; instead, she went into the depot building to write a letter (ibid., frame 436).

24. "Pictures—The Women and the War," *Montgomery Advertiser*, 15 June 1864.

25. "The Women and the War, Picture No. 3," ibid., 18 June 1864.

26. "The Women and the War, Picture Number Four," ibid., 28 June 1864.

27. Letter from Une Mere, ibid., 30 June 1864.

28. This clipping can be found in the Joseph Jones Collection, box 35, Tulane. It has neither a date nor the name of the newspaper on it; however, the surrounding articles are dated late January 1865. Many of the other clippings in the box came from the Augusta (Georgia) *Daily Constitutionalist*, so this one may have as well.

29. *Macaria* was reissued in 1992 by the Louisiana State University Press, with an excellent introduction by Drew Gilpin Faust. Faust provides a brief biographical sketch of Evans and places the novel in the context of Confederate nationalism. See Augusta Jane Evans, *Macaria; or, Altars of Sacrifice* (Baton Rouge: Louisiana State University Press, 1992).

30. "To the Ladies," Joseph Jones Collection, box 35, Tulane.

31. Annette Koch to Christian Koch, 13–23 May 1863, Christian D. Koch Papers, LSU; "Weekly Gossip with Readers and Correspondents," *Southern Field and Fireside*, 16 May 1863, 139. On female refugees, see Faust, *Mothers of Invention*, 40–45; Rable, *Civil Wars*, 181–92; Whites, *Civil War as a Crisis in Gender*, 96–103, 110–11, 115–16; and Mary Elizabeth Massey, *Refugee Life in the Confederacy* (Baton Rouge: Louisiana State University Press, 1964).

32. Kate Stone, *Brokenburn: The Journal of Kate Stone, 1861–1865*, ed. John Q. Anderson, Library of Southern Civilization (Baton Rouge: Louisiana State University Press, 1972), 30 August and 1 September 1863, 238–39; Cumming, *Kate*, 9 March 1865, 261.

33. Eliza Middleton Huger Smith to J. J. Pringle Smith, 4 July 1864, in Smith et al., eds., *Mason-Smith Family Letters*, 108; Stone, *Brokenburn*, 15 April 1864, 277; letter

to Henry H. Brownell, 18 February 1863, Layssard Family Papers, box 1, LSU. On the emotional impact of death on soldiers and civilians, see Drew Gilpin Faust, "The Civil War Soldier and the Art of Dying," *Journal of Southern History* 67 (February 2001): 3–38.

34. Eliza Middleton Huger Smith to daughters, 16 February 1864, in Smith et al., eds., *Mason-Smith Family Letters*, 80; Chesnut, *Mary Chesnut's Civil War*, 26 July 1864, 62; Edgeworth Bird to Sallie Bird, 18 July 1864, in John Rozier, ed., *The Granite Farm Letters: The Civil War Correspondence of Edgeworth & Sallie Bird* (Athens: University of Georgia Press, 1988), 178.

35. Chesnut, *Mary Chesnut's Civil War*, 3 March 1864, 577–78; Emma LeConte, *When the World Ended: The Diary of Emma LeConte*, ed. Earl Schenck Miers (New York: Oxford University Press, 1957), 18 and 19 January 1865, 14–15; Lancelot Minor Blackford to Mrs. William M. Blackford, 25 June 1864, Blackford Family Letters, vol. 3, UVA.

36. Chesnut, *Mary Chesnut's Civil War*, 1862–63, 430; November 1863, 492; 7 December 1863, 503. She includes several arguments over her socializing in the diary. For the history of Richmond during the war, see Ernest B. Furgurson, *Ashes of Glory: Richmond at War* (New York: Alfred A. Knopf, 1996); Emory M. Thomas, *The Confederate State of Richmond: A Biography of the Capital* (Austin: University of Texas Press, 1971); and Alfred H. Bill, *The Beleaguered City: Richmond, 1861–65* (New York: Alfred A. Knopf, 1946).

37. Sallie Bird to Sarah Hamilton Yancey, 8 January 1865, in Rozier, ed., *Granite Farm Letters*, 235; Benjamin Lewis Blackford to Mrs. William M. Blackford, 9 February 1863, Blackford Family Letters, vol. 2, UVA; Isaac Read to David Comfort III, 13 January 1864, Comfort Family Papers, VHS.

38. Jno. Doyle to Maggie Knighton, 13 November 1863, Josiah Knighton and Family Papers, box 1, LSU; Cumming, *Kate*, 5 January 1865, 248; Stone, *Brokenburn*, 26 June 1864, 292; Chesnut, *Mary Chesnut's Civil War*, 19 December 1864, 694.

39. See Faust, *Mothers of Invention*, 234–47, on the collision between self-interest and patriotism. The North also suffered from divided loyalties or instances where economic self-interest triumphed over patriotism in the form of labor unrest and, most famously, the New York City draft riots. See Phillip Shaw Paludan, *A People's Contest: The Union and the Civil War, 1861–65* (Lawrence: University Press of Kansas, 1988, 1996), 181–97; and Iver Bernstein, *New York City Draft Riots* (New York: Oxford University Press, 1990).

40. The classic study of Confederate conscription is Albert Burton Moore, *Conscription and Conflict in the Confederacy* (1924; reprint, New York: Hillary House Publishers, 1963). On Confederate conscription policy, see also Emory M. Thomas, *The Confederate Nation: 1861–1865* (New York: Harper Torchbooks, 1979), 152–55, 260–61; Paul D. Escott, *After Secession: Jefferson Davis and the Failure of Confederate Nationalism* (Baton Rouge: Louisiana State University Press, 1978), 63–64, 80–88; and George C. Rable, *The Confederate Republic: A Revolution against Politics* (Chapel Hill: University of North Carolina Press, 1994), 138–43, 248–49.

41. *Montgomery Advertiser*, 21 November 1863; "Promise and Performance," reprinted in *Southern Field and Fireside*, 13 February 1864, 4; "The Duties of the Hour,"

Montgomery Advertiser, 9 July 1864. On the issue of extortion, see Drew Gilpin Faust, *The Creation of Confederate Nationalism: Ideology and Identity in the Civil War South* (Baton Rouge: Louisiana State University Press, 1988), 41–55.

42. "More Men," Augusta (Georgia) *Daily Constitutionalist*, 9 December 1863, in box 35, Joseph Jones Papers, Tulane.

43. Albert Gallatin Brown, "The State of the Country. Speech of Hon. A. G. Brown in the Confederate Senate, December 24, 1863" (Richmond, 1863?), 1. The remaining five resolutions dealt with economic matters and provided for food and clothing for soldiers families; a direct tax on property, making Confederate notes legal tender for all debts after six months; a prohibition on buying or selling gold and silver coins and any U.S. government or bank notes; a prohibition on "running the blockade"; and a provision to make violators of any of these war measures subject to military, as opposed to civilian, courts.

44. Brown, "State of the Country," 6–10.

45. On women's role in encouraging enlistments, especially at the beginning of the war, see Faust, *Mothers of Invention*, 13–16; and Whites, *Civil War as a Crisis in Gender*, 19, 29, 39–40.

46. "An Appeal from Women," in Jackson, *Southern Women*, 27–28.

47. "Weekly Gossip with Readers and Correspondents," *Southern Field and Fireside*, 5 September 1863, 224; East, ed., *Sarah Morgan*, 30 September 1862, 283; Ella Gertrude Clanton Thomas, *The Secret Eye: The Journal of Ella Gertrude Clanton Thomas, 1848–1889*, ed. Virginia Ingraham Burr (Chapel Hill: University of North Carolina Press, 1990), 16 September 1864, 235; Mrs. Allen S. Izard to Eliza Middleton Huger Smith, in Smith et al. eds., *Mason-Smith Family Letters*, 116. I have taken the liberty of expanding Izard's abbreviations, e.g., sd. becomes should.

48. John C. Murray Diary, 7, 9, and 12 February 1864, Civil War Manuscripts Series, Tulane.

49. "Hoppleggs' War Dotts, by Achilles Hoppleggs, Esq.," *Southern Field and Fireside*, 10 September 1864, 5; "To Go, or Not to Go," *Montgomery Advertiser*, 11 July 1864.

50. "Croaker's Dialogue," *Montgomery Advertiser*, 3 June 1864.

51. "Special Service Hero! Self-Detailed," by the author of "The Rose of Shenandoah" (Richmond, 1863).

52. Number is from James M. McPherson, *Ordeal by Fire: The Civil War and Reconstruction* (New York: Alfred A. Knopf, 1982), 468. See also Reid Mitchell, *Civil War Soldiers: Their Expectations and Their Experiences* (New York: Viking, 1988), 168–73, 182–83. For a general study of desertion, see Ella Lonn, *Desertion during the Civil War* (Lincoln: University of Nebraska Press, 1998). On a comparison of conscription and desertion in the North and South, see Gary W. Gallagher, *The Confederate War* (Cambridge: Harvard University Press, 1997), 30–36.

53. Annette Koch to Christian Koch, 13–23 May 1863 and 1 July 1863, Christian O. Koch Papers, LSU. In an excellent article, Amy E. Murrell has argued that women who appealed to the Confederate government to release their relatives from Confederate service were demonstrating the depth of their loyalty to the Confederacy. See "'Of Necessity and Public Benefit': Southern Families and Their Appeals for Protec-

tion," in Catherine Clinton, ed., *Southern Families at War: Loyalty and Conflict in the Civil War South* (New York: Oxford University Press, 2000), 77–99.

54. Cumming, *Kate*, 13 September 1863, 143; J. Johnston Pettigrew to Zebulon B. Vance, 22 May 1863, GLC.

55. Clement S. Watson to Mary Watson, 2 June 1863 and 26 July 1863, Watson Family Papers, Tulane.

56. Gustave Cook to Lizzie Cook, 21 January 1865, Gustave Cook Papers, GLC; Henry P. Fortson to Rebecca A. Barnes, 27 February 1865, Barnes Family Papers, 1775–1873, Accession #4444, UVA; Lancelot Minor Blackford to Mrs. William M. Blackford, 22 January and 12 February 1864, 8–9 and 28–29, Blackford Family Letters, vol. 3, UVA.

Interlude: Only Not a Victory

1. The most recent example of this literature is Joseph E. Stevens, *1863: The Rebirth of a Nation* (New York: Bantam Books, 1999).

2. The historiography on Gettysburg is voluminous, but good narratives for the general reader can be found in James M. McPherson, *Battle Cry of Freedom: The Civil War Era* (New York: Oxford University Press, 1988), 646–65; and Champ Clark, *Gettysburg: The Confederate High Tide* (Alexandria: Time-Life Books, 1985). Military historians have contributed much to the literature; for a general account, see Herman Hattaway and Archer Jones, *How the North Won: A Military History of the Civil War* (Urbana: University of Illinois Press, 1983), 375–423, passim. Readers seeking more thorough discussions of strategy and tactics should see the three collections edited by Gary W. Gallagher, *The First Day at Gettysburg: Essays on Confederate and Union Leadership* (Kent, Ohio: Kent State University Press, 1992); *The Second Day at Gettysburg: Essays on Confederate and Union Leadership* (Kent, Ohio: Kent State University Press, 1993); and *The Third Day at Gettysburg and Beyond* (Chapel Hill: University of North Carolina Press, 1994). A well-researched, highly readable, and thoroughly enjoyable fictionalized account can be found in Michael Shaara, *The Killer Angels* (New York: Ballantine Books, 1974).

3. Richard Beringer, Herman Hattaway, Archer Jones, and William N. Still Jr., in *Why the South Lost the Civil War* (Athens: University of Georgia Press, 1986), for example, argue that the loss at Gettysburg "had a greater negative impact on the country that it should have had, and fear and foreboding stealthily crept in to take over the corners of Confederate hearts and minds, left vacant as morale and will withered away" (268). Paul Escott makes a similar point in *After Secession: Jefferson Davis and the Failure of Confederate Nationalism* (Baton Rouge: Louisiana State University Press, 1978), claiming that "for thousands of Southerners the first week of July turned hope to despair and swept away remaining illusions that the South could win the war. After July 1863, the leaders of the Confederacy had to communicate with a people who knew that their cause was probably lost" (189–90). This analysis, however, only works in retrospect and largely disregards the very powerful ways in which Confederates told themselves that this defeat was no worse than any other.

4. Gary Gallagher, "Lee's Army Has Not Lost Any of Its Prestige: The Impact of

Gettysburg on the Army of Northern Virginia and the Confederate Home Front," in *Third Day at Gettysburg*, 1–30; and *The Confederate War* (Cambridge: Harvard University Press, 1997), 20–23, 36–44.

5. *Richmond Examiner*, 16 July 1863; "The Capitulation of Vicksburg," *Southern Recorder*, 21 July 1863; "The Lesson Taught by the Fall of Vicksburg and Port Hudson," *Charleston Mercury*, 24 July 1863.

6. "Glorious News from the North—The Rioting Unabated—The Draft Definitely Suspended," *Richmond Examiner*, 21 July 1863; ibid., 18 July 1863. In *The New York City Draft Riots* (New York: Oxford University Press, 1990), Iver Bernstein argues that the riots, in fact, had less to do with resistance to the draft and more to do with tensions between labor and the upper classes (and Democrats and Republicans) in New York City.

7. Edgeworth Bird to Sallie Bird, 15 August 1863, in John Rozier, ed., *The Granite Farm Letters: The Civil War Correspondence of Edgeworth & Sallie Bird* (Athens: University of Georgia Press, 1988).

8. Josiah Gorgas, *The Journals of Josiah Gorgas*, ed. Sarah Woolfolk Wiggins, with a foreword by Frank E. Vandiver (Tuscaloosa: University of Alabama Press, 1995), 25 July 1863, 75; John B. Minor to William Blackford, 10 July 1863, Blackford Family Letters, vol. 2, UVA. On Gorgas's suffering from bouts of depression, see Gorgas, *Journals*, xviii–xix.

9. Mrs. Robert Smith to Eliza Middleton Huger Smith, 18 July 1863, in Daniel E. Huger Smith, Alice R. Huger Smith, and Arney R. Childs, eds., *Mason-Smith Family Letters: 1860–1868* (Columbia: University of South Carolina Press, 1950), 54–55; "Aggressive War," *Charleston Mercury*, 30 July 1863.

10. Lee to Davis, 8 August 1863, *OR*, ser 1, vol. 51, pt. 3, p. 752; Davis to Lee, 11 August 1863, *OR*, ser. 1, vol. 29, pt. 2, p. 639; "Resolution of Thanks," 8 January 1864, in James D. Richardson, ed., *The Messages and Papers of Jefferson Davis and the Confederacy* (New York: Chelsea House–R. Hector, 1966), 1:420. On Lee's resignation offer, see Emory M. Thomas, *Robert E. Lee: A Biography* (New York: W. W. Norton & Company, 1995), 307–8. Thomas believes that Lee's offer was part a pro forma gesture, part genuine. Michael Fellman (*The Making of Robert E. Lee* [New York: Random House, 2000], 150–53) sees it as more calculated, designed to elicit expressions of support from Davis.

11. Margaret Brown Wight Diary, 28 and 29 July 1863, Wight Family Papers, VHS; William Andy Heirs to Sue Carter, 4 August 1863, Sue Carter Letters, GLC. In *Confederate War* (8–9, 85–92, 140), Gary Gallagher argues that the Army of Northern Virginia and Robert E. Lee, not the Confederate government, became the focus of Confederate nationalism and morale.

12. Lancelot Minor Blackford to Mary W. Blackford, 12 August 1863, Blackford Family Letters, vol. 2, p. 399, UVA; Edgeworth Bird to Sallie Bird, 28–29 August 1863, in Rozier, ed., *Granite Farm Letters*, 145; William Andy Heirs to Sue Carter, 28 July 1863, Sue Carter Letters, GLC. For the text of the resolutions to which Edgeworth Bird referred, see *Richmond Examiner*, 22 August 1863.

13. Lee to Davis, 8 August 1863, *OR*, ser. 1, vol. 51, pt. 3, p. 752.

14. "Proclamation," 25 July 1863, in Richardson, ed., *Messages and Papers*, 1:328.

15. "Remarkable Phenomenon, Interpretation Suggested," "A Strange Phenomenon," and "For the Spectator—Remarkable Phenomenon," all in *Staunton Spectator*, 22 September 1863. For more about the *Staunton Spectator* and editor Richard Mauzy, see the Valley of the Shadow website, <http://valley.vcdh.virginia.edu>. A letter to the paper on 13 October put forth a more prosaic interpretation: that of "atmospheric condensation."

Chapter Three

1. I am not writing about Southern Unionists in this chapter, though they clearly represented an alternative Southern (as opposed to Confederate) identity. The literature on Southern Unionists is extensive; see William W. Freehling, *The South vs. the South: How Anti-Confederate Southerners Shaped the Course of the Civil War* (New York: Oxford University Press, 2001); Thomas Dyer, *Secret Yankees: The Union Circle in Confederate Atlanta* (Baltimore: Johns Hopkins University Press, 1999); Daniel E. Sutherland, ed., *Guerrillas, Unionists, and Violence on the Confederate Home Front* (Fayetteville: University of Arkansas Press, 1999); Daniel W. Crofts, *Reluctant Confederates: Upper South Unionists in the Secession Crisis* (Chapel Hill: University of North Carolina Press, 1989); Carl N. Degler, *The Other South: Southern Dissenters in the Nineteenth Century* (New York: Harper & Row, 1974); and Georgia Lee Tatum, *Disloyalty in the Confederacy* (Lincoln: University of Nebraska Press, 2000).

2. Zillah Haynie Brandon Diary, 29 May 1864 and 22 August 1863, *American Women's Diaries Microfilm, Segment II: Southern Women*, reel 3, frames 360, 350; "War," *Southern Field and Fireside*, 22 August 1863, 208.

3. Francis Williamson Smith to Francis Henney Smith, 24 November 1864, Smith Family Papers, VHS.

4. Emma LeConte, *When the World Ended: The Diary of Emma LeConte*, ed. Earl Schenck Miers (New York: Oxford University Press, 1957), 31 December 1864, 4; John W. Brown Diary, 24 April 1864, SHC; William R. Smith to Jeremiah Morton, 20 January 1863, Morton-Halsey Papers, box 1, UVA; Ella Gertrude Clanton Thomas, *The Secret Eye: The Journal of Ella Gertrude Clanton Thomas, 1848–1889*, ed. Virginia Ingraham Burr (Chapel Hill: University of North Carolina Press, 1990), 21 July 1864, 228.

5. For a discussion of the war against Confederate civilians, see Charles Royster, *The Destructive War: William Tecumseh Sherman, Stonewall Jackson, and the Americans* (New York: Alfred A. Knopf, 1991), 35, 79–89. Two recent books about the Union occupation of the Confederacy are Stephen V. Ash, *When the Yankees Came: Conflict and Chaos in the Occupied South, 1861–1865* (Chapel Hill: University of North Carolina Press, 1995), and Mark Grimsley, *The Hard Hand of War: Union Military Policy toward Southern Civilians, 1861–1865* (Cambridge: Cambridge University Press, 1995). For angry reactions to the occupiers, see Ash, *When the Yankees Came*, 38–73.

6. Josiah Gorgas, *The Journals of Josiah Gorgas*, ed. Sarah Woolfolk Wiggins, with a foreword by Frank E. Vandiver (Tuscaloosa: University of Alabama Press, 1995), 20 December 1863, 88; 7 July 1864, 120. Less than a month after the latter entry, Confederates gave Northerners a taste of war's destruction when a raiding party led by General John McCausland burned the town of Chambersburg, Pa. See Ted

Alexander and others, *Southern Revenge! Civil War History of Chambersburg, Pennsylvania* (Chambersburg: Greater Chambersburg Chamber of Commerce, 1989), and Everard H. Smith, "Chambersburg: Anatomy of a Confederate Reprisal," *American Historical Review* 96 (April 1991): 432–55.

7. Clement S. Watson to Mary Watson, 2 June 1863, Watson Family Papers, Tulane.

8. "What Subjugation Means," reprinted in *Charleston Mercury*, 12 and 16 January 1864.

9. "Subjugation," *Southern Field and Fireside*, 2 January 1864, 4.

10. "The Roll of the Drum," ibid., 18 February 1864, 4. For a general discussion of honor, see Bertram Wyatt-Brown, *Southern Honor: Ethics and Behavior in the Old South* (New York: Oxford University Press, 1982), 14–15, 25–27, 110–14.

11. Lise Mitchell Diary, 6 May 1865, Lise Mitchell Papers, Tulane; Mrs. Allen S. Izard to Eliza Middleton Huger Smith, 21 July 1864, in Daniel E. Huger Smith, Alice R. Huger Smith, and Arney R. Childs, eds., *Mason-Smith Family Letters: 1860–1868* (Columbia: University of South Carolina Press, 1950), 116; letter to Henry H. Brownell, 18 February 1863, Layssard Family Papers, box 1, LSU.

12. Mrs. L. P. Lewis to Mrs. D. 10 September 1864, in Emma Mordecai Diary, 109–13, *American Women's Diaries Microfilm*, reel 30. See also Grimsley, *Hard Hand of War*, and William Blair, *Virginia's Private War: Feeding Body and Soul in the Confederacy, 1861–65* (New York: Oxford University Press, 1998), 108–11, 118–19.

13. Mrs. L. P. Lewis to Mrs. D. 10 September 1864, in Emma Mordecai Diary, 109–13, *American Women's Diaries Microfilm*, reel 30. Mordecai noted that Mrs. Lewis was of Indian descent, through Governor Floyd.

14. John W. Brown Diary, 16 April 1864, SHC; Sally Armstrong Diary, 7, 12, 22 August 1863, VHS. Despite her distaste for the Federals, Armstrong was, like Margaret Wight, forced to concede that some were at least relatively trustworthy. The Armstrongs appear not to have been harassed, and Sally finally admitted that her neighbors were "the best Yankees in the north."

15. LeConte, *When the World Ended*, 18 February 1865, 42, 48; Emma Louise Walton to Col. James B. Walton, 22 April 1863, Walton-Glenny Family Papers, HNOC.

16. Cloe Tyler Whittle Greene Diary, 19 October 1863, *American Women's Diaries Microfilm*, reel 7, frame 403; ibid., 15 June 1863, frames 360–61.

17. "Union Sentiment in New Orleans," in Henry W. R. Jackson, *The Southern Women of the Second American Revolution. Our Naval Victories and Exploits of Confederate War Steamers, Capture of Yankee Gunboats, &c.* (Atlanta: Intelligencer Steam Power Presses, 1863), 52; LeConte, *When the World Ended*, 18 February 1865, 52; 18 March 1865, 82. See also Drew Gilpin Faust, *Mothers of Invention: Women of the Slaveholding South in the American Civil War* (Chapel Hill: University of North Carolina Press, 1996), 196–207; and George Rable, *Civil Wars: Women and the Crisis of Southern Nationalism* (Urbana: University of Illinois Press, 1989), 154–80.

18. Mary D. Robertson, ed. *A Confederate Lady Comes of Age: The Journals of Pauline DeCaradeuc Heyward, 1863–1888.* Women's Diaries and Letters of the Nineteenth-Century South (Columbia: University of South Carolina Press, 1992), 18 June 1864, 50; Kate Cumming, *Kate: The Journal of a Confederate Nurse*, ed. Richard Barksdale Harwell (Baton Rouge: Louisiana State University Press, 1959), 3 April 1865, 268;

Priscilla "Mittie" Munnikhuysen Bond Diary, 27 December 1863, LSU; Emma Mordecai Diary, 19 September 1864, 86–87, *American Women's Diaries Microfilm*, reel 30.

19. Lancelot Minor Blackford to Mrs. William M. Blackford, 23 April 1863, Blackford Family Letters, vol. 2, UVA; Kate Stone, *Brokenburn: The Journal of Kate Stone, 1861–1865*, ed. John Q. Anderson, Library of Southern Civilization (Baton Rouge: Louisiana State University Press, 1972), 9 March 1863, 177,

20. Cumming, *Kate*, 11 January 1864, 187; Cloe Tyler Whittle Greene Diary, 17 February 1863, *American Women's Diaries Microfilm*, frames 325–27.

21. Mahala Perkins Harding Eggleston Roach Diary, 24 October 1864 and 24 January 1865, VHS.

22. Ibid., 2 December 1863, 24 and 25 February 1865. The Eggleston-Roach Papers at LSU have copies of correspondence between Roach and the Danas regarding her mother's banishment.

23. See Harold Melvin Hyman, *The Era of the Oath: Northern Loyalty Tests during the Civil War and Reconstruction* (Philadelphia: University of Pennsylvania Press, 1954), 13–47.

24. Rev. B. M. Palmer, D.D. *The Oath of Allegiance to the United States, Discussed in Its Moral and Political Bearings* (Richmond: McFarlane & Fergusson, 1863), 6–7.

25. Ibid., 12–13, 15–17.

26. Ibid., 18, 20–21. Palmer's claim that people would be seen as believing in the Confederacy only as long as it could protect them forms the crux of several historians' arguments about failures of Confederate will. See Faust, *Mothers of Invention*, 6–8, 234–47; Paul Escott, *After Secession: Jefferson Davis and the Failure of Confederate Nationalism* (Baton Rouge: Louisiana State University Press, 1978); and Richard E. Beringer, Herman Hattaway, Archer Jones, and William N. Still Jr., *Why the South Lost the Civil War* (Athens: University of Georgia Press, 1986). I believe, as many Confederates did, that the oath was seen as one that could be broken, and one that had little bearing on feelings of national allegiance. Some newer work on loyalty in Union-controlled areas—Kentucky and the Shenandoah Valley—has made the case that loyalty to the Confederacy was more flexible and contingent than we have previously allowed it to be. See Kristin Streater, "Patriotism or Impropriety? Gendered Constructions of Loyalty in Civil War Kentucky," paper given at Southern Association of Women Historians Fifth Conference on Southern Women's History, June 2000; and Jonathan Berkey, "Nation and Neighborhood in Occupied Winchester, Va., Spring 1862," paper given at Southern Historical Association Annual Meeting, November 2002.

27. Charles East, ed., *Sarah Morgan: The Civil War Diary of a Southern Woman* (New York: Simon and Schuster, 1991), 31 March 1863, 449–50. On her half-brother, Philip Hickey Morgan, taking the oath, see ibid., 23 January 1863, 410.

28. East, ed., *Sarah Morgan*, 22 April 1863, 485–86; and 21 June 1863, 508–9.

29. Robert Andrews Wilkinson to Mary Farrar Wilkinson, 5 July 1863, Wilkinson-Stark Family Papers, HNOC; Margaret Brown Wight Diary, 16 December 1864, Wight Family Paper, VHS; "Union Sentiment in New Orleans," in Jackson, *Southern Women*, 51–52.

30. Alfred W. Smith to Nathan Stedman, 25 October 1863, Smith Family Letters,

Civil War Manuscripts, Tulane; Cloe Tyler Whittle Greene Diary, 18 September 1864, *American Women's Diaries Microfilm, Segment II: Southern Women*, reel 7, frame 494; Mahala Perkins Harding Eggleston Roach Diary, 28 January 1865, VHS.

31. Jno. Doyle to Maggie Knighton, 13 November 1863, Josiah Knighton and Family Papers, box 1, LSU; Gustave Arvilien Breaux Diary, 23 November 1863, Tulane. See also his entry for 17 January 1864, when he complains about the people of Iberia, Louisiana, having taken the oath.

32. John W. Brown Diary, 27 April 1864, 21 August 1864, and 29 August 1864, SHC.

33. All quoted in Drew Gilpin Faust, *The Creation of Confederate Nationalism: Ideology and Identity in the Civil War South* (Baton Rouge: Louisiana State University Press, 1988), 59–60.

34. Charles B. Dew, *Apostles of Disunion: Southern Secession Commissioners and the Causes of the Civil War* (Charlottesville: University Press of Virginia, 2001), 77–80.

35. *Constitution of the Confederate States of America*, 11 March 1861, <http://www .yale.edu/lawweb/avalon/csa/csa.htm>; "The Congress Removes to Richmond," *Charleston Mercury*, 22 May 1861.

36. Rt. Rev. Stephen Elliott, D.D., *A Sermon Preached in Christ Church Savannah, on Thursday, September 18th, 1862, Being the Day Set Forth by the President of the Confederate States as a Day of Prayer and Thanksgiving, for Our Manifold Victories and Especially for the Fields of Manassas and Richmond, KY.* (Savannah: Power Press of John M. Cooper & Co., 1862), 10; Faust, *Creation of Confederate Nationalism*, 60–61.

37. The historiography on the ways in which slaves, through their own efforts, contributed to the defeat of the Confederacy is voluminous. Leon Litwack's classic *Been in the Storm So Long: The Aftermath of Slavery* (New York: Random House, 1979) is still an excellent place to start; see also Armstead Louis Robinson, "Day of Jubilio: Civil War and the Demise of Slavery in the Mississippi Valley" (Ph.D. dissertation, University of Rochester, 1976), and Freehling, *South vs. the South*.

38. Elliot, *Sermon Preached in Christ Church Savannah*, 11.

39. "A War Problem," *Charleston Mercury*, 15 June 1864. For examples of similar rhetoric, see nearly identical (to each other) editorials in ibid., on 28 July 1862 and 5 November 1863. See also James L. Roark, *Masters without Slaves: Southern Planters in the Civil War and Reconstruction* (New York: W. W. Norton & Co., 1977), 77–108; and Litwack, *Been in the Storm So Long*, 104–66.

40. "The Effect of Nobility of Race and the Sense of Honor of the South," *Charleston Mercury*, 25 June 1862. An almost identical editorial, under the title "Contact Race and the Sense of Honor," appeared in the 29 November 1862 edition of the *Mercury*.

41. David Demus to Mary Jane Demus, 24 January 1865, Valley of the Shadow website, <http://jefferson.village.virginia.edu/vshadow2/cwletters.html>.

42. "Negroes," *Charleston Mercury*, 12 August 1863.

43. Michael Fellman, Lesley J. Gordon, and Daniel E. Sutherland, *This Terrible War: The Civil War and Its Aftermath* (New York: Longman, 2003), 163–65.

44. Ira Berlin et al., *Free at Last: A Documentary History of Slavery, Freedom, and the Civil War* (New York: New Press, 1992), 437–39.

45. For a comprehensive study of this issue, see Robert F. Durden, *The Gray and the Black: The Confederate Debate on Emancipation* (Baton Rouge: Louisiana State

University Press, 1972). See also Richard Beringer et al., *Why the South Lost*, 368–97; George Rable, *The Confederate Republic: A Revolution against Politics* (Chapel Hill: University of North Carolina Press, 1994), 287–92; Emory M. Thomas, *The Confederate Nation: 1861–1865* (New York: Harper Torchbooks, 1979), 290–93, 296–97; James M. McPherson, *Battle Cry of Freedom: The Civil War Era* (New York: Oxford University Press, 1988), 831–36; and Gary W. Gallagher, *The Confederate War* (Cambridge: Harvard University Press, 1997), 107–8.

46. Durden, *Gray and the Black*, 53–63.

47. Ibid., 67.

48. Ibid., 101–6.

49. Joseph Waddell Diary, 16 January 1865, Valley of the Shadow website, <http://valley.vcdh.virginia.edu>; *Richmond Enquirer*, 3 February 1865.

50. "Negroes in the Army," *Staunton Vindicator*, 18 November 1864; Thomas, *Secret Eye*, 17 November 1864, 243.

51. "Emancipation of Slaves by the Confederate Government," *Charleston Mercury*, November 3, 1864; "The Employment of Slaves," ibid., 12 November 1864.

52. "Whom the Gods Would Destroy they First Make Mad," ibid., 3 January 1865; "Lunacy," ibid., 13 January 1865; "Men Run Mad," ibid., 26 January 1865.

53. "Gen. Robert E. Lee—Federalism," ibid., 3 February 1865.

54. Joseph Waddell Diary, 16 January 1865, Valley of the Shadow website, <http://valley.vcdh.virginia.edu>.

55. Durden, *Gray and the Black*, 206–7.

56. B. H. Anthony to Callie J. Anthony, 20 February 1865, Anthony Family Letters, UVA.

57. David Schenck Diary, December 1864, David Schenck Papers, SHC.

58. *Richmond Enquirer*, 18 February 1865. On whites' misunderstanding the degree to which their slaves would remain "loyal" to them, see Litwack, *Been in the Storm So Long*, 3–63.

59. "Mass Meeting," *Staunton Vindicator*, 24 February 1865; "Public Meeting," ibid., 24 March 1865,.

60. Joseph Waddell Diary, 14 and 20 February 1865.

61. John W. Brown Diary, 6 April 1865, SHC; David Schenck Diary, 16 March 1865, David Schenck Papers, SHC; Durden, *Gray and the Black*, 274–75.

62. "Men Run Mad," *Charleston Mercury*, 26 January 1865.

Interlude: Peace (with Independence Always)

1. I am indebted to the work of Charles Royster for this idea, although he and I use it somewhat differently. Royster argues that Southerners' inability to conceptualize defeat fundamentally weakened their nation. I believe that their unwillingness to describe defeat actually strengthened Confederate loyalty, for a world without the Confederacy rapidly became unimaginable. Thus, Confederates encouraged each other to continue fighting even when it seemed futile. See Charles Royster, *The Destructive War: William Tecumseh Sherman, Stonewall Jackson, and the Americans* (New York: Alfred A. Knopf, 1991), 177–80.

2. On the Atlanta campaign, see Albert Castel, *Decision in the West: The Atlanta*

Campaign of 1864 (Lawrence: University of Kansas Press, 1992); James Lee McDonough and James Pickett Jones, *War So Terrible: Sherman and Atlanta* (New York: W. W. Norton & Company, 1987); and Thomas L. Connelly, *Autumn of Glory: The Army of Tennessee, 1862–1865* (Baton Rouge: Louisiana State University Press, 1971). On Lincoln's election, see John C. Waugh, *Reelecting Lincoln: The Battle for the 1864 Presidency* (New York: Crown Publishers, 1997); James M. McPherson, *Battle Cry of Freedom: The Civil War Era* (New York: Oxford University Press, 1988), 713–17; Phillip Shaw Paludan, *A People's Contest: The Union and Civil War, 1861–1865*, 2d ed. (Lawrence: University Press of Kansas, 1996), 249–52; and William Zornow, *Lincoln and the Party Divided* (Norman: University of Oklahoma Press, 1954). On Southern interest in the election, see Larry E. Nelson, *Bullets, Ballots, and Rhetoric: Confederate Policy for the United States Presidential Contest of 1864* (University: University of Alabama Press, 1980), and Albert Castel, *Winning and Losing in the Civil War* (Columbia: University of South Carolina Press, 1996).

3. Sallie Bird to Saida Bird, 7 September 1864, in John Rozier, ed. *The Granite Farm Letters: The Civil War Correspondence of Edgeworth & Sallie Bird* (Athens: University of Georgia Press, 1988), 199; Cumming, *Kate*, 7 September 1864, 231; Gustave Arvilien Breaux Diary, 18 September 1864, Tulane.

4. Ella Gertrude Clanton Thomas, *The Secret Eye: The Journal of Ella Gertrude Clanton Thomas, 1848–1889*, ed. Virginia Ingraham Burr (Chapel Hill: University of North Carolina Press, 1990), 22 September 1864, 236–37; Margaret Brown Wight Diary, 14 September 1864, Wight Family Papers, VHS; Mary Chesnut, *Mary Chesnut's Civil War*, ed. C. Vann Woodward (New Haven: Yale University Press, 1981), 21 September 1864, 645.

5. George C. Rable, *The Confederate Republic: A Revolution Against Politics* (Chapel Hill: University of North Carolina Press, 1994), 272–73.

6. Josiah Gorgas, *The Journals of Josiah Gorgas*, ed. Sarah Woolfolk Wiggins, with a foreword by Frank E. Vandiver (Tuscaloosa: University of Alabama Press, 1995), 24 September 1864, 133; Cloe Tyler Whittle Greene Diary, 22 September 1864, *American Women's Diaries Microfilm, Segment II: Southern Women*, reel 7, frames 496–97.

7. Thomas, *Secret Eye*, 21 October 1864, 239. To her credit, Thomas does not appear to have done anything to prevent her husband's service, but the fact that she was unwilling to see him die a hero's death illustrates the approaching limits of nationalist rhetoric.

8. Much has been made over the years of the notion that the election of 1864 represented a "turning point" in the war, that a McClellan victory would have led to Confederate independence. In his essay "The Turning Point that Wasn't: The Confederates and the Election of 1864," William C. Davis (*The Cause Lost: Myths and Realities of the Confederacy* [Lawrence: University Press of Kansas, 1996]) uses a series of counterfactual assumptions to argue that even a lame-duck Lincoln would have continued to pursue the war so aggressively that Northern victory was the only outcome. Davis looks at the event only from a political and strategic perspective; in examining it from the standpoint of emotion, it marks a shift in the attitude, hopes, and fears of the Confederate people.

9. Gorgas, *Journals*, 17 November 1864, 139; Thomas, *Secret Eye*, 17 November

1864, 243; Kate Stone, *Brokenburn: The Journal of Kate Stone, 1861–1865*, ed. John Q. Anderson, Library of Southern Civilization (Baton Rouge: Louisiana State University Press, 1972); 15 November 1863, 259; Frances Jane (Bestor) Robinson Diary, 16 November 1864, *American Women's Diaries Microfilm*, reel 3.

10. Annie B. Hays to John G. Dunlap, 23 November 1864, Dunlap Correspondence, Tulane; John W. Brown Diary, 11 November 1864, SHC; Edward Laight Wells to Mr. & Mrs. Thomas L. Wells, 17 November 1864, in Daniel E. Huger Smith, Alice R. Huger Smith, and Arney R. Childs, eds., *Mason-Smith Family Letters: 1860–1868* (Columbia: University of South Carolina Press, 1950), 148. On Confederates professing unconcern after Lincoln's election, see Gary W. Gallagher, *The Confederate War* (Cambridge: Harvard University Press, 1997), 41–42.

11. David Schenck Diary, January 1865, David Schenck Papers, SHC; "Weekly Record," *Southern Field and Fireside*, 21 January 1865.

12. William S. Oldham, "Speech of the Hon. W. S. Oldham, of Texas, on the Resolutions of the State of Texas Concerning Peace, Reconstruction, and Independence. In the Confederate States Senate, January 30, 1865" (Richmond: n.p., 1865), 1–2. The resolutions called first for a convention of Confederate and Union state representatives to "reform" the Constitution of the United States to "forever guarantee" slavery. They also announced that Texas would not entertain peace talks with the United States as an individual state, but only through the Confederacy as a whole, and condemned the United States for attempting to "divide and conquer." The third resolution asked that the Northern people understand "that the Southern states did not secede from the Union upon any question such as the mere preservation of the slave property of their citizens" and reiterated their right of secession. Northerners also needed to understand that the Southern states were determined in their fight and staunchly unwilling to reunite with the North because of both historical grievances and the growing atrocities of war.

13. Ibid., 8–9.

14. Ibid., 11–13.

Chapter Four

1. On the evacuation and occupation of Richmond, see Ernest B. Furgurson, *Ashes of Glory: Richmond at War* (New York: Alfred A. Knopf, 1996), 319–39; A. H. Hoehling and Mary Hoehling, *The Day Richmond Died* (Lanham, Md.: Madison Books, 1981); Robert Hendrickson, *The Road to Appomattox* (New York: John Wiley & Sons, Inc., 1998), 123–54; Rembert W. Patrick, *The Fall of Richmond* (Baton Rouge: Louisiana State University Press, 1960); and Nelson D. Lankford, *Richmond Burning: The Last Days of the Confederate Capital* (New York: Viking Press, 2002).

2. Harriet Boswell Anderson Caperton to John Caperton, 9 April 1865, Caperton Family Papers, VHS.

3. Emma Mordecai to Edward Cohen, 5 April 1865, Emma Mordecai Diary, 113–30, *American Women's Diaries Microfilm, Segment II: Southern Women*, reel 30.

4. Emma Mordecai Diary, 13 April 1865, *American Women's Diaries Microfilm*; Fanny Churchill Braxton Young to Mary Walker Tomlin Braxton, 11 April 1865, Fanny Churchill Braxton Young Papers, VHS.

5. John W. Brown Diary, 16 April 1865, SHC; Mary Chesnut, *Mary Chesnut's Civil War*, ed. C. Vann Woodward (New Haven: Yale University Press, 1981), 7 April 1865, 782; Kate Cumming, *Kate: The Journal of a Confederate Nurse*, ed. Richard Barksdale Harwell (Baton Rouge: Louisiana State University Press, 1959), 7 April 1865, 268.

6. Davis's final message can be found in James D. Richardson, ed., *Messages and Papers of Jefferson Davis and the Confederacy*, 1:568–70. On the government's and Davis's retreat to Danville and points south, see William C. Davis, *An Honorable Defeat: The Last Days of the Confederate Government* (New York: Harcourt, 2001); James C. Clark, *Last Train South: The Flight of the Confederate Government from Richmond* (Jefferson, N.C.: McFarland & Company, Inc., 1984); and Michael B. Ballard, *A Long Shadow: Jefferson Davis and the Final Days of the Confederacy* (Jackson: University Press of Mississippi, 1986).

7. William Lyne Wilson Diary, 2 April 1865, GLC.

8. Ibid., 4–8 April 1865, GLC.

9. J. E. Whitehorne Diary, 2–4, 8 April 1865, SHC. According to the typescript version in the Southern Historical Collection, the original was presented to the State Library of Virginia (now the Library of Virginia) in 1939. Chris M. Calkins, *The Battles of Appomattox Station and Appomattox Court House, April 8–9, 1865* (Lynchburg: H. E. Howard, 1987), provides a detailed account of the battles leading up to the surrender.

10. On the retreat from Richmond and the surrender itself, see Hendrickson, *Road to Appomattox*, particularly 187–206. See also Richard Wheeler's *Witness to Appomattox* (New York: Harper & Row, 1989), which is almost purely descriptive, quoting extensively from many first-person accounts of the campaign and the surrender. On the decision to surrender and disperse the Army of Northern Virginia rather than resort to guerrilla warfare, see Richard E. Beringer, Herman Hattaway, Archer Jones, and William N. Still Jr., *Why the South Lost the Civil War* (Athens: University of Georgia Press, 1986), 436–38; and Emory M. Thomas, *The Confederate Nation, 1861–1865* (New York: Harper Torchbooks, 1979), 302–4.

11. William Lyne Wilson Diary, 9 April 1865 and undated entry following it, GLC.

12. J. E. Whitehorne Diary, 9–13, 16, 22 April 1865, SHC.

13. Kena King Chapman Diary, 9–10, 19–20 April 1865, SHC.

14. Sabina Elliott Wells to Mrs. Thomas L. (Julia) Wells, 10 April 1865, in Daniel E. Huger Smith, Alice R. Huger Smith, and Arney R. Childs, eds., *Mason-Smith Family Letters: 1860–1868* (Columbia: University of South Carolina Press, 1950), 194; Margaret Brown Wight Diary, 12 April 1865, White Family Papers, VHS; Emma Mordecai Diary, 13 April 1865, *American Women's Diaries Microfilm*.

15. Charles East, ed., *Sarah Morgan: The Civil War Diary of a Southern Woman* (New York: Simon & Schuster, 1991), 19 April 1865, 606; Edwin H. Fay to Sarah Shields Fay, 5 May 1865, in Bell Irvin Wiley and Lucy E. Fay, eds. *This Infernal War: The Confederate Letters of Edwin Fay* (Austin: University of Texas Press, 1958), 442.

16. William Nalle Diary, 6, 12–14 April 1865, VHS.

17. Ibid., 17 and 21 April 1865.

18. C. W. Hutson letter fragment, presumably to Mrs. William Ferguson Hutson, 11 April 1865, and Frances S. O'R Hutson Journal, 24–26 April 1865, Hutson Family

Papers, Tulane; Cumming, *Kate*, 22, 26 April and 1 May 1865, 275, 277. As late as 1 May, a full three weeks after the surrender, Cumming reported her belief that the French had recognized the Confederacy at the eleventh hour.

19. Harriet Boswell Anderson Caperton to John Caperton, 9 April 1865, Caperton Family Papers, VHS.

20. Anna Maria Dandridge (Deans) Smith to Francis Smith, 16 April 1865, Smith Family Papers, VHS; Edwin Leet to Sarah Leet, 26 April 1865, Edwin Leet Letters, LSU.

21. Cumming, *Kate*, 16 April 1865, 270; Lise Mitchell Diary, 6 May 1865, Lise Mitchell Papers, Tulane; Pauline DeCaradeuc Heyward, *A Confederate Lady Comes of Age: The Journals of Pauline DeCaradeuc Heyward, 1863-1888*, ed. Mary D. Robertson, Women's Diaries and Letters of the Nineteenth-Century South (Columbia: University of South Carolina Press, 1992), 26 April 1865, 75.

22. On Lincoln's funeral and immediate reactions, both North and South, see Merrill D. Petersen, *Lincoln and American Memory* (New York: Oxford University Press, 1994), 3–26, 38–50. On the Southern reaction specifically, see Carolyn L. Harrell, *When Bells Tolled for Lincoln: Southern Reaction to the Assassination* (Macon: Mercer University Press, 1997).

23. Emma LeConte, *When the World Ended: The Diary of Emma LeConte*, ed. Earl Schenck Miers (New York: Oxford University Press, 1957), 21 April 1865, 91, 93; Kate Stone, *Brokenburn: The Journal of Kate Stone, 1861-1865*, ed. John Q. Anderson, Library of Southern Civilization (Baton Rouge: Louisiana State University Press, 1972), 28 April and 15 May 1865, 333, 340; Louis A. Bringier to "Shel" Bringier, 23 April 1865, Louis A. Bringier and Family Papers, LSU; Laura to Martha, 25 May 1865, William Alexander Hoke Papers, SHC.

24. East, ed., *Sarah Morgan*, 19 April 1865, 607; William R. Palmer to Dr. John Baylor, 25 April 1865, Baylor Family Papers, Accession #2257, UVA; Kena King Chapman Diary, 19 April 1865, SHC; William Nalle Diary, 22 April 1865, VHS.

25. Margaret Brown Wight Diary, 18 April 1865, Wight Family Papers, VHS; Mary Elizabeth Carter Rives Diary, 25 April 1865, LSU; John W. Brown Diary, 2 May 1865, SHC.

26. William M. Myers to William H. Henshaw, 12 May 1865, Anne Henshaw Gardiner Papers, Duke; David Schenck Diary, April 1865, David Schenck Papers, SHC; Harriet McLellan Diary, July 1865, 31–32, *American Women's Diaries Microfilm*, reel 6.

27. Mahala Perkins Harding Eggleston Roach Diary, 18 April 1865, LSU; East, ed., *Sarah Morgan*, 22 April 1865.

28. LeConte, *When the World Ended*, 27 June 1865, 110–11. Richmond incident quoted in Harrell, *When Bells Tolled for Lincoln*, 37.

29. John Lansing Burrows, D.D., *Palliative and Prejudiced Judgments Condemned: A Discourse Delivered in the First Baptist Church, Richmond VA, June 1, 1865, The Day Appointed by the President of the United States for Humiliation and Mourning on Account of the Assassination of President Lincoln, Together with an Extract from a Sermon, Preached on Sunday, April 23rd, 1865 upon the Assassination of President Lincoln* (Richmond: Office of the Commercial Bulletin, 1865), 4–5.

30. Ibid., 6–11.

31. Thomas T. Munford to Brigadier General Mackenzie, 17 April 1865, and "Head Quarters Munford's Cav. Brigade, Special Orders, April 21 1865," in Munford-Ellis Family Papers, Duke; "Headq'rs Dist. of Florida, Tallahassee, April 28th 1865," in Edward M. L'Engle Papers, SHC.

32. C. W. Hutson letter fragments, presumably to Mrs. William Ferguson Hutson, 9 and 11 April 1865, Hutson Family Papers, Tulane.

33. Ibid., 18 and 19 April 1865. Apparently, he did not emigrate, as he received a parole on 26 May, in Greensboro, but his desire to do so reflected many Confederate soldiers' first impulse.

34. Jared Y. Sanders to Bessie Wofford, 11 and 12 May 1865, Jared Y. Sanders and Family Papers, LSU.

35. Ibid.

36. Copy of a letter from James Longstreet in the *Lynchburg Virginian*, 25 April 1865, in Munford-Ellis Family Papers, Duke; J. R. Andrews to James Calvert Wise, 7 May 1865, James Calvert Wise Papers, LSU.

37. Stone, *Brokenburn*, 28 April and 15 May 1865, 333–34, 339–40.

38. "Lee's Surrender" in Mary E. Grattan Papers, SHC.

39. Louis A. Bringier to "Shel," 13 May 1865, Louis A. Bringier and Family Papers, LSU; Edward Conigland to "Mr. Editor," 28 July 1865, Edward Conigland Papers, SHC.

40. For a description of the trip through Virginia and North Carolina by a member of the Davis cabinet, see Josiah Gorgas, *The Journals of Josiah Gorgas*, ed. Sarah Woolfolk Wiggins (Tuscaloosa: University of Alabama Press, 1995), 30 April 1865, 158–62. See also James C. Clark, *Last Train South*; Ballard, *Long Shadow*; and William J. Cooper Jr., *Jefferson Davis, American* (New York: Alfred A. Knopf, 2000), 525–34.

41. Ella Gertrude Clanton Thomas, *The Secret Eye: The Journal of Ella Gertrude Clanton Thomas, 1848–1889*, ed. Virginia Ingraham Burr (Chapel Hill: University of North Carolina Press, 1990), 8 May 1865, 266; Cumming, *Kate*, 30 April and 7 May 1865, 275, 282–83; Laura to Martha, 25 May 1865, William Alexander Hoke Papers, SHC.

42. Nina Silber has produced a thorough and thought-provoking analysis of this gendered rhetoric and imagery in *The Romance of Reunion: Northerners and the South, 1865–1900* (Chapel Hill: University of North Carolina Press, 1993), 29–37.

43. Thomas, *Secret Eye*, 17 May 1865, 268–69; Mary Chesnut, *Mary Chesnut's Civil War*, ed. C. Vann Woodward (New Haven: Yale University Press, 1981), 21 May 1865, 819.

44. Heyward, *Confederate Lady*, 15 May and 9 July 1865, 76, 82.

Chapter Five

1. Two of the best studies of the politics of this period are Dan T. Carter, *When the War Was Over: The Failure of Self-Reconstruction in the South* (Baton Rouge: Louisiana State University Press, 1985), and Michael Perman, *Reunion without Compromise: The South and Reconstruction, 1865–1868* (Cambridge: Cambridge University Press, 1973).

2. On the "faithful slave" and white anger at realizing that that was a pose, see

Leon F. Litwack, *Been in the Storm So Long: The Aftermath of Slavery* (New York: Random House, 1979), 3–63, 167–221.

3. Emma Mordecai Diary, 19 April 1865, 141; 5 May 1865, 147, *American Women's Diaries Microfilm, Segment II: Southern Women*; Letitia A. Walton to Mollie Watkins, 23 July 1865, in E. Grey Dimond and Herman Hattaway, eds. *Letters from Forest Place: A Plantation Family's Correspondence* (Jackson: University Press of Mississippi, 1993), 336. For other examples of similar complaints (about slaves refusing to work, etc.), see Kate Stone, *Brokenburn: The Journal of Kate Stone, 1861–1865*, ed. John Q. Anderson, Library of Southern Civilization (Baton Rouge: Louisiana State University Press, 1972), 362–63; and Ella Gertrude Clanton Thomas, *The Secret Eye: The Journal of Ella Gertrude Clanton Thomas, 1848–1889*, ed. Virginia Ingraham Burr (Chapel Hill: University of North Carolina Press, 1990), 270–75. On white resistance to the use of free black labor, see James L. Roark, *Masters without Slaves: Southern Planters in the Civil War and Reconstruction* (New York: W. W. Norton & Co.), 1977.

4. Joseph Waddell Diary, entries for 2, 12, 14, 30 May and 7 June 1865, Valley of the Shadow website, <http://valley.vcdh.virginia.edu>.

5. Caroline R. Ravenel to D. E. Huger Smith, 26 July 1865, in Daniel E. Huger Smith, Alice R. Huger Smith, and Arney R. Childs, eds., *Mason-Smith Family Letters: 1860–1868* (Columbia: University of South Carolina Press, 1950), 225; Dr. Benjamin Huger to Thomas L. Wells, 17 June 1865, ibid., 232.

6. "To Be Amended," *Hinds County Gazette*, 17 August 1866.

7. Whitelaw Reid, *After the War: A Southern Tour*, 1 May 1865–1 May 1866 (New York: Moore, Wilstach & Baldwin, 1866), 295. Reid was a war correspondent for the *Cincinnati Gazette* and became well known for his reports from both Washington and the field. Immediately after the war ended, he made two extended tours of the South, the first with Chief Justice Chase. His book is one of several accounts of travels through the defeated South penned by Northern or foreign reporters. Others include Sidney Andrews, *The South Since the War* (1866; reprint, with an introduction by David Donald, Boston: Houghton Mifflin Company, 1971); John Richard Dennett, *The South As It Is: 1865–1866* (New York: Viking Press, 1965); and John T. Trowbridge, *The Desolate South, 1865–1866: A Picture of the Battlefields and of the Devastated Confederacy* (1866; reprint, edited with an introduction by Gordon Carroll, New York: Duell, Sloan and Pearce, 1956). A comprehensive bibliography of postwar travel accounts with an informative introduction can be found in Thomas D. Clark, *The Postwar South, 1865–1900: An Era of Reconstruction and Readjustment*, vol. 1 of *Travels in the New South: A Bibliography* (Norman: University of Oklahoma Press, 1962).

8. IWF to Col. J. W. Hinsdale, 30 June 165, Hinsdale Family Papers, Duke.

9. Mrs. J. J. Pringle Smith to Eliza Middleton Huger Smith, 5 June 1865, in Smith et al., eds., *Mason-Smith Family Letters*, 218; Emma LeConte, *When the World Ended: The Diary of Emma LeConte*, ed. Earl Schenck Miers (New York: Oxford University Press, 1957), 17 May 1865, 98; Mary Chesnut, *Mary Chesnut's Civil War*, ed. C. Vann Woodward (New Haven: Yale University Press, 1981), 26 July 1865, 834; William Lee Alexander to Mother, 9 July 1865, William Alexander Hoke Papers, SHC; Stone, *Brokenburn*, 20 July 1865, 355.

10. Robert Ferguson, *America during and after the War* (London: Longmans,

Green, Reader and Dyer, 1866), 213–15; Lewis D. Crenshaw to Samuel Barron, 8 August 1865, Barron, Waring, and Baylor Family Papers, Accession #10134-c, UVA; M. R. Shockley to Mrs. M. K. Texada, 30 June 1865, Ker-Texada Family Papers, Tulane.

11. J. J. Pringle Smith to Eliza Middleton Huger Smith, 4 May and 19 June 1865, Smith et al., eds., *Mason-Smith Family Letters*, 205, 219.

12. Thomas, *Secret Eye*, 8 May 1865, 266; Cumming, *Kate*, 29 May 1865, 295.

13. Reid, *After the War*, 79, 155, 220, 237, 263.

14. LeConte, *When the World Ended*, 5 July 1865, 113–14; Eveline Harden Jackson Diary, 4 July 1865, *American Women's Diaries Microfilm*, reel 22. On emancipation day celebrations by African Americans in the postwar South, see Kathleen Clark, "Celebrating Freedom: Emancipation Day Celebrations and African American Memory in the Early Reconstruction South," in *Where These Memories Grow: History, Memory, and Southern Identity*, ed. W. Fitzhugh Brundage (Chapel Hill: University of North Carolina Press, 2000), 107–32.

15. Cumming, *Kate*, 5 and 29 May 1865, 281–82, 302, 306–7.

16. LeConte, *When the World Ended*, 18, 28, and 29 May 1865, 102–3, 106, 108–9.

17. Margaret Brown Wight Diary, 29 April 1865, Wight Family Papers, VHS; Charles East, ed., *Sarah Morgan: The Civil War Diary of a Southern Woman* (New York: Simon & Schuster, 1991), 22 April 1865, 609–10.

18. Pauline DeCaradeuc Heyward, *A Confederate Lady Comes of Age: The Journals of Pauline DeCaradeuc Heyward, 1863–1888*, ed. Mary D. Robertson, Women's Diaries and Letters of the Nineteenth-Century South (Columbia: University of South Carolina Press, 1992), 18 June 1865, 79; Emma Mordecai to Edward Cohen, 5 April 1865, Emma Mordecai Diary, *American Women's Diaries Microfilm*, reel 3. White resentment toward black soldiers erupted into a race riot in Memphis in 1866; see George C. Rable, *But There Was No Peace: The Role of Violence in the Politics of Reconstruction* (Athens: University of Georgia Press, 1984), 24–25, 36–42. On attitudes toward black soldiers generally in the postwar period, see Litwack, *Been in the Storm So Long*, 267–74.

19. David Schenck Diary, 14 June 1865, David Schenck Papers, SHC; unsigned letter to George Scarborough Barnsley, 31 July 1865, George Scarborough Barnsley Papers, SHC.

20. Reid, *After the War*, 221, 73.

21. F. Turget to Dr. Stephen Duncan, 31 July 1865, Stephen Duncan Papers, LSU; LeConte, *When the World Ended*, 27 June 1865, 112.

22. Josiah Gorgas, *The Journals of Josiah Gorgas*, ed. Sarah Woolfolk Wiggins, with a foreword by Frank E. Vandiver (Tuscaloosa: University of Alabama Press, 1995), 26 May 1865, 172–74.

23. Chesnut, *Mary Chesnut's Civil War*, 7 and 15 May 1865, 801, 814; Margaret Brown Wight Diary, 13 April 1865, Wight Family Papers, VHS; James B. Walton to Mrs. M. A. Walton, 6 May 1865, Walton-Glenny Family Papers, HNOC.

24. Thomas, *Secret Eye*, 1 May 1865, 260.

25. J. T. McMurray to Dr. Stephen Duncan, 22 July 1865, Stephen Duncan Papers, LSU; "Editorial Brevities: Andrew Johnson and His Policy," *Scott's Monthly Magazine* 1 (January 1866): 133–34.

26. Reid, *After the War*, 321, 398; Dennett, *South As It Is*, 31, 359.

27. Dennett, *South As It Is*, 168; Andrews, *South Since the War*, 9, 37; Reid, *After the War*, 394.

28. "Put Them Away," *Southern Opinion*, 15 June 1867; "Editorial," *De Bow's Review*, After the War Series, 1 (May 1866): 555.

29. Reid, *After the War*, 379, 399; Dennett, *South As It Is*, 63.

30. Reid, *After the War*, 366–67.

31. For examples of this sort of language, see Andrews, *South Since the War*, 92, 283; and Trowbridge, *Desolate South*, 152.

32. "Is There Any Peace in the Land?" *Montgomery Advertiser*, 13 December 1865.

33. "Editorial," *The Land We Love* 2 (December 1866): 153.

34. "Civil Policy of America," *De Bow's Review*, After the War Series, 3 (January 1867): 33; "Editorial Notes," *Crescent Monthly* 1 (May 1866): 161.

35. David Schenck Diary, 1 September 1866 and 5 June 1867, David Schenck Papers, SHC; Harriet McLellan Diary, 28 October 1867, *American Women's Diaries Microfilm*, reel 6.

36. Col. Richard Jones to Thomas A. Watkins, in Dimond and Hattaway, eds., *Letters from Forest Place*, 22 April 1866, 344; R. H. Maury to Jeremiah Morton, 7 March 1866, Morton-Halsey Papers, UVA.

37. J. C. Delavigne, "The Future of the South," *De Bow's Review*, After the War Series, 5 (April 1868): 393; "Terribly in Earnest," ibid., 2 (August 1866): 173–74, 177.

38. "Editorial," ibid., 1 (March 1866): 331.

39. Hon. Charles Gayarré, "Oaths, Amnesties, and Rebellion," ibid., 1 (March 1866): 295.

40. For a discussion of Bledsoe's politics and their impact on his magazine, see Thomas O'Connor High, "Bledsoe's *Review*: A Southern Apologia" (MA thesis, Vanderbilt University, 1942).

41. "The Origin of the Late War," *Southern Review* 1 (April 1867): 257-72. The *Southern Review* contained several articles dealing with the legitimacy of secession. See "The Legal Status of Southern States," 1 (January 1867): 70–95; "North and the South," 2 (July 1867): 122–45; "Causes of Sectional Discontent," 2 (July 1867), 200–230; and "North and the South in 1787," 2 (October 1867), 358–70. For other invocations of Northern rebellions, see "Editorial," *The Land We Love* 2 (December 1866): 152–53.

42. Andrews, *South Since the War*, 333, 362–63, 378, 391, 392.

43. Eric Foner, *Reconstruction: America's Unfinished Revolution, 1863-1877* (New York: Harper & Row, 1988), 291–94; Litwack, *Been in the Storm So Long*, 545–46, 551–55.

44. Francis W. Dawson to Mother, 2 September 1867, Francis Warrington Dawson I and II Papers, Duke; David Schenck Diary, 1 September 1866, David Schenck Papers, SHC; Gorgas, *Journals*, 14 July 1867, 213; Charles Morris to William Cabell Rives Jr., 5 April 1868, Papers of the Rives, Sears, and Rhinelander Families, UVA.

45. Charles Morris to William Cabell Rives Jr., 4 May 1867, Papers of the Rives, Sears, and Rhinelander Families, UVA; "The South," *De Bow's Review*, After the War Series, 4 (July and August 1867): 13–15.

46. Rosalie Miller Murphy, "The Broken Idol," *Southern Opinion*, 13 July 1867; "The Unconstitutionality of Congress—The Paramount Unwritten Law," *De Bow's Review*, After the War Series, 4 (September 1867): 296–97.

47. "Political Carrion-Crows," *Southern Home Journal*, 21 March 1868; "Opinions of the Southern Press," *Southern Opinion*, 21 September 1867; "Editorial," *The Land We Love* 5 (June 1868): 188.

48. "Editorial," *The Land We Love* 5 (June 1868): 188; Jubal A. Early, *A Memoir of the Last Year of the War for Independence, in the Confederate States of America, Containing an Account of the Operations of His Commands in the Years 1864 and 1865* (Toronto: Lovell & Gibson, 1866), x; Frances Butler Leigh, *Ten Years on a Georgia Plantation Since the War* (London: R. Bentley & Son, 1883), 67.

Interlude: To Receive the Oath and Brand of Slave

1. A loyalty oath had been part of Reconstruction plans going back to the 1864 Wade-Davis bill, which called upon Confederates to swear that they had never voluntarily aided the Confederacy and to pledge to uphold the U.S. Constitution. On 29 May 1865, Johnson issued a proclamation offering amnesty and restitution of property (excluding slaves, of course) to anyone who took the oath of allegiance. There were, however, several categories of exemptions, including officials in the Confederate government; wartime governors; army officers above the rank of colonel and navy officers above the rank of lieutenant; people who had resigned their positions in the U.S. courts, military, or Congress to join the Confederacy; people who had committed military crimes or mistreated prisoners of war; and individuals with over $20,000 of taxable property. The last provision was Johnson's way of hurting the Southern aristocracy that he had long detested. Anyone in those exempted categories was required to get a presidential pardon. Such a provision, which demanded that they humble themselves before Johnson, upset and frustrated Southerners. However, Johnson's liberal granting of pardons quickly allayed their fears. The oath question, resolved initially in 1865, reared up again under Radical Reconstruction. The Reconstruction Acts of 1867 required Southerners who wished to vote to take another oath, the much more stringent "ironclad oath," which required that a person swear that he or she had never willingly aided the Confederacy (as opposed to merely swearing current loyalty to the Union). This repudiation of their first oaths, of Southerners words of honor, was seen as an insult, and Southerners railed against it. See Harold Melvin Hyman, *The Era of the Oath: Northern Loyalty Tests during the Civil War and Reconstruction* (Philadelphia: University of Pennsylvania Press, 1954), and Eric Foner, *Reconstruction: American's Unfinished Revolution, 1863–1877* (New York: Harper & Row, 1988), 185.

2. Henry Brown Richardson to his parents, 21 June 1865, Henry Brown Richardson and Family Papers, LSU.

3. Ibid.

4. On the relationship between oath-taking and honor, see Bertram Wyatt-Brown, *Southern Honor: Ethics and Behavior in the Old South* (New York: Oxford University Press, 1982), 55–59.

5. Emma LeConte, *When the World Ended: The Diary of Emma LeConte*, ed. Earl Schenck Miers (New York: Oxford University Press, 1957), 29 May 1865, 107–8.

6. Sidney Andrews, *The South Since the War* (1866; reprint, with an introduction by David Donald, Boston: Houghton Mifflin Company, 1971), 289. For a similar exchange, see Whitelaw W. Reid, *After the War: A Southern Tour* (New York: Moore, Wilstach & Baldwin, 1866), 360.

7. "The Oath of Office—Who Can Take It?" *Montgomery Advertiser*, 17 September 1865; David Comfort to James Comfort, 10 July 1865, Comfort Family Papers, VHS; Bradley T. Johnson to his wife, Accession #2239, GLC.

8. "Good Citizenship—The Oath of Amnesty," 27 July 1865, and "Qualifications for Voting," 19 October 1865, *Montgomery Advertiser*; "Let Every Man Register," 10 August 1867, *Southern Opinion*.

9. Reuban E. Wilson to Julia A. Jones, 13 May 1865, and W. A. Howser to Julia A. Jones, 22 July 1865, Jones Family Papers, SHC.

10. Foner, *Reconstruction*, 190–91; see also Michael Perman, *Reunion without Compromise: The South and Reconstruction, 1865-1868* (Cambridge: Cambridge University Press, 1973), 121–31; and Jonathan T. Dorris, *Pardon and Amnesty under Lincoln and Johnson* (Chapel Hill: University of North Carolina Press, 1953).

11. Andrews, *South Since the War*, 344; John T. Trowbridge, *The Desolate South, 1865-1866: A Picture of the Battlefields and of the Devastated Confederacy* (1866; reprint, edited with an introduction by Gordon Carroll, New York: Duell, Sloan and Pearce, 1956), 211.

12. Josiah Gorgas, *The Journals of Josiah Gorgas*, ed. Sarah Woolfolk Wiggins, with a foreword by Frank E. Vandiver (Tuscaloosa: University of Alabama Press, 1995), 22 August 1865, 186; 15 September 1867, 218; Stephen R. Mallory to Angela S. Mallory, 17 June 1865, Stephen R. Mallory Papers, SHC.

13. Hon. C. Gayarré, "Oaths, Amnesties, and Rebellion," *De Bow's Review*, After the War Series, 1 (January 1866): 302; John Richard Dennett, *The South As It Is: 1865-1866* (New York: Viking Press, 1965), 312–13; Andrews, *South Since the War*, 318–19. Earlier in his travels, Andrews came to a similar conclusion, opining that the former soldiers in South Carolina were "of a better disposition toward the government, toward Northerners, toward progression, than any other class of citizens" (94–95).

14. "Editorial," *The Land We Love* 5 (September 1868): 444.

15. "Noble Sentiments of a Virginia Lady," *Southern Opinion*, 19 October 1867; "A Lady's Letter of Approval" and "Wade Hampton's Manly Speech," *Southern Opinion*, 16 November 1867; Gorgas, *Journals*, 11 August 1867, 215.

Chapter Six

1. "'Young America' and 'Young South,'" *Montgomery Advertiser*, 16 August 1865.

2. The three main foreign destinations were Mexico, Brazil, and Venezuela. For a general discussion of Southern emigration, see James L. Roark, *Masters without Slaves: Southern Planters in the Civil War and Reconstruction* (New York: W. W. Norton & Co., 1977), 121–31. On Mexico, see Andrew F. Rolle, *The Lost Cause: The Confederate Exodus to Mexico*, with a foreword by A. L. Rowse (Norman: University of

Oklahoma Press, 1965); W. C. Nunn, *Escape from Reconstruction*, with a foreword by Austin L. Porterfield (Fort Worth: Leo Portishman Foundation, Texas Christian University, 1956); and Robert E. Shalhope, "Race, Class, Slavery, and the Antebellum Southern Mind," *Journal of Southern History* 37 (November 1971): 557–74. On Brazil, see Blanche Henry Clark Weaver, "Confederate Emigration to Brazil," *Journal of Southern History* 27 (February 1961): 33–53. On Venezuela, see Alfred Jackson Hanna, *Confederate Exiles in Venezuela* (Tuscaloosa: Confederate Publishing Co., 1960).

3. For an expanded analysis of this topic, see Bertram Wyatt-Brown, "Honor Chastened," in *The Shaping of Southern Culture: Honor, Grace, and War, 1760s–1880s* (Chapel Hill: University of North Carolina Press, 2001), 255–69.

4. "Editorial," *De Bow's Review*, After the War Series, 1 (January 1866): 217.

5. George Terrill to Jeremiah Morton, 5 January 1866, Morton-Halsey Papers, UVA; W. W. Corcoran to Samuel Barron, 7 June 1866, Barron, Waring, and Baylor Family Papers, Accession #10134-c, UVA; Laura [Alexander] to Martha, 3 July 1865, William Alexander Hoke Papers, SHC.

6. "Let Us Press Forward," *Southern Cultivator* 26 (April 1868): 120; W. H. Chase to W. Chase Morton, 21 July 1866, Morton-Halsey Papers, UVA; "Editorial Department," *De Bow's Review*, After the War Series, 3 (January 1867): 111; "Editorial Notes and Clippings," *De Bow's Review*, After the War Series, 5 (March 1868): 332–33.

7. "Our Condition and Prospects," *Southern Field and Fireside*, 16 December 1865; "Suggestions," *Southern Cultivator* 25 (September 1867): 278.

8. D. H. Hill, "Education," *The Land We Love* 1 (May 1866): 2–5, 8, 10. On the New South creed in general, see Paul M. Gaston, *The New South Creed: A Study in Southern Mythmaking* (New York: Alfred A. Knopf, 1970). On the role of ex-Confederates in New South promotion, see Peter S. Carmichael, "New South Visionaries: Virginia's Last Generation of Slaveholders, the Gospel of Progress, and the Lost Cause," in *The Myth of the Lost Cause and Civil War History*, ed. Gary W. Gallagher and Alan T. Nolan (Bloomington: Indiana University Press, 2000), 111–26.

9. Alexander H. H. Stuart, *The Recent Revolution, Its Causes and Its Consequences and the Duties and Responsibilities Which It Has Imposed on the People, and Especially the Young Men, of the South. Address of Alexander H. H. Stuart. Delivered Before The Literary Societies of the University of Virginia, June 29, 1866* (Richmond: Examiner Job Office, 1866), 25; General John Tyler Morgan, *Address to the Graduating Class of the Virginia Military Institute, on the Third of July, 1868, by J. T. Morgan* (Richmond: W. A. R. Nye, Book and Job Printer, 1868), 5–6.

10. James D. B. De Bow died of peritonitis on 27 February 1867 in Elizabeth, New Jersey. One month later, his brother, Benjamin, the *Review*'s Business editor also died. During this transitional period, the *Review* was actually being published in New York, although it never abandoned its regional leanings.

11. "The New Era of Southern Manufactures," *De Bow's Review*, After the War Series, 3 (January 1867): 56–68 (quotation on 59); "Manufactures—The South's True Remedy," ibid., 3 (February 1867): 172–78 (quotation on 173); "Exodus," ibid., 5 (November 1868): 979.

12. "Seeking a Situation," *Southern Boys and Girls Monthly* 2 (March 1868): 116;

"Editorial Brevities: Time—Faith—Energy," *Scott's Monthly Magazine* 1 (January 1866): 135.

13. *De Bow's Review*, After the War Series, 2 (December 1866): 667; "Virginia," ibid., 2 (July 1866): 55; Charles Morris to William Cabell Rives Jr., 4 May 1867, Papers of the Rives, Sears, and Rhinelander Families, Accession #10596, UVA.

14. "The South: Its Duty and Destiny," *De Bow's Review*, After the War Series, 1 (January 1866): 75.

15. William Lee Alexander to M. J. Wilson, 8 January 1868, William Alexander Hoke Papers, SHC; "Sowing Sorrow," *Field and Fireside*, 6 January 1866.

16. Charles Minor Blackford to Mrs. William (Mary B.) Blackford, 31 May 1865; Charles Minor Blackford to B. Lewis Blackford, 11 June 1865; Mrs. William (Mary B.) Blackford to B. Lewis Blackford, 14 June 1865; B. Lewis Blackford to Mrs. William (Mary B.) Blackford, 30 May 1865; all in Blackford Family Letters, vol. 3, Accession #6403, UVA.

17. Charles F. Barnes to Rebecca A. Barnes, 9 June 1865, Barnes Family Papers, Accession #4444, UVA.

18. James Comfort to David Comfort, 16 March 1866, Comfort Family Papers, VHS.

19. Charles F. Barnes to Rebecca A. Barnes, 26 July 1865, Barnes Family Papers, Accession #4444, UVA; Francis Warrington Dawson to Mother, 12 September 1865, Francis Warrington Dawson I and II Papers, Duke.

20. *Southern Opinion*, 19 October 1867; "They Who Ran Away and Came Back," ibid., 15 June 1867.

21. "Why Home Enterprise Does Not Prosper," ibid., 13 July 1867; "Home Enterprise," *The Land We Love* 6 (February 1869): 350.

22. Laurence Shore, *Southern Capitalists: The Ideological Leadership of an Elite, 1832–1885* (Chapel Hill: University of North Carolina Press, 1986), see esp. 99–124. See also Lawrence N. Powell, *New Masters: Northern Planters during the Civil War and Reconstruction* (New Haven: Yale University Press, 1980), 35–54; and Roark, *Masters without Slaves*, 165–68.

23. "Our Condition and Prospects," *Field and Fireside*, 16 December 1865.

24. "The Future of South Carolina," *De Bow's Review*, After the War Series, 2 (July 1866); "The South," ibid., 4 (July–August 1867): 16; "Emigration to the South," *Montgomery Advertiser*, 12 October 1865.

25. Dennett, *The South As It Is*, 307, 311.

26. E. C. Cabell, "White Emigration to the South," *De Bow's Review*, After the War Series, 1 (January 1866): 91–92.

27. "Northern Immigration," *Southern Cultivator* 25 (January 1866): 18–19.

28. "Northern Immigration," *Southern Cultivator* 25 (March 1866): 72.

29. *De Bow's Review*, After the War Series, 2 (December 1866): 667; "The Inducements Offered by the South to the Labor and Capital of the World," *Montgomery Advertiser*, 29 July 1865; "Emigration South," *Southern Cultivator* 24 (May 1866): 119.

30. All from *De Bow's Review*, After the War Series: "Alabama and Her Resources," 2 (October 1866): 362–72; "Florida—Past, Present, and Future," 2 (October 1866): 382–92; "Arkansas—Its Advantages to Immigrants," 2 (January 1867): 68–73; "The Inviting Fields of Arkansas," 3 (April 1867): 402–8; "The Wealth and Future of North

Carolina," 3 (January 1867): 89–90; "The State of Missouri," 2 (November 1866): 481–89; "The Vast Resources of Louisiana," 2 (September 1866): 274–85.

31. "North Carolina Land Agency" broadside and "Southern Land Company" pamphlet in Benjamin Sherwood Hedrick Papers, box 20, Duke; "The Florida Improvement Company" pamphlet in Edward M. L'Engle Papers, folder 112, SHC.

32. *Virginia: A Brief Memoir for the Information of Europeans Desirous of Emigrating to the New World* (Richmond: Wm. A. R. Nye, 1868), quotation on 13.

33. Jno. A. Wagener, "European Emigration," *De Bow's Review*, After the War Series, 3 (June 1867): 525–35. In a similar vein, see also "The Future of South Carolina—Her Inviting Resources," ibid., 2 (June 1866): 38–49, a report prepared by a committee of South Carolina citizens designed to attract immigrants to South Carolina.

34. John A. Wagener, *South Carolina: A Home for the Industrious Immigrant* (Charleston: South Carolina Bureau of Immigration, 1867). Quotation is on p. 6.

35. John A. Wagener, *South Carolina: A Home for the Industrious Immigrant, Supplement 1* (Charleston: Joseph Walker's, 1867), 3–4, 6–7, 10.

36. On postwar literary and political magazines in general, see Ray Morris Atchison, "Southern Literary Magazines, 1865–1887" (Ph.D. dissertation, Duke University, 1956); Calvin Ellsworth Chunn, "History of News Magazines" (Ph.D. dissertation, University of Missouri, 1950); Aliene Johnson, "Southern Literary Magazines of the Reconstruction Period" (MA thesis, Duke University, 1935); and Francis Elliott Hall McLean, "Periodicals Published in the South Before 1880" (Ph.D. dissertation, University of Virginia, 1928). Sam G. Riley, *Magazines of the American South* (Westport, Conn.: Greenwood Press, 1986), and Frank Luther Mott, *A History of American Magazines* (Cambridge: Harvard University Press, 1938–68), both provide brief discussions of several Reconstruction-era publications.

37. *Richmond Eclectic* 1 (November 1866): 1, 96; "Prospectus of the Southern Home Journal," *Southern Home Journal* 1 (28 December 1867): 7.

38. *De Bow's Review*, After the War Series, 1 (January 1866); introduction is unpaged. For biographies of De Bow, see Ottis Clark Skipper, *J. D. B. De Bow, Magazinist of the Old South* (Athens: University of Georgia Press, 1958), and Wills D. Weatherford, *James Dunwoody Brownson De Bow* (Charlottesville: The Historical Publishing Co., Inc., 1935).

39. R. G. Barnwell and Edwin Q. Bell took over publication of the *Review*, ultimately shifting its place of publication to New Orleans during the spring of 1868.

40. "Our Book Table," *Field and Fireside*, 3 February 1866, 36.

41. "Editorial Notes and Clippings," *De Bow's Review*, After the War Series, 3 (June 1867): 595, and 4 (September 1867): 366.

42. "Education," *The Land We Love* 1 (May 1866): 2. For a general history of the magazine, see Ray M. Atchison, "*The Land We Love*: A Southern Post-Bellum Magazine of Agriculture, Literature, and Military History," *North Carolina Historical Review* 37 (October 1960): 506–15.

43. *Field and Fireside*, 4 August 1866, 244. Rumors that *The Land We Love* was printed in the North persisted long after publication was moved to Charlotte. See Hill's response in his editorial, *The Land We Love* 3 (August 1867): 268–69.

44. Editorials in *The Land We Love*, 2 (April 1867): 473–74; 3 (May 1867): 87; 3 (August 1867): 358.

45. For a brief biography of H. Rives Pollard and a description of an altercation with a rival, see Michael B. Chesson, "'Editors Engaging in Double-leaded Matter': The Shoot-out at the Capitol in 1866," *Virginia Cavalcade* 30, no. 3 (Winter 1981): 100–109.

46. "Editors Statement," *Southern Opinion*, 15 June 1867.

47. "The Heading of Our Paper," *Southern Opinion*, 15 June 1867.

48. "The Paper for the People," ibid., 8 August 1868.

49. "Introductory Note" (on the inside front cover) and "Editorial Notes," *Crescent Monthly* 1 (April 1866): 66–67.

50. "Editorial Notes," *Crescent Monthly* 1 (April 1866): 67.

51. Ibid., 1 (May 1866): 156–57.

52. "Resumed," *Field and Fireside*, 16 December 1865, 4; "Literary Notices, ed. by Paul Hayne of SC—A Glance at Magazinedom—Southern Literary Magazines and Weeklies," *Southern Opinion*, 28 September 1867.

53. "Our Tripod: Southern Literature," *Scott's Monthly Magazine* 1 (May 1866): 429.

54. "Southern Literature," reprinted in *Field and Fireside*, 21 April 1866, 126. The article opened with praise for the *Field and Fireside*'s efforts, which may explain the editors' eagerness to reprint it.

55. "The Press Dispatches," *Montgomery Advertiser*, 24 October 1865; "Editorial Notes," *Crescent Monthly* 1 (April 1866): 72.

56. "Yankee Papers in the South," *Southern Opinion*, 6 July 1867; "Editorial," *The Land We Love* 6 (November 1868): 88–89; description of *Harper's* in "Editorial," *The Land We Love* 2 (January 1867): 227.

57. *Field and Fireside*, 1 September 1866, 276.

58. Ibid., 3 November 1866, 343. This article foreshadowed controversies over textbooks during the height of the Lost Cause movement, spearheaded by the United Daughters of the Confederacy. See Gaines Foster, *Ghosts of the Confederacy: Defeat, the Lost Cause, and the Emergence of the New South, 1865–1913* (New York: Oxford University Press, 1987), 188–90.

59. "Educational Department," *De Bow's Review*, After the War Series, 3 (January 1867): 93–94; "Southern Text Books," *Southern Cultivator* 24 (October 1866): 241.

60. For an example of the argument that Southerners needed to improve their educational systems in order to improve the South's industrial economy, see "Educational Interests of the South," *The Land We Love* 3 (July 1867): 476–78.

61. "The Yankee Attempting the Intellectual Conquest of the South," *Southern Opinion*, 3 August 1867, 1.

Interlude: The Vicarious Sufferer

1. On wartime dislike of Davis, see Paul D. Escott, *After Secession: Jefferson Davis and the Failure of Confederate Nationalism* (Baton Rouge: Louisiana State University Press, 1978), and George C. Rable, *The Confederate Republic: A Revolution against Politics* (Chapel Hill: University of North Carolina Press, 1994). Recent biographies

of Davis include William C. Davis, *Jefferson Davis: The Man and His Hour* (New York: HarperCollins Publishers, 1991); William J. Cooper Jr., *Jefferson Davis, American* (New York: Alfred A. Knopf, 2000); Herman Hattaway and Richard E. Beringer, *Jefferson Davis, Confederate President* (Lawrence: University Press of Kansas, 2002); and Brian R. Dirck, *Lincoln and Davis: Imagining America, 1809–1865* (Lawrence: University Press of Kansas, 2001).

2. "Mr. Davis—His Trial, His Punishment, and the Duty the Southern People Owe Him," *Montgomery Advertiser*, 15 August 1865.

3. George Anderson Mercer Diary, 4 November 1865, SHC; "Memorial in Behalf of Jefferson Davis," *Montgomery Advertiser*, 3 October 1865.

4. Vindex, "Ex-President Davis, of the Southern Confederacy, in Chains," n.d. The opening passage is actually a passage from John J. Craven's *Prison Life of Jefferson Davis* (New York: Carleton, 1866).

5. Craven, *Prison Life of Jefferson Davis*. In 1987, an edition with annotations from Davis's own copy was published by Mercer University Press. It also contains a lengthy and useful introduction stressing the role of *Prison Life* in creating a new myth of Jefferson Davis, and provides a narrative of Davis's two years at Fortress Monroe culled from a variety of sources, and correcting many of Craven's misstatements. See Edward K. Eckert, ed., *Fiction Distorting Fact*, annotated edition of John J. Craven, *Prison Life of Jefferson Davis* (Macon, Ga.: Mercer University Press, 1987); and Cooper, *Jefferson Davis, American*, 554–56.

6. Quoted in Eckert, ed., *Fiction Distorting Fact*, xlii. For a discussion of the relationship between Halpine and Craven and the genesis of *Prison Life of Jefferson Davis*, see ibid., xlii–xlvii. See also William Hanchett, "Reconstruction and the Rehabilitation of Jefferson Davis: Charles G. Halpine's Prison Life," *Journal of American History* 56 (September 1969): 280–89.

7. D. H. Hill, "Prison Life of Jefferson Davis," *The Land We Love* 1 (August 1866); S. G. H. Jr., "Prison Life of Jefferson Davis," *Scott's Monthly Magazine* 2 (October 1866): 750.

8. *Field and Fireside*, 7 July 1866, 212.

9. Cooper, *Jefferson Davis, American*, 558–65.

10. David W. Blight, *Race and Reunion: The Civil War in American Memory* (Cambridge: Harvard University Press, 2001), 57–58; Eckert, ed., *Fiction Distorting Fact*, xvii, xl; Cooper, *Jefferson Davis, American*, 565–67.

11. Blight, *Race and Reunion*, 59–60.

12. George Rose [Arthur Sketchley], *The Great Country; or, Impressions of America* (London: Tinsley Brothers, 1868), 112.

13. "Ex-President Davis and His Persecutors," *Southern Opinion*, 10 August 1867.

14. "A Confederate Hero Lies Neglected in Jail," *Southern Opinion*, 14 September 1867. See also briefer mentions in the 9 November 1867 and 8 January 1868 issues.

Chapter Seven

1. For a provocative study of the intersection of race, class, gender, and Reconstruction in Granville County, North Carolina, see Laura F. Edwards, *Gendered Strife and Confusion: The Political Culture of Reconstruction* (Urbana: University of Illinois

Press, 1997). See also Drew Gilpin Faust, *Mothers of Invention: Women of the Slaveholding South in the American Civil War* (Chapel Hill: University of North Carolina Press, 1996), 248–54; LeeAnn Whites, *The Civil War as a Crisis in Gender: Augusta, Georgia, 1860–1890* (Athens: University of Georgia Press, 1995), 132–59; and Catherine Clinton, *Tara Revisited: Women, War, and the Southern Plantation Legend* (New York: Abbeville Press, 1995), 160–74.

2. Nina Silber, *The Romance of Reunion: Northerners and the South, 1865–1900* (Chapel Hill: University of North Carolina Press, 1993), 26–28. I am looking at these stories only as they appeared in Southern publications and through Southern eyes, since other historians, Nina Silber in particular, have examined the Northern writings. Silber argues that Northerners used these stories as further evidence of the degraded state of Southern gender roles and relations. Southern men, already emasculated by their losses on the battlefield, were seen as all the more weak because of their inability to control their womenfolk.

3. Gail Hamilton [Mary Abigail Dodge], *Wool-Gathering* (Boston: Tichnor & Fields, 1867), 301–2; Whitelaw Reid, *After the War: A Southern Tour* (New York: Moore, Wilstach & Baldwin, 1866), 46; Robert Ferguson, *America during and after the War* (London: Longmans, Green, Reader, and Dyer, 1866), 208; Silber, *Romance of Reunion*, 26–28; Gaines Foster, *Ghosts of the Confederacy: Defeat, the Lost Cause, and the Emergence of the New South, 1865–1913* (New York: Oxford University Press, 1987), 29–31.

4. John Richard Dennett, *The South As It Is: 1865–1866* (New York: Viking Press, 1965), 279; Reid, *After the War*, 380; Sidney Andrews, *The South Since the War* (1866; reprint, with an introduction by David Donald, Boston: Houghton Mifflin Company, 1971), 361; J. E. Hilary Skinner, *After the Storm; or, Jonathan and His Neighbors in 1865–6* (London: Richard Bentley, 1866), 38; John Henry Kennaway, *On Sherman's Track; or, The South After the War* (London: Seeley, Jackson, and Halliday, 1867), 207.

5. Dennett, *South As It Is*, 75–76, 49–50.

6. Andrews, *South Since the War*, 13–16; Dennett, *South As It Is*, 278–79.

7. Charles F. Barnes to Rebecca A. Barnes, 9 June 1865, Barnes Family Papers, Accession #4444, UVA; Ferguson, *America during and after the War*, 204.

8. Henry Deedes, *Sketches of the South and West; or, Ten Months Residence in the United States* (Edinburgh: William Blackwood & Sons, 1869), 88; Andrews, *South Since the War*, 10; Ferguson, *America during and after the War*, 193, 208; Dennett, *South As It Is*, 11, 305. See also *South Since the War*, 31, where Andrews writes, "Whatever else the South Carolina mothers forget, they do not seem likely in this generation to forget to teach their children to hate Sherman."

9. "Memories of the War," *De Bow's Review*, After the War Series, 3 (February 1867): 145; Andrews, *South Since the War*, 234.

10. Reid, *After the War*, 416; Dennett, *South As It Is*, 347.

11. Jeremiah Morton to C. Walker, 23 July 1866, Morton-Halsey Papers, UVA.

12. William Wallace McMillan to Mary Cave, 29 November 1865, Comfort Family Papers, VHS; Henry F. Haywood to Col. J. W. Hinsdale, 15 November 1865, Hinsdale Family Papers, Duke.

13. C. N. Bennet Letter, 2 February 1866, Tulane; "'Your Fondly Attached' &c.,"

Southern Opinion, 6 July 1867; John T. Trowbridge, *The Desolate South, 1865–1866: A Picture of the Battlefields and of the Devastated Confederacy* (1866; reprint, edited with an introduction by Gordon Carroll, New York: Duell, Sloan and Pearce, 1956), 231.

14. John W. De Forest, *A Union Officer in the Reconstruction*, edited with an introduction and notes by James H. Croushore and David Morris Potter (New Haven: Yale University Press, 1948), 46. De Forest is much better known for his fiction, especially the 1867 novel, *Miss Ravenel's Conversion from Secession to Loyalty*.

15. Dennett, *South As It Is*, 234, 242; William E. Huger to Isabella Middleton Smith, 29 October 1865, in Daniel E. Huger Smith, Alice R. Huger Smith, and Arney R. Childs, eds., *Mason-Smith Family Letters: 1860–1868* (Columbia: University of South Carolina Press, 1950), 242; reprinted in "Opinions of the Southern Press," *Southern Opinion*, 16 November 1867.

16. Ella Gertrude Clanton Thomas, *The Secret Eye: The Journal of Ella Gertrude Clanton Thomas, 1848–1889*, ed. Virginia Ingraham Burr (Chapel Hill: University of North Carolina Press, 1990), 20 September 1866, 286; Kennaway, *On Sherman's Track*, 88.

17. Fred Reanick to Sue Carter, 15 February 1866, Sue Carter Letters, GLC; "A Great Mistake," *Southern Opinion*, 15 June 1867; George Fitzhugh, "The Return of Good Feeling," *De Bow's Review*, After the War Series, 4 (December 1867): 558.

18. See Silber, *Romance of Reunion*, 39–65.

19. I. W. F. to Col. J. W. Hinsdale, 8 October 1865, 2 November 1865, and 15 November 1865, Hinsdale Family Papers, Duke.

20. "Sic Transit," *Crescent Monthly* 1 (October 1866): 323. The same poem also appeared in *The Land We Love* 2 (November 1866): 16.

21. Beck to Sue Carter, 27 March 1867, Sue Carter Letters, GLC; "An Opening for Destitute Young Men," *Southern Opinion*, 10 August 1867.

22. Madge Rutledge, "The Stamina of My Herbarium," *Field and Fireside*, 9 June 1866, 179.

23. The *Southern Home Journal* was published by John Y. Slater & Co. in Baltimore between November 1867 and mid-1869. Its masthead proclaimed it "Devoted to Choice Literature, Biography, History, Poetry and the News," and its eight pages were filled with a mixture of serialized fiction, poetry, humorous pieces, reminiscences of the war, and general essays. The paper gradually became more politicized, particularly in 1868 when it ran editorials expressing opposition to the impeachment of Andrew Johnson and opposing the presidential candidacy of Ulysses S. Grant. I have transcribed these letters as is, without using [*sic*]. Unless otherwise indicated, spellings and punctuation are original.

24. "Florence Fay Arrows: Small Fry," *Field and Fireside*, 23 December 1865; "Florence Fay Arrows: Mushroom Aristocracy," ibid., 30 December 1865. These columns appeared in late 1865 and early 1866, about two years before Betsey's letters in the *Southern Home Journal*. The *Field and Fireside* was a continuation of the wartime *Southern Field and Fireside*, a weekly paper published first in Augusta, Georgia, but then in Raleigh, North Carolina. It, too, consisted of a mixture of serial fiction, poetry, and political writings.

25. Interestingly, the first Arp letters written during the war by Charles Henry Smith were written in dialect, but his postwar humor columns were not. See David B. Parker, *Alias Bill Arp: Charles Henry Smith and the South's "Goodly Heritage"* (Athens: University of Georgia Press, 1991).

26. Betsey Bittersweet was actually written by Mary Bayard Clarke, a prolific author best known for her poetry and essays. The Bittersweet letters represent somewhat of a departure for her, in terms of both their angry tone and satirical style. Her criticisms of the Radicals are especially interesting in light of her husband's joining the Republican Party in late 1868. Florence Fay's author is unknown. See Terrell Armistead Crow and Mary Moulton Barden, *Live Your Own Life: The Family Papers of Mary Bayard Clarke, 1854–1886* (Columbia: University of South Carolina Press, 2003), xlv, 250–53. I want to thank Jane Turner Censer for alerting me to this reference.

27. "Letter from Betsey Bittersweet," *Southern Home Journal*, 23 November 1867, 7.

28. "Florence Fay Arrows: Patriotism," *Field and Fireside*, 1 January 1866.

29. Ibid.

30. "Florence Fay Arrows: Blue Devils," *Field and Fireside*, 24 March 1866.

31. "Letter from Betsey Bittersweet," *Southern Home Journal*, 21 December 1867, 8.

32. Ibid., 7 December 1867, 8.

33. Ibid., 21 December 1867, 8.

34. Ibid., 4 January 1868, 8.

35. Ibid., 21 March 1868, 5. Betsey's letter is dated 21 February.

36. See Whites, *Civil War as a Crisis in Gender*, 132–50; and Foster, *Ghosts of the Confederacy*, 26–29.

37. "Letter from Betsey Bittersweet," *Southern Home Journal*, 21 December 1867, 8; Suzanne D. Lebsock, "Radical Reconstruction and the Property Rights of Southern Women," in *Half Sisters of History: Southern Women and the American Past*, ed. Catherine Clinton (Durham: Duke University Press, 1994), 110–35.

38. "Letter from Betsey Bittersweet," *Southern Home Journal*, 4 January 1868, 8.

39. Ibid., 7 December 1867, 8; 2 February 1868, 8.

40. "Florence Fay Arrows: Wee Women," *Field and Fireside*, 20 January 1866. Florence Fay also sent arrows flying in the direction of grumblers and saloon-keepers. See "Florence Fay Arrows: Grumblers," ibid., 27 January 1866; and "Florence Fay Arrows: Stray Arrows," ibid., 3 February 1866.

41. "Florence Fay Arrows: 'Whom Shall We Marry?'" ibid., 3 March 1866.

42. "Memories of the War: The Women of the Confederacy," *De Bow's Review*, After the War Series, 3 (February 1867): 144.

43. The idea of republican motherhood comes from Linda Kerber, *Women of the Republic: Intellect and Ideology in Revolutionary America* (Chapel Hill: University of North Carolina Press, 1980). On idealized roles for women, see Edwards, *Gendered Strife and Confusion*, 129–44.

44. "Women of the Confederacy," 144–45.

45. A. J. Requier, "The Belle of the Blue Cockade," *Southern Home Journal*, 28 December 1867; William Gilmore Simms, ed., *War Poetry of the South* (New York: Richardson & Company, 1866); John Esten Cooke, "Heroic Women of the South," 1866, VHS.

46. "The Women of the South," *Southern Opinion*, 27 July 1867; *Field and Fireside*, 7 April 1866, 108.

47. "Spartan Virtues," *De Bow's Review*, After the War Series, 2 (July 1866): 150; Eliza Middleton Huger Smith to Mrs. Edward L. Cottenent, 12 July 1865, in Smith et al., eds., *Mason-Smith Family Letters*, 220.

48. Fanny Downing (Mary J. Upshur), "Too Proud to Work," *The Land We Love* 2 (April 1867): 444.

49. *The Land We Love* 3 (July 1867): 269; ibid., 1 (August 1866): 304.

50. *Field and Fireside*, 20 January 1866, 20.

51. "Women as Compositors," ibid., 19 May 1866, 158.

52. Foster, *Ghosts of the Confederacy*, 36–46; Whites, *Civil War as a Crisis in Gender*, 182–95; David W. Blight, *Race and Reunion: The Civil War in American Memory* (Cambridge: Harvard University Press, 2001), 77–86.

53. Reid, *After the War*, 319; Frank Alfriend, "Recollections of O. Jennings Wise," *Field and Fireside*, 3 February 1866, 37.

54. "The Duty of the Hour," *The Land We Love* 6 (December 1868): 118.

55. David Wills, "War—The Departed Heroes and Patriots of Macon," *Scott's Monthly Magazine* 5 (March and April 1868); quotation on page 126.

56. "An Eloquent Address," *Field and Fireside*, 14 April 1866, 117.

57. Typescript of letter to *Columbus (Georgia) Times*, 12 March 1866, Memorial Associations Collection, Louisiana Historical Association Collection, Tulane. On the history of Confederate Memorial Day, see Foster, *Ghosts of the Confederacy*, 42–45; and G. Kurt Piehler, *Remembering War the American Way* (Washington: Smithsonian Institution Press, 1995), 58–59, 61–62.

58. "Flowers for the Dead," *East Feliciana Patriot*, 21 and 28 April 1866, clippings found in Lee H. Farrar Family Papers, Tulane; Pherrie Muse to Ellie Knighton, 26 April 1867, Josiah Knighton and Family Papers, LSU.

59. "Editorial," *De Bow's Review*, After the War Series, 1 (June 1866): 663.

60. R. A. M. to George S. Barnsley, 11 June 1866, George Scarborough Barnsley Papers, SHC.

61. "Desecration of Confederate Graves," *Southern Opinion*, 23 November 1867; John Greville Chester, *Transatlantic Sketches in the West Indies, South America, Canada and the United States* (London: Smith, Elder & Co., 1869), 207. The incident had such an effect on Chester that he returns to it again, as an indication of the profound hatred Southerners still felt for Northerners (Chester, *Transatlantic Sketches*, 382).

62. Abram J. Ryan, "Lines Respectfully Inscribed to the Ladies Memorial Association of Fredericksburg, VA. By the Author of the Conquered Banner," 31 December 1866, VHS; Sallie Badger Hoke to Aunt Sallie, 2 August 1866, William Alexander Hoke Papers, SHC.

63. Regarding the Manassas Memorial Association, see "Our Dead," *Southern Opinion*, 3 August 1867; regarding cemeteries in Marietta and Resaca, see "Cemeteries for our Dead," ibid., 10 August 1867; "Confederates at Sharpsburg," ibid., 6 July 1867; and "The Antietam Dedication," ibid., 21 September 1867.

64. Josiah Gorgas, *The Journals of Josiah Gorgas*, ed. Sarah Woolfolk Wiggins,

with a foreword by Frank E. Vandiver (Tuscaloosa: University of Alabama Press, 1995), 3 February 1867, 206.

65. "Confederate Memorial Monument," *Southern Opinion*, 9 November 1867.

Conclusion

1. David Schenck Diary, March 1867, David Schenck Papers, SHC.

2. The editors of the *Harvard Encyclopedia of American Ethnic Groups* (Cambridge: Belknap Press, 1980) included Southerners in their project (along with Appalachians and Yankees) because "they are not the same in character as immigrant or racial groups, but possess a historical identity of their own." For discussions of Southerners as an ethnic group, see John Shelton Reed's entry for "Southerners" in the *Harvard Encyclopedia*, 944–48. See also George B. Tindall, *The Ethnic Southerners* (Baton Rouge: Louisiana State University Press, 1977) and *Natives and Newcomers: Ethnic Southerners and Southern Ethnics* (Athens: University of Georgia Press, 1995).

3. David Schenck Diary, 26 March 1867, David Schenck Papers, SHC.

4. William Alexander to William A. Hoke, 10 August 1867, William Alexander Hoke Papers, SHC; Thomas Read Rootes to Sarah A. Rootes, 18 May 1867, Sarah A. Rootes Papers, Duke; George Anderson Mercer Diary, 3 November 1867, SHC.

5. Josiah Gorgas, *The Journals of Josiah Gorgas*, ed. Sarah Woolfolk Wiggins, with a foreword by Frank E. Vandiver (Tuscaloosa: University of Alabama Press, 1995), 30 June 1867, 210; "The Elective Franchise in the South," *Southern Opinion*, 3 August 1867; "Marching On," *Southern Opinion*, 27 June 1868.

6. "Registration and Reconstruction," *Hinds County Gazette*, 28 June 1867.

7. "The Return of Good Feeling," *De Bow's Review*, After the War Series, 4 (December 1867): 557. For another example of pleasure at the results of Northern elections, see "Light is Breaking," *Southern Opinion*, 14 September 1867, and "Opinions of the Southern Press," *Southern Opinion*, 16 November 1867.

8. "The South," *De Bow's Review*, After the War Series, 4 (July–August 1867): 15; "Publick Apathy in the South," *Southern Opinion*, 13 July 1867.

9. "The Right Spirit in Alabama," *Hinds County Gazette*, 17 January 1868.

10. "Editorial Notes," *De Bow's Review*, After the War Series, 5 (March 1868): 332–33 and (July 1868): 667.

11. David Schenck Diary, 24 March and 12 April 1868, David Schenck Papers, SHC.

12. On violence and Reconstruction politics, see George C. Rable, *But There Was No Peace: The Role of Violence in the Politics of Reconstruction* (Athens: University of Georgia Press, 1984), and Allen W. Trelease, *White Terror: The Ku Klux Conspiracy and Southern Reconstruction* (New York: Harper Torchbooks, 1971).

13. David Schenck Diary, October 1868, David Schenck Papers, SHC. In Camilla on 19 September 1868, Democrats determined to crush their opposition ambushed and opened fire on blacks on their way to a Republican meeting (Rable, *But There Was No Peace*, 73–74). In Opelousas, whites attacked a Republican schoolteacher, precipitating a conflict that left over 200 African Americans dead and Democrats securely in political control (Trelease, *White Terror*, 128–29).

14. David Schenck Diary, October 1868, David Schenck Papers, SHC.

BIBLIOGRAPHY

Primary Sources

MANUSCRIPTS
Historic New Orleans Collection, New Orleans, La.
    Walton-Glenny Family Papers
    Wilkinson-Stark Family Papers
Gilder Lehrman Collection, Pierpont Morgan Library, New York, N.Y.
    Sue Carter Letters
    Gustave Cook Papers
    Bradley T. Johnson Letter
    J. Johnston Pettigrew Letter
    James A. Seddon Letter
    William Lyne Wilson Diary
Library of Congress, Washington, D.C.
    George Stanton Denison Papers
    Fannie Page Hume Diary
    Diary of M. Shuler, 1862
    Ward Family Papers
Louisiana and Lower Mississippi Valley Collections, Louisiana State University
    Libraries, Baton Rouge, La.
    Benson Family Papers
    John H. Bills and Family Papers
    Priscilla "Mittie" Munnikhuysen Bond Diary and Papers
    Samuel C. Bonner and Family Papers
    Louis A. Bringier and Family Papers
    John C. Burruss Papers
    Eli J. Capell Papers
    Stephen Duncan Papers
    Eggleston-Roach Papers
    Josiah Knighton and Family Papers
    Christian D. Koch Papers
    Layssard Family Papers
    Edwin Leet Letters
    Robert A. Newell Papers
    Henry Brown Richardson and Family Papers
    Mary Elizabeth Carter Rives Diary
    Jared Y. Sanders and Family Papers
    M. J. Scott Letter
    James Calvert Wise Papers

Manuscript Department, Alderman Library, University of Virginia,
    Charlottesville, Va.
        Anthony Family Letters
        Baker Family Papers
        Barnes Family Papers
        Samuel Barron Papers
        Barron, Waring, and Baylor Family Papers
        Baylor Family Papers
        William M. Blackford Diaries
        Blackford Family Letters
        Mollie C. Buckalew, Letters Received from Confederate Soldiers
        Henry Chapin Letter
        Nancy Emerson Diary
        Basil Gildersleeve Letter
        Josiah Hodges Letter
        Erastus Hoskins Letters
        Bradley T. Johnson Papers
        William Preston Johnston Letter
        Jean Reynaud Jacques Prosper Landry Letter
        John Singleton Millson Letter
        Morton-Halsey Papers
        Papers pertaining to Virginia
        Letter to Gov. Thomas C. Reynolds
        Papers of the Rives, Sears, and Rhinelander Families
        Letter to Rev. Philip Slaughter
        Louis A. Wise Letters
Manuscript Department, Howard-Tilton Memorial Library, Tulane University,
    New Orleans, La.
        Dr. Noah Bennet Benedict Papers
        C. N. Bennet Letter
        Gustave Arvilien Breaux Diary
        Civil War Manuscripts Series
            Alfred Huger Letter
            Smith Family Letters
        Confederate wine recipe
        Dunlap Correspondence
        Lee H. Farrar Family Papers
        John M. Galbraith Papers
        Herron Family Correspondence
        Hutson Family Papers
        Joseph Jones Collection
        Ker-Texada Family Papers
        Lise Mitchell Papers
        Louisiana Historical Association Collection
            J. A. Chalaron Papers

Civil War Papers
Confederate Personnel Files
Memorial Associations Papers
Watson Family Papers
Manuscript Department, William R. Perkins Library, Duke University,
Durham, N.C.
George M. Brown Papers
Patrick H. Cain Papers
Thomas Carroll Papers
Francis Warrington Dawson I and II Papers
Anne Henshaw Gardiner Papers
Benjamin Sherwood Hedrick
Hinsdale Family Papers
Munford-Ellis Family Papers
Lizzie Nelms (Smith) Parker Papers
Sarah A. Rootes Papers
Southern Historical Collection, University of North Carolina Library,
Chapel Hill, N.C.
David Alexander Barnes Papers
George Scarborough Barnsley Papers
John W. Brown Diary
Kena King Chapman Diary
Edward Conigland Papers
Creagh Family Papers
Mary E. Grattan Papers
William Alexander Hoke Papers
Jones Family Papers
James Thomas Leach Papers
Edward M. L'Engle Papers
Stephen R. Mallory Papers
George Anderson Mercer Diary
North and South Carolina Oaths of Allegiance
J. D. Porter Letters
David Schenck Papers
Annie Blackwell Thorne, Collector
J. E. Whitehorne Diary
Virginia Historical Society, Richmond, Va.
Sally Armstrong Diary
Bailey Family Papers
Caperton Family Papers
Comfort Family Papers
Cooke, John Esten, "Heroic Women of the South," 1866
Sarah Scarborough Butler Henry French Papers
Lucas Family Papers
William Nalle Diary

Mahala Perkins Harding Eggleston Roach Diary
Ryan, Abram J., "Lines Respectfully Inscribed to the Ladies Memorial
    Association of Fredericksburg, VA. By the Author of the Conquered
    Banner," 31 December 1866
Smith Family Papers
Thomas Family Papers
Wight Family Papers
Fanny Churchill Braxton Young Papers

PERIODICALS

The Age

Burke's Weekly for Boys & Girls

The Charleston Mercury

The Cosmopolite

The Crescent Monthly

De Bow's Review

The Hinds County (Miss.) Gazette

The Land We Love

The Magnolia Weekly

The Memphis Daily Appeal

The Montgomery Advertiser

The Raleigh Register

The Richmond Eclectic

The Richmond Enquirer

The Richmond Examiner

Scott's Monthly Magazine

The Southern Boys and Girls Monthly

The Southern Confederacy

The Southern Cultivator

The Southern Field and Fireside
    and The Field and Fireside

The Southern Home Journal

The Southern Illustrated News

The Southern Literary Messenger

The Southern Magazine (New Eclectic)

The Southern Monthly

The Southern Opinion

Southern Punch

The Southern Recorder

The Southern Review

The Staunton Spectator

The Staunton Vindicator

PUBLISHED PRIMARY SOURCES

Allen, Henry W. "To the Citizens of New Orleans: I Greet You as the Governor of
    Louisiana. . . ." Shreveport: n.p., 1864.

American Women's Diaries Microfilm, Segment II: Southern Women: Zillah Haynie
    Brandon Diary, Emma Mordecai Diary, Cloe Tyler Whittle Greene Diary, Eveline
    Harden Jackson Diary, Harriet McLellan Diary.

Atkinson, Rev. Joseph M. God the Giver of Victory and Peace. A Thanksgiving
    Sermon, Delivered in the Presbyterian Church, September 18, 1862. Raleigh: n.p.,
    1862.

Beneath, William W. A Narrative of the Great Revival in the Southern Armies.
    Philadelphia: Claxton, Remsen and Haffelfinger, 1877.

Brown, Albert Gallatin. "The State of the Country. Speech of Hon. A. G. Brown in
    the Confederate Senate, December 24, 1863." Richmond, 1863[?].

Buck, Lucy Rebecca. Sad Earth, Sweet Heaven: The Diary of Lucy Rebecca Buck
    during the War between the States, Front Royal, Virginia, December 25, 1861–
    April 15, 1865. Edited by William P. Buck. Birmingham: Cornerstone Press,
    1973.

Burrows, John Lansing, D.D. Palliative and Prejudiced Judgments Condemned:

A Discourse Delivered in the First Baptist Church, Richmond VA, June 1, 1865, the
Day Appointed by the President of the United States for Humiliation and Mourning
on Account of the Assassination of President Lincoln, Together with an Extract
from a Sermon, Preached on Sunday, April 23rd, 1865 upon the Assassination of
President Lincoln. Richmond: Office of the Commercial Bulletin, 1865.

Campbell, William A. The Child's First Book. Richmond: Ayres & Wade, 1864.

The Cavalier Songster. Staunton: n.p., 1865.

Caylat, Charles E. "Southern Victories Chickahominy, Fredericksburg,
Chancellorsville, Chickamauga, etc.: A Warning to All Such Fanatics as Lincoln,
Greely & Co." N.p., 1863.

Chesnut, Mary. Mary Chesnut's Civil War. Edited by C. Vann Woodward. New
Haven: Yale University Press, 1981.

The Confederate Receipt Book: A Compilation of Over One Hundred Receipts Adapted
to the Times. Edited with an introduction by E. Merton Coulter. Athens:
University of Georgia Press, 1960.

The Confederate States Almanac and Repository of Useful Knowledge for the Year
1864. Vol. 3. Augusta, Ga.: H. C. Clarke, 1863.

Confederate States Almanac for the Year of Our Lord 1864. Macon, Ga.: Burke,
Boykin & Co., S. H. Goetzel, 1863.

The Confederate States Almanac and Repository of Useful Knowledge for the Year
1865. Vol. 4. Mobile: H. C. Clarke, 1864.

Crandall, Marjorie Lyle. Confederate Imprints: A Checklist Based Primarily on the
Collection of the Boston Athenaeum. Boston: Boston Athenaeum, 1955.

Craven, John J. Prison Life of Jefferson Davis. New York: Carleton, 1866.

Crow, Terrell Armistead, and Mary Moulton Barden. Live Your Own Life: The
Family Papers of Mary Bayard Clarke, 1854–1886. Columbia: University of South
Carolina Press, 2003.

Cumming, Kate. Kate: The Journal of a Confederate Nurse. Edited by Richard
Barksdale Harwell. Baton Rouge: Louisiana State University Press, 1959.

Dabney, Robert Lewis. A Defense of Virginia and Through It of the South. New York:
E. J. Hale & Son, 1867.

De Jarnette, D. C. The Monroe Doctrine. Richmond: n.p., 1865.

Dimond, E. Grey, and Herman Hattaway, eds. Letters from Forest Place:
A Plantation Family's Correspondence. Jackson: University Press of Mississippi,
1993.

Doggett, Rev. David Seth. A Nation's Ebenezer: A Discourse Delivered in the Broad
Street Methodist Church, Richmond, Virginia, Thursday, September 18, 1862: The
Day of Public Thanksgiving Appointed by the President of the Confederate States.
Richmond: Enquirer Book and Job Press, 1862.

Duncan, Rev. James A. "The Southern Soldier." No. 53. Richmond: Soldiers' Tract
Association, 1863.

Early, Jubal A. A Memoir of the Last Year of the War for Independence, in the
Confederate States of America, Containing an Account of the Operations of His
Commands in the Years 1864 and 1865. Toronto: Lovell & Gibson, 1866.

East, Charles, ed. *Sarah Morgan: The Civil War Diary of a Southern Woman*. New York: Simon and Schuster, 1991.

Eckert, Edward K., ed. *Fiction Distorting Fact*. Annotated edition of John J. Craven, *Prison Life of Jefferson Davis*. Macon, Ga.: Mercer University Press, 1987.

Elliott, Rt. Rev. Stephen, D.D. *A Sermon Preached in Christ Church Savannah, on Thursday, September 18th, 1862, Being the Day Set Forth by the President of the Confederate States as a Day of Prayer and Thanksgiving, for Our Manifold Victories and Especially for the Fields of Manassas and Richmond, KY*. Savannah: Power Press of John M. Cooper & Co., 1862.

Evans, Augusta Jane. *Macaria; or, Altars of Sacrifice*. Edited with an introduction by Drew Gilpin Faust. Baton Rouge: Louisiana State University Press, 1992.

Farrar, Ferdinando R. "Johnny Reb, The Confederate: A Lecture." Richmond: W. A. Nye, 1869.

The First Reader, for Southern Schools. Raleigh: N.C. Christian Advocate Publishing Company, 1864.

Flanders, Henry. *Observations on Reconstruction*. Philadelphia: n.p., 1866.

Fowler, Abidjah. *The Southern School Arithmetic or Youth's Assistant*. Richmond: West and Johnston, 1864.

Free Masonry and the War: Report of the Committee under the Resolutions of 1862, Grand Lodge of Virginia, in Reference to our Relations as Masonic Bodies and as Masons in the North and South, Growing out of the Manner in Which the Present War Has Been Prosecuted. Richmond: Chas. H. Wynne, 1865.

Gorgas, Josiah. *The Journals of Josiah Gorgas*. Edited by Sarah Woolfolk Wiggins. With a foreword by Frank E. Vandiver. Tuscaloosa: University of Alabama Press, 1995.

Hall, Rev. William A. *The Historic Significance of the Southern Revolution*. Petersburg: A. F. Crutchfield & Co., 1864.

Harrisonburg, Virginia: Diary of a Citizen from May 9, 1862–August 22, 1864. Edited by E. R. Grymes Heneberger. Privately published, n.d. (LC no. F234.H3 H37).

Harwell, Richard Barksdale. *The Confederate Hundred: A Bibliophilic Selection of Confederate Books*. 2d ed. Wendell, N.C.: Broadfoot's Bookmark, 1982.

Henry, Gustavus Adolphus. "Speech of Hon. Gustavus A. Henry of Tennessee in the Senate of the Confederate States, November 29, 1864." Richmond: n.p., 1864.

Heyward, Pauline DeCaradeuc. *A Confederate Lady Comes of Age: The Journals of Pauline DeCaradeuc Heyward, 1863–1888*. Edited by Mary D. Robertson. Women's Diaries and Letters of the Nineteenth-Century South. Columbia: University of South Carolina Press, 1992.

Jackson, Henry W. R. *Historical Register and Confederates Assistant to National Independence*. Augusta, Ga.: Office of the Constitutionalist, 1862.

———. *The Southern Women of the Second American Revolution. Our Naval Victories and Exploits of Confederate War Steamers, Capture of Yankee Gunboats, &c*. Atlanta: Intelligencer Steam Power Presses, 1863.

Jones, J. William. *Christ in the Camp; or, Religion in Lee's Army*. Richmond: Johnson, 1887.

Lamar, L. Q. C. "Speech of the Hon. L. Q. C. Lamar of Mississippi on the State of the Country. Delivered in the Athenaeum, Atlanta, Georgia, April 14, 1864. Reported by A. E. Marshall." Atlanta: J. J. Toon & Co., 1864.

LeConte, Emma. *When the World Ended: The Diary of Emma LeConte*. Edited by Earl Schenck Miers. New York: Oxford University Press, 1957.

Lyons, James. *Four Essays on the Right and Propriety of Secession by the Southern States, by a Member of the Bar of Richmond*. Richmond: Ritchie & Dunnavant, Printers, 1861.

MacMahon, T. W. *Cause and Contrast: An Essay on the American Crisis*. Richmond: West and Johnston, 1862.

Mason, Emily V. *The Southern Poems of the War*. Baltimore: John Murphy & Co., 1867.

Meade, William. *"Address on the Day of Fasting and Prayer Appointed by the President of the Confederate States, June 13, 1861; Delivered at Christ Church, Millwood, VA, by Bishop Meade Published by Request."* Richmond: Enquirer Book and Job Press, 1861.

Miranda. "The Battle of the Fair." New Orleans: n.p., 1863.

Moore, M[arinda] B[ranson]. *The Dixie Primer*. Raleigh: Branson & Farrar, 1864.

————. *The Dixie Speller*. Raleigh: Branson & Farrar, 1864.

————. *The Geographical Reader for the Dixie Children*. Raleigh: Branson, Farrar & Co., 1863.

Morgan, Gen. John T. *Address to the Graduating Class of the Virginia Military Institute, on the Third of July, 1868, by J. T. Morgan*. Richmond: W. A. R. Nye, Book and Job Printer, 1868.

Neely, John, Rev. *The Confederate States Speller and Reader*. Augusta, Ga.: A. Bleakley, 1864.

"Official Report of the Battle of the Oyster Shells." N.p., 1863.

Oldham, William S. "Speech of the Hon. W. S. Oldham, of Texas, on the Resolutions of the State of Texas Concerning Peace, Reconstruction, and Independence. In the Confederate States Senate, January 30, 1865." Richmond: n.p., 1865.

Palmer, Rev. B. M., D.D. "The Oath of Allegiance to the United States, Discussed in Its Moral and Political Bearings." Richmond: McFarlane & Fergusson, 1863.

Pollard, Edward A. *The First Year of the War*. Richmond: West and Johnston, 1862.

————. *The Lost Cause: A New Southern History of the War of the Confederates*. New York: E. B. Treat & Co., 1866.

————. *The Lost Cause Regained*. New York: G. W. Carleton & Co, 1868.

————. *Memoir of the Assassination of Henry Rives Pollard*. Lynchburg: Schafeter & Bryant, 1869.

————. *Southern History of the War: The Third Year of the War*. New York: Charles B. Richardson, 1865.

Prayers and Other Devotions for the Use of the Soldiers of the Army of the Confederate States. Charleston: Published for the Female Bible, Prayer-Book and Tract Society. Evans & Cogswell, 186[?]

Richardson, David (calculator). *The Southern Almanac for 1864*. Lynchburg: Johnson & Schaffter, 1863.

Richardson's Virginia and North Carolina Almanac, for the Year of Our Lord 1868. Lynchburg: J. P. Bell & Co., 1867.

Rozier, John, ed. *The Granite Farm Letters: The Civil War Correspondence of Edgeworth & Sallie Bird*. Athens: University of Georgia Press, 1988.

St. Paul, Henry. *Our Home and Foreign Policy*. Mobile: Printed at the Office of the Daily Register and Advertiser, 1863.

Shepperson, William G., ed. *War Songs of the South*. Edited by "Bohemian," *Correspondent Richmond Dispatch*. Richmond: West and Johnston, 1862.

Simms, William Gilmore, ed. *War Poetry of the South*. New York: Richardson & Company, 1866.

Smith, Daniel E. Huger, Alice R. Huger Smith, and Arney R. Childs, eds. *Mason-Smith Family Letters: 1860-1868*. Columbia: University of South Carolina Press, 1950.

Smith, Richard McAllister. *The Confederate Primer*. Richmond: George L. Bidgood, 1864.

———. *The Confederate Spelling Book with Reading Lessons for the Young Adapted to the Use of Schools or for Private Instruction*. Richmond: George L. Bidgood, 1865.

Smith, Roswell Chamberlain. *Louisiana English Grammar*. Shreveport: Printed at the Office of the Southwestern, 1865.

Southall, Stephen O. "Inaugural Address Delivered to the Law Class of the University of Virginia." Charlottesville: Chronicle Steam Printing House (1883 reprint), 1866.

A South Carolinian. *The Confederate "Respice Finem."* Mobile: S. H. Goetzel & Co., 1863.

"Special Service Hero! Self-Detailed." By the author of "The Rose of Shenandoah." Richmond: Published for the author, 1863.

Stewart, Rev. K[ensey] J[ohns]. *A Geography for Beginners*. Palmetto Series. Richmond: J. W. Randolph, 1864.

Stone, Kate. *Brokenburn: The Journal of Kate Stone, 1861–1865*. Edited by John Q. Anderson. Library of Southern Civilization. Baton Rouge: Louisiana State University Press, 1972.

The Stonewall Song Book: Being a Collection of Patriotic, Sentimental and Comic Songs. 11th ed., enl. Richmond: West and Johnston, 1865.

Stuart, Alexander H. H. *The Recent Revolution; Its Causes and Its Consequences, and the Duties and Responsibilities Which It Has Imposed on the People, and Especially the Young Men, of the South: Address of Alexander H. H. Stuart. Delivered before the Literary Societies of the University of Virginia, June 29, 1866*. Richmond: Examiner Job Office, 1866.

Thomas, Ella Gertrude Clanton. *The Secret Eye: The Journal of Ella Gertrude Clanton Thomas, 1848-1889*. Edited by Virginia Ingraham Burr. Chapel Hill: University of North Carolina Press, 1990.

Thornwell, J. H. "Our Danger and Our Duty." Raleigh: Raleigh Register Steam Power Press, 1863.

"To the Citizens of the State and The People of Richmond." 1865.

"To the People of the Southern Confederacy." 186?.

"To Win or To Die"; air—"Rock Me to Sleep." 1863?.

Turner's North Carolina Almanac for the Year of our Lord 1865. Raleigh: Henry D. Turner, 1864.

The Valley of the Shadow website. <http://valley.vcdh.virginia.edu>.

Virginia: A Brief Memoir for the Information of Europeans Desirous of Emigrating to the New World. Richmond: Wm. A. R. Nye, 1868.

The Virginia Primer. Richmond: J. R. Kennigham, 1864.

Wake Forest Broadside Poetry Collection website. <http://www.wfu.edu/Library/rarebook/>.

The War and Its Heroes. Illustrated. Richmond: Ayres & Wade, 1864.

War of the Rebellion: A Compilation of the Official Records of the Union and Confederate Armies. 128 vols. Washington, D.C.: Government Printing Office, 1880–1901.

Warrock's Virginia and North Carolina Almanac for the Year of Our Lord 1864. Richmond: James E. Goode, 1864.

Warrock's Virginia and North Carolina Almanac for the Year of our Lord 1865. Richmond: James E. Goode, 1865.

Warrock's Virginia and North Carolina Almanac for the Year of Our Lord 1866-1868. Richmond: James E. Goode, 1865–67.

Woodbridge, George. "A Tract for the Times: Appeal for the Church and Ministry." Richmond: Chas. H. Wynne, 1866.

Wynne, T. H., ed. *The Narrative of David Fanning, (A Tory in the Revolutionary War with Great Britain) Giving an Account of his Adventures in North Carolina, from 1775 to 1783*. Richmond: n.p., 1861.

Wynne's Edition of Richardson's Virginia and North Carolina Almanac, for the Year of our Lord 1864. Richmond: Chas. H. Wynne, 1864.

TRAVEL ACCOUNTS

Andrews, Sydney. *The South Since the War*. 1866. Reprint, with an introduction by David Donald, Boston: Houghton Mifflin Company, 1971.

Avary, Myrta Lockett. *Dixie after the War*. 1906. Reprint, with an introduction by General Clement A Evans, Boston: Houghton Mifflin Company, 1937.

Biddle, Ellen McGowan. *Reminiscences of a Soldiers Wife*. Philadelphia: Lippincott, 1907.

Botume, Elizabeth Hyde. *First Days among the Contrabands*. Boston: Lee and Shepard, 1893.

Chester, John Greville. *Transatlantic Sketches in the West Indies, South America, Canada and the United States*. London: Smith, Elder & Co, 1869.

Clark, Thomas D., *The Postwar South, 1865-1900: An Era of Reconstruction and Readjustment*. Vol. 1 of *Travels in the New South: A Bibliography*. Norman: University of Oklahoma Press, 1962.

Conser, Rev. Samuel M. *Virginia after the War: An Account of Three Years' Experience in Reorganizing the Methodist Episcopal Church in Virginia.* Indianapolis: Baker-Randolph, 1891.

Deedes, Henry. *Sketches of the South and West; or, Ten Months Residence in the United States.* Edinburgh: William Blackwood & Sons, 1869.

De Forest, John William. *A Union Officer in the Reconstruction.* Edited with an introduction and notes by James H. Croushore and David Morris Potter. New Haven: Yale University Press, 1948.

Dennett, John Richard, ed. *The South As It Is: 1865-1866.* New York: Viking Press, 1965.

Ferguson, Robert. *America during and after the War.* London: Longmans, Green, Reader and Dyer, 1866.

Hamilton, Gail [Mary Abigail Dodge]. *Wool-Gathering.* Boston: Tichnor & Fields, 1867.

Kelley, William Darrah. *The Old South and the New: A Series of Letters.* New York: G. P. Putnam's Sons, 1888.

Kennaway, John Henry. *On Sherman's Track; or, The South after the War.* London: Seeley, Jackson, and Halliday, 1867.

Latham, Henry. *Black and White: A Journal of a Three Months' Tour in the United States.* London: Macmillan and Co., 1867.

Leigh, Frances Butler. *Ten Years on a Georgia Plantation Since the War.* London: R. Bentley & Son, 1883.

Mitchell, A. *Notes of a Tour in America in August & September, 1865.* Glasgow: Printed for private circulation, 1868.

Muir, John. *A Thousand-Mile Walk to the Gulf.* Edited by William Frederic Badé. Boston: Houghton Mifflin Company, 1916.

Oliphant, Laurence. *The Present Style of Political Parties in America.* Edinburgh: William Blackwood & Sons, 1867.

Parker, Nathan H. *Missouri as It Is in 1867: An Illustrated Historical Gazetteer of Missouri.* Philadelphia: Lippincott, 1867.

Pattison, Margaret Amanda. *The Emigrant's Vade-Mecum or Guide to the "Price Grant" in Venezuelan Guyana.* London: Published for the American, English, and Venezuelan Trading & Commercial Company, 1868.

Peters, Theodore Curtis. *A Report upon the Condition of the South, with Regards to Its Needs for a Cotton Crop and its Financial Wants in Connection therewith as Well as the Safety of Temporary Loans.* Baltimore: H. A. Robinson, 1867.

Reid, Whitelaw W. *After the War: A Southern Tour.* New York: Moore, Wilstach & Baldwin, 1866.

Skinner, J. E. Hilary. *After the Storm; or, Jonathan and His Neighbors in 1865-6.* London: Richard Bentley, 1866.

Smith, Samuel. *Reflections Suggested by a Second Visit to the United States of America.* Liverpool: David Marples, 1867.

Swett, Charles. *A Trip to British Honduras and to San Pedro, Republic of Honduras.* New Orleans: Price Current Print, 1868.

Trowbridge, John T. *The Desolate South, 1865-1866: A Picture of the Battlefields and*

of the Devastated Confederacy. 1866. Reprint, edited with an introduction by
Gordon Carroll, New York: Duell, Sloan and Pearce, 1956.

Wagener, John A. *South Carolina: A Home for the Industrious Immigrant*.
Charleston: South Carolina Bureau of Immigration, 1867.

———. *South Carolina: A Home for the Industrious Immigrant, Supplement 1*.
Charleston: Joseph Walker's, 1867.

Secondary Sources

BOOKS AND ARTICLES

Alexander, Ted, and others. *Southern Revenge! Civil War History of Chambersburg,
Pennsylvania*. Chambersburg: Greater Chambersburg Chamber of Commerce,
1989.

Anderson, Benedict R. *Imagined Communities: Reflections on the Origin and Spread
of Nationalism*. Rev. ed. London: Verso, 1991.

Ash, Stephen V. *When the Yankees Came: Conflict and Chaos in the Occupied South,
1861–1865*. Chapel Hill: University of North Carolina Press, 1995.

Atchison, Ray M. "*The Land We Love*: A Southern Post-Bellum Magazine of
Agriculture, Literature, and Military History." *North Carolina Historical Review*
37 (October 1960): 506–15.

Ballard, Michael B. *A Long Shadow: Jefferson Davis and the Final Days of the
Confederacy*. Jackson: University Press of Mississippi, 1986.

Behlohlavek, John, and Lewis N. Wynne, eds. *Divided We Fall: Essays on
Confederate Nation Building*. Saint Leo, Fla.: Saint Leo College Press, 1991.

Beringer, Richard E., Herman Hattaway, Archer Jones, and William N. Still Jr. *Why
the South Lost the Civil War*. Athens: University of Georgia Press, 1986.

Berlin, Ira, et al. *Free at Last: A Documentary History of Slavery, Freedom, and the
Civil War*. New York: New Press, 1992.

Bernstein, Iver. *The New York City Draft Riots: Their Significance for American
Society and Politics in the Age of the Civil War*. New York: Oxford University
Press, 1990.

Bill, Alfred H. *The Beleaguered City: Richmond, 1861–65*. New York: Alfred A. Knopf,
1946.

Blair, William. *Virginia's Private War: Feeding Body and Soul in the Confederacy,
1861–65*. New York: Oxford University Press, 1998.

Blight, David W. *Race and Reunion: The Civil War in American Memory*. Cambridge:
Harvard University Press, 2001.

Brooks, Carlton P. "The *Magnolia*: A Literary Magazine for the Confederacy."
Virginia Cavalcade 32 (Spring 1983): 150–57.

Brown, Richard D. *Knowledge Is Power: The Diffusion of Information in Early
America*. New York: Oxford University Press, 1989.

Buruma, Ian. *The Wages of Guilt: Memories of War in Germany and Japan*. New
York: Farrar, Straus, Giroux, 1994.

Bynum, Victoria. *Unruly Women: The Politics of Social and Sexual Control in the Old
South*. Chapel Hill: University of North Carolina Press, 1992.

Calkins, Chris M. *The Battles of Appomattox Station and Appomattox Court House, April 8–9, 1865*. Lynchburg: H. E. Howard, 1987.

Callahan, James Morton. *The Diplomatic History of the Southern Confederacy*. 1901. Reprint, New York: Greenwood Press, 1968.

Carmichael, Peter S. "New South Visionaries: Virginia's Last Generation of Slaveholders, the Gospel of Progress, and the Lost Cause." In *The Myth of the Lost Cause and Civil War History*, edited by Gary W. Gallagher and Alan T. Nolan, 111–26. Bloomington: Indiana University Press, 2000.

Carter, Dan T. *When the War Was Over: The Failure of Self-Reconstruction in the South, 1865–1867*. Baton Rouge: Louisiana State University Press, 1985.

Castel, Albert. *Decision in the West: The Atlanta Campaign of 1864*. Lawrence: University of Kansas Press, 1992.

————. *Winning and Losing in the Civil War*. Columbia: University of South Carolina Press, 1996.

Chatterjee, Partha. *The Nation and Its Fragments: Colonial and Postcolonial Histories*. Princeton: Princeton University Press, 1993.

Chesbrough, David B., ed. *"God Ordained This War": Sermons on the Sectional Crisis, 1830–1865*. Columbia: University of South Carolina Press, 1991.

Chesson, Michael B. "'Editors Engaging in Double-leaded Matter': The Shoot-out at the Capitol in 1866." *Virginia Cavalcade* 30, no. 3 (Winter 1981): 100–109.

Clark, Champ. *Gettysburg: The Confederate High Tide*. Alexandria: Time-Life Books, 1985.

Clark, James C. *Last Train South: The Flight of the Confederate Government from Richmond*. Jefferson, N.C.: McFarland & Company, Inc., 1984.

Clark, Kathleen. "Celebrating Freedom: Emancipation Day Celebrations and African American Memory in the Early Reconstruction South." In *Where These Memories Grow: History, Memory, and Southern Identity*, edited by W. Fitzhugh Brundage, 107–32. Chapel Hill: University of North Carolina Press, 2000.

Clinton, Catherine. *Tara Revisited: Women, War, and the Southern Plantation Legend*. New York: Abbeville Press, 1995.

————, ed. *Southern Families at War: Loyalty and Conflict in the Civil War South*. New York: Oxford University Press, 2000.

Clinton, Catherine, and Nina Silber, eds. *Divided Houses: Gender and the Civil War*. New York: Oxford University Press, 1992.

Confino, Alon. *The Nation as a Local Metaphor: Württemberg, Imperial Germany, and National Memory, 1871–1918*. Chapel Hill: University of North Carolina Press, 1997.

Connelly, Thomas L. *Autumn of Glory: The Army of Tennessee, 1862–1865*. Baton Rouge: Louisiana State University Press, 1971.

Connelly, Thomas L., and Barbara L. Bellows. *God and General Longstreet: The Lost Cause and the Southern Mind*. Baton Rouge: Louisiana State University Press, 1982.

Cooper, William J., Jr. *Jefferson Davis, American*. New York: Alfred A. Knopf, 2000.

Craven, Avery O. *The Growth of Southern Nationalism, 1848–1861*. A History of the South, vol. 6. Baton Rouge: Louisiana State University Press, 1953.

Crofts, Daniel W. *Reluctant Confederates: Upper South Unionists in the Secession Crisis*. Chapel Hill: University of North Carolina Press, 1989.

Crook, David Paul. *The North, the South, and the Powers, 1861–1865*. New York: Wiley, 1974.

Cullen, Jim. *The Civil War in Popular Culture: A Reusable Past*. Washington: Smithsonian Institution Press, 1995.

Current, Richard Nelson. *Lincoln's Loyalists: Union Soldiers from the Confederacy*. Boston: Northeastern University Press, 1992.

Daniel, W. Harrison. "Protestantism and Patriotism in the Confederacy." *Mississippi Quarterly* 24 (Spring 1971): 117–134.

Davis, William C. *The Cause Lost: Myths and Realities of the Confederacy*. Lawrence: University Press of Kansas, 1996.

———. *"A Government of Our Own": The Making of the Confederacy*. New York: Free Press, 1994.

———. *An Honorable Defeat: The Last Days of the Confederate Government*. New York: Harcourt, 2001.

———. *Jefferson Davis: The Man and His Hour*. New York: HarperCollins Publishers, 1991.

Degler, Carl N. *The Other South: Southern Dissenters in the Nineteenth Century*. New York: Harper & Row, 1974.

Dew, Charles B. *Apostles of Disunion: Southern Secession Commissioners and the Causes of the Civil War*. Charlottesville: University Press of Virginia, 2001.

Dirck, Brian R. *Lincoln and Davis: Imagining America, 1809–1865*. Lawrence: University Press of Kansas, 2001.

Dorris, Jonathan T. *Pardon and Amnesty under Lincoln and Johnson*. Chapel Hill: University of North Carolina Press, 1953.

Durden, Robert F. *The Gray and the Black: The Confederate Debate on Emancipation*. Baton Rouge: Louisiana State University Press, 1972.

Dyer, Thomas. *Secret Yankees: The Union Circle in Confederate Atlanta*. Baltimore: Johns Hopkins University Press, 1999.

Edelman, Murray. *Politics as Symbolic Action: Mass Arousal and Quiescence*. Chicago: Markham Publishing Company, 1971.

Edwards, Laura F. *Gendered Strife and Confusion: The Political Culture of Reconstruction*. Urbana: University of Illinois Press, 1997.

Emery, Edwin. *The Press and America: An Interpretative History of the Mass Media*. Englewood Cliffs: Prentice-Hall, 1972.

Escott, Paul D. *After Secession: Jefferson Davis and the Failure of Confederate Nationalism*. Baton Rouge: Louisiana State University Press, 1978.

———. "Southern Yeomen and the Confederacy." *South Atlantic Quarterly* 77 (Spring 1978): 146–58.

———. "The Uses of Gallantry: Virginians and the Origins of J. E. B. Stuart's Historical Image." *Virginia Magazine of History and Biography* 103 (January 1995): 47–72.

Faust, Drew Gilpin. "Altars of Sacrifice: Confederate Women and the Narratives of War." *Journal of American History* 76 (March 1990): 1200–1228.

———. "Christian Soldiers: The Meaning of Revivalism in the Confederate Army." *Journal of Southern History* 53 (February 1987): 63–90.

———. "The Civil War Soldier and the Art of Dying." *Journal of Southern History* 67 (February 2001): 3–38.

———. *The Creation of Confederate Nationalism: Ideology and Identity in the Civil War South*. Baton Rouge: Louisiana State University Press, 1988.

———. *Mothers of Invention: Women of the Slaveholding South in the American Civil War*. Chapel Hill: University of North Carolina Press, 1996.

Fehrenbacher, Don E. "The Confederacy as a Constitutional System." *Constitutions and Constitutionalism in the Slaveholding South*. Mercer University Lamar Memorial Lectures No. 31. Athens: University of Georgia Press, 1989.

Fellman, Michael. *The Making of Robert E. Lee*. New York: Random House, 2000.

Fellman, Michael, Lesley J. Gordon, and Daniel E. Sutherland, *This Terrible War: The Civil War and Its Aftermath*. New York: Longman, 2003.

Flanders, Bertram Holland. *Early Georgia Magazines: Literary Periodicals to 1865*. Athens: University of Georgia Press, 1944.

Foner, Eric. *Reconstruction: American's Unfinished Revolution, 1863–1877*. New York: Harper & Row, 1988.

Foster, Gaines M. *Ghosts of the Confederacy: Defeat, the Lost Cause, and the Emergence of the New South, 1865–1913*. New York: Oxford University Press, 1987.

Fredrickson, George M., ed. *A Nation Divided: Problems and Issues of the Civil War and Reconstruction*. Minneapolis: Burgess Publishing Co., 1975.

Freehling, William W. *The South vs. the South: How Anti-Confederate Southerners Shaped the Course of the Civil War*. New York: Oxford University Press, 2001.

Furgurson, Ernest B. *Ashes of Glory: Richmond at War*. New York: Alfred A. Knopf, 1996.

———. *Chancellorsville, 1863: The Souls of the Brave*. New York: Vintage Books, 1992.

Gallagher, Gary W. *The Confederate War*. Cambridge: Harvard University Press, 1997.

———, ed. *Chancellorsville: The Battle and Its Aftermath*. Chapel Hill: University of North Carolina Press, 1996.

———. *The First Day at Gettysburg: Essays on Confederate and Union Leadership*. Kent, Ohio: Kent State University Press, 1992.

———. *The Second Day at Gettysburg: Essays on Confederate and Union Leadership*. Kent, Ohio: Kent State University Press, 1993.

———. *The Third Day at Gettysburg and Beyond*. Chapel Hill: University of North Carolina Press, 1994.

Gaston, Paul M. *The New South Creed: A Study in Southern Mythmaking*. New York: Alfred A. Knopf, 1970.

Genovese, Eugene D. *The World the Slaveholders Made: Two Essays in Interpretation*. New York: Pantheon Books, 1969.

Grant, Susan-Mary. *North over South: Northern Nationalism and American Identity in the Antebellum Era*. Lawrence: University Press of Kansas, 2000.

Greenfeld, Liah. *Nationalism: Five Roads to Modernity*. Cambridge: Harvard
University Press, 1992.

Grimsley, Mark. *The Hard Hand of War: Union Military Policy toward Southern
Civilians, 1861–1865*. Cambridge: Cambridge University Press, 1995.

Hahn, Steven. "Class and State in Postemancipation Societies: Southern Planters
in Comparative Perspective." *American Historical Review* 95 (February 1990):
75–99.

Hanchett, William. "Reconstruction and the Rehabilitation of Jefferson Davis:
Charles G. Halpine's Prison Life." *Journal of American History* 56 (September
1969): 280–89.

Handler, Richard. *Nationalism and the Politics of Culture in Quebec*. Madison:
University of Wisconsin Press, 1988.

Hanna, Alfred Jackson. *Confederate Exiles in Venezuela*. Tuscaloosa: Confederate
Publishing Co., 1960.

Harrell, Carolyn L. *When Bells Tolled for Lincoln: Southern Reaction to the
Assassination*. Macon, Ga.: Mercer University Press, 1997.

Harvard Encyclopedia of American Ethnic Groups. Cambridge: Belknap Press, 1980.

Hattaway, Herman, and Richard E. Beringer. *Jefferson Davis, Confederate President*.
Lawrence: University Press of Kansas, 2002.

Hattaway, Herman, and Archer Jones. *How the North Won: A Military History of
the Civil War*. Urbana: University of Illinois Press, 1983.

Hendrickson, Robert. *The Road to Appomattox*. New York: John Wiley & Sons, Inc.,
1998.

Hobsbawm, Eric, and Terence Ranger, eds. *The Invention of Tradition*. Cambridge:
Cambridge University Press, 1983.

Hobson, Fred. *Tell about the South: The Southern Rage to Explain*. Baton Rouge:
Louisiana State University Press, 1983.

Hoehling, A. H., and Mary Hoehling. *The Day Richmond Died*. Lanham, Md.:
Madison Books, 1981.

Hyman, Harold Melvin. *The Era of the Oath: Northern Loyalty Tests during the Civil
War and Reconstruction*. Philadelphia: University of Pennsylvania Press, 1954.

Jimerson, Randall C. *The Private Civil War: Popular Thought during the Sectional
Conflict*. Baton Rouge: Louisiana State University Press, 1988.

Kammen, Michael. *A Season of Youth: The American Revolution and the Historical
Imagination*. New York: Alfred A. Knopf, 1978.

Kerber, Linda. *Women of the Republic: Intellect and Ideology in Revolutionary
America*. Chapel Hill: University of North Carolina Press, 1980.

Kobre, Sidney. *Development of American Journalism*. Dubuque, Iowa: Wm. C.
Brown Company, 1968.

Lankford, Nelson D. *Richmond Burning: The Last Days of the Confederate Capital*.
New York: Viking Press, 2002.

Lawson, Melinda. *Patriot Fires: Forging a New American Nationalism in the Civil
War North*. Lawrence: University Press of Kansas, 2002.

Lebsock, Suzanne D. "Radical Reconstruction and the Property Rights of Southern

Women." In *Half Sisters of History: Southern Women and the American Past*, edited by Catherine Clinton, 110–35. Durham: Duke University Press, 1994.

Leonard, Thomas C. *News for All: America's Coming-of-Age with the Press*. New York: Oxford University Press, 1995.

Linden, Glenn M., and Thomas P. Pressly. *Voices from the House Divided: The United States Civil War as Personal Experience*. New York: McGraw Hill, 1995.

Linderman, Gerald F. *Embattled Courage: The Experience of Combat in the American Civil War*. New York: Free Press, 1987.

Litwack, Leon F. *Been in the Storm So Long: The Aftermath of Slavery*. New York: Random House, 1979.

Lonn, Ella. *Desertion during the Civil War*. Lincoln: University of Nebraska Press, 1998.

Marten, James. *The Children's Civil War*. Chapel Hill: University of North Carolina Press, 1998.

Massey, Mary Elizabeth. *Ersatz in the Confederacy: Shortages and Substitutes on the Southern Homefront*. With a new introduction by Barbara L. Bellows. Columbia: University of South Carolina Press, 1993.

———. *Refugee Life in the Confederacy*. Baton Rouge: Louisiana State University Press, 1964.

May, Robert E. "Southern Elite Women, Sectional Extremism, and the Male Political Sphere: The Case of John A. Quitman's Wife and Female Descendants, 1847–1931." *Journal of Mississippi History* 50 (November 1988): 251–85.

McCardell, John. *The Idea of a Southern Nation: Southern Nationalists and Southern Nationalism, 1830–1860*. New York: W. W. Norton & Co., 1979.

McCaslin, Richard B. *Lee in the Shadow of Washington*. Baton Rouge: Louisiana State University Press, 2001.

McDonough, James Lee, and James Pickett Jones. *War So Terrible: Sherman and Atlanta*. New York: W. W. Norton & Company, 1987.

McPherson, James M. *Abraham Lincoln and the Second American Revolution*. New York: Oxford University Press, 1991.

———. *Battle Cry of Freedom: The Civil War Era*. New York: Oxford University Press, 1988.

———. *For Cause and Comrades: Why Men Fought in the Civil War*. New York: Oxford University Press, 1997.

———. *Ordeal by Fire: The Civil War and Reconstruction*. New York: Alfred A. Knopf, 1982.

Mitchell, Reid. *Civil War Soldiers: Their Expectations and Their Experiences*. New York: Viking, 1988.

Moore, Albert Burton. *Conscription and Conflict in the Confederacy*. 1924. Reprint, New York: Hillary House Publishers, 1963.

Mott, Frank Luther. *American Journalism: A History of Newspapers in the United States through 250 Years, 1690–1940*. New York: Macmillan Company, 1941.

———. *A History of American Magazines*. Cambridge: Harvard University Press, 1938–68.

Nelson, Larry E. *Bullets, Ballots, and Rhetoric: Confederate Policy for the United*

States Presidential Contest of 1864. University: University of Alabama Press, 1980.

Norton, Anne. *Alternative Americas: A Reading of Antebellum Political Culture*. Chicago: University of Chicago Press, 1986.

Nunn, W. C. *Escape from Reconstruction*. With a foreword by Austin L. Porterfield. Fort Worth: Leo Portishman Foundation, Texas Christian University, 1956.

O'Brien, Michael, ed. *All Clever Men Who Make Their Way: Critical Discourse in the Old South*. Athens: University of Georgia Press, 1992.

———. *An Evening When Alone: Four Journals of Single Women in the South, 1827–1867*. Charlottesville: University Press of Virginia, 1993.

Osthaus, Carl R. *Partisans of the Southern Press: Editorial Spokesmen of the Nineteenth Century*. Lexington: University Press of Kentucky, 1994.

Owens, Harry P., and James J. Cooke, eds. *The Old South in the Crucible of War*. Jackson: University of Mississippi Press, 1983.

Owsley, Frank L. *King Cotton Diplomacy: Foreign Relations of the Confederate States of America*. Chicago: University of Chicago Press, 1959.

Palmer, Benjamin Morgan. *The Life and Letters of James Henley Thornwell, D.D.* Richmond: Whittet & Shapperson, 1875.

Paludan, Phillip Shaw. *A People's Contest: The Union and Civil War, 1861–1865*. 2d ed. Lawrence: University Press of Kansas, 1996.

Parish, Peter. "An Exception to Most of the Rules: What Made American Nationalism Different in the Mid-Nineteenth Century?" *Prologue: The Journal of the National Archives* 27 (Fall 1995): 219–29.

Parker, David B. *Alias Bill Arp: Charles Henry Smith and the South's "Goodly Heritage."* Athens: University of Georgia Press, 1991.

Patrick, Rembert W. *The Fall of Richmond*. Baton Rouge: Louisiana State University Press, 1960.

Perman, Michael. *Reunion without Compromise: The South and Reconstruction, 1865–1868*. Cambridge: Cambridge University Press, 1973.

Perry, James M. *A Bohemian Brigade: The Civil War Correspondents—Mostly Rough, Sometimes Ready*. New York: John Wiley & Sons, 2000.

Peterson, Merrill D. *Lincoln and American Memory*. New York: Oxford University Press, 1994.

Piehler, G. Kurt. *Remembering War the American Way*. Washington: Smithsonian Institution Press, 1995.

Potter, David Morris. *The South and the Sectional Conflict*. Baton Rouge: Louisiana State University Press, 1968.

Powell, Lawrence N. *New Masters: Northern Planters during the Civil War and Reconstruction*. New Haven: Yale University Press, 1980.

Rable, George C. *But There Was No Peace: The Role of Violence in the Politics of Reconstruction*. Athens: University of Georgia Press, 1984.

———. *Civil Wars: Women and the Crisis of Southern Nationalism*. Urbana: University of Illinois Press, 1989.

———. *The Confederate Republic: A Revolution against Politics*. Chapel Hill: University of North Carolina Press, 1994.

Radford, J. P. "Identity and Tradition in the Post–Civil War South." *Journal of Historical Geography* 18 (January 1992): 91–103.

Richardson, James D., ed. *The Messages and Papers of Jefferson Davis and the Confederacy*. 2 vols. New York: Chelsea House–R. Hector, 1966.

Riley, Sam G. *Magazines of the American South*. Westport, Conn.: Greenwood Press, 1986.

Roark, James L. *Masters without Slaves: Southern Planters in the Civil War and Reconstruction*. New York: W. W. Norton & Co., 1977.

Rolle, Andrew F. *The Lost Cause: The Confederate Exodus to Mexico*. With a foreword by A. L. Rowse. Norman: University of Oklahoma Press, 1965.

Romero, Sidney J. *Religion in the Rebel Ranks*. Lanham, Md.: University Press of America, 1983.

Royster, Charles. *The Destructive War: William Tecumseh Sherman, Stonewall Jackson, and the Americans*. New York: Alfred A. Knopf, 1991.

Schudson, Michael. *Discovering the News: A Social History of American Newspapers*. New York: Basic Books, 1978.

Schwartz, Barry. *George Washington: The Making of an American Symbol*. New York: Free Press, 1987.

Shalhope, Robert E. "Race, Class, Slavery, and the Antebellum Southern Mind." *Journal of Southern History* 37 (November 1971): 557–74.

Shibutani, Tamotsu. *Improvised News: A Sociological Study of Rumor*. Indianapolis: Bobbs-Merrill Educational Publishing, 1966.

Shore, Laurence. *Southern Capitalists: The Ideological Leadership of an Elite, 1832–1885*. Chapel Hill: University of North Carolina Press, 1986.

Silber, Nina. *The Romance of Reunion: Northerners and the South, 1865–1900*. Chapel Hill: University of North Carolina Press, 1993.

Silver, James Wesley. *Confederate Morale and Church Propaganda*. New York: W. W. Norton & Co., 1967.

Skipper, Ottis Clark. *J. D. B. De Bow, Magazinist of the Old South*. Athens: University of Georgia Press, 1958.

Smith, Everard H. "Chambersburg: Anatomy of a Confederate Reprisal." *American Historical Review* 96 (April 1991): 432–55.

Stevens, Joseph E. *1863: The Rebirth of a Nation*. New York: Bantam Books, 1999.

Stout, Harry S., and Christopher Grasso. "Civil War, Religion, and Communications: The Case of Richmond." In *Religion and the American Civil War*, edited by Randall M. Miller, Harry S. Stout, and Charles Reagan Wilson, 313–59. New York: Oxford University Press, 1998.

Stowe, Steven. *Intimacy and Power in the Old South: Ritual in the Lives of the Planters*. Baltimore: Johns Hopkins University Press, 1987.

Sutherland, Daniel E., ed. *Guerrillas, Unionists, and Violence on the Confederate Home Front*. Fayetteville: University of Arkansas Press, 1999.

Sydnor, Charles S. *The Development of Southern Sectionalism, 1819–1848*. A History of the South, vol. 5. Baton Rouge: Louisiana State University Press, 1948.

Tatum, Georgia Lee. *Disloyalty in the Confederacy*. Lincoln: University of Nebraska Press, 2000.

Taylor, William Robert. *Cavalier and Yankee: The Old South and American National Character*. New York: Harper & Row, 1969.

Thomas, Emory M. *The Confederacy as a Revolutionary Experience*. Englewood Cliffs: Prentice-Hall, 1971.

———. *The Confederate Nation: 1861–1865*. New York: Harper Torchbooks, 1979.

———. *The Confederate State of Richmond: A Biography of the Capital*. Austin: University of Texas Press, 1971.

———. *Robert E. Lee: A Biography*. New York: W. W. Norton & Company, 1995.

Tindall, George B. *The Ethnic Southerners*. Baton Rouge: Louisiana State University Press, 1977.

———. *Natives and Newcomers: Ethnic Southerners and Southern Ethnics*. Athens: University of Georgia Press, 1995.

Trelease, Allen W. *White Terror: The Ku Klux Klan Conspiracy and Southern Reconstruction*. New York: Harper Torchbooks, 1971.

Waldstreicher, David. *In the Midst of Perpetual Fetes: The Making of American Nationalism, 1776–1820*. Chapel Hill: University of North Carolina Press, 1997.

Waugh, John C. *Reelecting Lincoln: The Battle for the 1864 Presidency*. New York: Crown Publishers, 1997.

Weatherford, Wills D. *James Dunwoody Brownson De Bow*. Charlottesville: The Historical Publishing Co., Inc., 1935.

Weaver, Blanche Henry Clark. "Confederate Emigration to Brazil." *Journal of Southern History* 27 (February 1961): 33–53.

Wheeler, Richard. *Witness to Appomattox*. New York: Harper & Row, 1989.

Whites, LeeAnn. *The Civil War as a Crisis in Gender: Augusta, Georgia, 1860–1890*. Athens: University of Georgia Press, 1995.

Wiley, Bell Irvin, and Lucy E. Fay, eds. *This Infernal War: The Confederate Letters of Edwin Fay*. Austin: University of Texas Press, 1958.

Wilson, Charles Reagan. *Baptized in Blood: The Religion of the Lost Cause, 1865–1920*. Athens: University of Georgia Press, 1980.

Wish, Harvey. *George Fitzhugh, Conservative of the Old South*. Charlottesville: University Press of Virginia, 1938.

———. *George Fitzhugh, Propagandist of the Old South*. Baton Rouge: Louisiana State University Press, 1943.

Wolfe, Margaret Ripley. *Daughters of Canaan: A Saga of Southern Women*. Lexington: University Press of Kentucky, 1995.

Wood, Gordon S. "The Greatness of George Washington." *Virginia Quarterly Review* 68 (Spring 1992): 189–207.

Wyatt-Brown, Bertram. *The Shaping of Southern Culture: Honor, Grace, and War, 1760s–1880s*. Chapel Hill: University of North Carolina Press, 2001.

———. *Southern Honor: Ethics and Behavior in the Old South*. New York: Oxford University Press, 1982.

Zelinsky, Wilbur. *Nation into State: The Shifting Symbolic Foundation of American Nationalism*. Chapel Hill: University of North Carolina Press, 1988.

Zornow, William. *Lincoln and the Party Divided*. Norman: University of Oklahoma Press, 1954.

DISSERTATIONS AND THESES

Atchison, Ray Morris. "Southern Literary Magazines, 1865–1887." Ph.D. dissertation, Duke University, 1956.

Chunn, Calvin Ellsworth. "History of News Magazines." Ph.D. dissertation, University of Missouri, 1950.

High, Thomas O'Connor. "Bledsoe's *Review*: A Southern Apologia." MA thesis, Vanderbilt University, 1942.

Johnson, Aliene. "Southern Literary Magazines of the Reconstruction Period." MA thesis, Duke University, 1935.

Kennerly, Sarah Law. "Confederate Juvenile Imprints: Children's Books and Periodicals Published in the Confederate States of America, 1861–1865." Ph.D. dissertation, University of Michigan, 1956.

McLean, Francis Elliott Hall. "Periodicals Published in the South Before 1880." Ph.D. dissertation, University of Virginia, 1928.

Robinson, Armstead Louis. "Day of Jubilio: Civil War and the Demise of Slavery in the Mississippi Valley." Ph.D. dissertation, University of Rochester, 1976.

INDEX

Fourth of July, 147, 227
Freedmen's Bureau, 148, 151, 219

Gettysburg, 80–82, 84
Gorgas, Josiah: quoted, 82, 87, 113, 114, 152, 164, 171, 241
Greeley, Horace, 205–6
Guerrilla war, 119, 120, 130–33; Reconstruction violence as, 145

Hard work: valued in Reconstruction, 172–75, 176–77, 183, 184, 188; women praised for, 231. *See also* Class distinctions; Honor; Masculinity; Reconstruction economy
Honor, 24–25, 31, 44, 52, 64, 78, 90, 159, 169–71, 184, 206–7, 240; and loyalty oaths, 95–96, 164–65; challenged by black troops, 103; and Confederate surrender, 121, 133–34; challenged by Reconstruction, 144, 156–57; and labor, 183. *See also* Loyalty oaths, wartime; Loyalty oaths, reconstruction; Masculinity; Women
Home Guard, 71
Humor columns, 218–29

Immigration to the South, 179–80, 183–90; racial overtones of, 183; argument against inviting, 184; political overtones of, 185, 188; idealized image of, 185; promotional literature for, 185–90; calls for, to Mississippi, 185; calls for, to Florida, 187; calls for, to North Carolina, 187; calls for, to Virginia, 187; calls for, to South Carolina, 187–90; threatened by anger, 214. *See also* Northerners
Industrialization, postwar, 175–77, 179. *See also* Reconstruction economy

Jackson, Thomas J., 37, 48, 136
Johnson, Andrew, 4, 126–29, 136, 152, 153. *See also* Reconstruction, Presidential
Johnston, Joseph, 126, 132, 135

Ku Klux Klan, 171, 245

Ladies Aid Societies, 56, 60
Ladies Memorial Associations, 233–39. *See also* Memorialization
Literary independence, Southern, 25–28, 190–200; and regional appeals, 191–94; and criticism of Northern publishers, 197–99. *See also* Confederate States of America, identity of; Confederate States of America, nationalism of Southern identity, postwar
LeConte, Emma: quoted, 23–24, 67, 87, 91, 127, 129, 147, 148–49, 151
Lee, Richard Henry (Light Horse Harry), 14, 22
Lee, Robert E., 20, 48, 82–84, 120, 124, 136; on arming slaves, 105–9; blamed for surrender, 123
Lincoln, Abraham, 24, 47, 112, 112–14, 124; assassination of, 126–30
Loss of will thesis, 110–11, 250–51 (n.)
Lost Cause, 193, 252 (n. 6)
Loyalty oaths, wartime, 2, 86, 94–100. *See also* Honor; Loyalty oaths, Reconstruction; Masculinity
Loyalty oaths, Reconstruction, 164–71, 243, 282 (n.). *See also* Honor; Loyalty oaths, wartime; Masculinity; Pardons

Manassas, second battle of, 39–40, 43, 47–48
Marriage and nationalism, 93, 215–18, 228. *See also* Romance and nationalism; Women
Masculinity, 54–55, 88, 99–100, 156, 169–71, 183, 203–4, 208–9, 213, 226–27; and African Americans, 102; and arming slaves, 107; and Jefferson Davis, 136–37; and loyalty oaths, 164–65; redefined in Reconstruction, 172–76
Memorialization, 56, 233–39. *See also* Ladies Memorial Associations